Beginning RPG Maker VX Ace

Darrin Perez

Apress®

Beginning RPG Maker VX Ace

ISBN-13 (pbk): 978-1-4842-0785-7

ISBN-13 (electronic): 978-1-4842-0784-0

Managing Director: Welmoed Spahr
Lead Editor: Ben Renow-Clarke
Technical Reviewer: Michael Lin
Editorial Board: Steve Anglin, Mark Beckner, Ewan Buckingham, Gary Cornell, Louise Corrigan, Jim DeWolf, Jonathan Gennick, Robert Hutchinson, Michelle Lowman, James Markham, Matthew Moodie, Jeff Olson, Jeffrey Pepper, Douglas Pundick, Ben Renow-Clarke, Dominic Shakeshaft, Gwenan Spearing, Matt Wade, Steve Weiss
Coordinating Editor: Christine Ricketts
Copy Editor: Michael Laraque
Compositor: SPi Global
Indexer: SPi Global
Artist: SPi Global
Cover Designer: Anna Ishchenko

Distributed to the book trade worldwide by Springer Science+Business Media New York, 233 Spring Street, 6th Floor, New York, NY 10013. Phone 1-800-SPRINGER, fax (201) 348-4505, e-mail orders-ny@springer-sbm.com, or visit www.springeronline.com. Apress Media, LLC is a California LLC and the sole member (owner) is Springer Science + Business Media Finance Inc (SSBM Finance Inc). SSBM Finance Inc is a Delaware corporation.

For information on translations, please e-mail rights@apress.com, or visit www.apress.com.

Apress and friends of ED books may be purchased in bulk for academic, corporate, or promotional use. eBook versions and licenses are also available for most titles. For more information, reference our Special Bulk Sales–eBook Licensing web page at www.apress.com/bulk-sales.

Any source code or other supplementary material referenced by the author in this text is available to readers at www.apress.com. For detailed information about how to locate your book's source code, go to www.apress.com/source-code/.

This book is dedicated to the important people in my life; my family and my friends. You are the reason why I press on.

Contents at a Glance

Contents

About the Author

Darrin Perez (1988-) was born in Alexandria, Virginia and currently resides in Puerto Rico. His debut fantasy novel, *Whispers of Dawn*, was written as a self-imposed challenge in the spirit of NaNoWriMo (National November Writing Month). He has also written many video game related articles over at Hubpages and published an ebook concerning RPG Maker VX Ace (a video game development engine) as well. His newest non-fiction book, *Beginning RPG Maker VX Ace*, is a robust expansion of that ebook and is published by Apress.

About the Technical Reviewer

Michael Lin is an experienced RPG Maker developer and has created scripts for RMVX Ace since 2012. He is the founder of HimeWorks, a website dedicated to resources for RPG Maker including a wealth of scripts and tutorials on game development and programming.

Acknowledgments

It has been a long journey to reach this point. This book started as a much smaller (self-published) offering titled The RPG Maker VX Ace Help Guide for Beginners: Tips and Tricks You Can Use For Your Very Own RPG (quite the mouthful, right?) that was released exclusively in e-book format for the Amazon Kindle. I was contacted by Ben Renow-Clarke in early June of this year concerning writing a RPG Maker book for Apress. He even specifically noted that we could expand on my e-book; a sentiment I promptly agreed on. Work on Beginning RPG Maker VX Ace started a few months later. Several iterations of editing, proofreading, and formatting culminated in what you are now reading. I started using RPG Maker VX Ace a few years ago and even made my own game (albeit unpolished) with it.

This book is the manifestation of my desire to teach other people the things that I have learned during my time using the game development engine. But, this is an acknowledgement section, so enough about the book for now; you'll be reading it soon enough, after all!

I would like to acknowledge the efforts of everyone in Apress who has worked with me, especially Ben Renow-Clarke, who approached me to actually expand on my previous work, and Christine Ricketts, who has served as this book's coordinating editor; the glue that binds the project together, if you will. Honorable mentions include Michael Laraque (copy editor), and Dhaneesh Kumar (formatting and composition). Without the efforts of those working in Apress, you would not be reading this book at this time.

Michael Lin served as this book's technical reviewer, and I would like to thank him for helping me to make this book the best it can be. His expertise with Ruby and the RMVXA engine were essential in making the scripting sections of this book as beginner-friendly as possible.

I would like to thank the RPG Maker VX Ace community as a whole for all that they have done to make exploring and using RMVXA as easy as humanly possible. They have provided countless resources (both in the form of tutorials and other essential assets such as sprites and music). Working with a game development engine can be a daunting task, but they are always willing to lend a helping hand to anyone who needs it. There are far too many people to name, but I hold the community fondly in my heart (even if it has been seemingly forever since I've visited).

On a personal level, I have to thank my parents, Jose Perez and Victoria Diaz, who provided (and still provide) me with the support I needed to push through the barriers that one faces when writing a work such as this. It wasn't easy, but here we are, and we have survived!

I also have to thank my closest friends for being constant bulwarks of support and always listening to me rant about this or that.

Finally, I thank you, my dear reader. At the end of the day, all writers make sacrifices to get a solid book out to you and everyone else who desires to read about a certain subject. It is when I see the number of people who read my work that I can boldly say that the sacrifices were worth it. May you enjoy reading this book as much as I enjoyed writing it!

Introduction

If you're reading this book, you are probably interested in learning about RPG Maker VX Ace. If you've just started using RPG Maker VX Ace, the amount of features it offers for your roleplaying game development may be confusing. That's what I'm here for. During the course of this book, I will give a basic overview of the engine, give tips and tricks that will help you start getting a foothold on understanding RPG Maker VX Ace, and even give you some of the code I've personally used for some of the neater events in my game. So, take a deep breath, and let's go!

What is RPG Maker VX Ace (RMVXA)?

RMVXA is the latest roleplaying game development engine created by Enterbrain. It was designed with ease of use in mind and allows a total beginner to create a complete RPG without needing a single day of programming experience. It was released internationally in 2012, and many RPGs have already been developed with it. Here's a list of features that RMVXA brings to the table:

- A powerful eventing system. Events are essentially precoded instances that allow you to do many of the most common RPG things, such as create treasure chests, a shop, an inn, force player movement and non-player characters (NPCs for short) that change what they say based on the player's actions.

- A fully developed turn-based battle system. If you don't mind the forward-facing view of old classics such as Final Fantasy: Mystic Quest and Phantasy Star, this will work great for you. If you don't like it, then you can script your own battle system. However, that is an advanced topic and I will not be touching upon it in the context of this book.

- A character generator. This generator allows you to create your very own characters by using and mixing predetermined art assets. It can create both the character sprite and the portrait.

- Modifiable skills and item damage formulas. If you want to change the default formula for the Attack command, you can. Likewise, you can change different skills and items so they damage or heal based on both the user's and the enemy stats.

- The ability to create and use multiple tile sets, and edit the passability and terrain tags of those tile sets. Terrain tags can be used with switches and variables to create damage floors, among other things.

- The ability to create enemy encounters and define the regions they spawn in, all with the help of the self-titled Region Tool.

- The ability to use events and scripts to give additional effects to items and skills above and beyond the already extensive functionality that RPG Maker VX Ace provides out of the box.

What is a roleplaying game (RPG)?

Chances are that, if you've picked up this book, you probably already know what an RPG is. Most likely you've played some of them by now. Sticklers would say that every game is technically a roleplaying game given the fact that you control a character or group of characters in your attempt to win the game. So, on that note, here's a list of criteria I feel are essential for a game to be considered an RPG.

- A system that rewards character progression. The most common of these is the experience system. By gaining a certain amount of experience (commonly abbreviated to XP or EXP), the player's character gains a level. The higher the character's level, the stronger they are. Leveling up normally grants new abilities and perks for the character as well.

- A predetermined storyline. While most other genres of video games have a story, nowhere is it as important as in an RPG. It is, usually, the main reason why people play RPGs.

- A player character (PC for short). This is the human player's persona within the in-game universe. The player experiences the game's story through the eyes of his character.

- Non-player characters (NPCs). Real life would be boring if you were the only one in it, right? In the same way, a video game would be fairly dull if you were in a completely blank slate devoid of all interaction. NPCs help give the RPG world life as well as serve the many roles required in virtual society. By definition, every character that the player cannot control is an NPC.

There are surely other criteria by which an RPG can be defined, but the ones listed above are, in my appraisal, the most important.

## PART I

Creating a Solid Foundation

Everything worth doing starts with a single step. It is the same with creating your very own video game, whether with a development engine such as RPG Maker VX Ace (RMVXA) or utilizing your own programming skills. During the course of this part of the book, I will cover the following topics:

- Installing and starting up RMVXA, as well as a short overview of story and game play in the role-playing game (RPG) genre of video games.

- The use of switches and variables to create quests and area exits, among other things.

- Adding maps to your project to encompass various typical RPG locales, such as towns and dungeons, manually and with RMVXA's own Load Sample Map function.

- A detailed overview of the RMVXA database and how it pertains to player characters, enemies, collectible items such as weapons and potions, and other RPG essentials.

- Populating our first dungeon, complete with enemies, treasure chests, and a boss encounter.

I hope you're as excited as I am! Without further ado, let's begin!

CHAPTER 1

■ ■ ■

Starting Out with RPG Maker VX Ace

This chapter will cover the following subjects:

- Installing RPG Maker VX Ace (RMXVA)
- A short overview of story and game play in role-playing games (RPGs)
- Starting up RPG Maker and taking your first steps toward creating your very own game

---

■ **Note**   This book will exclusively cover RPG Maker VX Ace. If you have an earlier version of the engine (such as XP or VX), you will have to upgrade to VX Ace, to follow along.

Before you can use RMVXA, you must have it installed. First, I'll walk you through the process of getting and installing your own copy of RMVXA.

Where Can I Get RMVXA?

RMVXA (and a slew of related products, while we're on the subject) can be purchased from the official site at www.rpgmakerweb.com. The exact link is www.rpgmakerweb.com/products/programs/rpg-maker-vx-ace.

When not on sale, RMVXA usually costs $69.99, but you can try it for free for an entire month by grabbing the trial version. In addition, there is currently a light version of RMVXA (aptly named RMVXA Lite) that allows you to try out a large part of the RMVXA functionality. As the link path is different from that of the full version, I'll provide it: www.rpgmakerweb.com/download/free-programs/rpg-maker-vx-ace-lite.

If you like the engine, you can upgrade at any time and export your Lite project into the full version. Finally, if you use Steam, RMVXA is available through, and frequently on sale, on that platform.

You will be asked for your name and e-mail address, if you attempt to download the full version of RMVXA (whether you pay for it at that time, wait until later, or decide not to keep using the product). No such prompt will appear in the Lite version of RMVXA.

What Restrictions Does RMVXA Lite Have?

The chief restriction is that you cannot use RMVXA's Script Editor in the Lite version. There are many other restrictions set in place, mostly so that you cannot make a full commercial RPG out of the Lite version, such as being able to use only twenty maps and ten classes in your project. In any case, if you managed to make a full game out of the Lite version, be forewarned that you *must* upgrade to release your game commercially.

So, I Downloaded a Copy of RMVXA/RMVXA Lite. What Next?

No matter the version of RPG Maker VX Ace that you have acquired, what follows next is finding the downloaded archive and running the Setup.exe located within it. Afterward, installing it is as easy as following the steps in the installer.

I Got RMVXA Lite!

Once the installation is complete, loading up RMVXA Lite for the first time will initiate the Product Activation pop-up screen. From there, you can choose to upgrade to the full version (Buy Now) or activate your Lite version. All you have to do to activate your copy of RMVXA Lite is provide your full name and an e-mail address. Once that is done, you have unlimited access to the limited functionality of RMVXA's Lite version.

I Got RMVXA!

Once the installation is complete, loading up RMVXA for the first time will initiate a similar Product Activation screen. However, the options offered will be to activate your copy for use or a link to buy the full version. If you choose to activate, the program will ask if you wish to use your 30-day trial or input a purchase code. You should have received a trial code when you gave your information for the RMVXA download. Likewise, you should have a purchase code, if you decided to buy the full version of RMVXA. Provide the relevant information exactly as you initially gave it (don't change your name/e-mail), and you should be ready to go.

So, I'm Done.

Welcome to the world of video game development ! I hope you enjoy your stay! Now that you have a functioning copy of RMVXA or RMVXA Lite, we can continue. Before we start using the application, it would be good to talk about RPG design in general. Let us begin with the most important aspect.

Story

As mentioned previously, perhaps the most important thing about an RPG is its story. Even in the days of old, when the first *Dragon Quest* (known as *Dragon Warrior* in the United States until the eighth entry in the series was released) and *Final Fantasy* games were in their prime and storage was an issue with the earliest consoles, RPG developers sought to invest their players into the simple plot that they managed to fit within the cartridge. Perhaps the most important thing that I can point out is that not every story needs to be complex. Complexity helps, sure, *if you can make it work*. Sometimes, it's the little things that have the greatest impact. The basic facets of *any* basic RPG story are virtually identical to those used in your standard fantasy or sci-fi book with a heroic protagonist.

- *You have a protagonist*: In an RPG, this is the main character controlled by the player. The protagonist is a distinct entity, with goals, dreams, and desires.

- *You have a conflict*: The most typical fantasy conflict for both books and video games is a great evil that rises, and only the hero/chosen one/protagonist (whether alone or with help) can defeat them. With that said, don't limit yourself. If you come up with a great plot that involves a conflict between the protagonist and himself, for example, feel free to take that ball and run with it.

- *You have obstacles*: Think back to the last RPG you played or fantasy book you read. The protagonist did not start the adventure and defeat the main villain within ten minutes/pages (if they did, it was probably a fake-out and not an actual victory). The protagonist probably started from a position of relative weakness and set out into the world to defeat the antagonist, being deterred every so often by hostile forces (some aligned with evil, and some not) and hindrances such as a broken bridge or a collapsed mine shaft.

- *You have a climax and a resolution*: The protagonist, after countless tribulations, finally reaches the castle of the "Dark Lord." With a carefully calculated strike of his weapon of choice, he defeats his timeless foe. Or does he? Depending on the type of story you want to tell, perhaps your antagonist escapes to live another day. Perhaps he was merely subordinate to an even greater evil.

A great story can save an otherwise mediocre RPG, but a mediocre story can ruin even great RPGs. You must define what type of story your RPG will have. Following are a bunch of questions that should get you thinking along the right track:

- *Will it be a fantasy RPG?* If so, will magic be prominent? Will alternate forms of abilities, such as technology or something else altogether, take center stage?

- *Or will you have a sci-fi RPG?* That's neat too. Will technology be prominent, or will the setting be a devastated future where everyone is basically surviving with sticks and stones?

- *When will the story take place?* You can have a modern-day story set in a high school, for example, or a historical spy thriller set during the cold war. Maybe you want your story to take place in prehistory!

- *Who is your protagonist?* Is he young? Old? Is your protagonist female? Define why your protagonist is doing what he/she is doing. A good backstory can set the stage for greater things during the actual story.

- *Who are your protagonist's allies?* Do they know each other at the time of the game's events, or will they meet one another during the game? Define their backstories. Or perhaps you want a mysterious type in your party? Those are cool too, if you know how to create them.

- *What is your protagonist's quest?* Is he/she seeking an artifact to save the world? Or perhaps the end of the world will be brought about by a heinous villain. Of course, you could just do something else entirely and have your party go on a journey of self-discovery.

- *Who are some important nonplayer characters in the story?* Will they aid or hinder the party? Are any of them related to any of your party members?

All of those questions are good to consider for getting the ball rolling on a great story. It's important to take some time to think about the story you want for your game before you get too invested in trying to actually create it. Yet, maybe you don't want to make an RPG at all? Although this book is meant to teach you about the intricacies of RMVXA via the creation of an RPG, there's nothing to prevent you from applying the knowledge you will learn from reading this book to create something completely different. You could use RMVXA's framework to create a game that eschews battles and magic systems altogether! In fact, there have been many games created with RMVXA that are not RPGs. Off the top of my head, I can offer *You Are Not the Hero* (YANTH, for short), which is a quirky action-platformer with many minigames and a self-aware sense of humor. Also, you could take it even further by creating, with the engine, an interactive novel in the same vein as *To the Moon*. At the end of the day, the only limits to your story are those that you place on yourself.

Game Play

Of course, while the story of an RPG is important, you want your game play to be just a bit more enticing than just going into a single 30-floor dungeon and killing things (although that *has* worked on more than one occasion as well, especially for other genres, such as the action RPG). Basically, ask yourself this question: Would I play this game from start to finish? If you can't answer yes to that question with a straight face, you have to reevaluate your game, or have friends do it for you. A tried-and-true template for an RPG's game flow is listed below.

- A town gives the player quests with objectives located at a nearby dungeon.

- Said dungeon is filled with said objectives and a boss.

- After defeating the boss, the player unlocks the next area.

- This is a new town and a new dungeon.

- Repeat until the final dungeon with the final boss.

It may seem ridiculously simple and boring, but several famous RPG franchises (*Dragon Quest* and *Final Fantasy* come to mind) had plots for most of their earlier iterations that followed that general sequence. Of course, there's no problem with making the game a bit more nonlinear and allowing your players to branch off into areas they perhaps shouldn't be in yet (as long as there is an appropriate risk-to-reward ratio). Also, evaluate whether you want to add vehicles to your game, such as airships, submarines, or horses. You might even make certain vehicles available only after lengthy sidequests but reward the player for doing said sidequests by allowing the special vehicle to access otherwise inaccessible areas. Here are some other things to consider concerning your game's game play.

- *What type of progression will you be using?* Will you have the conventional system of gaining experience via combat/quest completion and then grant skills/spells/abilities as your characters level up? Or maybe you will go for something a little less conventional, perhaps a system similar to *Final Fantasy 2* (the real *FF2*, not the one released in the West that is technically *Final Fantasy 4*), in which you get stats by doing, so that if you take hits, you gain health. If you cast a spell, you gain magic points, and so forth.

- *How difficult do you want the game to be?* Easier isn't always equal to boring, mind you. *Chrono Trigger* is one of the most renowned Japanese RPGs of all time, and I've always felt that the battle system and encounters were on the easier side for such a game. *Shin Megami Tensei*, on the other hand, is rather fair, if extremely challenging, for newer players. Fairness is ultimately more important than difficulty when it comes to RPG game play.

- *How many characters will the player's party have?* Is the protagonist an army of one, or does he/she have allies? I'll elaborate on the importance of this in the following paragraph.

Balance is an important consideration when you are designing your game. A preceding bullet point asks you, the reader, about your party size. There is a concept in video game theory, especially when related to turn-based games, called *action economy*. Generally, each character only gets a certain number of actions in the period of time defined as a turn. The more characters you have, the more actions your party receives in total. For example, the original *Dragon Quest* had the player control a single hero. That meant that effects that caused the player character to miss a turn (such as sleep) were particularly dangerous. It also created a trade-off whereby if you were close to defeating an enemy but your hero was near death, you had to decide whether to heal yourself or attack again. If you were making an RPG with a single playable character, you would have to keep such facts in mind.

On the flip side, if you have a party of three or four characters, you must design some of the party's potential enemies around that. Maybe the party will face off against venomous plants that can spew poison at the entire group. When you have multiple characters, you can be a little more liberal with effects that cause turn-skipping, as the player would still have other characters to defeat those effects or otherwise continue fighting. A game's balance is one of the hardest things to perfect but is, thankfully, something you can work toward with the feedback you receive from your game's players and your own play-testing.

Entire works have been written about video game design, and it is beyond the scope of this book to discuss it further at this time. Let us move on to a basic overview of RMVXA itself. So, you've probably already started up RMVXA and have taken a cursory look around. If you have just recently installed the software and gotten past the Product Activation screen, you'll notice that you're dumped into a lifeless screen, like the one in Figure 1-1.

Figure 1-1. *The opening screen of RPG Maker VX Ace*

The first thing you'll want to do is go to the File menu at the top-left part of the interface and select New Project. That will bring up a prompt asking for three things.

- *Folder Name*: Whatever name you put in this field will also populate the Game Title field. As the field suggests, it is the name of the folder that will be created to store your RMVXA data.

- *Game Title*: Self-explanatory. This gets auto-populated by whatever you write in the Folder Name, but you can change the contents of this field manually just by manually overwriting the text.

- *Location*: Where the RMVXA Project folder will be saved. You can press the small button to the right labeled "..." to change the destination.

Once you have worked out what you want your project to be called, press OK. I simply called mine "Test" and saved it in the default location. Take a look at Figure 1-2 to see where that leads.

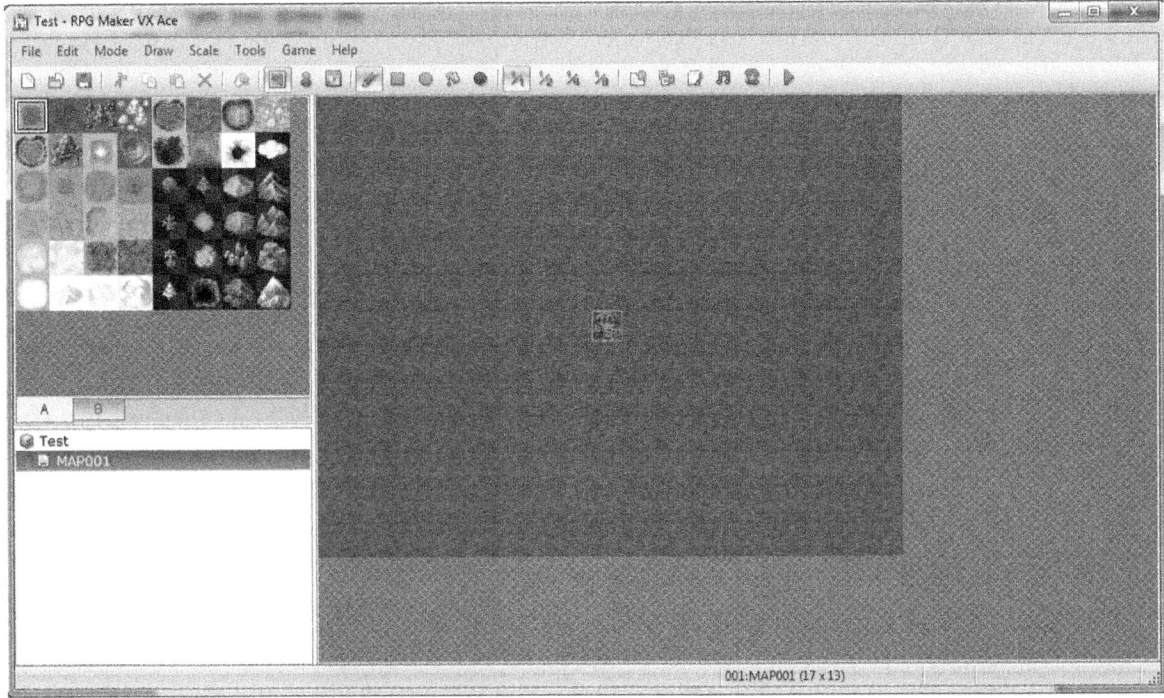

Figure 1-2. *Your first world*

Looks much better now, doesn't it? You should now be seeing a white-haired character in the middle of an empty ocean. On the top-left part of the screen, you can see various graphics, each of a specific pixel size. Those graphics are called tiles and make up the pieces that you can use to create your own RPG locations. RMVXA comes with a fairly robust Run-Time Package (RTP, for short) that includes all sorts of things that you will need for making your very own game. It will serve you well up to the moment you decide to use completely custom assets for your game development.

For now, let us mess around a bit. At the top of the screen, find the menu option named Game and click it. Then click Playtest. You will get a title screen with a nice song and the following options:

- *New Game*

- *Continue*: This should be grayed out, as there are no saved games to continue from.

- *Shutdown*: I've always thought that Shutdown should be called Exit Game or Quit, but that's just me. The name of certain hard-coded terms is actually something you can change in RMVXA, and I'll explain how to do this in a bit.

Use your keyboard's arrow keys (there's no mouse support built into RMVXA out of the box; you'd have to script it in) to select New Game and then press Enter. Now you should be able to control the character with your arrow keys. You'll quickly find that, while you can make him turn every which way, you cannot actually make him walk. That is because you're on top of impassable terrain (water, in this case), as defined by RMVXA itself. Press X or Esc to access the Character menu. You will see several options, including Save (which allows you to record your progress; RMVXA defaults to Save Anywhere, but you can use simple eventing in combination with defined save points to have a save system similar to many of the *Final Fantasy* games, for example). Feel free to poke around in the various menus. (You can use the spacebar or the Enter key to select and X or Esc to cancel/deselect.) Once you're done, hit Game End (which should probably be called End Game or Quit).

Now that we're back where we started, let's integrate everything I've talked about. First, let's change those terms I mentioned. If you click on the Tools item in the menu toolbar for RMVXA, you will see several options.

- *Database (Hotkey: F9)*: The Database is the meat and bones of RMVXA in its stock form (even if you make ample use of the Script Editor). It contains a whopping 14 tabs that contain very nearly everything you could ever think of needing for an RPG.

- *Resource Manager (Hotkey: F10)*: The Resource Manager allows you to sample, import, and export assets from your RMVXA project.

- *Script Editor (Hotkey: F11)*: The Script Editor is where most of RMVXA's hard-coded data is contained, as well as where you can add, remove, and tweak from what has been coded to make your game even more unique. Discretion is advised when you tamper with the included code, as most of it is essential for the proper functioning of RMVXA. Experience in Ruby is useful, as RMVXA runs on RGSS (Ruby Game Scripting System) 3, although you can still do a few things even if you're a total novice. I will touch upon some scripting opportunities later on in this text.

- *Sound Test (Hotkey: N/A)*: As the name suggests, you can listen to sounds contained within your project. The four different types of sounds are the following:

  - *BGM—Background Music*: Such things as the default title screen song are considered BGM.

  - *BGS—Background Sounds*: If you can hear something constant in an area, but it is not music, it is probably a BGS. Rain and Wind are two of the stock examples present within RMVXA.

  - *ME—Music Effects*: Mini-songs, if you will, such as the tune played when you rest at an inn.

  - *SE—Sound Effects*: The simplest of sounds, yet so important as well. A slew of things are SE. The sounds of fire spells and sword attacks are but two of the types of SE present within RMVXA's stock content.

- *Character Generator (Hotkey: N/A)*: Allows you to create new character (human-based) models by mixing and matching hair, eye, and skin color with 20 other customization options. If you'd rather, you can always click Generate Random and see what pops up.

- *Options*: Allows you to change the color that is considered "transparent" by RMVXA. Defaults to 0 Red/0 Green/128 Blue. Additionally, you can toggle the map grid (minimum size 2x2) from here as well.

So, much like most other things we'll be seeing during the course of this book, we will want to go to the Database. Once there, you will see the 14 tabs I mentioned previously. To change the menu options, we have to click the Terms tab (which happens to be the last one). You'll see three major categories.

1. A block of four lists denoting types of skills and attacks

2. A block of three groups of terms I'll call "Character Terms," as they're relevant to the player characters

3. A block of terms called Commands

The Commands section of the Terms tab is what we're looking for, as displayed in Figure 1-3.

Commands

Fight:	Escape:	Weapon:	Armor:
Fight	Escape	Weapons	Armours
Attack:	Guard:	Key Item:	Equip:
Attack	Guard	Key Items	Change
Item:	Skill:	Optimize:	Clear:
Items	Skills	Optimize	Clear
Equip:	Status:	New Game:	Continue:
Equipment	Status	New Game	Continue
Formation:	Save:	Shutdown:	To Title:
Formation	Save	Shutdown	To Title
Game End:		Cancel:	
Game End		Cancel	

Figure 1-3. *The Commands section of the Terms tab, edited to better fit on the page*

As you can see, from here we can change the name of any of those listed terms. So, let's change "Game End" to "End Game" and "Shutdown" to "Quit." Press Apply to save the changes and then press OK to close the Database menu. Now, let's see if we can get our protagonist onto solid ground. Figure 1-4 shows my own efforts. Use the provided tiles to replicate it as best you can.

Figure 1-4. *A simple map*

From inner to outer layer, the tiles are

- Grass

- Desert

- Clouds

- High Mountain (Rock) on top of Wasteland

There are a few drawing tools that you can use (RMVXA defaults to the pencil, which draws in tiles as you click/drag your mouse). They are located almost directly below the Help item of the menu toolbar. You can choose to draw rectangles, ellipses, or fill a large area with the same tile. I used the Fill tool to add the Wasteland tile and then the High Mountain on top of the Wasteland.

■ **Tip**   You can find the name of tiles by mousing over them. The name of the tile will be displayed on the lower-left corner of the application.

Once you have added the terrain to your map, load up the game again, and you should be able to move all the way to the clouds. The mountains will stop you from moving any further. Simple, isn't it?

Summary

This chapter has covered the installation and initialization of RPG Maker VX Ace, as well as providing a short overview of game play and story design considerations and a first look at the game-development engine. However, there's not much of a game here yet. Let's move on to a topic that is rather important to video games of all genres, RPGs included.

CHAPTER 2

Switches and Variables

If you have any amount of programming experience, you're probably familiar with the use of switches and variables (especially the latter) in coding programs.

Switches? Variables? Pizza?

Yes. Yes. With pepperoni, please. Seriously, though, let me explain. Switches and variables in RPG Maker VX Ace (RMVXA) are similar to boxes in real life. They both hold information you would want to use later on. They are ubiquitous in video games as well. Don't believe me? Here's a small list of things that, with the use of switches and variables, you can influence in any video game:

- The ability to keep track of the number of chests opened during the course of the game (variables)

- The ability to determine whether a boss has been defeated or not (switches)

- Preventing the player from accessing a certain area without a key or some other device (switches)

- Changing a quest reward based on the method the player used to complete the quest. For instance, you could give a 300 gold reward for killing a group of bandits, and give a reduced reward if the player drives them off, sparing them, instead. (variables)

- Counting the amount of enemies left on a certain screen (variables)

- Counting the amount of steps your party has taken. (variables) This has several applications, such as causing a nonstandard Game Over when the player exceeds a certain number of steps or granting the player an achievement or skill. You could use a variable to increase or decrease the power of a skill as well.

As you must have noticed, you cannot make a video game without switches and variables!

Switches and Variables Do the Same Thing, Then?

Mostly, but there are differences. For switches, think of a light switch that has an on and an off state. You can set conditionals that only trigger when a certain switch is on or when said switch is off. Variables, on the other hand, can hold a number—any number that you can think of. Want to have-327 contained within a variable you call Bob? Sure, go right ahead! Basically, both switches and variables are used for storing relevant game information, but they are best used in different types of situations.

It is best to use a switch when you want to create a button/lever/switch in-game that is binary (that is to say, has exactly two states). It is best to use a variable when you have a situation that cannot be covered with a simple on/off state. For example, if you wanted to count how many goblins a player has defeated, you would have to store that information in a variable. On the other hand, if someone gave your character a quest to slay five goblins, you could have a switch flip to the "on" state after the fifth goblin is defeated.

While switch and variable theory is nice and all, let's take some time to apply it.

Objectives:

- Add a button to the previously made map that creates an exit through which our intrepid hero can reach another map. After all, if I were him, I wouldn't want to be cooped up in a single 13×17 map for eternity!

- Create the exit itself.

So, how do we go about adding the necessary items to the map? We are finally going to start dabbling with the functionality that gives RMVXA its reputation as a robust game-development engine that even a novice can use. If you look directly below the Game item on the menu toolbar, you'll notice a trio of icons (they are to the left of the drawing tool icons).

- The first icon, which should have an orange square around it, if you haven't interacted with these icons previously, is Map Mode. As the name suggests, having Map Mode selected allows you to add/remove tiles on your currently selected map. You can press F5 to switch to Map Mode at any time.

- The second icon is the Event Editing Mode. (You can also press F6 to switch to that mode without having to click the icon.) Events form a large part of RMVXA's stock functionality.

- An event is an object that occupies a single square on an RMVXA map and carries out processing for pretty much all essential game functions. For example, we can create a shop run by a horse or a doorway that requires a key. Without events, you won't be able to do much, if anything, at all. All nonplayer characters (NPCs) are events, for example.

- The final icon is for Region Editing Mode. I will elaborate on what Regions do in RMVXA, once it becomes relevant. (Teaser: It involves encounters with monsters). You can also press F7 to switch to this mode without having to click the icon.

Click the Event Editing Mode icon (or press F6), and you'll notice that a grid appears on the map. If you right-click any square of the grid, you'll see a menu pop up, as seen in Figure 2-1.

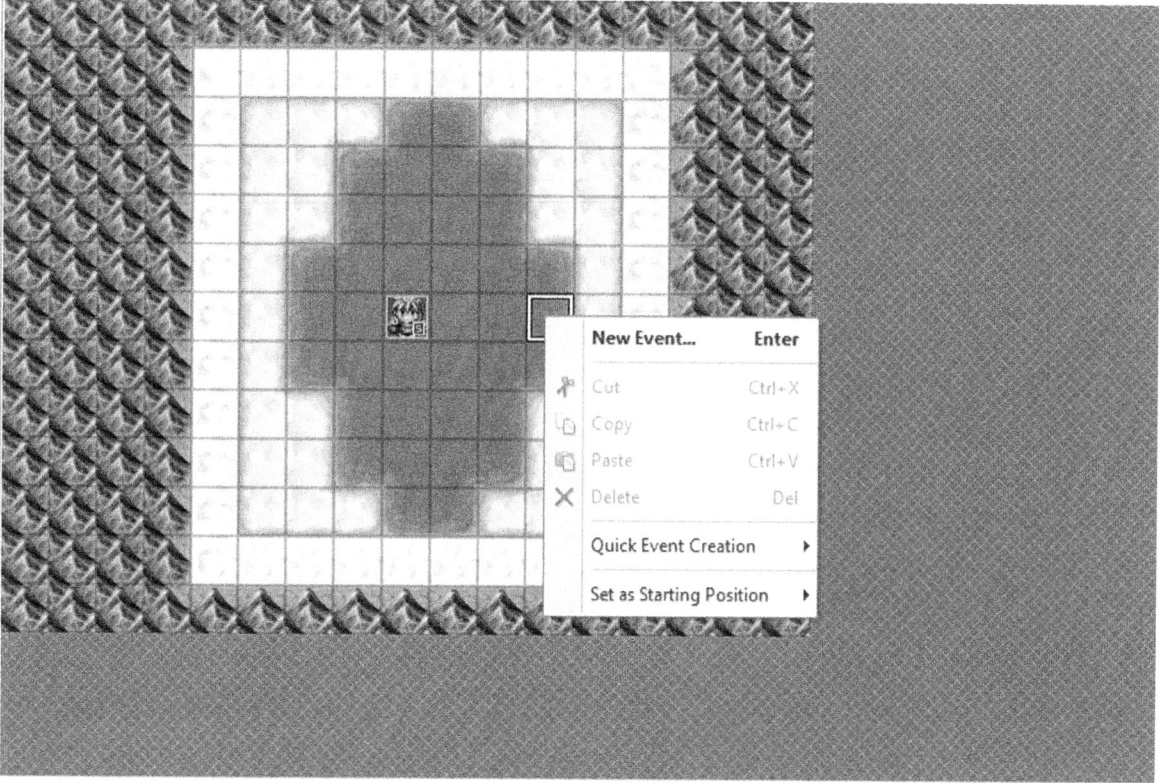

Figure 2-1. *The Event pop-up menu*

The available options are as follows:

- *New Event*: This allows you to place a new event on the map. We'll be using this frequently throughout the course of this book.

- The editing tools (Cut/Copy/Paste/Delete) are grayed out because there is no event in the selected square.

- *Quick Event Creation*: RMVXA comes with four quick events for things that are essential to any RPG experience.

  1. **Transfer.** Creates an event that allows you to transfer a player from one place to another

  2. **Door.** A situational type of transfer event, usually used for entrances to buildings

  3. **Treasure Chest.** Creates an event that gives items or currency (default name "gold") to the player when he/she interacts with it

  4. **Inn.** Heals the player and his/her party (if applicable) for a predefined cost in currency

- *Set Starting Position*: Allows you to set the starting position for the player character and three types of vehicles (boat, ship, airship). Setting a starting position for the player character is mandatory, but starting vehicle locations is optional.

Click New Event and you'll wind up on a large blank slate, as seen in Figure 2-2.

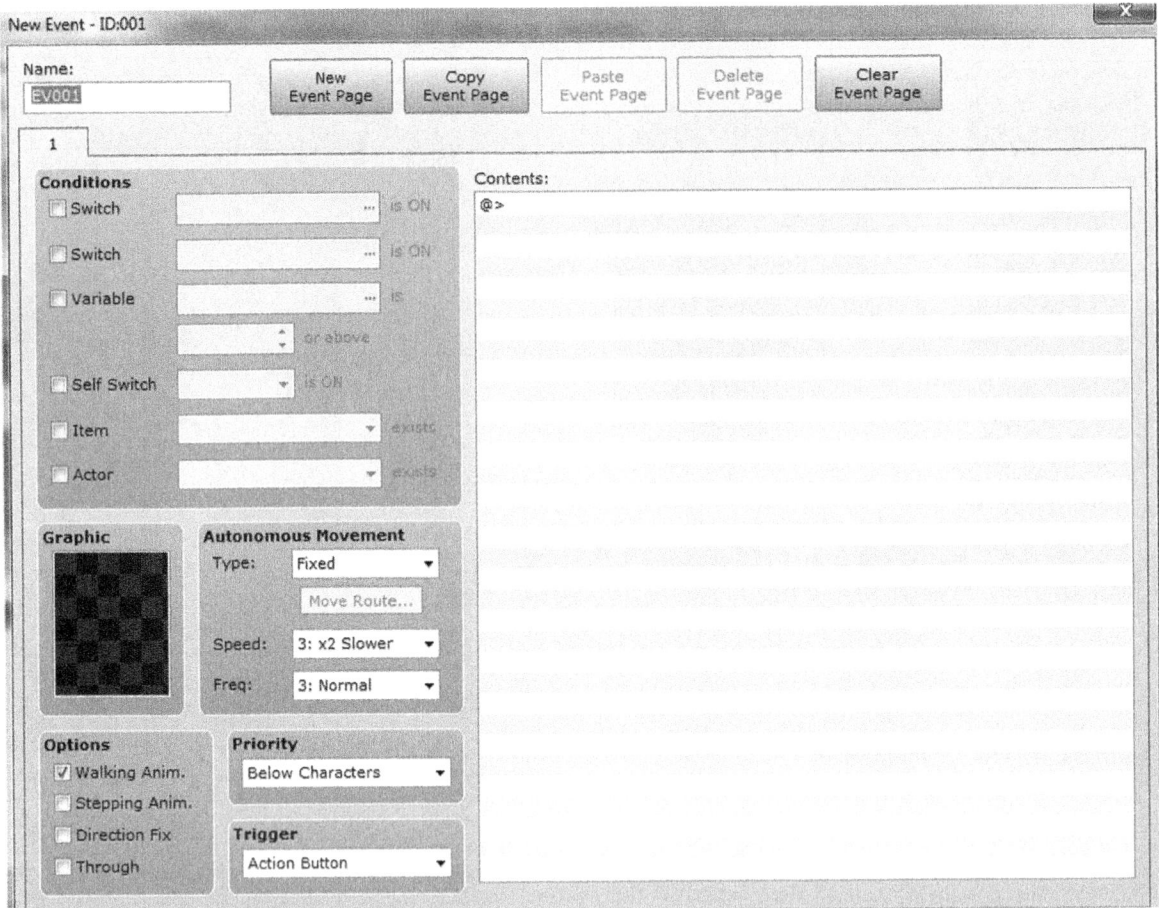

Figure 2-2. *The New Event window*

There are many aspects to the Event screen, so let's break them down.

- In the upper-left corner, you have several *Conditions*. If you don't set any event conditions, the event in question will always be active.

- The checkerboard directly under *Graphic* can be double left-clicked to display a list of graphics present within the project. You can then choose a graphic to represent the event. For example, you could use a graphic for a villager or a monster. We'll be using a button graphic later in the chapter.

- Below the checkerboard, you have a list of four *Options*.

  1. **Walking Anim.** is short for "Walking Animation" and displays character movement. If you turn off Walking Anim. and have an NPC that moves, the character will appear to be sliding on the ground.

  2. **Stepping Anim.** is short for "Stepping Animation." When the check box is ticked, the NPC will walk in place. A neat use of Stepping Anim. is if you want to simulate gesturing during conversations.

  3. **Direction Fix**. As the option implies, clicking this check box will cause the event to be unable to switch directions. You could use this for a shooting gallery–type of mini-game, in which you want the player to face forward no matter what arrow key he/she presses.

  4. **Through**. The player character can pass through an event that has this option toggled on. Logically, the event can also pass through the player character (in the case of a mobile event such as an NPC). This is cool for ghosts and other such apparitions.

- *Autonomous Movement* is divided into three functions.

  1. **Type**. Defines what kind of movement the event uses. There are four types of movement.

     - *Fixed*: An event with this type of movement will remain in its starting location. This is perfect for the many kinds of immobile things that you will need for your RPG.

     - *Random*: Events with a random movement type will wander wherever they feel like, with no rhyme or reason. I'd use this movement type sparingly, as it can cause some annoying situations if you have thin corridors in your game.

     - *Approach*: An event with this movement type will try to approach the player character. It is good for making a scene involving enemies chasing your players.

     - *Custom*: This allows the Move Route button to be clicked, which, in turn, lets you set a movement pattern for the event in question.

  2. **Speed**. This sets how quickly the event executes its movement pattern. The higher the speed, the quicker the event will step.

  3. **Freq**. Short for "Frequency." Sets how frequently the event executes its movement pattern. The higher the frequency, the more often the event takes a movement action.

- *Priority* defines what graphical layer an event is rendered on, relative to the player character.

  1. **Below Characters**. Means that the event is located beneath the player character's feet. This is good for floor switches and staircases.

  2. **Same As Characters**. Means that the event is located on the same graphical layer as the player character. This is perfect for NPCs and inanimate objects, such as cabinets and trees.

  3. **Above Characters**. Means that the event is located over the player character's head. This is useful for chandeliers and ceilings, among other things.

- *Trigger* defines how the event can be activated.

    1. **Action Button**. An event that activates via the use of the Action Button (spacebar or Enter, by default) when appropriate. If the event has *Below Characters* priority, the player character will have to stand on top of the event, to activate it. If the event has *Same as Characters* priority, the player character will have to stand next to the event while facing it, to activate it. Last, if the event has *Above Characters* priority, the player character will have to stand under the event, to activate it.

    2. **Player Touch**. An event that activates when the player character touches the event by walking into it. It is affected by Priority much like the Action Button.

    3. **Event Touch**. An event that activates when it touches the player character. It is similarly affected by Priority as the previous two options. I prefer to use Player Touch, but you'll need Event Touch on the map, if you're trying to make moving projectiles that your players must dodge, for example.

░ **Note**   An easy way to determine if you need Player Touch or Event Touch is the following: for something that you want the player to trigger at his/her convenience, use Player Touch. For something that the player must avoid or is otherwise triggered outside of his/her control, use Event Touch.

---

    4. **Autorun**. An event with the Autorun trigger is always on and will repeat its actions until interrupted somehow. This is probably the easiest way to crash your game when you're just starting out in RMVXA. I generally only use it for cinematic sequences (such as events in which you have the game auto-control the player character in an in-game cut scene).

    5. **Parallel Process**. Similar to an Autorun trigger, a Parallel Process event is always on. However, it will not interrupt other game functions. This is the type of event you should use to handle large-scale area transitions, among several other things.

- The entire right half of the New Event screen contains its *Contents*. By right-clicking (and left-clicking Insert) or double left-clicking anywhere inside of the window boundaries, you'll find yourself looking at a large list of event commands. They represent the many things that we can do with RMVXA without having an inkling of Ruby knowledge. I will be covering a few of these later in this chapter and many more throughout the book.

- At the very top of the page, you'll see five buttons involved in the creation and deletion of Event Pages. A single event can have up to 99 pages.

An Event Can Have 99 Event Pages!

Yes, seriously. I'm hard-pressed to think of any situation in which you'd have to make use of all 99 pages, but most events you create for your RPG will require more than one. Multiple event pages are how you can make NPCs change conversations as you progress within the game, to name but one thing you can do with them. As a matter of fact, the button event I will create shortly is going to have two pages.

Ready?

Let us begin. First of all, check Figure 2-3 for the end result.

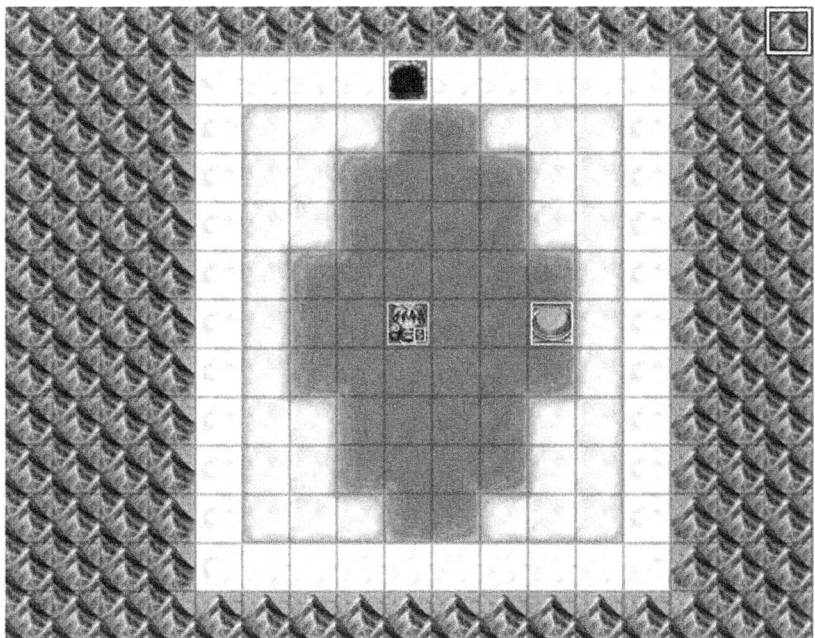

Figure 2-3. *The finished button and exit in place*

That's a green button three steps to the player character's right and the exit located five steps to the north. The button event is two pages, and the exit event is one page. Before I explain what commands to add, let's think about the situation critically. Our player starts the game and sees nothing of note, save a single button. You want the player to press the button and receive some sort of feedback after the fact, so that he/she knows he/she did. So, page 1 of the button event will have a graphic of the green button in a raised position, while page 2 of that event will have a graphic of the same button in a lowered position. We will inform the player via a text box that the button has been pressed, before we do that.

Pressing the button will reveal the exit to the north. You are starting to see how this will all work out. In essence

- We want a button that the player can press to reveal an exit.

- We do not want the exit to be revealed before the player presses the switch.

- We want the switch to reflect the fact that the player has pressed it.

How do we do that? With a switch! The final results for the pages are shown in Figures 2-4 to 2-6. We'll step through the required instructions for reaching this state next.

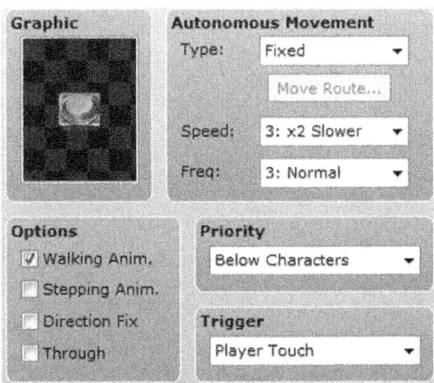

Figure 2-4. *The first page of our button*

```
@>Text: -, -, Normal, Bottom
:                : You stepped on the switch!
@>Play SE: 'Jump1', 80, 100
@>Control Switches: [0001:Switch] = ON
```

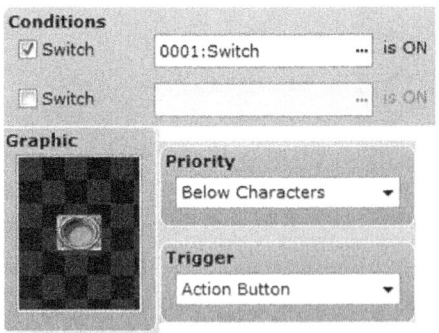

Figure 2-5. *The second page of our button*

```
@>Text: -, -, Normal, Bottom
:                : You see a button pushed into the earth.
```

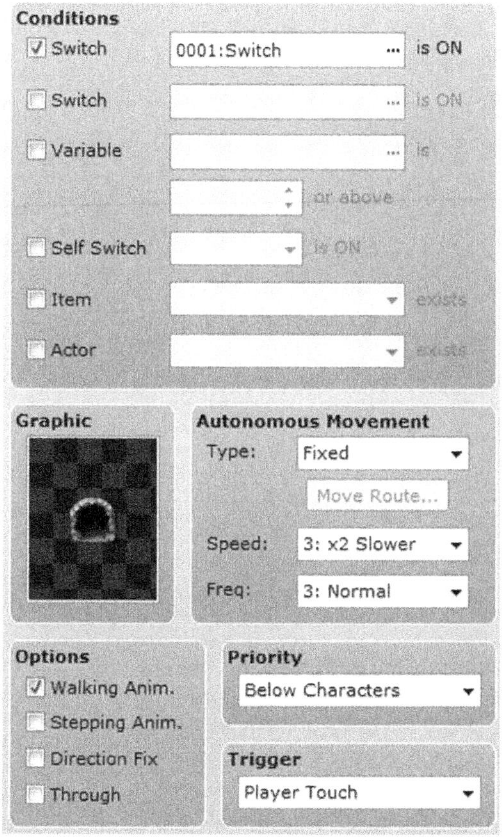

Figure 2-6. *Our exit event for transferring the player to the next map*

```
@>Transfer Player:[001:MAP001] (008,001)
```

■ **Note** If an event has a single page with a condition that has yet to be met, it will be invisible in-game. Thus, the player will not be able to see the exit until the "Switch" Switch is on.

Creating the Events

- While in Event Mode, right-click the square three grids to the right of the player's starting position and then left-click New Event. We'll be making the button first.

- On the blank event page, you can rename the event on the upper-left corner. It is currently unimportant, but if you make your own game, you'll want to have your events properly identified. Trust me when I say that trying to figure out which of your 38 events on a map is supposed to represent a rolling boulder is nigh impossible when they're named EV001, EV002, EV003, etc.

- Right-click the @ sign in the Contents part of the event page and then left-click Insert. Alternatively, you can double left-click to achieve the same effect.

Now you can see a large list of appropriately named Event Commands. There are three pages full of many useful commands for your eventing needs. The first command we need is called *Show Text*. Show Text will allow you to write in some text that will be displayed in a box when the event is triggered; see Figure 2-7.

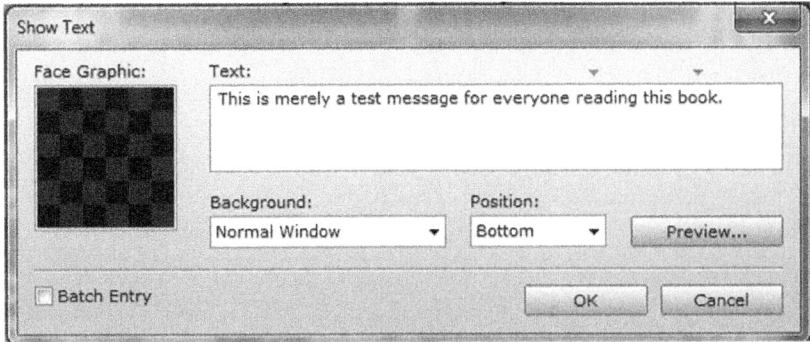

Figure 2-7. *The Show Text event window*

As you can see in Figure 2-7, there are a few things you can do with this command.

- You can add a character portrait to the text box. Keep in mind that doing so reduces the amount of text that you can fit in each line.

- On that note, you may have already noticed the pair of arrows on top of the text box. The left arrow marks the limit of text that can be displayed in a line if you have a character portrait, while the right arrow marks the limit if you do not have a portrait in the box. If you had a character portrait, the preceding line would read roughly as follows in-game: "This is merely a test message for everyone re." Otherwise, it would read, "This is merely a test message for everyone reading this bo." You can use Enter to break up your lines, so that they don't hit that limit. A text box can fit up to four lines of text.

- The *Batch Entry* option can be toggled to allow you to write more than four lines of text. (It adds a scrollbar to the right of the text box). Additional Show Text commands will automatically be created after every fourth line of text that you have, once you select OK.

- *Background* affects the appearance of the text box itself. The default is Normal Window, which will display the text box in the color set within RMVXA. The default is -34 Red/0 Green/68 Blue and can be changed with the use of the *Change Window Color* event command. You can also set the text box to Dim Background and Transparent. Transparent can be quite useful if you have a scene in which you have blacked out the screen and just want to show the text, without the accompanying text box.

- *Position* is fairly self-explanatory. You can set the position of the text box on the screen when it is displayed. It defaults to Bottom and can also be set to Middle or Top, as desired.

Let's write "You stepped on the switch!" and then click OK.

- The next step is not strictly required but adds a little atmosphere to the event. By using the *Play SE* command (available on the second page of the Event Command list), you can set a sound effect to be played after you step on the switch. I chose the Jump1 SE and left it at default volume and pitch. You can play around with one or the other, to see how they affect the sound effect in question.

- Last, we toggle the switch! The *Control Switches* event command is on the first page of the Event Commands list.

When you click on it, it will show you the screen shown in Figure 2-8. The Control Switches command is rather simple. You choose a single switch or a batch of switches to flip, and then you decide whether you want to set them to on or off. You can press the button labeled ".." to change the switch you are affecting (as well as give the switch a proper name, as all switches and variables default to having a blank name). Here, I've given Switch #0001 the name of Switch, but you can rename it to something like "ButtonPress" or "ButtonSwitch." Once that is ready, all you have to do is set the other options, so that they match mine shown following:

- Options
  - Toggle on Walking Anim.
- Autonomous Movement
  - Type: Fixed
  - Speed: 3: ×2 Slower
  - Freq 3: Normal

- Priority: Below Characters
- Trigger: Player Touch

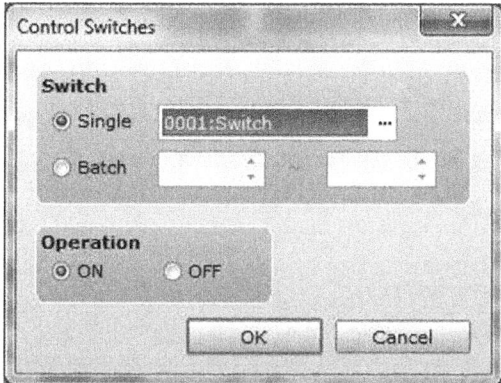

Figure 2-8. *The Control Switches window*

■ **Note** The green switch that I used is from the tileset called !Switch1, namely, the one in the top-left corner.

That concludes the first event page for the button. Now, what you need to do is click New Event Page. You will see a new tab numbered 2 appear. Make sure to toggle the conditional, as I did, and set the relevant options, as shown following:

- Conditions: Switch 0001: Switch is ON
- Priority: Below Characters
- Trigger: Action Button

I also added some text reading: "You see a button pushed into the earth." Once that is done, you can press OK, which will place you back at the map screen.

▪ **Note** The green button graphic used in page 2 is the one on the lower-right corner of the group of relevant graphics in !Switch1.

Finally, right-click the square five steps to the north of the player's starting position and set the parameters for the Exit Event as I have done below.

- Conditions: Switch 0001: Switch is ON

- Options: Toggle on Walking Anim.

- Autonomous Movement

  - Type: Fixed

  - Speed: 3: ×2 Slower

  - Freq: 3: Normal

- Priority: Below Characters

- Trigger: Player Touch

▪ **Note** The graphic used for the exit can be found in the Tileset-B graphics group. It is two tiles down and one tile right from the upper-left corner.

As for the contents of the exit event, there are two ways to create a transfer event, as follows:

1. Create it manually. You should do so for the practice, but keep in mind option 2 for the future.

2. Use the Quick Event Creation ➤ Transfer option to achieve the same effect.

If you prefer to do it the long way, *Transfer Player* can be found on the second page of the Event Command List. Clicking on Transfer Player in the event command menu will present you with an image similar to that shown in Figure 2-9.

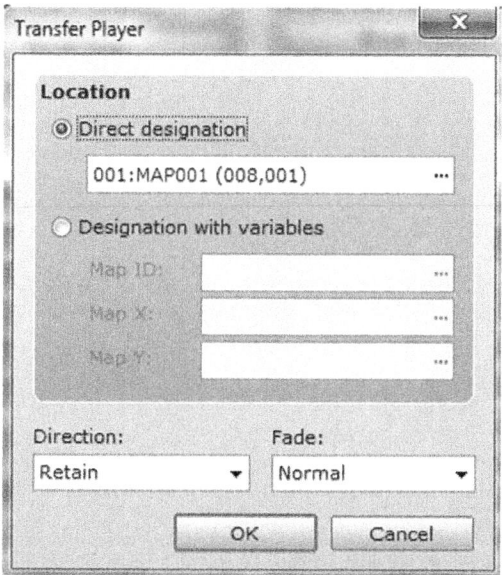

Figure 2-9. *The Transfer Player event dialog screen*

For now, just leave the settings as displayed in Figure 2-9. We'll expand on this in the next section. Once all is said and done, you can play-test the game in its current state. Feel free to move around and interact with the button. If you have set up the map events correctly, all of the following should be true.

- Walking onto the button will cause the button event to trigger a text box pop-up, as well as the sound effect to play and the switch to sink into the ground.

- After the switch is pressed, you should see the exit reveal itself at the upper part of the screen.

- Pressing the spacebar or Enter when you are on top of the pressed button will give you the relevant text, telling you that the button is already pressed.

- Walking into the exit will just place you back on top of the exit.

■ **Note**　When an event has multiple pages, the *right-most* page with valid conditions is executed. That is the reason why we have the button event ordered as it is. If it were backward, the event would keep repeating itself every time you stepped onto the square.

Creating Your Second Map

You may have noticed beforehand that the destination for the map exit has been set to the same coordinates as the exit itself. What we need to do now is create a new map and change the Transfer event command to send us to the new map. To do that, take a look at the lower-left corner of the map screen, shown in Figure 2-10.

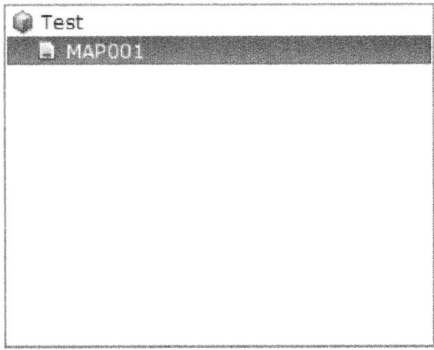

Figure 2-10. *This portion of the screen displays all of the maps in your game*

You should see something similar to the preceding screenshot. On your end, Test will be whatever you decided to call your project. MAP001 is the default 13×17 map that automatically gets inserted into every new project. Right-click MAP001, and you'll see the following options:

- *Map Properties (Hotkey: Space)*: Allows you to edit the currently selected map

- *New Map (Hotkey: Ins)*: Creates a new map

- *Load Sample Map (Hotkey: N/A)*: RMVXA comes with a wide range of premade maps that will allow you to see how to lay out many areas typical of the standard RPG experience.

- *Copy/Paste/Delete*: These are the editing tools available when dealing with maps.

- *Shift (Hotkey: Ctrl+T)*: Allows you to move the map a certain number of squares in the direction you choose

- *Generate Dungeon (Hotkey: Ctrl+D)*: Randomly generates a maze, based on the map size and a selection of wall and floor tiles. I should note that exceedingly small maps will result in a dungeon that has only one or two rooms, as RMVXA is very liberal with creating a wall border (it's something like 10 squares big) around the maze.

For now, let's click New Map. You will land on the screen shown in Figure 2-11.

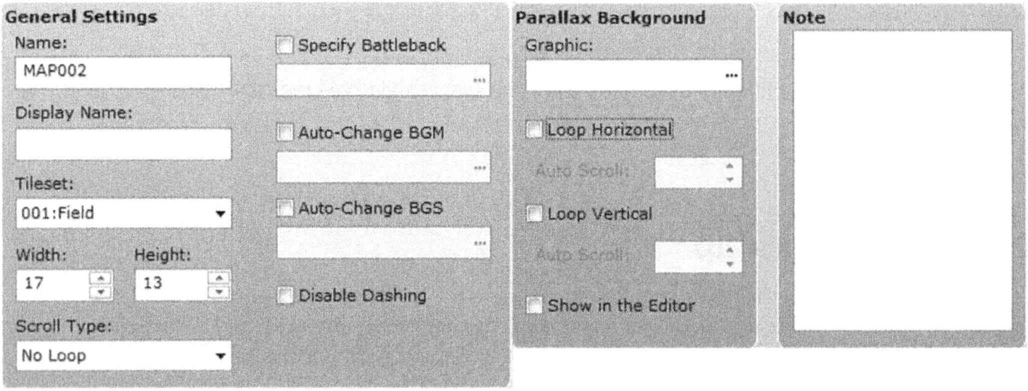

Figure 2-11. *The New Map dialog screen*

As with several of the preceding screenshots, I have tweaked it, so that it can fit neatly within the confines of this page. I've left out the Encounters section on the right side of the window. Encounters are relevant to monster spawning, and I will be touch on them at a later time. Anyway,

- *Name* is the internal name of your map, that is to say, the name the map has while you're working on your game in RMVXA. This can be edited, if desired. For example, MAP001 is the internal name of the default map included in all RMVXA projects when they are created.

- *Display Name* is the name of the area as displayed in-game. When your player reaches an area that has a non-blank display name, the game will display the area name in a small box near the upper-left corner of the screen.

- *Tileset*: If you're using RMVXA Lite, the four tilesets available will be the only ones you can use. In the full version of RMVXA, you can add more tilesets of your own choosing. In any case, and as you might imagine, each tileset is created with a distinct graphical goal in mind. The map properties default to Field, which is the tileset you would use for a world map.

- *Width/Height* control the map's size.

- *Scroll Type* allows you to make a map that loops in on itself horizontally, vertically, or both. This is very good for a world styled much like our own planet.

- *Specify Battleback* allows you to set a background that will be displayed during combat with enemies.

- *Auto-Change BGM/BGS*: This pair of options allows you to change the background music and sounds when the player first enters the new map.

- *Disable Dashing*: Players can move in double time during game play by holding down the Shift button as they move. You can disable this functionality on a map by toggling this check box.

- *Parallax Background*: This can be used to make a dynamic background that moves when the player moves. It can be used for such things as simulating an elevator going up or down floors.

- The *Notes* field is pretty much self-explanatory. It can be used to write down things related to the map in question. If you want to write up a list of important events that occur on a certain map, this would be the perfect place to put it.

Those are the relevant options. Let us set them, like so:

- Name/Display Name: Second Area

- Tileset: Exterior

- Width/Height: 30/30

- Auto-Change BGM: Field3

When you're ready, press OK. You will be greeted with a large checkerboard of nothing.

Why Is the Map Empty?

While MAP001 comes with water tiles already set, subsequently created maps are completely blank (to be precise, that's the transparent tile). To answer the question posed by the section heading, it's just the way RMVXA works. Worthy of note is the fact that 30×30 is large enough a map size to require you to use the scrollbars (even if you've been following this book while using RMVXA full-screen). Make sure your editing mode is set to Map Mode (click the relevant icon or press F5) and then draw a rectangle with the Meadow tile that starts at (0,0) and ends on (23,15).

Tips

- As a reminder, the rectangle drawing tool for tiles is directly to the right of the pencil tool.

- You can find the specific coordinates for a certain square on your map by looking near the lower-right corner of the map screen while your cursor is over said square.

- I specified (23,15), as this is the limit of how much of the map I can see while keeping RMVXA in a non-maximized form and not using the scrollbars. If you can see more or less of the map, you may have to drag, squish, or expand your program size to be able to use the rectangle as I intend.

As you can see, the tileset for Exterior has different tiles than the Field tileset. Find (11,0) on the new map and the Dirt (Meadow) tile and draw a vertical line to (11,4). After that, take some time to add some terrain and play with the tileset.

Notes

- Adding certain types of terrain, such as ledges and walls, will cause small shadows to be rendered automatically. This is meant to simulate the effects of sunlight. You can use the Shadow Pen (the final drawing tool I have not mentioned as of yet) to remove those shadows or add some more of your own.

- Tilesets have multiple pages. The Exterior tileset has three pages. Page A of a tileset is dedicated to major terrain, such as grass/dirt/snow, ledges, and structures. Other pages contain doodads to flesh out what would otherwise be a fairly dull map.

You can find my rendition of the 23×15 area in Figure 2-12. Make sure your road is in the right place (and I'd highly recommend having at least the ledges directly to the sides of that road as well). Once that is done, switch to Event Mode and right-click (11,0). It's time to create another transfer event.

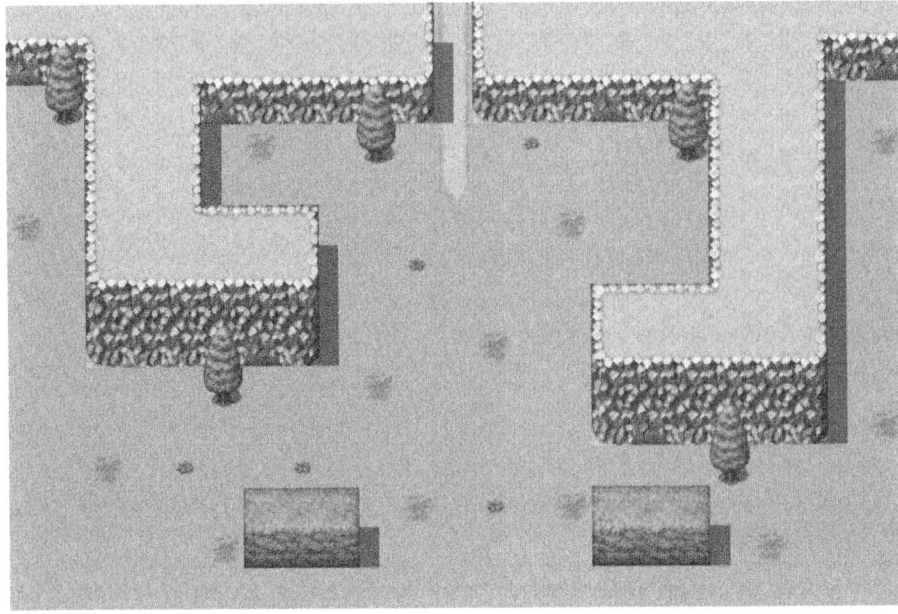

Figure 2-12. *My final map for the second area*

Don't forget to switch the event trigger to Player Touch; otherwise, the player will have to press spacebar or Enter to activate the event. Set the destination to one square south of the exit on MAP001. (You can left-click the map list within the Transfer Player menu to change which map you are looking at.) If you have followed the book up to now, that should be (8,2). Then, left-click MAP001 in the main map screen, to return to the first map. Right-click the Exit event and then left-click Edit. What you want to do is edit the Transfer Player command so that it points to the dirt road in our second map. For the sake of this tutorial, let's place the destination at (11,2). Right-click the Transfer Player command and choose Edit, to make the appropriate changes. What you *don't* want to do is place it right where you have the event to transfer to MAP001, as that has the potential to cause issues.

If you have done all of the above, you are now set. Play-test the game and see what happens.

▩ **Note**   If your character is going through the exit and facing north instead of south, it is because you must manually change the direction he/she faces after said transition. You can do this by changing the Direction setting in the Transfer Event dialog screen from Retain to Down.

Cool! Now, About Those Variables . . .

Okay fine, you're right. Let's apply the usage of variables before we end this chapter and move on to meatier subjects. Take a look at your second map. Place five trees (wherever you like, so long as you stay within that 23×15 area we populated with grass) around the area. If you managed to copy the map I created earlier, then the five trees you already have will be perfect.

▩ **Note**   For larger graphics (such as the trees we've used) that take up more than a single tile of space, you will have to place each individual tile accordingly. Trees have a top tile for foliage and a trunk as the bottom tile.

What we're going to do now is have each tree increase the value of a variable by one when the player interacts with them. We have to make sure that the player can't just interact with the same tree five times. In other words, each tree can only be counted once. So, how do we do this? There are several ways, but I'm going to take advantage of the fact that this is the switches and variables chapter to talk a little about self-switches.

Each event can contain up to four self-switches. While switches and variables have global scope (that is to say, the value of a switch or variable can be accessed from any other part of RMVXA), self-switches are local in scope. The rest of your game's events care not if Event #441 on Map #72 has its self-switch B (self-switches go from A to D) set to the "ON" state. It only holds importance to that one specific event itself.

So, we need an event that does the following:

- Displays a text box telling the player a little about the tree.

- Increases the value of the Tree variable by 1, if it is the first time the player has interacted with that tree. Otherwise, do nothing.

With that said, if you like a challenge or have previous coding experience, I invite you to try and figure this one out by yourself. You'll need to keep in mind the following:

- The tree is a solid object, unlike the cave entrance/clearing we have used as our pair of exits so far during the book. That means the player will not be able to step on the event square.

- It is preferable that the player interact with the tree rather than having to run into it to trigger the event.

- You will need a new Event Command called *Conditional Branch* to check for the self-switch.

- On that note, you'll have to make use of *Control Variables* as well.

- And *Control Self Switch*. Otherwise, using the Conditional Branch command would be in vain.

- You're essentially using the same event five times.

Did you figure it out? If you think you have (or are stumped), let's resume. The crux of this particular exercise is in those new event commands that I have not explained yet. I wholeheartedly recommend experimentation throughout your use of RMVXA. After all, video game design is basically one long sequence of problems to be solved. (The same can be said of programming.) With that in mind, let's take a look at the Conditional Branch command shown in Figure 2-13.

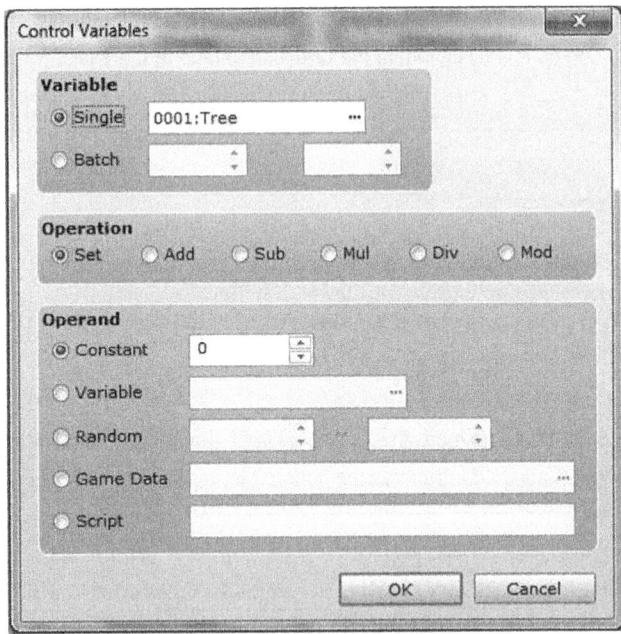

Figure 2-13. *The Conditional Branch event dialog*

■ **Note**   In Ruby, and programming in general, a conditional is something that happens when a certain condition is met. In this case, we're talking about a simple if/else condition. For example, if I have more than three cats, I am a cat person; else, I am not.

The Conditional Branch command in RMVXA automatically defaults to the switch option. Click the self-switch bubble and then set it so that the branch check for A is OFF. There's a check box I didn't include in Figure 2-13 that's titled "Set handling when conditions do not apply." It defaults with a check mark, but I usually untoggle it. Why, you may ask? I find it generally easier to make a pair of conditional branches rather than having to handle the exception (in this case, A is ON) within a single branch. As you work in RMVXA, you'll realize that my way of working with conditional branches actually results in less clutter. In any case, we won't need the Else that leaving that check box checked would create, as we don't want the event to execute anything within that branch if the self-switch is already on.

The second new event command we should take a look at is *Control Variables*. See Figure 2-14 for an image of the Control Variables menu, as seen when accessed.

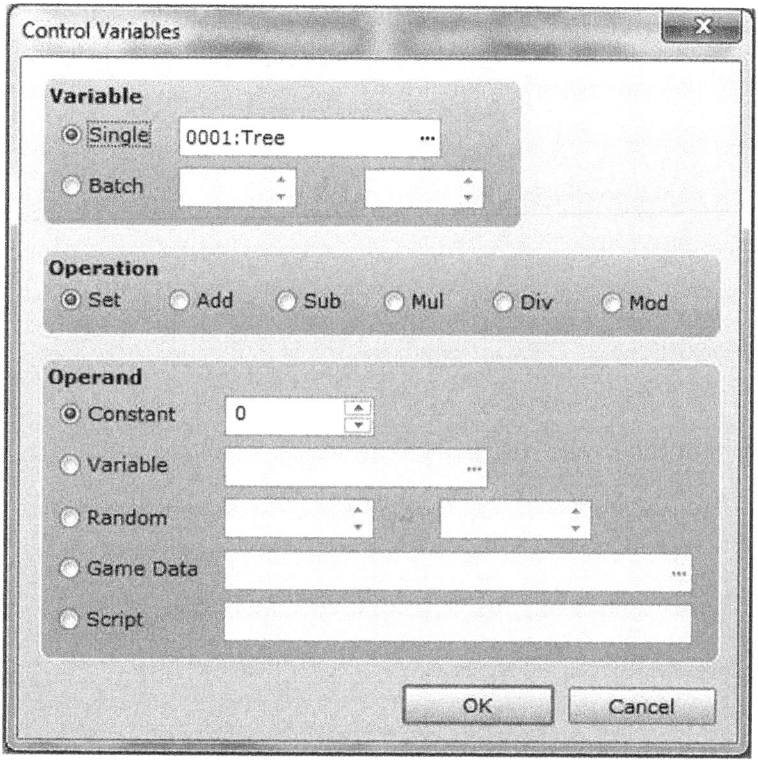

Figure 2-14. *The Control Variables event dialog*

Like Control Switches, Control Variables allows you to manipulate a single variable or a batch (group) of variables at the same time. Unlike Control Switches, there are many more things you can do with a variable. This is mostly owing to the fact that a variable can hold any number, while a switch can only hold an *off* or an *on* state. In what may seem as a rather meta thing, you can have a variable be affected by the value of *another* variable. *Final Fantasy* uses variables in such a way to great effect. For example, a certain character's weapon in *Final Fantasy* IX causes greater damage the more dragons it has killed during the course of the game. While making a weapon stronger based on such a variable requires scripting in RMVXA, you *can* create a skill that does much the same, and it does *not* require scripting.

For this exercise, all we have to do is name the variable in question (I called it Tree), change the operation to Add, and set the Operand to Constant with a value of 1. If you leave the operation on Set, it will make the value of the variable 1. You want the variable to gain 1, not stay at 1, when the player interacts with a tree. To summarize, when the player performs an action on the tree the first time, the variable "Tree" will be increased by 1.

Finally, we need to add a Control Self Switch event. Control Self Switch is a simple enough event command that I won't use an image on it. All you can do with that command is select one of the four self-switches and set its state to ON or OFF. Set self-switch A to ON, and there you have it.

In simpler terms, here's the solution. Figure 2-15 shows the necessary Priority and Trigger settings.

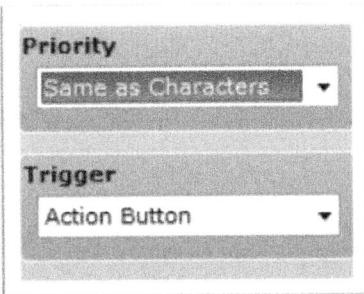

Figure 2-15. *The Priority and Trigger settings for the tree*

```
@>Text: -, -, Normal, Bottom
:              : This tree looks rather peculiar.
@>Conditional Branch: Self Switch A == OFF
   @>Control Variables: [0001:Tree] += 1
   @>Control Self Switch: A =ON
   @>
: Branch End
@>
```

- As noted earlier, an event with the priority "Same as Characters" exists on the same graphical layer as the player.

- On that note, you won't be able to step on top of the event's square, so the trigger should be Action Button.

- The conditional branch checks to see if the event's self-switch A is off. If it is, then it adds one to the value of Tree and turns self-switch A on, preventing a single tree from adding more than one to the variable.

- Copy-paste this exact event to the four other trees you have placed on the map, and you're done. You can do this by right-clicking the event on the map editor and selecting *Copy*, then right-clicking the square you wish to paste the event to and selecting *Paste*. Alternatively, you can use the *Copy Event Page* button within the event properties.

What's the Point?

There is no greater honor than botany. No? Okay, fair enough. Let's add a final event that requires the Tree variable to be at 5. We'll make it a treasure chest, to show off the relevant Quick Event.

- First, find a nice unoccupied space on your second map.

- Right-click and select the Treasure Chest event from Quick Event Creation.

- Because the quest involved trees, let's give the player something made with wood as a reward. Select the Longbow from the list of weapons and then press OK.

■ **Note** The default character, Eric, cannot equip the Longbow in his current state. I'll cover how to allow him to do so in the next chapter.

- Now, right-click that event and click Edit. What we want to do is make it so the chest is invisible until the player has taken a look at all five of the trees. To do that, check the Variable condition on the first page of the event and set it so it says "Tree is 5 or above." Once that is ready, you're done!

Check Figure 2-16 to see how the relevant part of the second map looks for me. Besides the five trees and the road, your map will probably look different.

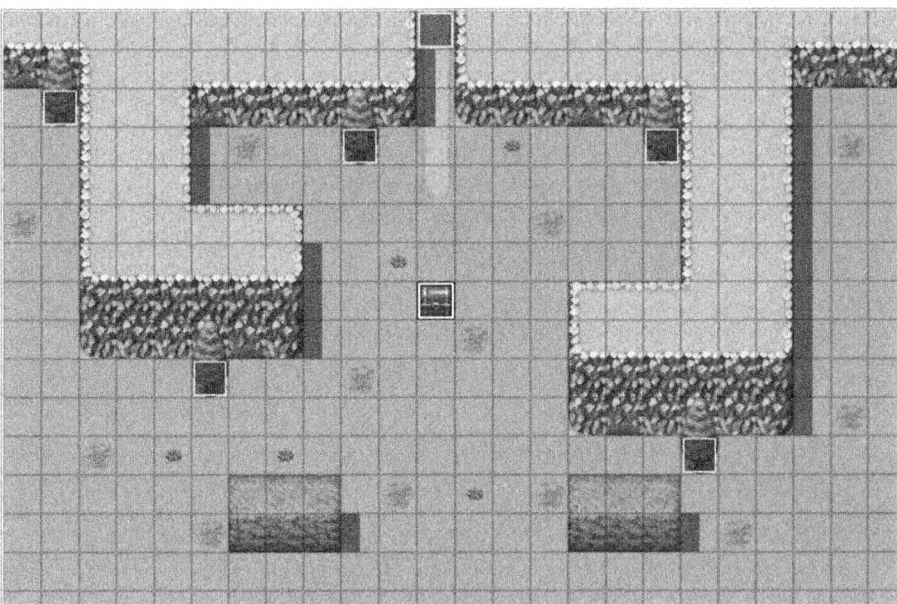

Figure 2-16. *The final second area map, showing the events*

Before I close this chapter, here's one final application of variables that will most likely be of great use to you as you work on your RMVXA game.

Advanced Challenge: Using Variables to Handle an Area Transition!

Up to now, we have dealt with area transitions that are one square wide. However, what happens if we make an expansive area, such as a desert, and want to make exits for the player? It could take dozens of events to cover a single direction. For those of you following this book using the Lite version of RMVXA, that is unacceptable (as RMVXA Lite only allows ten events to be placed per map). Truly, it is unacceptable, period, even if you have the full version. Why spend 10–40 events for area transitions on a single map when you can cover them all in one? This exercise requires the use of the following:

- The Parallel Process event trigger

- A pair of variables to hold the character's coordinates

- Liberal use of the Conditional Branch event command

First, switch to Event editing mode. Then, find a nice spot in the second map that the player cannot reach. In my case, I'll be using one of the squares on the mountaintop. Afterward, create a new event at that square. Set the event trigger to Parallel Process. Next, we'll have to check for the player's x and y positions at all times. That is the reason why we use Parallel Process. (Remember: Autorun is meant more for cinematic sequences. Trying to use it for an event such as this will only cause the game to hang.) The secret lies in the Control Variables command, specifically the Game Data category of operand. The Game Data category defaults to Map ID. Click the button labeled "…" on the far end of the bar, to change what type of data you want to assign to your variable.

Once you click the button, you'll notice a slew of possible things you can plug into a variable. What we're looking for is the player's position on the map (a.k.a. his/her x and y coordinates). Thus, we click the Character option, which defaults to Player's Map X. Exactly what we need! Select that, then make sure you're saving the value to a new variable (I'm calling it variable 2 X and variable 3 Y). Afterward, create a new Control Variable command and repeat the process up to the point where you are looking at the Player's Map X setting. Click the arrow on the drop-down menu for Map X, and it will reveal four more settings. The one we want, of course, is Map Y.

Here's where it gets interesting. I'm going to recommend that you lower the map size down to 23×15 (the size of the grass rectangle we made in starting our second map). To be fair, it doesn't particularly matter for this exercise, but it'll help you visualize the boundaries in-game. Now what you have to do is figure out the boundaries of each side of the map on which you want to have area transitions. Let me use some Region numbering, shown in Figure 2-17, to help you visualize what I mean.

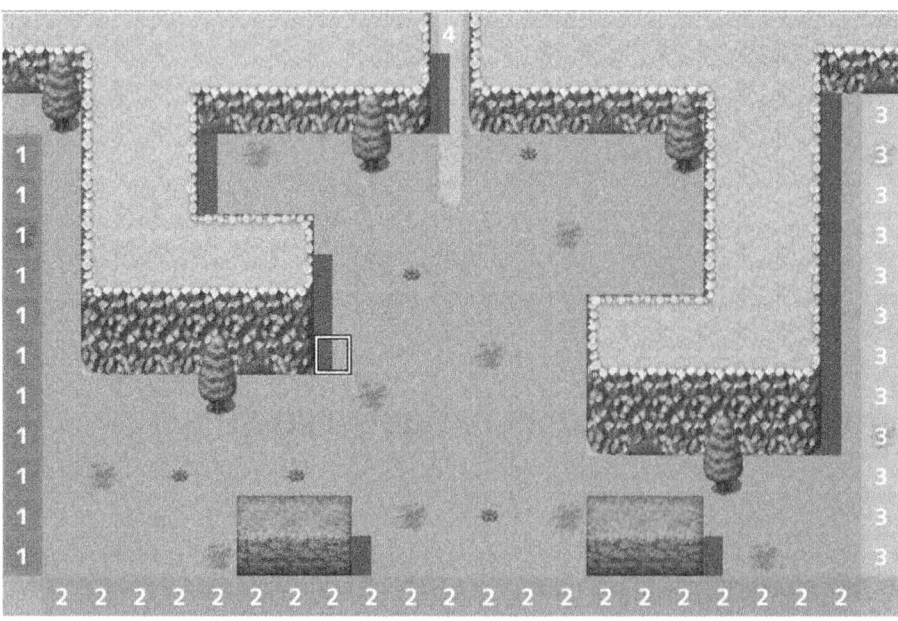

Figure 2-17. *The map Regions for our transitions*

We have a single transition marked by the number four to the north. Additionally, we have 11 squares on the left, 21 squares on the bottom, and 12 squares on the right. That would be 45 transition events, if we did them one by one. So, let's not.

Let's Crunch Those Map Boundaries, Shall We?

The topmost square of the left boundary is (0,3), while the bottommost square of the left boundary is (0,13). The left-most square of the bottom boundary is (1,14), while the right-most square of the bottom boundary is (21,14). The topmost square of the right boundary is (22,2), while the bottommost square of the right boundary is (22,13).

What does this mean? Well, we can see some trends.

- When you trace a horizontal boundary, you will find that the value of Y stays the same.

- When you trace a vertical boundary, the value of X stays the same.

Thus, our conditional branches should read as follows:

```
@>Control Variables: [0002:X] = Player's Map X
@>Control Variables: [0003:Y] = Player's Map Y
@>Conditional Branch: Variable [0002:X] == 0
  @>
: Branch End
@>Conditional Branch: Variable [0003:Y] == 14
  @>
: Branch End
@>Conditional Branch: Variable [0002:X] == 22
  @>
: Branch End
@>
```

Keeping in mind that == is the equal sign when used in this context (a single equal sign means that a value is assigned in programming), you can probably tell what is going on. Note how every conditional branch event ends with a Branch End. The first conditional branch covers the left border. The second branch covers the southern border, and the third branch covers the right border.

But You Don't Have Anything Inside the Branches!

Keen eye! Indeed, you would be correct. Feel free to put in transfer events, as you see fit, to wherever you want them to lead. The best use of such a transition in practice is to send the player to the world map (on which it doesn't particularly matter where the player exits from, only that he or she exits the area map from a certain direction).

```
@>Control Variables: [0002:X] = Player's Map X
@>Control Variables: [0003:Y] = Player's Map Y
@>Conditional Branch: Variable [0002:X] == 0
  @>Transfer Player: [001:MAP001] (013,006), Left
  @>
: Branch End
@>Conditional Branch: Variable [0003:Y] == 14
  @>Transfer Player: [001:MAP001] (008,011), Up
  @>
: Branch End
```

```
@>Conditional Branch: Variable [0003:Y] >= 2
  @>Conditional Branch: Variable [0002:X] == 22
  @>Transfer Player: [001:MAP001] (004,006), Right
  @>
: Branch End
@>
```

Summary

That concludes this chapter on switches and variables. Here are two more exercises for you to stretch your mind with.

1. Using an event with Autorun, create a two-page event that greets the player with a text box upon arriving at the second area.

    - As with Parallel Process events, I recommend you place this event somewhere that the player cannot access.

    - Only the first page of the event should be Autorun. The second page should be blank, with a trigger that is not Autorun or Parallel Process. Flipping a self-switch on page 1 and using it as a conditional on page 2 would probably work best.

2. Using an event with Autorun, use the Fadeout and Fadein event commands to cause the screen to black out momentarily and then reveal the treasure chest, instead of it popping immediately into being.

    - The easiest way to accomplish this is by cheating a little. The chest is set to appear when Tree is equal to 5. Make it so that the chest appears when Tree is equal to *6*. Then, with Fadeout, you can create an Autorun when Tree is equal to 5, add 1 to the value of Tree, and Fadein, in that order.

    - The use of a self-switch also comes recommended for this event. An Autorun left unchecked *will* hang your game.

3. Tweak the five tree events so that they also display a text box that tells players how many trees they have looked at up to that point.

    - Tool tips are your friend here. Place your cursor over the text box in the Show Text event command and leave it there until the tool tip appears. You'll see a text option that allows you to print the value of a variable as text.

Next, let's talk about a large part of what makes RPGs what they are: characters and enemies!

CHAPTER 3

▓ ▓ ▓

Of Friends and Foes

We spent the last chapter talking about the use of switches and variables within RPG Maker VX Ace (RMVXA). What was mentioned there is just the tip of the iceberg in terms of what you can do with them, but it's time to start populating our role-playing game (RPG) world. One thing every video game needs is a character for the player to control. Even the simplicity that is *Pong* has the player controlling a paddle and trying to get a ball past an opponent's own paddle. We have been controlling RMVXA's default character for the entirety of the last chapter. It's time we got to know him a little better. Make your way to the Database (by pressing F9 or finding it in the Tools item of the menu toolbar) and make your way to the Actors tab. When you first install RMVXA, your first foray into the Database will automatically lead you to the Actors tab, but recall that we already poked our heads in there to change some of the game's terms. Take a look at Figure 3-1.

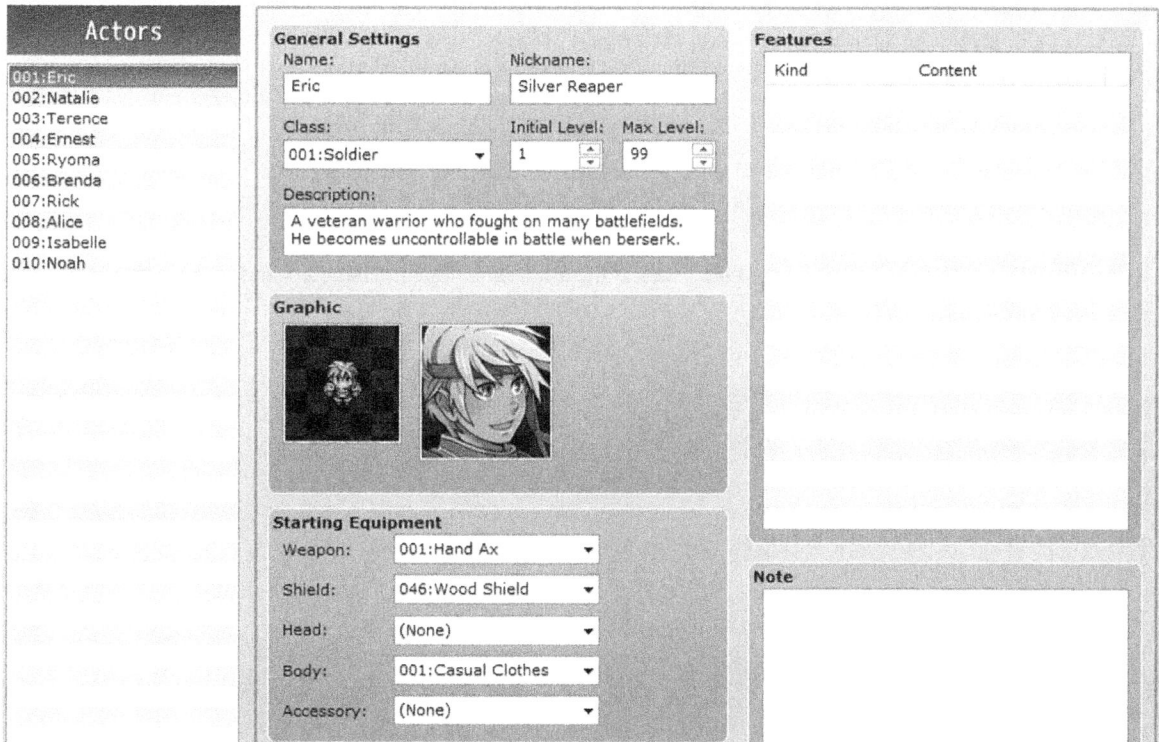

Figure 3-1. *The Actors tab in RMVXA's Database*

In RMVXA, player characters (those that the player can mix and match in his/her party) are called Actors. As you can see at the upper left of the preceding screenshot, the program comes with ten premade actors. If you're using the full version, you can change the maximum number of characters and add some more of your own. With either version, you can edit or erase the ones present, for the same effect.

There are various things to cover here, so let's work our way through this part of the Database.

- *General Settings* cover an actor's basic information and are largely self-explanatory. Of note is *Class*, which will be discussed when we reach the appropriate tab of the Database.

- You can tweak an actor's initial level, which will determine at what level he/she joins the party when placed in the game. You can also change an actor's max level as well, limiting his/her growth, if you should have a reason to do so. One common use of limiting a character's maximum level is when you have a temporary party member. You can set his/her initial level equal to its maximum, and he/she will stay at the same level for the duration.

- There is a pair of graphics. The one to the left is the character's sprite set, which covers his/her appearance as well as his/her movement patterns, while the one to the right is his/her character portrait.

- *Starting Equipment* determines what items a given actor starts with. A character should generally start with some manner of equipment, although there are times when it would not be appropriate (such as when a protagonist starts the game as a prisoner; he or she might have the clothes on his/her back and nothing else).

- *Features* are kind of a big thing in RMVXA. You'll quickly see that the ten actors have a blank Features list, and that's because the default characters have all of their features contained within their classes and not themselves. The way RMVXA manages this by default is fine, although there are niche cases in which it would be best to have some differentiating features at the Actor level. If you have two characters of the same class, and they are not identical twins, you could differentiate some of their stats through the use of Features at the Actor level. For example, you could give one of the characters the [HP] * 80% and the other [MP] * 110%.

- Finally, *Note* is just a notepad of sorts. If you have to make notes about a certain character, you can write them here. Most parts of RMVXA have a Note section. It's awfully convenient, if I may say so myself.

That covers the Actors tab. Feel free to take a look at the other nine default characters and see how they differ from Eric. Afterward, let's move on to the Classes tab (see Figure 3-2).

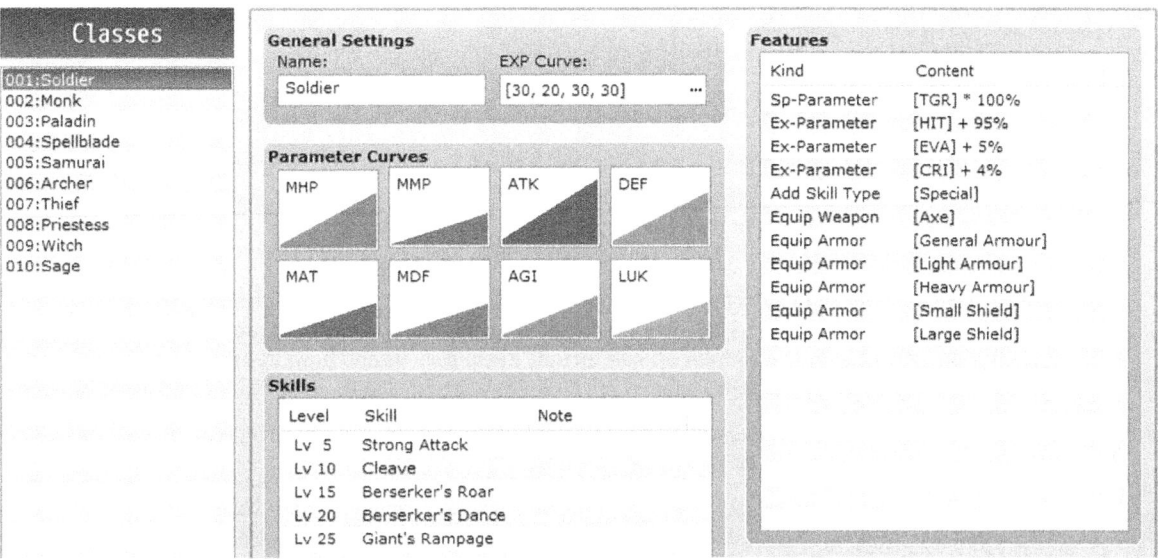

Figure 3-2. *The Classes tab in RMVXA's Database*

The ten actors each have their own class. Eric's class is Soldier. Take a look at each of the classes and note how its features, parameter curves, and skills differ. RMVXA prefers to place character-defining features within the Classes tab, as an actor's class highly defines him/her. Case in point, look at everything that is governed strictly by class.

- *EXP Curve: EXP* is short for "Experience." If you click the " . . . " button to the right of the bracketed numbers, you'll see what those four values relate to and how you can use them to tinker with the rate of advancement. You can make levels easier or harder to get, via the use of this property. By default, the ten premade classes all have the same experience curve. If you want actors to level up based on their class, you can tweak their curves here. To take a predominantly pen-and-paper example, *Advanced Dungeons & Dragons* (video game adaptations of that ruleset include *Dark Sun* and *Baldur's Gate*) had an experience system in which classes leveled up at a rate proportionate to their power. So, the spellcasters, who, arguably, had more power, took a longer time to gain a single level, while the "weaker" classes, such as Thief, leveled up faster, to compensate for their lower overall power level.

- *Parameter Curves*: These affect the rate at which a given class gains its stats. You can edit a parameter by double-clicking it, which will bring up a graph. There are eight stats in RMVXA.

  1. **MHP (Maximum Hit Points)**. If these drop to 0, the character is dead and requires some form of revival.

  2. **MMP (Maximum Magic Points)**. Used to cast all manner of magic spells

  3. **ATK (Attack)**. Influences the amount of damage that a character does with his/her weapon of choice

  4. **DEF (Defense)**. Influences the amount of damage that a character suffers from enemy attacks. The default damage formula for the basic Attack command is [ATK * 4 - DEF * 2]. Essentially, the basic formula favors boosting your attack over your defense.

  5. **MAT (Magic Attack)**. Can be used in spell formulas to determine damage

39

6. **MDF (Magic Defense)**. Can be used in spell formulas to determine damage mitigation

7. **AGI (Agility)**. The higher a character's AGI, the sooner he/she acts in a given battle turn.

8. **LUK (Luck)**. Much as it is in many other games that have such a stat, Luck in RMVXA is the wildcard stat. The official help file for RMVXA states that Luck "affects the chance of adding a state or debuffing a parameter." The default formula is [Chance (%) = 100 + (user's luck – target's luck) ÷ 10].

- *Skills*: These are one of the most intrinsic aspects of an RPG character. If a character did not have any skills, it would only be able to attack with its weapon, and that would probably get boring after a while. Some examples of skills include healing spells and power attacks. Eric's class specializes in powerful attacks that inflict great physical damage.

- *Features*: These define many miscellaneous, but important, aspects of a certain class. Let's break down the Soldier class, feature by feature.

    1. *TGR* is short for "TarGet rate" and marks the rate at which a member of this class is targeted by enemies. The default rate is 100% and can be increased or decreased as desired. A particularly large warrior might warrant a higher TGR, while a smaller thief would probably warrant a lower TGR. Say you have a party of three: a large warrior with 200% TGR, a normal-sized guard with 100% TGR, and a small thief with 50% TGR. It is four times more likely that the warrior will be attacked than the thief. It is half as likely that the thief will be attacked than the guard.

    2. *HIT* is short for "HIT rate." In RMVXA, a character's accuracy is equal to its HIT plus any HIT it is gaining from its equipment. A character's ability to land its attacks and skills is negatively modified by any EVA (Evasion) the enemy has. The stock functionality of RMVXA is set up so that the game calculates first to see if an actor lands its attack and, if so, checks if the enemy dodges the attack.

    3. *CRI* is short for "Critical rate." When a character lands a critical hit, it deals triple the normal damage. An actor's chance to land a critical hit is reduced, based on the enemy's CEV (Critical Evasion rate).

    4. *Add Skill Type* is a feature that allows a chosen class to use a category of skills. In this case, Soldiers can use Special-type skills. By default, RMVXA has two skill types: Special and Magic. A class requires access to a skill type to be able to use skills from that type.

    5. *Equip Weapon/Armor* are both fairly self-explanatory. They define what kinds of weapons and armor a given class can use. If you don't assign any Equip features to a class, it will be unable to equip anything (which, to be fair, might be good for a completely unusual player character type, such as a wolf or a yeti).

From the Classes tab, let's move on to the Skills tab, which has a lot of information. The first time I laid eyes on that part of the Database, I nearly fainted. Rest assured that it is not as overwhelming as it initially seems. Let's break up this tab into two parts. Check Figure 3-3 for the first half.

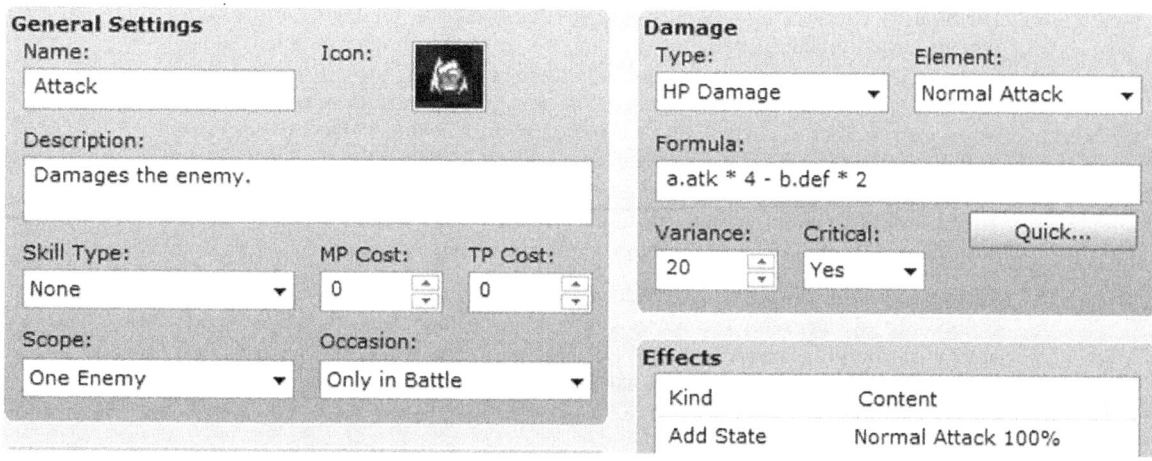

Figure 3-3. *The upper half of the Skills tab in RMVXA*

We're looking at the very first skill in the list of 126 (!) provided by default within RMVXA. If you're following along with the Lite version, you will have to edit/erase skills to make room for your own, as you are disallowed from tweaking the maximum value. Skills 1 and 2 are internally important for RMVXA, so take care not to edit them, unless you're sure of your changes. The first skill in RMVXA is the basic attack.

- *General Settings* provide basic, yet essential, values to be tweaked. Skill Type denotes what type of skill category must be unlocked for a player to use that skill. As Attack is a generic basic attack, anyone can use it. Similarly, it has no MP cost or TP (Technique Points). A character gains TP from taking damage and using skills, including Attack.

- *Scope* defines what gets affected by said skill. The basic attack hits a single, targeted enemy.

- *Occasion* toggles when a skill can be used.

    1. **Always**. The skill can be used in and out of battle.

    2. **Only in Battle – The skill can only be used in battle.**

    3. **Only from the Menu**. This is the character menu that we accessed back in Chapter 1, to be precise.

    4. **Never**. Seems pointless, but it's actually useful for a skill that you only want to be used under highly specific circumstances. (You would probably want to create an event to trigger the skill, in that case.)

- *Damage*: Besides having a marginally misleading name (as you can use the formula for healing spells as well), this has a few intricacies of its own.

    1. **Type**. The type of effect you want this skill to have. To confuse the issue even more, you have HP and MP Recover as two of the seven possible options. The *None* type can be useful for skills that cause status effects but do not do any actual damage in causing them.

    2. **Element.** Determines the elemental typing of the skill. Normal Attack is its own special element, which leads me to believe that it is coded in that way so that Attack can benefit from the elemental properties of a character's weapon, to take one example.

3. **Formula**. That little box you see there carries nearly infinite potential. Entire forum threads have been filled throughout the Internet on making unconventional damage formulas for seemingly anything you can think of in RMVXA. I'll be showcasing some of the ones I've personally used, later on. For now, you should know that the user of a skill is expressed by a (a.atk in the case of Attack) and the target of a skill is expressed by b (b.def, for this skill). Leaving your cursor over the formula box for a few seconds will cause a very helpful tool tip to appear, so I'll leave that as a short exercise for you. The Quick button underneath the formula box allows you to nearly instantly crunch basic damage formulas, based on the criteria it gives you.

4. **Variance**. Determines the range of values a skill returns. Attack has a variance of 20(%). To give an example, a character able to do 100 damage with Attack would actually do anywhere between 80 and 120. I prefer my skill variance to be low, but then again, I prefer my characters to have low stats rather than the high stats that the default characters come with in RMVXA.

5. **Critical**. Determines whether a skill can land a critical hit or not.

- *Effects*: These are to skills what Features are to actors (and, as we'll see later, enemies and other items as well). When used, Attack has a special effect to add a state named Normal Attack. I wouldn't tamper with that. You can add other effects to the basic attack if you're curious, though.

The Database Skill tab doesn't seem so intimidating now, does it? We're more than half done looking at it as well! Take a look at Figure 3-4, for the other half of the Skills tab.

Figure 3-4. *The lower half of the Skills tab in RMVXA*

- *Invocation*: This affects the use of the skill itself.

  1. **Speed**. This adjusts the user's AGI upward or downward when using the skill. (Speed can be a negative value.) You can make a skill that's guaranteed to strike first by giving it high Speed. You can also make a skill that causes its user to act last by giving it highly negative Speed.

  2. **Success %**. The chance of the skill to actually connect. I tend to use a non-100% Success rate for skills that cause nasty status effects, such as instant death or petrification.

  3. **Repeats**. How many times the skill is triggered when used once. Most skills should only trigger once, but multi-hit skills work precisely by repeating.

  4. **TP Gain**. The amount of TP a character gains from skill use is governed by this value right here. So, you could easily make a skill with the sole purpose of boosting your character's TP to 100. (TP caps at 100, unlike MP, which can go all the way to 9999.) Likewise, you could make a skill that doesn't grant TP to its user.

  5. **Hit Type**. There are three possible hit types for any given skill.

     - *Certain Hit*: A skill with this hit type ignores the user's accuracy and the target's evasion stats. The only determinant of whether a Certain Hit skill will work is its Success %.

     - *Physical Attack*: A skill with this hit type connects based on the user's hit rate and is affected by the target's evasion rate, as well as its own Success %.

     - *Magical Attack*: A skill with this hit type connects based on the target's magical evasion rate and the skill's Success %.

  6. *Animation*: What is displayed when you use the skill in battle.

- *Using Message*: This is fairly self-explanatory. The only thing I would note is that you need a single space before your skill message. Take a look at the message for the Attack skill and you'll see what I mean. Otherwise, in-game, it will look like "Characterattacks!" instead of "Character attacks!" when you use the skill.

- Below Using Message, there are three buttons: *casts *!*, *does *!*, and *uses *!*. The tool tip for the buttons is "**Generate Use Message**: A button that automatically sets the message." Clicking one of those buttons replaces the text in the *Using Message* text boxes with predetermined text. For Attack, the text would read "casts Attack!", "does Attack!", and "uses Attack!", respectively.

- *Required Weapon*: This is the last item in the Skills tab, and it does what it implies. You can adjust it so that a certain skill requires a certain weapon type (such as a rain of arrows ability requiring a bow or crossbow). You can be strict and leave it at one weapon type or relax the restriction a little and add a second weapon type. (A powerful swing of your weapon can be done with both a sword and an axe, for example.)

You can see a screenshot of the Items tab (Figure 3-5), but you'll probably understand why I'm going to gloss over the details rather than actually explain it. It holds many similarities to the Skills tab. (Neat fact: Internally, Skills are also considered items, so this is merely a case of the stock functionality matching the code.) So there's only one or two new things to even mention.

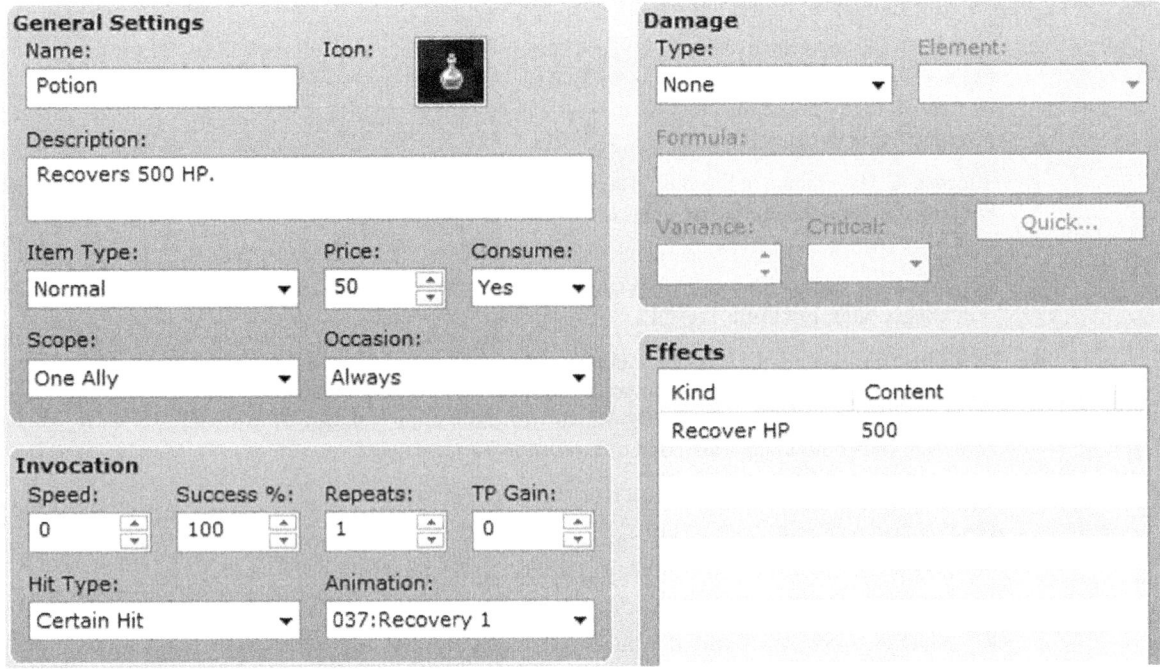

Figure 3-5. *The Items tab of the RMVXA Database*

- *Item Type*: These are subdivided into Normal (very nearly every type of item you could think of) and Key Items. Key Items are important things that the player acquires and should never get rid of (or is required to use for a specific purpose). A potion, food, and a smoke bomb are but three examples of Normal items, while an ancient key or a royal missive are good examples of Key Items.

- *Price*: Items, weapons, and armor can have a set price (in in-game currency). Items with a value of 0 cannot be sold (but, you can have an item that costs 0 for sale in a shop; I usually don't recommend that, mind you). Items sell for half of their value.

▪ **Note** With very few exceptions, you should set the price of your Key Items to 0, so that they cannot be sold. You would think that Key Items have protection from being sold, but that is not the case in RMVXA.

- *Effects*: Much as in the case of skills, your items can have a variety of effects. If you'd prefer, you can even use the damage formula for curative items or consumable damage items (think bombs and throwing stars).

As you can see, it is pretty much identical to the Skills tab. For those of you with RMVXA Lite, you are stuck with a 16-item limit. It is, perhaps, one of the more painful restrictions, as you will probably use many different types of items for your game. In any case, I will be elaborating on the Weapons tab and glossing over the Armors tab for the same reason that I skimmed over the Items tab. Refer to Figure 3-6 for a screenshot of the Weapons tab.

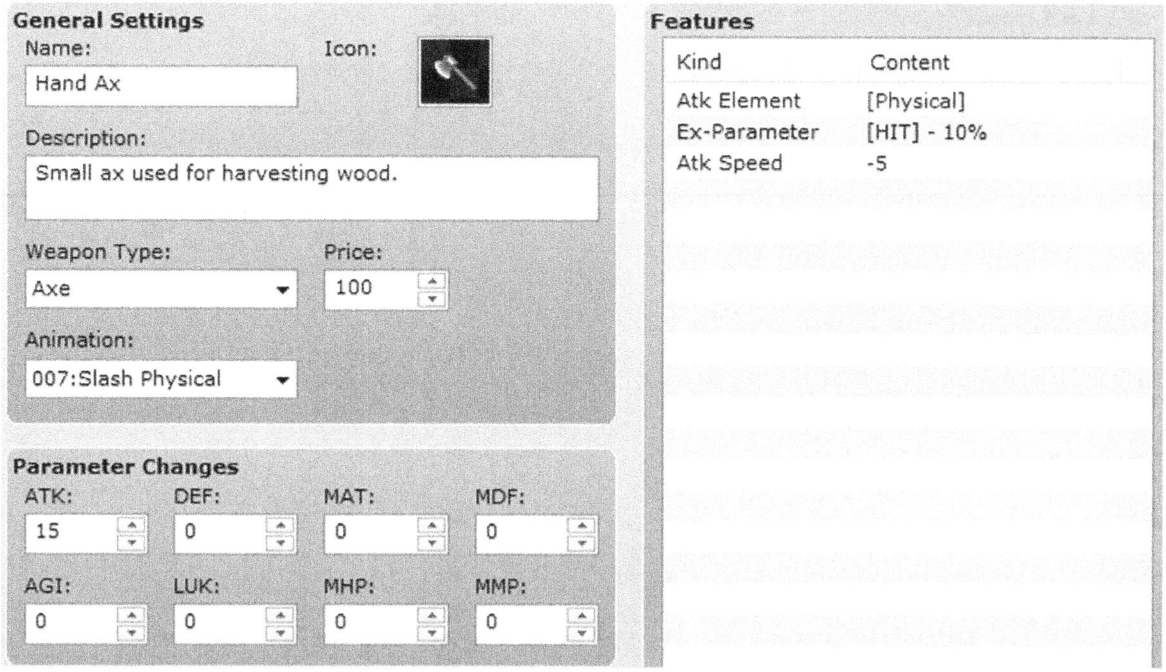

General Settings

Name: Hand Ax

Icon:

Description: Small ax used for harvesting wood.

Weapon Type: Axe

Price: 100

Animation: 007:Slash Physical

Features

Kind	Content
Atk Element	[Physical]
Ex-Parameter	[HIT] - 10%
Atk Speed	-5

Parameter Changes

ATK:	DEF:	MAT:	MDF:
15	0	0	0

AGI:	LUK:	MHP:	MMP:
0	0	0	0

Figure 3-6. *The Weapons tab of the RMVXA Database*

Just as items have two different types, you can define your weapon (and armor, for that matter) type as well. The Weapon Type drop-down menu will be populated with the terms listed in the Terms tab for that category. What makes weapons and armor different from items is their ability to be equipped by eligible actors. As equipment, they grant parameter changes (usually bonuses, but you could have cursed items that reduce stats as well) and have features that further add to their properties. In the case of weapons, you have to define their attack element. Most weapons do physical damage, but a flaming blade would do fire damage, while a bow of Ice could inflict extreme cold or water damage. In the case of RMVXA's Hand Ax, it also has a HIT penalty (making the wielder more inaccurate) and an attack speed penalty. (Similar to skill speed, attack speed adds or subtracts from the character's artificial general intelligence [AGI] to determine how fast it acts when using a normal attack.)

■ **Note**   Unlike some other RPG systems, weapons do not have an inherent damage range (such as Greatswords in *Dungeons & Dragons* having a 2–12 damage range, modified by the wielder's Strength). What you see in a weapon's Parameter Changes is what you get.

The Armors tab is essentially identical. (See Figure 3-7.)

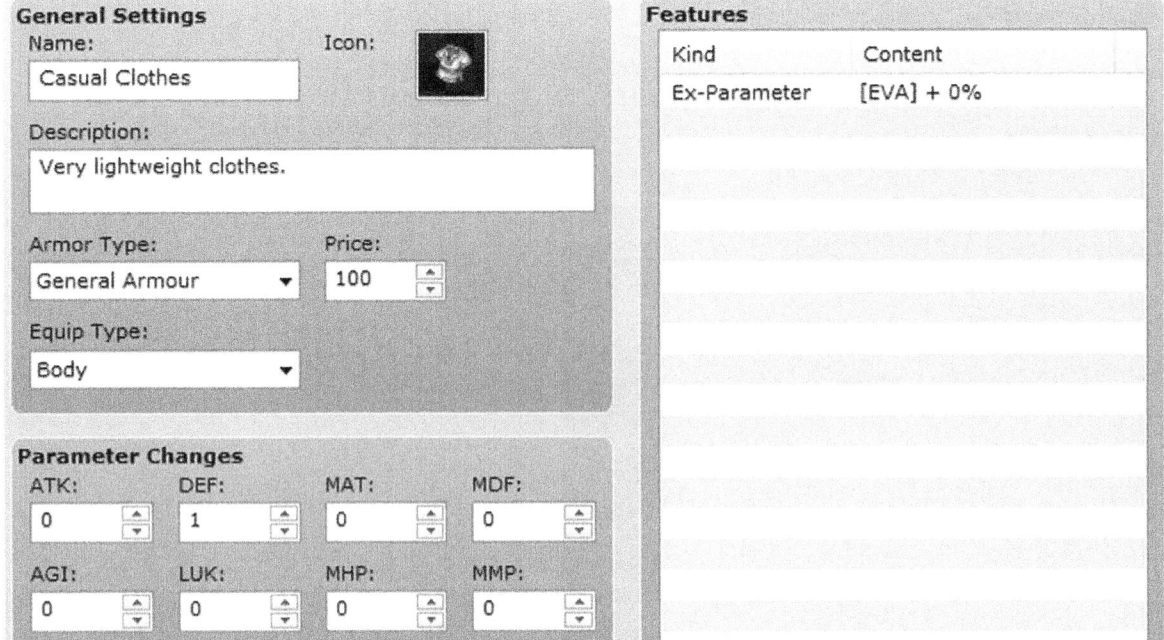

Figure 3-7. *The Armors tab of the RMVXA Database*

The main difference is that the Armors tab also has an *Equip Type*. As you can see, shields and accessories are also considered armor in RMVXA (the former making sense, while the latter is a bit odd).

Time for Enemies!

Yes, indeed. An RPG wouldn't be much of one if there weren't foes to serve as obstacles for the player and his/her companions. If you have RMVXA Lite, the monster limit is 30. Check Figure 3-8 to see a screenshot of the Enemies tab.

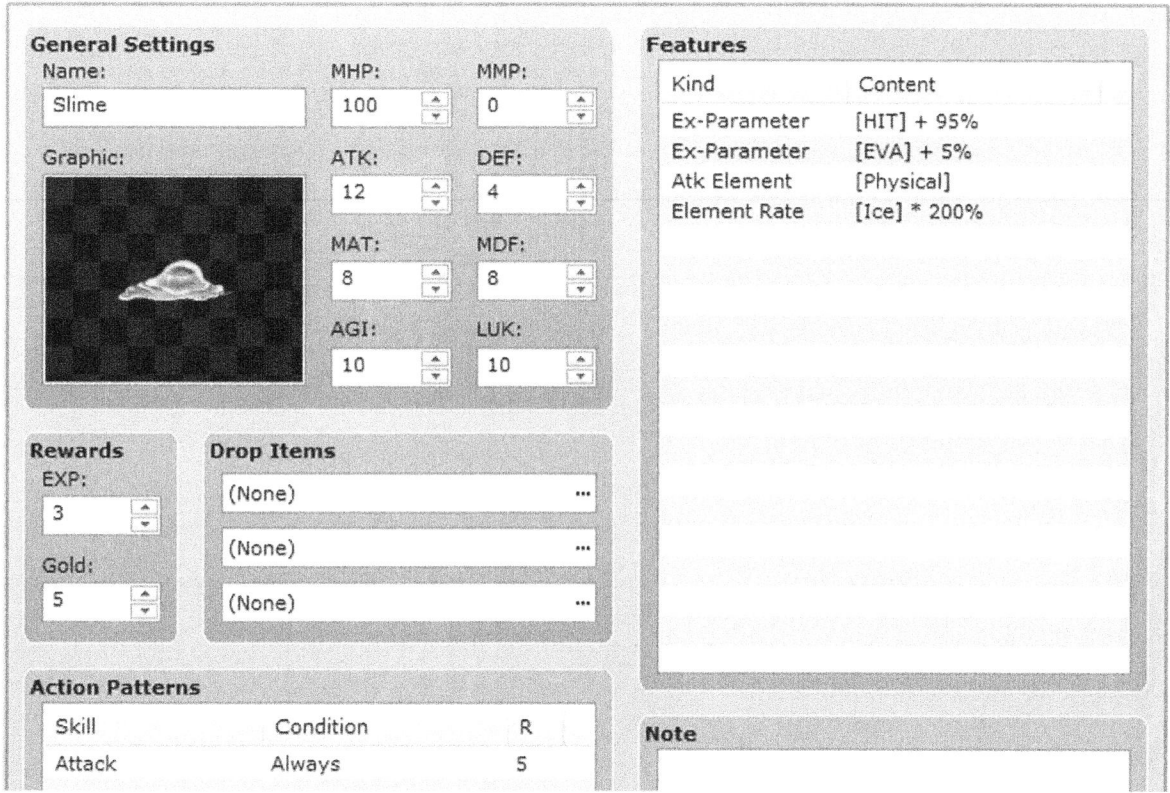

Figure 3-8. *The Enemies tab of the RMVXA Database*

In the preceding figure, we can see Slime, one of the Japanese RPG genre's weakest but most iconic monsters. The *Dragon Quest* series has cute slimes, while RMVXA's rendition is more of an amorphous blob. Like actors, enemies have eight stats. They also confer rewards—in experience and gold—when defeated and can also potentially drop items for the player. Slime has no items to drop, however. You can set up to three items for an enemy to drop, with a probability of 1/X (where X can be any number from 1 to 1000). I personally don't recommend drop rates lower than 1/128, but that's mostly because I have not played an RPG in which most of the item drops are rarer than that (*Dragon Quest 8*, if I recall correctly, had a few 1/256 drops, but they were situational at best).

Action Patterns are what give an enemy most of its bite. The lowly Slime can only use the basic attack that we saw a few pages back. With its 12 ATK, it won't be winning any damage records in the near future. I'll be discussing *Ratings* in detail later in the chapter. Last, *Features* are back and used for enemies in much the same way that they are for actor classes. Slime has a 5% chance of missing on its attacks (95% HIT), as well as a 5% chance of dodging physical attacks (5% EVA). Its attacks render physical damage, and it suffers double damage from ice-based attacks. You can give enemies resistances and immunities to types of damage and status effects (defined with States in RMVXA). This discussion has been a bit long, so let's touch on one last section before applying all that we have talked about so far. Figure 3-9 shows off the Troops tab. You could design a thousand monsters, but you must actually form them into a troop for them to initiate a valid encounter. The RMVXA Lite troop limit is 30. The very first troop in the list is a pair of Slimes. Let's talk a bit about each of the commands available.

Figure 3-9. *The Troops tab of the RMVXA Database*

- *Autoname* names the troop based on the number and type of monsters contained within. The default troops are all named in the Autoname style.

- *Change Battleback* allows you to change the background during battle testing. This has no effect on the Battlebacks in your game.

- *Battle Test* allows you to create a party of up to four actors equipped with items you choose to face off against the currently selected troop. During a Battle Test, the party gains 99 copies of every item in the Database.

- *Add* allows you to include a monster in a troop while, clicking an individual monster and pressing *Remove* clears it from the troop. If you want to *Clear* out the troop completely, that would be the option to click.

- Dragging on a monster placed in a troop allows you to change its in-battle position. This is merely for aesthetic purposes and has no actual effect on combat. You can use *Arrange* to return all monsters to their default positions.

- Events return with a vengeance in the Troops tab, in the form of *Battle Events*. They have six different conditionals, available from the drop-down menu.

  1. If you don't use *any* of the conditionals, the event will default to *Don't Run*. As implied, an event with Don't Run will never trigger.

  2. **When the end of turn - An event with this conditional will trigger after all battlers (party members and enemies) have taken their turn.**

  3. **Turn No**. Allows you to set a determined turn for the event to trigger. You will see that there are two number boxes. The first determines the turn in which the event triggers, while the second defines the interval at which the event repeats. (You can leave that blank, and the event will only trigger once.)

  4. **Enemy's HP is X% or Below**. You have to specify a specific enemy within the troop for this conditional. When that enemy reaches the HP value you designated, the event will trigger.

  5. **Actor's HP is X% or Below**. Same as the preceding, but for actors instead of enemies. You can declare an actor that doesn't even exist within your game (as long as the actor exists within the Database), so be mindful of that.

  6. **Switch X is ON**. Switches! This is really useful for a boss monster in the style of Zoma from *Dragon Quest 3*, who was nigh unbeatable, unless you used the Orb of Light. You can flip a switch, based on any relevant conditions elsewhere that causes your boss monster to be a weaker version of its peers (by lowering their stats permanently, for example).

- Battle Events also have three types of **Span**, determining how many times the event triggers.

  1. **Battle**. An event with the Battle span triggers only once per battle, even if its conditions continue to be met throughout combat.

  2. **Turn**. An event with this span triggers once per turn, even if its conditions are met multiple times within the same turn.

  3. **Moment**. An event with this span triggers repeatedly, once conditions are met. I rarely use this type of span, as it has a fair chance of causing your game to hang in an infinite loop if you mess up.

Playing with the Database

There you have it. We have seen most of the Database by now, so let's integrate into an exercise all that we have learned.

Objectives:

- Change Eric so that he can use bows as well as axes.

- Erase skill 126 (Mystic Spell) and create a skill that requires the use of a bow.

- Give Eric the skill that you have created.

- Erase items 15 and 16 (Speed Up/Luck Up). Create a normal item that can be used to attack enemies and is consumed on use and a key item.

- Erase weapon 60 (Etherblast Gun) and create a bow for Eric to use.

- Erase enemy 30 (Demon God) and come up with a new enemy.

- Erase troop 30 (Demon God) and make a troop containing one Slime and one of the new enemy you create.

Given the information already provided, the preceding should be fairly easy to accomplish. Take some time to read the various things in each tab, so that you can make a more measured decision in tweaking your creations, and it should be as easy as counting. RMVXA is nothing if not intuitive. Let me write up the changes that I made.

- **Change Eric so that he can use bows as well as axes.** To do this, you can add the Equip Weapon (Bow) feature to Eric or his class, and it will have the same overall effect for our purposes. I chose to add it to his class.

- **Erase skill 126 (Mystic Spell) and create a skill that requires the use of a bow.**

  1. I made a new skill that I named Arrow Rain. It is of the Special skill type and costs 10 MP per use. It has a scope of All Enemies and can only be used in battle. Its hit type is Physical Attack, while its animation is 013: Pierce Physical. As intended, I set it to require the use of a bow.

  2. For my skill's damage formula, I used the default of [a.atk * 4 - b.def * 2]. It does Physical HP Damage with a variance of 10 and can inflict Criticals. It has no special effects.

- **Give Eric the skill that you have created.**

  1. To add a skill to a class, double left-click (or right-click and then select Edit) within the Skills list of that class. You can do the same on an already added skill, to edit or erase it.

  2. Because we want to add the new skill, let's add it to the blank slot directly below Giant's Rampage. For the purposes of this exercise, let's set the level at which to learn our bow skill at 1. That means that Eric will have that bow skill level from **the start of the game**.

- **Erase items 15 and 16 (Speed Up/Luck Up). Create a normal item that can be used to attack enemies and is consumed on use and a key item.**

  1. My normal item is a Bomb. It deals exactly 50 physical damage to all enemies when used (you can write in numbers into the damage formula). It is Consumed when used and costs 200 gold to purchase from a shop (which means that it sells for 100 gold). It has a Physical Hit Type and the 059: Fire All 1 animation.

  2. My key item is an Old Key. It has no price, cannot be consumed, and has a scope of None and an occasion of Never. Such an item seems useless at first glance, but it can be used in conjunction with the Item conditional. It is mainly used for events involving locked doors/gates, to allow players to open them, if they have the appropriate key item.

- **Erase weapon 60 (Etherblast Gun) and create a bow for Eric to use.**

  1. I created a new bow called Eric's Bow and, after looking at the Longbow and Crossbow, decided to give it an attack value halfway (33) between the two bows.

  2. It has no value, so it cannot be sold, and it has the Pierce Physical animation.

  3. For Features:

     - Does physical damage

     - Grants a bonus of 5% HIT to its wielder

     - Prevents shields from being used (via the use of the Seal Equip feature) at the same time as the bow

     - Grants a 5% bonus to the wielder's CRI

Note   So, this is Eric's Bow. What stops another bow user from using this bow? Good question. The easiest, if clunky, way, outside of scripting, to make a weapon that only a certain character can use is to make a whole new weapon type for said character. You could call the new weapon type EBow (short for "Eric's Bow") and then allow Eric to use weapons of the EBow type. Anyway, let's resume.

- **Erase enemy 30 (Demon God) and come up with a new enemy.**

  1. I made a new enemy called the Hill Orc. I used *Hue* to make the Orc graphic have a tinge of reddish pink. Using Hue is awesome for the shameless, but necessary, RPG convention of having recolored enemies. Rather than have to manually recolor the same sprite multiple times, you could just have a single sprite and tweak it with Hue within RMVXA.

  2. It has 110 MHP, no MMP, 24 ATK, 10 DEF, 8 MAT, 8 MDF, 8 AGI, and 12 LUK.

  3. The Hill Orc gives 20 EXP and 30 Gold when defeated and has a 1/8 chance of dropping a Bomb.

  4. For features, it has 95% HIT, 5% EVA, and physical damage for its normal attacks.

  5. Its attack pattern consists solely of attacking normally.

I Want My Monster to Do More Than Just Attack with a Weapon!

A good wish—and easy to do as well. Let's take a closer look at *Action Patterns*. As you have probably noticed by now, many lists in RMVXA can be edited in the same way. That is, double left-click or right-click and select Edit. When you do the same in the Action Patterns area of an enemy page, Figure 3-10 shows what comes up.

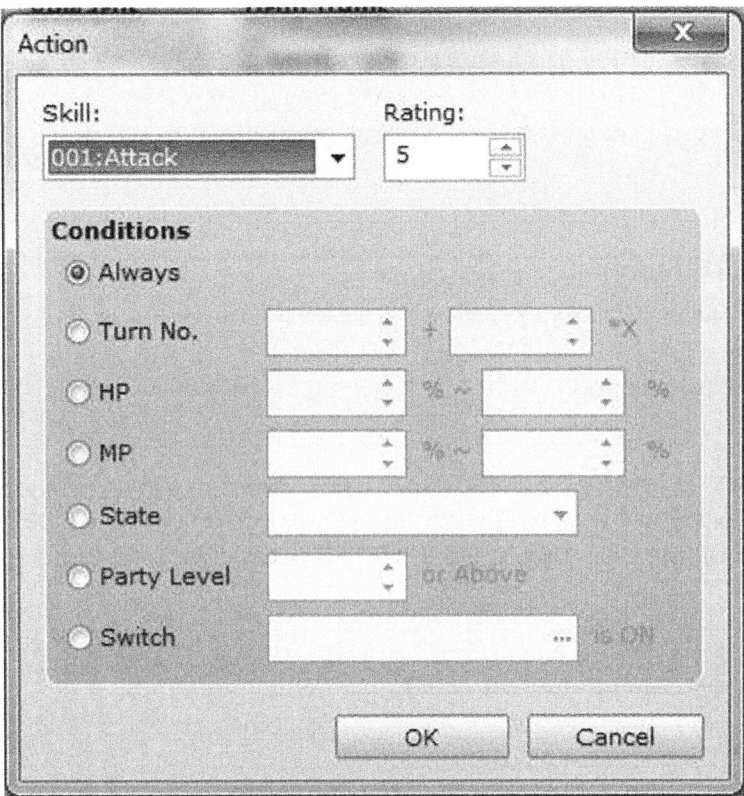

Figure 3-10. *The screen displayed by choosing to add or edit a skill to an enemy's Action Patterns*

- *Skill* is a drop-down menu that allows you to select the skill that you want the enemy to use.

- *Rating* is a value that does nothing in of itself. However, when an enemy has multiple skills, it looks to its rating value to determine what to use. I've always felt that the official explanation for Rating is ridiculously clunky yet somehow manages to convey the intended message. RMVXA says: "Actions 1 rating point away from the highest priority rating will be used 2/3 of the time and those 2 rating points away will be used 1/3 of the time. If there are actions with the same ratings, their probability of use will be the same."

An Explanation of Ratings

Confusing, isn't it? I'll do my best to explain! Suppose we give our new enemy two new skills. Let's just call them Skill A and Skill B. So now, the enemy has Attack, Skill A, and Skill B in its action pattern list. If we leave Attack's rating at 5, give Skill A a rating of 4, and Skill B a rating of 3, here is how the probabilities work.

- Attack: The standard/baseline for the action pattern, as it has the highest rating

- Skill A: Will be used two-thirds of the time, as compared to Attack

- Skill B: Will be used one-third of the time, as compared to Attack

Doesn't seem like my explanation helps, but let's go deeper. If our hypothetical enemy uses a total of 100 actions, we can roughly expect the following number of uses of each skill:

- Attack: 50/100 uses

- Skill A: 50*2/100*3 = 100/300. When we simplify that, so it becomes 33.3(repeating)/100. Let's call that 33/100.

- Skill B: 17/100 (to add up to 100 actions)

If we go back to the previous set of bullets, we realize that the math checks out. Attack is used most frequently, followed by Skill A, and, last, by Skill B.

Okay, what happens if the rating difference is more than two points? Skills that have a rating more than two points lower than the highest usable skill will never be used. Never, ever.

How about those conditions? Do they affect rating? They most certainly do. The game checks for *usable* skills. So, if you have a skill with rating 10 and a condition to only be used on every third turn, then it doesn't matter what rating any other skills have on the other, non-third, turns. Let's take our initial example and add a Skill C that relies on such a conditional.

- Skill C—Rating 10: 100% chance to use on every third turn; 0% chance on every non-third turn

- Attack—Rating 5: 50% chance to use on every non-third turn;.no chance to use on every third turn

- Skill A—Rating 4: 33% chance to use on every non-third turn; no chance to use when Skill C's turn rolls around

- Skill B—Rating 3: 17% chance to use when Skill C is unavailable; nil on those chances when Skill C is usable

Feel free to test the rating system for yourself, by giving Slimes extra skills and using Battle Test to see how often Slimes use each ability.

■ **Hint**   For that one skill to be used on every third turn, you would place a 3 in the second number box for the Turn No. conditional. You can determine the first time an enemy uses a skill, based on what turn number you put in the first box.

By skillful use of conditionals, you can create enemies that have predetermined patterns of attack. For example, here's a boss pattern I came up with when working on my own game. The pattern in Figure 3-11 is for a Sand Scorpion. It attacks on the first turn, then skips a turn, and then uses a power attack (Poison Tail). That sequence is repeated until the player or the boss is defeated. The turn skip is a skill that has no effects save for displaying a message (in that particular case: "is about to unleash a powerful attack!").

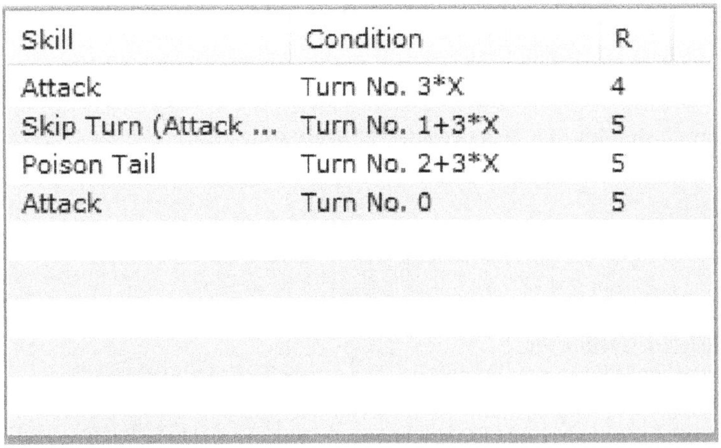

Skill	Condition	R
Attack	Turn No. 3*X	4
Skip Turn (Attack ...	Turn No. 1+3*X	5
Poison Tail	Turn No. 2+3*X	5
Attack	Turn No. 0	5

Figure 3-11. *The action pattern for a boss I came up with when working on my game*

Let's finish this exercise!

- **Erase troop 30 (Demon God) and make a troop containing one Slime and one of the new enemy you create.**

  1. Highlight Slime on the list to the right of the troop graphic and click Add. Afterward, highlight your new enemy and repeat the action.

  2. You can manually name the troop or use Autoname (screenshot of my new troop provided on the next page).

There you have it! Look at Figure 3-12 to see the finished troop. We now have several new things to make the game just a bit more unique. Before we move on, make sure to edit the treasure chest on the second map, so that it gives the player the new bow we created before, instead of the stock Longbow.

Figure 3-12. *The newly created troop*

With that done, let's add the new content to the map.

- To add the new troop to the map, you'll have to go to the second map's Properties by right-clicking its name in the map screen and selecting *Map Properties*. We have not covered map *Encounters* yet, but they are plug and play. Basically, interact (as usual, double left-click or right-click and then select Edit) with the currently empty list, and you'll get the following pop-up (see Figure 3-13).

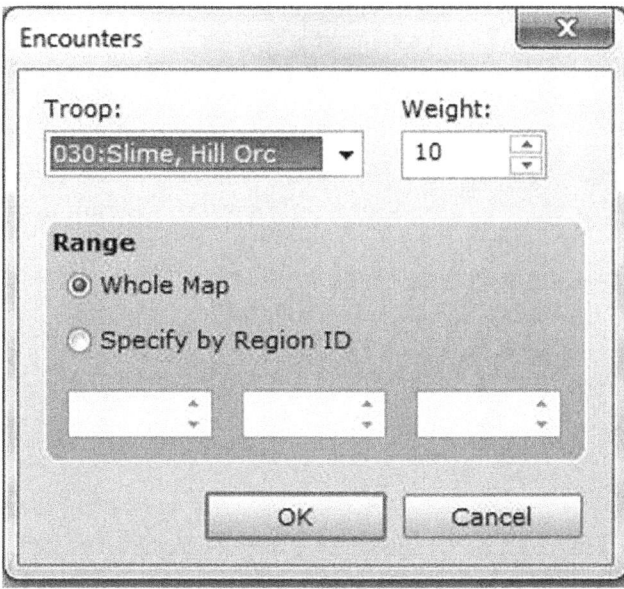

Figure 3-13. *Editing an encounter in a map's properties*

- *Troop* is a drop-down menu that lets you select which troop of enemies you wish to add to the encounter table. Scroll all the way down to the bottom and select the new troop you created.

- *Weight* determines how often the encounter appears. As we have just the one encounter, the actual value of Weight is unimportant. When you have multiple encounters, the chance of encountering any particular troop is equal to [Troop Weight ÷ Total Weight]. So, if we had three troops with the same weight, the chance to encounter each troop would be 1 in 3.

- *Range* specifies whether the troop can be encountered anywhere on the map or if its absence/presence is determined by a particular Region (I'll cover Regions in the next section). Let's make it so that our troop only has a chance to appear from Region 1. Click Specify by Region ID, and you'll see the three number boxes brighten. You can specify up to three regions in which that troop can be encountered on the current map. Let's just write in a 1 in the first box. You'll notice that the Range of the troop is 1. Had you set the range to Whole Map, it would indicate "Whole" instead.

▤ **Note** Once you click OK, you might notice a single option named Steps Average at the bottom of the list. It determines the average of how many steps the player must take to encounter enemy troops within appropriate areas. The default is 30.

Regions

As already noted, Regions define where certain troops of enemies can be found. RMVXA allows you to place up to 63 distinct regions on a single map, although you'll be hard-pressed to use that many anywhere but on a larger world map. You can reach the Region Editor by pressing F7 or clicking the icon to the right of the Event editing mode icon. Find a solitary corner of your map and make a small square or rectangle Region 1. Following is my own map, for reference (see Figure 3-14).

Figure 3-14. *A map with Regions added*

Let's play-test the game with the appropriate changes! If you did not set an appropriate battleback beforehand, the combat screen will look something like Figure 3-15.

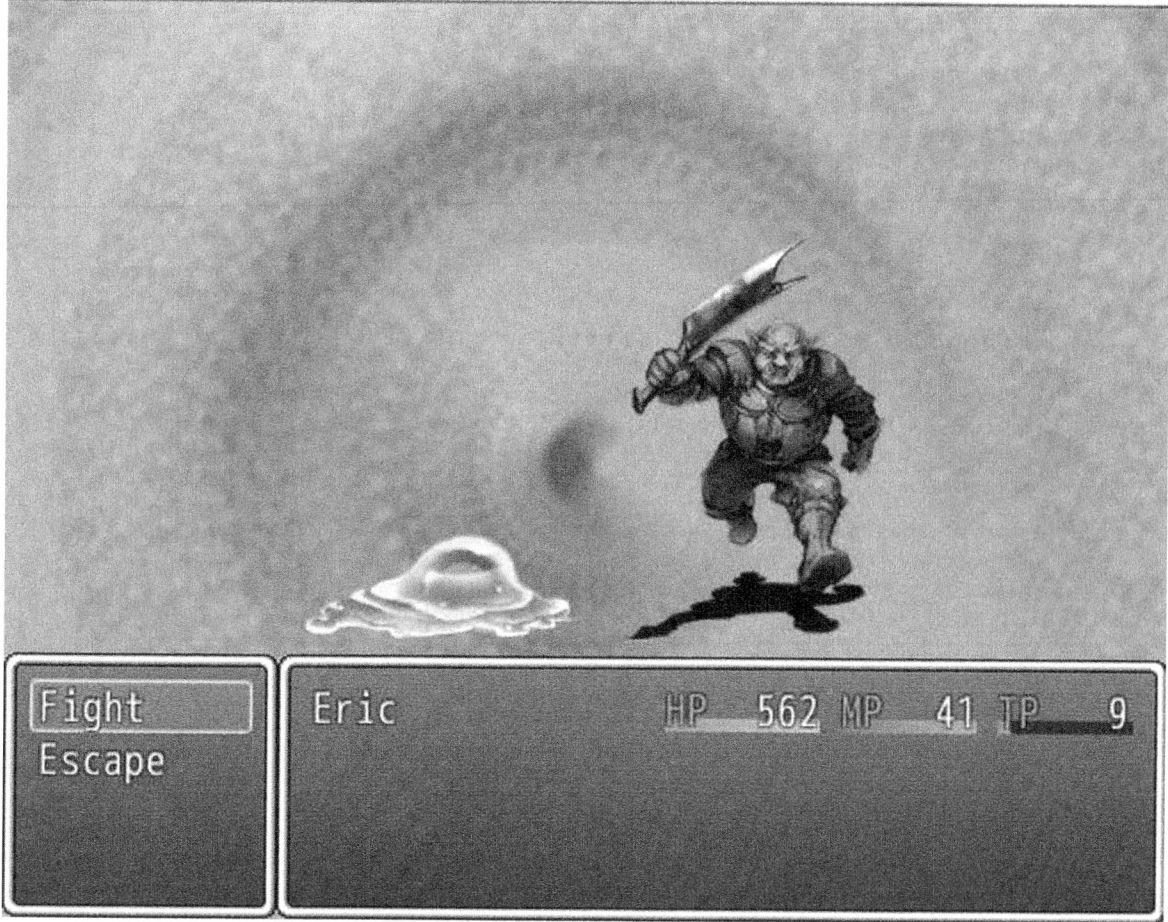

Figure 3-15. *The combat screen with the new troop created previously*

The Strange Battleback

Indeed it is. That's RMVXA's attempt to try and generate a battleback based on the available terrain. As you can see, it's a bit . . . underwhelming. And swirly. So, close your play-test and make your way to the second map's properties once again. Find *Specify Battleback*, toggle the check box, and browse through the graphics. I used Grassland for both the foreground and background, but feel free to choose something different. When you encounter the troop once again, you'll see that the battleback is now an actual defined background and not a strange swirl.

We're nearing the end of this chapter, but I think it's time to have a little discussion about damage formulas.

Damage Formulas

Up to now, we have created one new skill, as well as one item that used the damage formula box. However, we have used the default formula. What if we wanted to use different formulas? If you take a look at the many premade skills in RMVXA, you'll see that not all skills are created equal. Following are some examples of different circumstances that can be covered by different damage formulas.

- *An attack that pierces the enemy's defense*: If you want to alter the basic formula, use [a.atk*4] instead of [a.atk*4 - b.def*2]. A skill that doesn't factor in an enemy's defense in the damage formula will do damage based on the user's attack. Likewise, you can make a spell in the format [a.mat], instead of [a.mat - b.mdf], to have a magic defensive piercing skill.

- *An attack that does damage based on the target's HP*: You can plug MHP (Maximum HP) and HP (current HP) into formulas as well (MMP and MP too). What if you wanted to make a gravity attack in the vein of *Final Fantasy*'s Demi spells? Gravity skills, by definition, cannot kill their target. So, let's use HP. Writing in [b.hp/4] would result in a skill that causes damage equal to a quarter of the enemy's remaining HP. If we were to switch HP with MHP, said skill would do a quarter of its maximum HP in damage instead.

- *A skill that boosts the user's stats while damaging the enemy*: If you look at the stock functionality of RMVXA, you'll notice that this is seemingly impossible. If you create an attack and use Effects to add states or buff/debuff stats, you'll see that the target will get them as well. But, perhaps I want a skill that increases my AGI for two turns every time I connect with it. We can use .add_buff() to accomplish that (.add_debuff() lowers a stat instead). So, a skill that boosts the user's AGI for two turns while damaging an enemy would look something like this: [a.add_buff(6,2); a.atk*4 - b.def*2].

What's with the numbers in the .add_buff *parentheses?* Perhaps I should explain, eh? When you add buffs or debuffs via the damage formula box, you can declare the parameter (stat) to affect, as well as the turn duration. Parameter 6 is AGI, and the turn duration is 2.

Parameter Abbreviations

If you head into the Script Editor (in which your functionality is essentially nil, if you're using RMVXA Lite), you will see a bunch of code. Make your way to Game_BattlerBase under the Game Objects section of the available code and left-click it. If you scroll down that page of code, you'll find a list of parameters and their internal values. Take a look at the following code, which shows which parameter the numbers refer to.

```
#-------------------------------------------------------------------------
# * Access Method by Parameter Abbreviations
#-------------------------------------------------------------------------
def mhp;  param(0);   end            # MHP  Maximum Hit Points
def mmp;  param(1);   end            # MMP  Maximum Magic Points
def atk;  param(2);   end            # ATK  ATtacK power
def def;  param(3);   end            # DEF  DEFense power
def mat;  param(4);   end            # MAT  Magic ATtack power
def mdf;  param(5);   end            # MDF  Magic DeFense power
def agi;  param(6);   end            # AGI  AGIlity
def luk;  param(7);   end            # LUK  LUcK
def hit;  xparam(0);  end            # HIT  HIT rate
def eva;  xparam(1);  end            # EVA  EVAsion rate
def cri;  xparam(2);  end            # CRI  CRItical rate
def cev;  xparam(3);  end            # CEV  Critical EVasion rate
def mev;  xparam(4);  end            # MEV  Magic EVasion rate
def mrf;  xparam(5);  end            # MRF  Magic ReFlection rate
def cnt;  xparam(6);  end            # CNT  CouNTer attack rate
def hrg;  xparam(7);  end            # HRG  Hp ReGeneration rate
def mrg;  xparam(8);  end            # MRG  Mp ReGeneration rate
def trg;  xparam(9);  end            # TRG  Tp ReGeneration rate
def tgr;  sparam(0);  end            # TGR  TarGet Rate
def grd;  sparam(1);  end            # GRD  GuaRD effect rate
def rec;  sparam(2);  end            # REC  RECovery effect rate
def pha;  sparam(3);  end            # PHA  PHArmacology
def mcr;  sparam(4);  end            # MCR  Mp Cost Rate
def tcr;  sparam(5);  end            # TCR  Tp Charge Rate
def pdr;  sparam(6);  end            # PDR  Physical Damage Rate
def mdr;  sparam(7);  end            # MDR  Magical Damage Rate
def fdr;  sparam(8);  end            # FDR  Floor Damage Rate
def exr;  sparam(9);  end            # EXR  EXperience Rate
```

Mind you, buffs and debuffs only apply for the first eight in the list (in other words, MHP through LUK).

So, States Work in the Same Way, Right?

Mostly. You can declare `.add_state(X)`, where X is the database entry for the state you wish to use. The number of turns a state will last is determined by the state's properties in the Database. So, if we have the default list of states (of which there are 25), we can make an attack that poisons the user and damages the enemy as follows: `a.add_state(2); a.atk*4 - b.def*2`.

It is good to note that you only really need to use the commands when you want to apply effects to both the user and the target. If you have a healing spell that also increases AGI, you can cover that just fine with a damage formula and the Add Buff Effect (or you could use a Recover HP effect for the healing part of the spell as well).

With all that said, let's take a peek at the States tab of the Database (Figure 3-16).

Figure 3-16. *The States tab of the RMVXA Database*

As previously noted, using `.add_state` requires that you set which state you actually want to add, and it looks at the database value to determine what to add. So, Death is 1, while HP Regen is 14, for example. States have one or two new things, but not much that we haven't seen in a similar form already.

- *Restriction* defines what happens to someone affected by the state. Most of them are more forced actions than restrictions. In the case of Death, the actor or enemy *cannot move* (logically, as they are dead!). However, you also have *None, Attack an enemy, Attack anyone*, and *Attack an ally*.

- *Removal Conditions* define when a state is removed. This is more important for actors, given that enemies cease to be after you are done battling with them. If you don't define any removal conditions, the only way to remove the state would be to have an item or event that does just that.

  1. **Remove at Battle End** is self-explanatory. Once the battle ends, so does the state.

  2. **Remove by Restriction**, on the other hand, is downright misleading. The RMVXA tool tip says: "Automatically remove a restriction if [Restriction] has been set to anything other than [None]". That's a bald-faced lie. The tool tip contradicts what Remove by Restriction implies. How it actually works is that a state with that condition will be removed if its owner is affected by another state that causes a restriction. For example, you can have a Rage state that is affected by restrictions so that, if your actor affected by Rage is stunned or otherwise hindered, he/she loses the state.

3. **Auto-removal Timing** allows you to set whether the state is removed automatically after a certain number of turns or not. *Action End* means that the state will be removed after the affected actor or enemy takes a certain number of actions. *Turn End* means that the state will be removed after a certain number of battle turns.

4. **Duration in Turns** can only be edited if you have selected Action End or Turn End in Auto-removal Timing. The first box defines the minimum number of turns the state will last, while the second box notes the maximum number of turns.

5. **Remove by Damage** gives a percentage chance based on the number placed in the appropriate box to remove the state when the actor or enemy suffers damage.

6. **Remove by Walking**. The state is automatically removed after the actor takes a certain number of steps on the map. You can have any number from 0 to 9999 in that box.

7. There are four kinds of messages you can edit. They display when an actor is affected by a state, an enemy is affected by a state, the end of a turn when an actor or enemy is still affected by a state, and when the state is removed.

8. Last, **Features** return once again but don't bear additional explaining, as they do mostly the same that they do in other sections. One thing that does bear mentioning is that state 001 is a special state that is automatically applied whenever a character's HP reaches 0. By default, it is called Death.

Back to Damage Formulas?

Back to damage formulas! We already scratched the tip of the figurative iceberg by noting the existence of `add_buff()` and `add_state()`. Incidentally, `remove_buff()` and `remove_state()` exist as well. The remove methods only accept a single parameter within their parentheses. In the case of `remove_buff`, you declare which of the eight main stats you wish to remove a buff for. For `remove_state`, you define which state is to be removed.

You may have noticed that, in my use of those mentioned methods, I used a semicolon to divide them from the damage formula. There is a little-known rule about damage formulas that is not mentioned within RMVXA, but here it is: *In any formula, you must end the formula with a damage value (or healing, as the case applies).* The easiest way to prove or disprove that assertion is by editing the damage formula of your new bow skill and adding a semicolon after the damage with an `add_state` or `add_buff` command (remember that "a" before the command denotes user, while "b" denotes target). If you did it correctly, you'll see that your skill now does nothing except apply the buff or state. Now, switch the two halves of the formula around, and you'll do damage again.

Here are some other neat things you can do with damage formulas:

- *Making a skill that does more damage based on the target's active states*: Say you want an enemy that poisons the player's party and then tries to consume that poison to do massive damage to its victims. You could have a formula like so: `if b.state?(x); b.remove_state(x);Winter.phys(1.0,a,b);else 0;end`.

  1. `state?` is another method within RMVXA. As the name might suggest, `state?` checks if the target has x state, where x is the number of the state in the Database.

  2. If the target has x state, the skill removes the state and then applies a custom damage formula I came up with (that's the `Winter.phys` part). *If you are using the full version of RMVXA, I'll be covering how to add extensive damage formulas into the script editor for you to call as in the preceding.*

  3. If the target does not have x state, then the skill does 0 damage.

  4. The end terminates the formula.

Those of you with programming experience (especially in Ruby, but even if not) will probably recognize the preceding formula as an if conditional branch. The damage formula box is fully robust. It will hold any amount of Ruby you can fit in there.

So, About That Winter up There . . .

Okay, first let's list some extra exercises for you to do. Then, I will cover what that strange method up there involves.

1. **Make a troop with a single monster that says some words before dying.**

   - Death is prioritized over any other consideration in battle, so you'll have to make the enemy immortal (there's a default state in RMVXA that covers exactly that), have a conditional that triggers when the monster drops to 0% HP, have the monster say its words, and then remove the Immortal state, so that Death can trigger.

   - This troop event can be done with two event pages. The first one should have a Turn No. 0 conditional and a Battle Span (as we only want this event to execute once per battle). You can use the Change Enemy State event command to set the monster's Immortal state.

   - The second event page for this exercise should have a Condition of HP 0% or below and a Battle Span. Because Death is prioritized, the monster must say its words before you remove the state.

2. **Create an enemy with five different skills (including the normal Attack skill). Have one skill require the enemy to be in a state to use, and have another one of its skills grant that state.**

3. **Create an enemy that uses a single skill on a three-turn countdown.**

   - Perhaps the best way to do so within the confines of RMVXA is to create one "skill" for each countdown turn, much like I did for the Sand Scorpion attack pattern I showed you some time ago. If you look at the message box for a skill, you'll see it has two lines. On line 1, you can write "is charging up a massively powerful attack," and on line 2, you can write the appropriate number (3, 2, or 1).

   - Remembering the whole thing about ratings and conditional uses of skills, you can also have the monster use a normal attack pattern that changes to the countdown when the monster is down to half HP or less.

4. **Create a damage formula that includes a variable.**

   - A variable has to be expressed in the form $game_variables[n], where n is the variable's ID.

   - Remember that a variable is, after all considerations, a number. You can use the variable as an attack multiplier, for example.

If you're following along with the Lite version of RMVXA, you will not be able to perform this next exercise, so feel free to skip ahead to Chapter 4, as this will be the last thing I post within this chapter. For the rest of you, let's go.

■ **Objective**   Add a formula to the script editor that we can call from the damage formula box.

You may be wondering the purpose of writing your formula somewhere else and calling it via code, instead of just typing it into the formula box. Well, as I have noted already, the damage box has limited space. Take a look at the formula that I used at one point in a game I was making using RMVXA.

```
a.atk>b.def ? a.atk*0.5*(1.0+(1.0-(b.def*1.0/a.atk*1.0))) : a.atk*0.5*(a.atk*1.0/b.def*1.0)
```

And that's *after* I applied some basic Ruby to shorten the expression. The above formula is written as a ternary expression. In simpler terms, it's another way to write out an `if` conditional branch. It reads out as such.

- If a.atk > b.def

- then a.atk*0.5*(1.0+(1.0-(b.def*1.0/a.atk*1.0))

- else (if a.atk < b.def) a.atk*0.5*(a.atk*1.0/b.def*1.0)

The damage formula may seem alien, but the net effect that it achieves is that a character can never deal more damage than its total Attack stat (which is the sum of a character's Attack and the Attack that it receives from its equipment). This formula favors lower stats a lot better than the default formula does. A similar formula is used for games in the *Dragon Quest* series (where the HP cap is 999 instead of 9999, as in *Final Fantasy*, and thus damage/healing has to be lower across the board).

Of course, as cool as the formula is, writing it out completely within the damage box takes up very nearly every inch of space there is. So, I read up a bit and decided to create a module within the Script Editor instead. How do we do that?

- From the main map screen, press F11 or click Tools and find the Script Editor option.

- Enter the Script Editor and then scroll all the way down to Materials. You will see a single option titled "(Insert Here)." Click it and read what it entails.

- Afterward, do as the help note recommends and insert a new page under the Materials section of the Script Editor by right-clicking Insert Here. Here's what the filled out page looks like for me:

```ruby
module Winter
  module_function

  def phys(p, a, b, v = $game_variables)
    if a.atk > b.def
      return (a.atk*p*(1.00+(1.00-(b.def*1.00/a.atk*1.00))))
    else
      return (a.atk*p*(a.atk*1.00/b.def*1.00))
  end
end

#Express in the form Winter.phys(p, a, b)
#p is the power multiplier for the ATK stat of the caster.

def sitva(bd, p, a, b, v = $game_variables)
  return ((bd + a.mat*p)*(a.mat*1.00/b.mdf*1.00))
end

#Express in the form Winter.sitva(bd, p, a, b)
#bd is the base damage of the Sitva
#p is the power multiplier for the MAT stat of the caster.

end
```

It's not much to look at, but it is basic-level Ruby programming at its finest. You'll be happy to know that you can copy-paste this for use in your game. However, programming is, at its heart, a journey of problem-solving and discovery. Let me walk you through these lines of code.

- We are creating a *module* to contain *methods* related to damage formulas for use in our game.

- This particular module is named Winter (you could rename it anything else, and it would be fine).

- `module_function` is needed for the module to work correctly. Alternately, you could add `self` to each of the method definitions (`def self.phys`, for example) for the same effect.

- Below we have `def phys` along with parentheses filled with several variables. Methods are expressed in the form method (parameters). Notice that the method is on a higher indentation level compared to module Winter. Indents are necessary in Ruby coding, to determine what goes where. Everything below the module is part of it, so it has to be indented. Likewise, everything under `def phys` until the second end is contained within said method; hence, it is a higher indentation level than def phys.

  1. As noted a few lines later in a comment tag, p is the power multiplier for the user's ATK stat.

  2. a and b are the standard uses in a damage formula (user and target).

  3. v is used for any variables you decide to use within a formula. You can use the value of a variable by expressing it as `$game_variables[n]` within a damage formula.

- Next, we have an `if` statement that's true if `a.atk` is greater than `b.def`. If the statement is true, then the first formula is the one to be used, If the statement is false, then the second formula is used instead.

  1. **return** is used within Ruby to exit a method early (in a case such as the one preceding, where we have the formula we want already). While it is not strictly necessary to use at any point of the code I placed in the previous page, it does no harm either, so I left it as is.

  2. The first end in the method terminates the `if` statement. The second end terminates the method itself.

- `def sitva` is the other method present here. Sitva is what I called magic in my own game. You can rename *sitva* to *magic*, and it will make no difference.

  1. As noted in the comment tags following this method, bd represents the base damage of the spell in question, and p is the power multiplier for the caster's MAT stat.

  2. You'll notice that there's no `if` statement for this method, as there's only the one damage formula to plug. I took my inspiration from many Japanese RPGs, in which spell damage tends to be a little more constant than physical damage. (So, barring the target having a massive amount of MDF compared to the user's MAT, damage spells should always do some good damage.)

  3. Because you have only the method itself, you only need the one end statement.

- Last, you'll notice a solitary end past the `def sitva` comment tags. That end closes out the module itself.

See Figure 3-17 for two examples of damage formulas using my new methods.

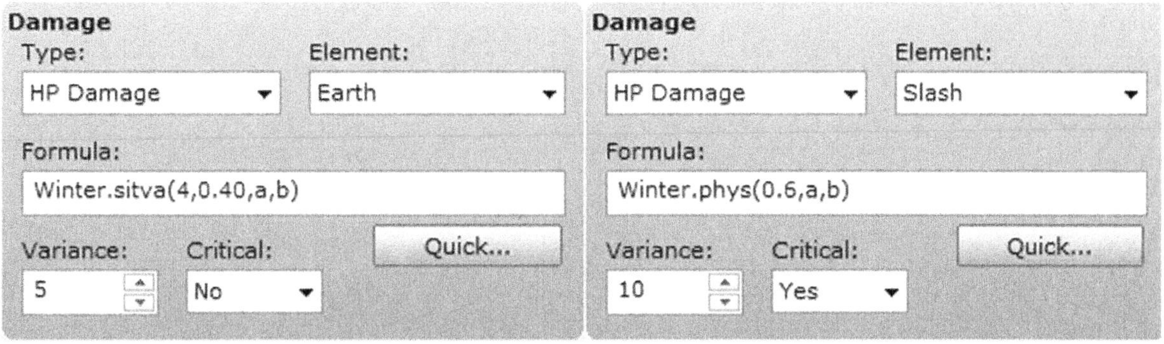

Figure 3-17. *A pair of damage formula examples using methods*

- As you can see, the code is called in the form Module.method. So, you have Winter.sitva and Winter.phys, respectively, in the two preceding examples. Compare the expressed methods with the code listed previously, and you'll see that we utilize every variable within the method parentheses. For sitva, we have base damage, the MAT multiplier, a, and b, in that order. For phys, we have the ATK multiplier, a, and b.

Summary

During the course of this chapter, we covered a great part of the Database. The Database is required to create playable character, enemies, and items for the player to collect. We created new items for our protagonist to use. In addition, we touched upon the Region tool and used it to create an area in which the player can engage a newly created troop. That concludes this chapter. In the next chapter, we will work on fleshing out our game a little more. How, you may wonder? We'll be adding more locations to the game!

CHAPTER 4

Fleshing Out Your World

During the course of the past two chapters, I've covered many basic but important aspects of RPG Maker VX Ace (RMVXA). Now it is time to build on what you have learned, to start making our very own game. The first order of business is to add a few more maps, as we only have the two we created so far. To make sure that we are using the same content, and also to show off the relevant feature, let's use some premade maps.

Adding Content to Our Game World

Two role-playing game (RPG) mainstays are towns and dungeons. Additionally, most RPGs have a world map that connects the various locations that the player can visit during the game. So, on that note, let's add three new maps from the premade selection that RMVXA has available.

1. From the main map screen, right-click your project's name on the lower-left corner and select Load Sample Map.

You could have done the same thing by right-clicking MAP001 or your second map. That would have caused the new map to be placed under the previous map. Doing so is rather useful for organizing maps that share a similar purpose. Figure 4-1 shows an example of what I mean.

Figure 4-1. A screenshot of a sample map list

Note In a sense, nesting related locations makes it easier to see what goes where on a meta level. This becomes more important as the size of the game increases. This is not actually necessary but can be a time-saver.

---

2. After clicking Load Sample Map, you'll see a wide variety of maps to use. First, let's choose our world map. I picked Field 3, a world map with many smaller continents and islands.

3. Next, let's add a town map. Right-click Field 3 and select Load Sample Map. Given that the world map has plenty of water, let's use the Port Town for our very first town.

4. Last, let's add a dungeon. Right-click Field 3 again and load up the sample map list. The Goblin Cave is a nice and simple dungeon layout, so let's select Goblin Cave F1F.

Now, what if I told you that I want you to place *both* of the Goblin Caves within the same map? Sounds like a cue to painstakingly spend a few hours drawing Goblin Cave FB1, right? Actually, wrong! It took me longer than I care to admit to realize that you can copy-paste terrain as easily as you can an event. How do we do this?

1. First, right-click Goblin Cave F1F and use Load Sample Map to add Goblin Cave FB1 to your project. Note that it is a 46×46 map.

2. Next, let's prepare Goblin Cave F1F to receive its own basement level. Go to Goblin Cave's map properties and increase its width by 56 (FB1's width plus 10 more squares, to effectively split the two maps). You'll see transparent tiles fill the extra space.

3. Now, switch over to Goblin Cave FB1 and display the map in 1/4 scale.

You can find scale buttons for 1/1 (default), 1/2, 1/4, and 1/8 to the right of the map drawing tools.

1. After making sure that you're in Map editing mode and using the Pencil tool, right-click the upper-left corner of Goblin Cave FB1 and drag the cursor all the way to the lower-right corner. If done correctly, your cursor should now be moving around a huge white square.

2. Switch back to F1F and scroll to the part of the map filled with transparent tiles. Once you have the square in a good spot, left-click once. Like magic, you'll see Goblin Cave FB1 appear. You can fill in the transparent tiles with the Darkness tile from tileset A, or just leave them as they are (transparent tiles show up black in-game). Your Goblin Cave map should look like Figure 4-2. (This screenshot was taken at 1/8 map scale).

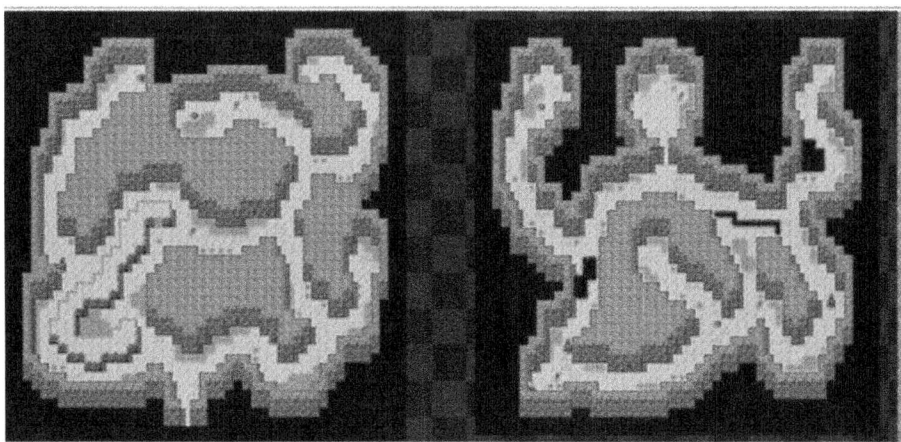

Figure 4-2. *Both levels of the Goblin Cave placed on a single map*

Populating the World Map

Now we are ready to start populating our game world. Let's make our way to Field 3. RMVXA's premade maps come with already defined terrain but none of the other trappings that make a world map what it is. What we're going to do is place appropriate graphics for our newly created town and dungeon and our previously created map. I'm placing the three doodads on the southern end of the largest landmass of the world map. (It's the left-side continent that's two parts dirt and one part grasslands.) All of the graphics are on the B tab of the Field tileset. Take a peek at Figure 4-3 to see what the area looks like after adding the new content.

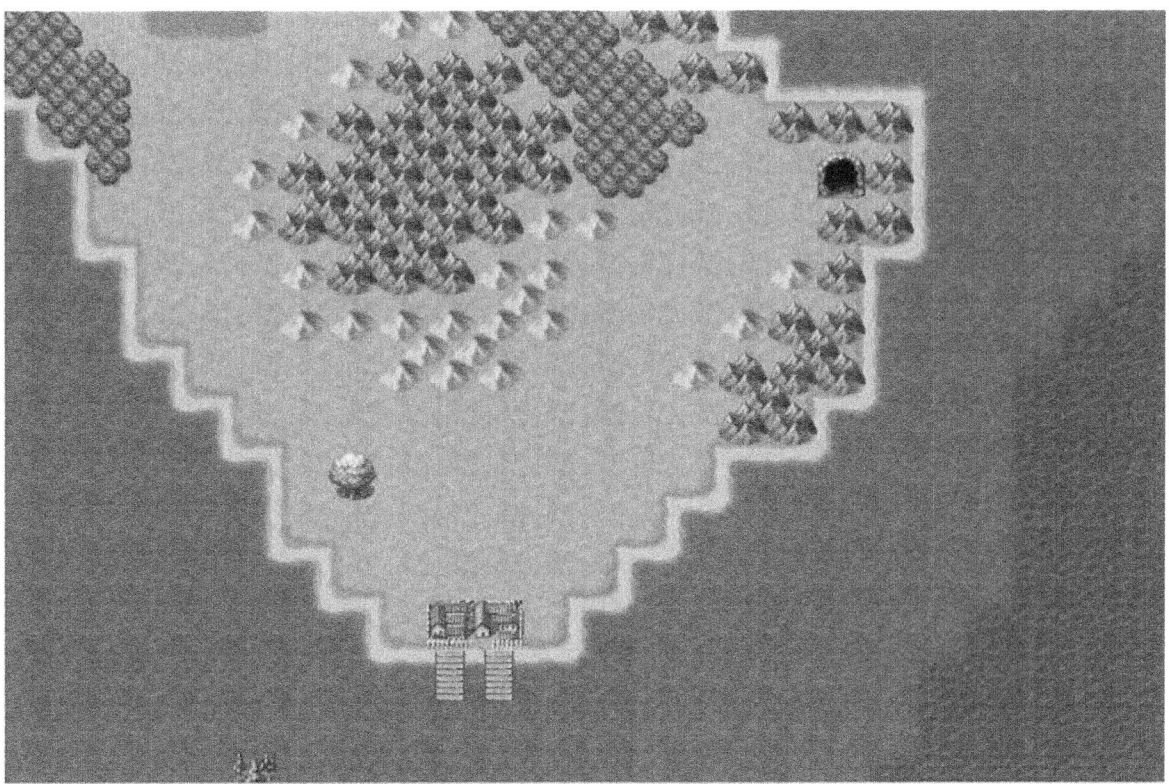

Figure 4-3. *The world map after adding appropriate graphics for each currently created area*

The giant tree to the northwest of the port town is the location from where our protagonist will exit the second area. I placed the dungeon entrance in a conveniently sized hole to the northeast of the port town and the giant tree. Of course, for as cool as they look placed as they are on the map, we must still create transfer events that actually take us to our new locations. If there was ever a place to use the Parallel Process event I mentioned back in Chapter 2 to cut down on overall event use, the world map is definitely it. Think back to your last RPG and how many locations you could reach from its world map. You're going to run out of events in a hurry, even if you're using the full version of RMVXA that has a much more lenient restriction on the number of events per map. You can copy-paste the relevant event from the second map and tweak it for the world map. We want the giant tree to take the player to the second map, the town graphic to take the player to the port town, and the cave graphic to take him/her to the Goblin Cave. It should look something like this:

```
@>Control Variables: [0002:X] = Player's Map X
@>Control Variables: [0003:Y] = Player's Map Y
@>Conditional Branch: Variable [0002:X] == 18
   @>Conditional Branch: Variable [0003:Y] == 88
      @>Transfer Player: [002:Second Area] (011,012), Up
      @>
   : Branch End
   @>
: Branch End
@>Conditional Branch: Variable [0002:X] >= 20
   @>Conditional Branch: Variable [0002:X] <= 21
      @>Conditional Branch: Variable [0003:Y] == 91
         @>Transfer Player: [004:Port Town] (019,004), Down
         @>
      : Branch End
      @>
   : Branch End
   @>
: Branch End
@>Conditional Branch: Variable [0002:X] == 28
   @>Conditional Branch: Variable [0003:Y] == 82
      @>Transfer Player: [005:Goblin CaveF1F] (020,043), Up
      @>
   : Branch End
   @>
: Branch End
@>
```

Once you have done that, you can fix the Transfer event in the second map to allow the player to reach the world map. I will leave those tasks as exercises for you. Let's move on to the port town. It's time to populate it! (Take a look at Figure 4-4 to see a picture of RMVXA's premade port town).

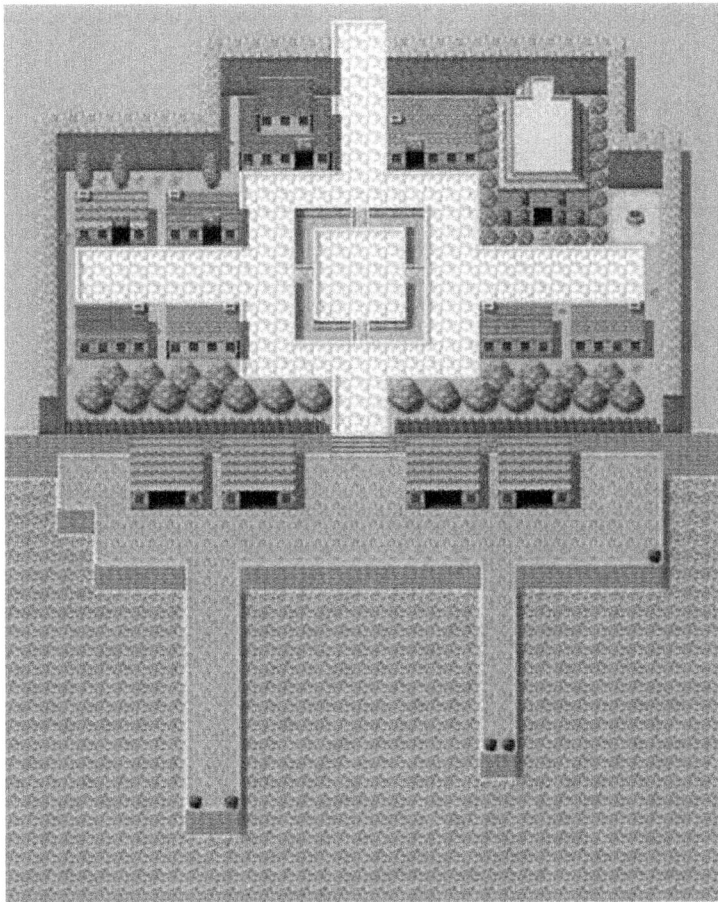

Figure 4-4. *The Port Town sample map in RMVXA*

Populating the Port Town

As you can see in Figure 4-4, the port town has two shops set in place, as well as an inn, a pub, and a temple. RMVXA has premade maps for all of the above-mentioned locales, as well as several house templates.

Of course, if we were to make one map for each of the buildings, RMVXA Lite users would run smack-dab into the map limit. Also, it's rather more efficient (in terms of map slots) to have all of the buildings contained within the same map. In the case of our port town, we save eight map slots (as we have nine locations) by doing so. Generally, I prefer to use a single map for town interiors, as they tend to have the largest amount of locations. For dungeons, I usually have one map per floor (with the obvious exception of the Goblin Cave, but I did that to illustrate the concept of having multiple locations in one map).

■ **Note**   The full version of RMVXA has a rather generous 999 map limit that you probably won't hit unless you make a particularly large game. However, the preceding discussion is good to keep in mind, if you decide to make the next 50-hour epic RPG.

So, let's create a new map of a whopping 500×500 in size that uses the Interior tileset. Then, using premade maps and copy-paste, add all of the following to said map:

- An inn with two floors
- An item shop
- A pub
- A weapon and armor shop
- Two houses
- A temple

Keep in mind that you'll want to separate each individual building by roughly 10 spaces; otherwise, the player will be able to see the different buildings present on the same map if he/she strays too far to the left or right. What I usually do to make sure the gap between two buildings is exactly 10 squares wide is draw a line of distinct terrain to the right of the first building. Then you place the new building adjacent to the end of the line. Once you're done placing your buildings, you can erase the lines you made. The first three buildings mentioned above are available as premades (the pub is covered by the Drinking Bar premade map). For the weapon and armor shop, I took the weapon shop premade and tweaked it a little to show off armor and place a second seat for the armor vendor. (See Figure 4-5).

Figure 4-5. *The weapon and armor shop map based off of the weapon shop sample map*

As for the two houses, there are several premades that you can use. I'm going to use House A and House B. Finally, the temple exterior looks more like the Church premade than the Temple, so let's use the former instead of the latter. Once you're done, you can reduce the size of the map. As I lined up all my buildings in one row, I went from 500×500 to 225×40. Figure 4-6 is a 1/8 scale screenshot.

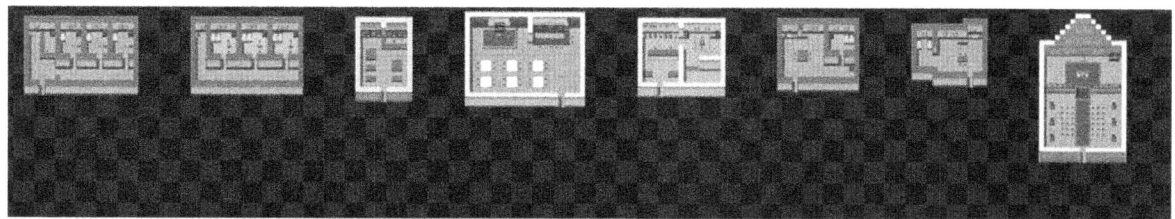

Figure 4-6. *The interior map for the port town's buildings*

Now let's get to work populating the port town! We're going to want non-player characters (NPCs) for each of the buildings. For the inn, you need the innkeeper. For each of the shops, you need shopkeepers. The pub needs a barkeeper, and the temple needs a priestly-type character. This is as good a time as any to use the character generator that RMVXA provides, so make your way to the Tools tab of the menu toolbar and click the Character Generator.

Creating Characters to Populate Seaside

This section will take you through the process of creating an NPC and placing him/her in the game world. You should be looking at the Character Generator at the moment. (See Figure 4-7.)

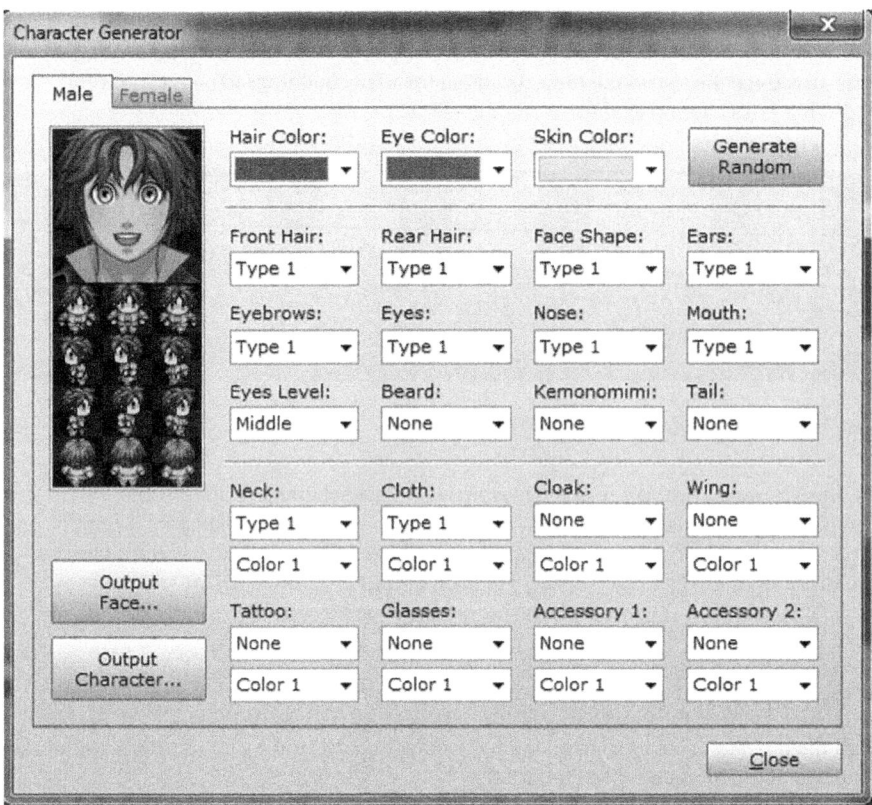

Figure 4-7. *The Character Generator dialog menu*

As mentioned earlier in the book, the Character Generator is awesome for making a diverse range of characters without any graphical know-how. Mess around with the settings for a bit and note how each feature change affects the character's face and sprite. Once you're done, you can save the character sprite by clicking Output Character and writing a file name in the prompt that appears. I don't usually have character faces for my less important characters, but you can save your character's face via Output Face, if you wish. Make a total of eight characters. Once you're done, placing a character on a map is as easy as switching to Event Mode, creating a new event, and adding your freshly made character sprite to the event. Here is where we're going to place the character events:

- Place one character on the stool behind the counter at the inn. That character will be your innkeeper. Place a second character on one of the stools on the inn's second floor.

- Place a character on the stool at the item shop. This will be the item shopkeeper.

- Place two characters at the pub/drinking bar. One of them will be the barkeeper, so place him/her behind the counter. Place the second in front of the piano.

- Place a pair of characters at the weapon/armor shop, one for each type of equipment.

- Place one character at each of the two houses.

- Place two characters at the temple. Leave the area behind the altar empty. We have special plans for the priestly type character (we'll be using a stock graphic for him).

After all that is said and done, we have to link the buildings to the port town exterior. Use a Parallel Process event, as we have already, and plug in the relevant Transfer events. With that done, make your way to the port town map. We have some tweaking to do! First of all, we have to add doors to the top buildings. Doors, as noted in Chapter 2, are a type of transfer event used for buildings. Add a door event to each of the buildings, making sure to link it to the correct destination on the other map. Figure 4-8 is a screenshot example of where the player should land after being transferred to the port town's inn interior.

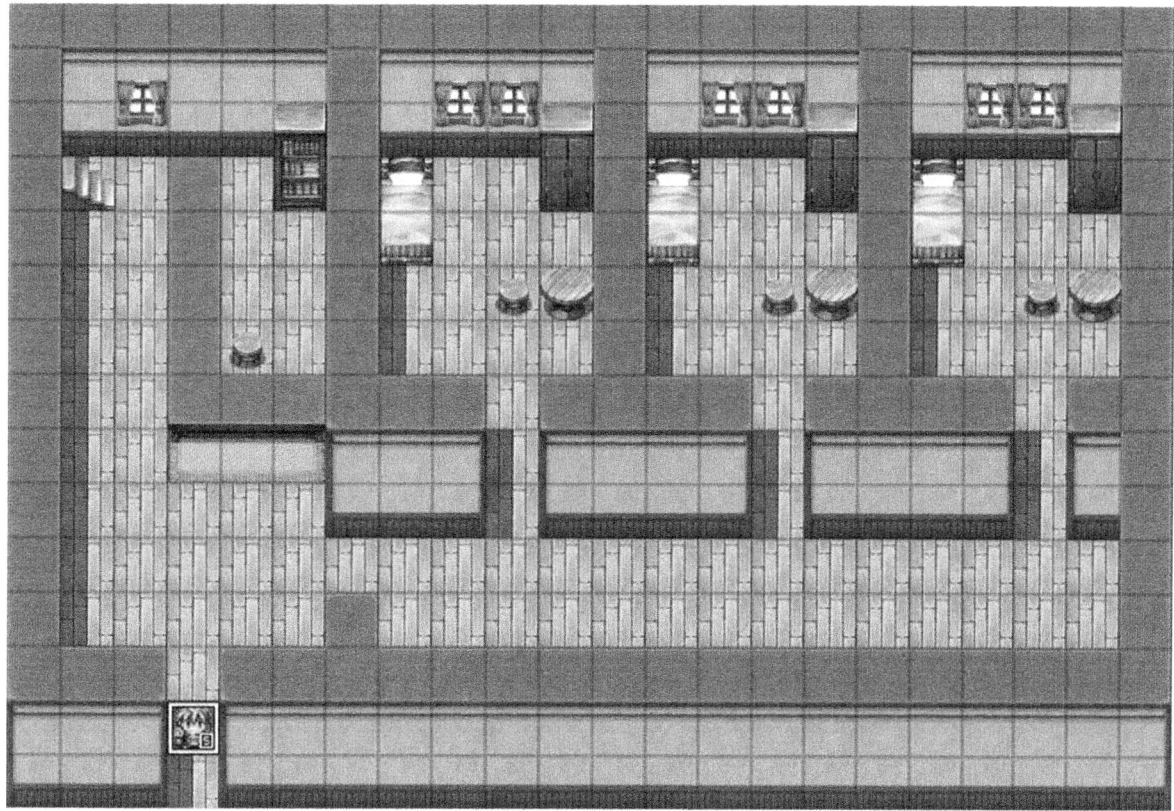

Figure 4-8. *The first floor of the port town's inn. Note the player character's location*

As you can see, there is one square below the player in the inn. We can use that square in the Parallel Process event on that map to serve as the inn's exit. You'll also want to connect that staircase with its sibling on the inn's second floor.

Going back to the port town map, if we scroll down, we'll see four buildings with two-square-wide entrances. What we're going to do is decrease the size of the entrances to one square and then place door events on two of them. For the other two houses, you'll want to create an event with a door graphic that tells the player that the door is locked. To do that

1. Create a new event covering the entrance with a door from the !Door1 graphic set. You'll notice that as soon as you set a graphic for the event, its priority will default to Same As Characters. In this case, that's exactly what we want. In other cases, such as the button event we created back in Chapter 2, we'll want to revert the event to Below Characters.

2. For the sake of consistency with the door transfer events, set the "locked door" events to Player Touch.

3. Afterward, add a Text Box that says: "This door is locked."

Note   If you're using the Lite version of RMVXA, which happens to have a ten-event cap on each individual map, it will probably be better if you wall off the buildings that would otherwise be locked, so you can save two event slots.

Now we have two houses that are linked to the interior map and two houses that give a message for the player when he/she tries to enter. Make three more characters using the Character Generator and place them as so:

- Place one at the longer pier, between the two mooring bollards (in simpler words, the two things that look like pins).

- Place one at the plaza at the northern end of town.

- Place the last one looking over the well to the east of the temple.

Note   Adding all three characters, if you have RMVXA Lite, will put you right at ten events. To compensate, remove one of the NPCs, so that you have an available event with which to create the transfer event for the player to leave the port town.

So, we've done a lot of character placing throughout the exterior and interior of the port town. But what are the NPCs doing there? What should they say to the player when he/she talks to them? Here's some setting info you can use to flavor what they could be talking about:

Eric awakes from an age-old slumber, finding himself within a ring of mountains that has only one exit. He appears within a small glen and finds his trusty bow after noticing some peculiar trees. Afterward, he finds himself to the northwest of a port town and makes his way there. The people of the port town of Seaside are frustrated with the current situation: ships have not docked there for the better part of a decade, crippling trade between Seaside and the rest of the world. Only the efforts of farmers living on the far end of the continent have kept them alive and well. Now, monsters from a cave to the northeast are attacking the farms and stealing their food. The people of the continent need a hero.

The only things I'll require are the following:

- That the barkeeper inform the player of the threat of monsters from the nearby cave, explaining that they are threatening the town's livelihood. Set a switch to ON after the initial conversation and then have the barkeeper talk about something else, if the player speaks to him/her again. You can use Show Text events for the greater part of the conversation and Show Choices when you want the player to weigh in with a response.

- Noah is the tenth premade actor in RMVXA. Use his graphic as an event placed behind the altar at the temple. If the player has already talked to the barkeeper (the relevant switch is ON), have Noah join Eric's party. If the player has not, Noah should recommend that they speak to the various townsfolk, to get a feel for what's going on. This should be a three-page event, with the third page removing the Noah event from the screen after he is added to the party. You can use the Change Party Member event command to have Noah join the player's party.

If you're unclear on how to tackle those two character events, I will explain them in detail later in the chapter. With that said, I should take some time to cover *how* to make the various NPCs that will be running the inn and the shops. If you check the third page of the Event Commands list, you'll find a command called *Shop Processing.* Clicking it brings up a relatively simple window (as shown in Figure 4-9).

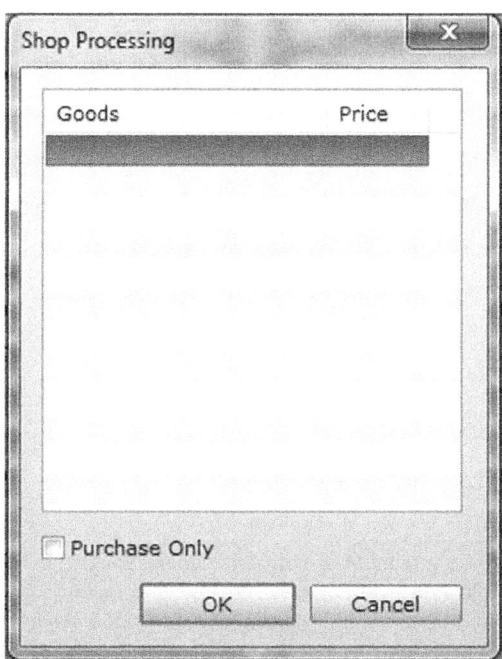

Figure 4-9. *The window that appears when Shop Processing is selected*

Essentially, Shop Processing allows you to create a list of items that the shopkeeper will then sell in-game. Double-click to add a new item. You can also set the item price here, if you want it to differ from the standard. The check box at the bottom allows you to create a shop that disallows selling. Here's a simple example of how the item shop NPC event could look like:

```
@>Text: -, -, Normal, Bottom
:     : What can I do for you, sir?
@>Shop Processing: [Antidote]
:               : [Potion]
:               : [Dispel Herb]
:               : [Hi-Potion]
:               : [Stimulant]
:               : [Magic Water]
:               : [Elixir]
@>
```

In the same way, you can use a similar event for the weapon and armor shop NPCs. As for the innkeeper, there's no Inn Processing equivalent in the event command list, but Inns *are* a Quick Event. Clicking the Inn Quick Event will bring up the following window (Figure 4-10).

Figure 4-10. *The Inn Quick Event*

Rather unassuming, isn't it? Select the character graphic that you designated to be your innkeeper, change the cost of staying the night if you wish, and then click OK. Next, take a look at the event that was created. Quite a few things in there, aren't there? The most important thing to note is the pair of screen fade commands. When the player pays the innkeeper for the room, the screen fades out, music is played, and then the screen fades back in. You could use a similar fade-out/fade-in coupling to add Noah to the player's party without showing the event disappearing simultaneously (as that would look clunky, at best). So, let me explain how I laid out the events I required.

- The barkeeper
    1. Right-click any square behind the counter of the drinking bar and create the new event.
    2. Create a conversation between Eric and the barkeeper whereby a switch is turned on after the player accepts the quest.

Take a look below for the conversation that I created, complete with an old RPG trope: the false choice.

```
@>Text: -, -, Normal, Bottom
:      : Hello there, young one. What brings you to fair
:      : Seaside?
@>Text: -, -, Normal, Bottom
:      : Eric explains what has happened recently.
@>Show Balloon Icon: This event, Exclamation, Wait
@>Text: -, -, Normal, Bottom
:      : Could it be?
@>Text: 'Actor4', 0, Normal, Bottom
:      : What is it?
@>Text: -, -, Normal, Bottom
:      : Legends speak of a hero that was sealed within a
:      : glen in times long past.
@>Text: -, -, Normal, Bottom
:      : We have dire need of a hero, lad. This port town is
:      : in danger, you see. Monsters have taken up residence
:      : at the cave to the northeast and are affecting our
:      : livelihood. Farmers live on the far end of this
@>Text: -, -, Normal, Bottom
:      : continent and provide for our many food-related
:      : needs. Traders have not visited Seaside for nearly
:      : a decade. Ships that we send out do not return.
:      : Please aid us, hero!
@>Label: Repeat
@>Text: -, -, Normal, Bottom
:      : What say you?
@Show Choices: Yes, No
: When [Yes]
   @>Text: -, -, Normal, Bottom
   :      : Thank you very much, lad! Please speak to Noah at
   :      : Seaside's temple. He has been searching for someone
   :      : to aid him in defeating the monsters.
   @>Control Switches: [0002:PlotAdvance] = ON
   @>
: When [No]
   @>Text: -, -, Normal, Bottom
   :      : But thou must!
   @>Jump to Label: Repeat
   @>
: Branch End
```

As usual, I took the time to add a few new things for us to look at.

- *Show Balloon Icon* is a neat little event command that places a balloon over someone's head. (You can choose between the player, the current event, or another event on the same map). In this case, the barkeeper gets an exclamation point, for reasons that make themselves obvious a few lines of text later. That Wait after Exclamation means that the game will wait until that event command has resolved to continue event processing. If you don't toggle that option, the conversation will continue as the balloon appears.

- *Label* (and the subsequent *Jump to Label*) are a pair of event commands that let you control event processing. Normally, events work much like regular computer programs. That is, they start resolving from the top of the code and end at the bottom. However, there are many situations in which we don't want this to be the case. For example, here we want the player to accept the quest given. Of course, it wouldn't be much of a game if he/she decided to say no. So, we invoke one of RPG's most classic tropes and pull a literal "But thou must!" on them if they do say no. The Jump to Label command then finds the designated label (in this case, called *Repeat*) and rewinds back to that point.

- *Show Choices* is what allows us to set the yes/no question in the first place. This event command can hold up to four choices and allows you to decide what to do when the player tries to opt out of the choice branch (with the Esc key, for example). You can set the choice branch so that the player cannot opt out of it, designate the choice to be picked if the player opts out, or create another branch when the player tries to opt out of the first one.

With that done, let's add Noah to the game! First, make your way to the Actors tab in the database and increase Noah's starting level to 5. Next, go to the port town building map that you created and make your way to the temple. Behind the altar, add a new event with a total of three pages.

Page 1 should look like this:

```
@>Conditional Branch: Self Switch A == OFF
   @>Text: 'Actor5', 6, Normal, Bottom
   :      : What brings you to this temple, traveler?
   @>Wait: 60 frame(s)
   @>Show Balloon Icon: This event, Exclamation, Wait
   @>Text: 'Actor4', 0, Normal, Bottom
   :      : Everything all right?
   @>Text: 'Actor5', 6, Normal, Bottom
   :      : Yes, you looked like somebody familiar.
   :      : That is all.
   @>Control Self Switch: A = ON
   @>
: Branch End
@>Conditional Branch: Self Switch A == ON
   @>Text: 'Actor5', 6, Normal, Bottom
   :      : If you'll be staying with us, you might
   :      : wish to speak with the barkeep over at
   :      : the local pub. He has eyes and ears all
   :      : over the continent.
   @>
: Branch End
@>
```

Remember to set Noah's character graphic, as well as keep the event trigger as Action Button. As the preceding event page displays, there is a *Wait* event command that can be used when you want to force the game to pause for a certain amount of time. Sixty frames is equal to a single second for Wait's purposes.

For page 2, you'll want to set a conditional for PlotAdvance to be ON (the switch I used during the conversation with the barkeeper). Then, once you have done that, take a look at the next page to see what you should add.

```
@>Text: 'Actor5', 6, Normal, Bottom
:       : I can see it in your eyes. The barkeep
:       : has told you of my wishes. I would see
:       : the monsters felled as soon as possible.
:       : When do we leave?
@>Play ME: 'Item', 100, 100
@>Text: -, -, Normal, Bottom
:       : Noah has joined your party!
@>Fadeout Screen
@>Wait: 120 frame(s)
@>Change Party Member: Add [Noah]
@>Control Self Switch: B =ON
@>Fadein Screen
@>
```

The first half of the event leading up to Fadeout Screen is pretty self-explanatory. What the second half does is create a transition that allows Noah to join the player's party without making it obvious that you're removing the event version of him. The screen fades out with a two-second delay, and Noah is added to the party via the use of the *Change Party Member* event command (which, incidentally, can also be used to remove party members, should the need arise). After that, we switch on the B Self Switch and have the screen fade back in. However, if we leave the event at that, you will have two Noahs. The third event page will have a conditional of "Self Switch B = ON" and nothing else, not even a character graphic. Once Noah has joined your party, the related event will, for as far as the player knows, cease to exist. Internally, though, it still does.

Now that we are done with that, I will list the items I have placed for sale from each of the shop NPCs (Figure 4-11). The left-most list is the item shop, the center list is the weapon shop, while the right-hand list is the armor shop.

Figure 4-11. *The three shops of Seaside*

Those are the most important things to do within this port town.

Creating Random Encounters for the World Map

Next, let's add some random encounters to the part of the world map to which we currently have access. For this, we can use Regions. (See Figure 4-12).

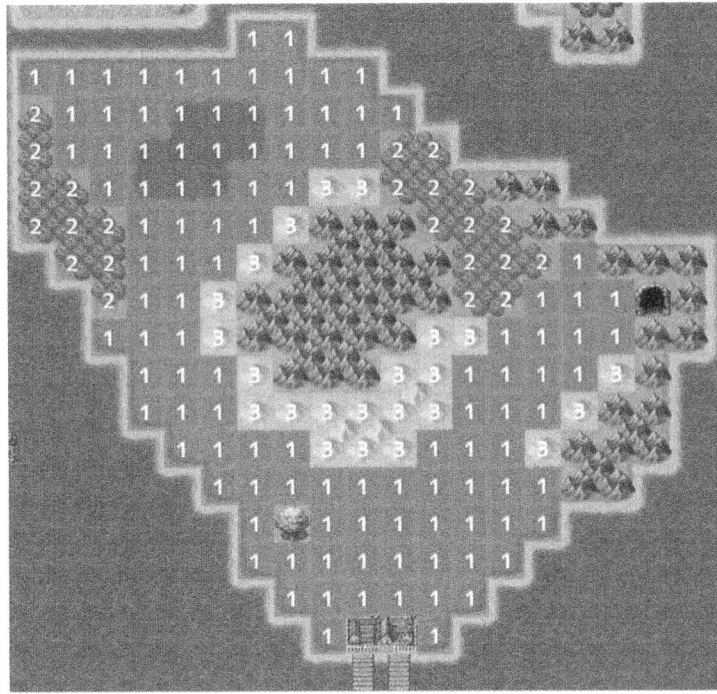

Figure 4-12. *The world map. Regions have been added*

Region 1 encompasses the entirety of the area's grasslands. We have Region 2 for the forests and Region 3 for the hills. Let's add some encounters to each region. In this particular case, I numbered the areas based on encounter difficulty, which is a good way to go, so that you can remember what you want appearing in a certain area. If you take a look at the Monsters tab, you'll notice that the monsters are roughly subdivided for such a purpose already. Monsters 001 through 005 all have similar power levels, then 006 (the Wisp, by default) is much stronger than 005 (the Rat). Similar power spikes appear at regular intervals. I'm going to use troops with the first six unit types to create my encounter tables for this part of the world. See Figure 4-13 for a list of encounters that I set for the world map as of now.

Encounters

Troop	Weight	Range
001:Slime*2	30	1
002:Bat*2	20	1, 2
003:Hornet*2	15	2
004:Spider*3	10	2
005:Rate*3	20	1, 2, 3
006:Wisp*3	5	3

Figure 4-13. *The encounters table for the world map*

As you can see, I made the total weight of the encounters 100, although that is not strictly true. For example, there are only three total encounters available in Region 1, with a total weight of 70. That means that you have a 30/70 chance of meeting two Slimes, a 20/70 chance of seeing two Bats, and a 20/70 chance of engaging three Rats (the Rat typo is present by default in RMVXA; it's as easy to fix as a single press of Backspace, should it particularly bug you). Wisps, being the strongest enemy type by far, are a rare sight in Region 3 (5/25 chance of seeing them, as compared to a 20/25 chance of seeing Rats). Now, we need to speak more about battlebacks.

A Discussion on Battlebacks

Up to now, we've had a single area with a single encounter. When you have a map that has uniform terrain (much like most dungeons), you can just set the area's battleback in the map properties. However, the world map is a conglomeration of various types of terrain (a cursory peek at Field 3 reveals snow and lava areas). It would be rather odd to have a forest battleback for a brawl in the snow, wouldn't you say? So, what we can do is apply past knowledge in a neat little exercise.

▪ **Objective**   Create an event that allows the battleback to change, based on the region the player is in when an encounter occurs.

How do we go about this? If you think back to Chapter 2, we used a Parallel Process event that wrote the values of the player's X and Y to variables to determine map boundaries for area transitions. Here, we can use the *Get Location Info* event command in conjunction with *Control Variables*, conditional branching, and *Change Battleback* within a Parallel Process to make sure the battle background is always appropriate to the area in question. As *Change Battleback* is pretty much equivalent to just setting a default area battleback in a map's properties, let me speak a little more of *Get Location Info*. Figure 4-14 is a screenshot of that event command.

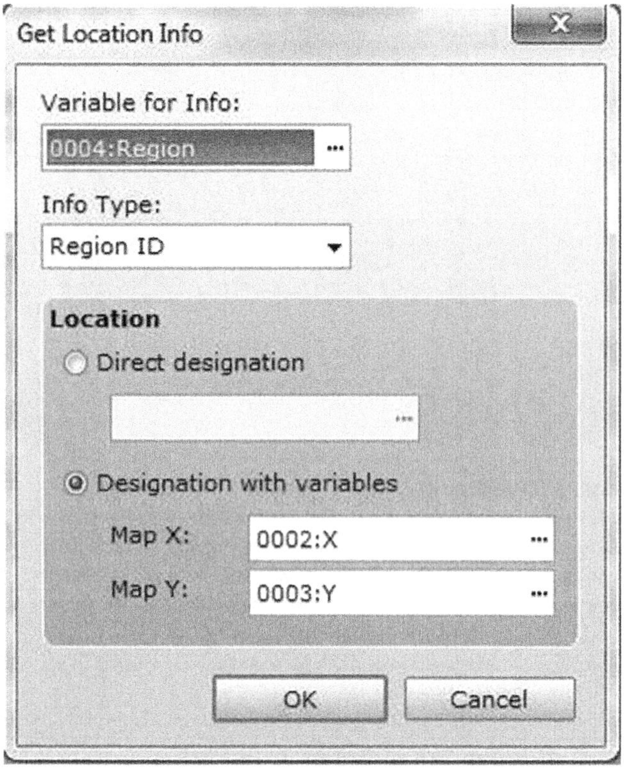

Figure 4-14. *The Get Location Info event command*

As you can see, *Get Location Info* first asks for the variable in which you wish to store your relevant information. I created a new variable named Region just for this occasion. Next, you have to use the second drop-down menu to define what information you wish to write to said variable. Region ID is preselected here, but it is the last item on the *Info Type* list. The others are

1. **Terrain Tag**. If you go to the Tilesets tab in the Database, you'll notice a series of buttons on the right-hand side of the screen that range from Passage at the top to Terrain Tag itself at the bottom. Terrain Tags are a minor, but useful, way to define different areas, without the use of Regions. All tiles default to 0 and can go up to 7. A little more on this (and more general terrain considerations) later.

2. **Event ID**. If the player is currently on top of an event square, using this option will write the specific Event ID to your variable of choice.

3. **Tile ID (Layers 1–3)** are the final three items before Region ID. This refers to the tile's ID internally. I'll leave it as an exercise to you to figure out uses for this particular command. (I prefer Terrain Tags, to be honest.)

Last, we want to select *Designation with Variables*, as we want the event to poll the player's position on a continuous basis.

As for the rest of the event, you can use Conditional Branches to check for the player's current region and change the battlebacks accordingly, like so:

```
@>Control Variables: [0002:X] = Player's Map X
@>Control Variables: [0003:Y] = Player's Map Y
@>Get Location Info: [0004], Region ID, Variable [0002][0003]
@>Conditional Branch: Variable [0004:Region] == 1
   @>Change Battle Back: Grassland & Grassland
   @>
 : Branch End
@>Conditional Branch: Variable [0004:Region] == 2
   @>Change Battle Back: Grassland & Forest1
   @>
 : Branch End
@>Conditional Branch: Variable [0004:Region] == 3
   @>Change Battle Back: Grassland & Cliff
   @>
 : Branch End
@>
```

RMVXA Lite has only a sampling of the total backgrounds that the full version contains. Still, the preceding battlebacks should give some form of differentiation of locales for the player's benefit.

Adding Transfer Events to the World Map

While you're on the world map, you should add another Parallel Process event for area transfers as well, given that we have three locations on this map already. Now, let's take some time to go back to our first two maps and add to them. We want to give the game a coherent direction in plot, rather than just dump the player in the middle of a map unceremoniously. So, on the first map, let's add an Autorun event with no conditionals. That means that it will activate as soon as the player enters the game. The first order of business is fading out the screen. Then, use transparent text boxes aligned with the center of the screen to give a relevant backstory. Just make sure you don't start the game with an overly long text dump, as most players hate that. A paragraph or two should be enough. Here's what I did:

```
@>Fadeout Screen
@>Text: -, -, Transparent, Middle
 :     : A young man awakens from his slumber. He knows only
 :     : that his name is Eric. He knows not where he is, nor
 :     : why. What adventures await him? It is time to find
 :     : out!
@>Wait: 60 frame(s)
@>Control Self Switch: A =ON
@>Fadein Screen
@>
```

Make sure you create a second page within the event that is empty and only active once that self-switch has been turned on, or your game will loop that event page forever. On the second map, add an NPC blocking the road that speaks of the five trees that block access to Eric's Bow and then disappears. Here's what I did:

```
@>Text: 'Actor'4, 0, Normal, Bottom
:      : Who are you?
@>Text: -, -, Normal, Bottom
:      : Me? I am but a man who used to be a king, in ages
:      : long past. Your bow has been sealed within this
:      : glade for as long as you. Examine the five trees
:      : and claim your birthright. Fare thee well.
@>Text: 'Actor'4, 0, Normal, Bottom
:      : Wait, what are you-
@>Fadeout Screen
@>Text: -, -, Normal, Bottom
:      : Before Eric can finish his sentence, the enigmatic
:      : figure disappears.
@>Control Self Switch: A =ON
@>Fadein Screen
@>
```

As in the previous event, have a second blank page after this one. We need to do two more things. First, to the Treasure Chest event, add a new switch that is set to ON once Eric opens the treasure chest revealed by the trees. Have a text box appear telling the player to head to Seaside once he/she receives the bow. Second, add a conditional to the Parallel Process event on this map that requires said switch to be turned on. This prevents the player from leaving before taking the chest's contents. Once all is said and done, the player will know that he/she is a mysterious being awoken from a deep slumber and has a first objective in the game world.

Our next task is to populate our very first dungeon, but that is a subject best left to its own chapter. Before ending this chapter, however, let's talk a little more about tilesets and terrain tags, as promised previously.

A Little More on Terrain Tags and Tilesets!

To talk about Terrain Tags is to talk about tilesets, as they are intrinsically linked. As mentioned previously, each tile can have a Terrain tag value between 0 and 7. Off the top of my head, here are a few of the cool things that terrain tags allow you to do:

- You can have a Parallel Process event running that turns all floor tiles with a certain terrain tag into damage floor tiles.

- You can have a minigame, in which you have to step on tiles in a certain order, just by setting the terrain tags of each set of tiles to a different number.

- You can have skills that have differing effects, based on the current terrain tag, similar to *Geomancy* from some of the *Final Fantasy* games. A skill could do more damage in the grasslands but have a chance to freeze victims in the snow.

For a little number, terrain tags sure can do a lot, eh? Of course, the Tilesets part of the Database is as robust as any other. Given that we have not looked at it yet, let's take some time to do so. Look at Figure 4-15.

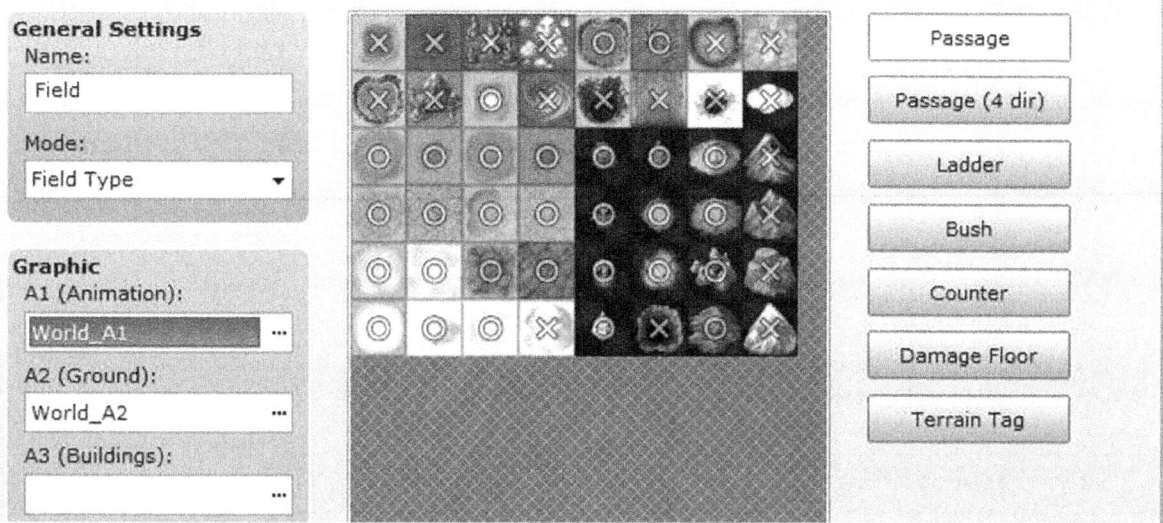

Figure 4-15. *The Tilesets tab in the RMVXA Database*

While *Name* in *General Settings* is self-explanatory, *Mode* is far from it. I leave it as an exercise to you to read up on Resource Standards in the Help file, as RMVXA itself recommends in the Mode tool tip. Most of that will be of little interest to you, unless you want to add your own custom tilesets (whether created by yourself or purchased from a graphic designer) to RMVXA. What is most relevant to beginner-level RMVXA users is those buttons I mentioned a few pages back when talking about Terrain Tags. Let's start from the top.

- *Passage* determines whether or not a player character can walk over the specific tile.

- *Passage (4 dir)* is for specific tiles. On tiles that allow the use of this property, you can control from which directions the player is allowed to enter that square of terrain. This is really useful for maps such as desert areas with rapidly moving sand that only allow movement in certain ways.

- *Ladder*, as the name implies, is used for ladder-type graphics. Basically, whenever you want the character to climb, you use the ladder property.

- *Bush* makes it so that the bottom part of the character is obscured when passing through a tile with that property.

- *Counter* is of particular interest. You probably noticed that we have placed several NPCs behind counters at the port town. If you have been doing some experimentation on your own, you will know that you must be standing adjacent to an event to trigger it via the use of Action Button/Player Touch/Event Touch. However, if your event is separated from the player by a tile considered a counter, you can still interact with him/her. It allows us to have NPCs like the barkeeper, who are otherwise trapped, but permits interaction with the player nonetheless.

- While you can use Terrain Tags for the same effect, there is a specific terrain property for *Damage Floors*. Designate a tile as a damage floor, and it will damage players who pass over them for 10 damage.

A Discussion of Floor Damage

How do I know how much damage such tiles cause? Well, it's all contained within a few lines of code (which you cannot edit unless you own the full version of RMVXA). To note: These lines are contained within Game_Actor.

```
#-------------------------------------------------------------------------
# * Get Base Value for Floor Damage
#-------------------------------------------------------------------------
def basic_floor_damage
    return 10
end
```

You'll probably be interested to know that you can have variable floor damage, depending on the type of floor. Here, let me illustrate with some code that I hammered out in about a minute on my full version of RMVXA.

```
#-------------------------------------------------------------------------
# * Get Base Value for Floor Damage
#-------------------------------------------------------------------------
def basic_floor_damage
    return 2 if $game_variables[3] == 1
    return 5 if $game_variables[3] == 2
    return 10 if $game_variables[3] == 3
    return 25 if $game_variables[3] == 4
end
```

Instead of a single global value for floor damage, we can have multiple values, as set by a particular variable. In this case, $game_variables[3] (where 3 is the variable ID in the Database), signifying the variable containing the Region ID, is the one I chose to use. You could consider leaving a simple return value (like the default number) for damage floors set within the Tileset tab and then have other damage floors marked by regions or terrain tags.

Additional Exercises

Here are some final exercises for you to close out this chapter with a bang!

1. **Expand the innkeeper so that you can choose to rest in the morning or nighttime.**

Having night in your game is as simple as applying a filter on the graphics. The *Tint Screen* command is perfect for this and, in fact, even has a specific color setting for nighttime. However, if you want nighttime to influence random encounters, that is quite a bit harder. It takes a small amount of scripting, and a fair amount of eventing, to have different encounters based on the time of day. Even so, you can stop the player character from leaving town and have certain events happen only at night.

I recommend having a Daytime switch and a Nighttime switch, if you're going to do this. Then, you can differentiate what events trigger when using the relevant conditionals. Just make sure you set one of the switches to on at the very start of the game. (Switches default to off and variables to 0 when a new game is created).

2. **Have some NPCs in Seaside give the player items when they're talked to.**

You have already used *Change Party Member* to add Noah to the player's party in Seaside. However, there are four other event commands in the Party category, and they can be used to grant items, weapons, gold, or armor to the player. Treasure chest events actually use those event commands to give items.

A common mistake is to give players an item and not tell them that they received it. Make good use of the *Show Text* command!

3. Make it so that the player cannot access the dungeon until Noah has joined the party.

This is as easy as adding a conditional branch to the relevant transfer event. If Noah is in the player's party, then they are transferred to the dungeon. Otherwise, they take a step back from the dungeon entrance on the world map and say that they would rather find help first.

4. Make it so that the player cannot even see the dungeon until Noah has joined the party.

Event slot conservation be darned, at this point you'll probably want to eliminate the dungeon transfer part from the main Parallel Process event. Then, you make a two-page event at the dungeon location where the *first* page is blank, and then the *second* page has the relevant graphic and only appears when Noah is in your player's party. The second page would be Below Characters, with a Player Touch trigger taking them to the dungeon as normal.

Summary

This chapter took us from a two-map prototype to the beginnings of an actual RPG. We added a port town and the foundation of our first dungeon to the game. We populated the port town with shops, a plot hook for our player to grab, and a new companion. In the next chapter, we will be populating our first dungeon with treasure chests and enemies.

## CHAPTER 5

Your First Dungeon

In the previous chapter, we fleshed out our small game, adding many features to it to make it feel more like an actual game and less like a disjointed mess. Our player now has an idea of what he or she should be doing. So, in this chapter, we will be tackling the task of populating the dungeon that we created (or, rather, copy-pasted) in the previous one. The first order of business is to determine how you want the enemies to appear.

Random or Static?

The heading poses a very important question without an easy answer.

Random

By default, RPG Maker VX Ace (RMVXA) has a random encounter system in place that allows the user to cause enemies to attack the player after a certain average of steps (determined by Steps Average).

Static

The alternative is to do as games such as *Final Fantasy: Mystic Quest* have done. That is, place enemy troops directly on the map. In RMVXA, you can do this much as you would any other event.

Really, it all depends on the type of game that you want. There's nothing wrong with having a game in which every single enemy is placed on the map already (as is the case with *Final Fantasy: Mystic Quest*). In any case, even if you use a random encounter system, you'll still want to place bosses accordingly.

Note   If you're using the Lite version, you won't have the event slot capacity to add all of the things listed below. In that case, just set up random encounters as normal, to save the slots for the treasure chests and other later dungeon content.

Creating Static Encounters

For the sake of completeness, let's have both types of encounters within our dungeon. As we have not placed a static encounter before, let's start with those. To place a static enemy, create an event, use an appropriate graphic, and find the *Battle Processing* event command. When you click it, you'll get the menu displayed in Figure 5-1.

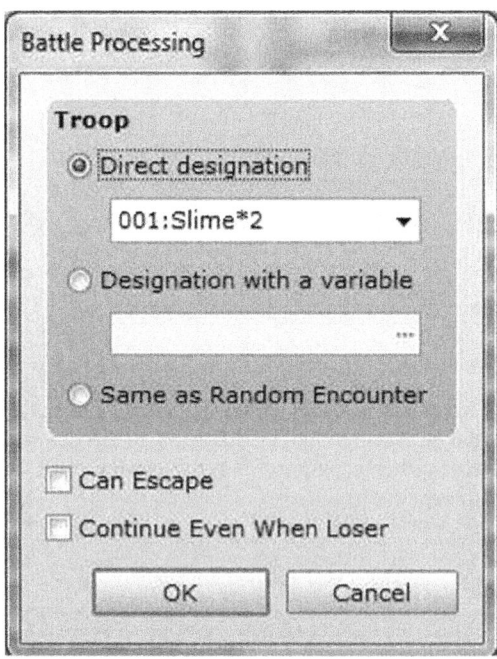

Figure 5-1. *The Battle Processing event command*

- The *Troop* section allows you to decide what encounter to place within the event. It defaults to *Direct designation*, which is the option I most frequently use. However, you can also use *Designation with a variable*, in which case the encounter you get is based on the troop ID in the Database. Or, you can just have Battle Processing act like a random encounter and roll on the encounters table in that map's properties.

- *Can Escape* can be toggled if you want to have an encounter that you can run away from. For most boss battles, I would leave this one off. For everything else, you can turn this on.

- *Continue Even When Loser* is self-explanatory. This is good for those battles in which you want the player to lose to advance the plot or for an optional battle with a nonplayer character (NPC) that ostensibly wouldn't kill the player if it wins (such as a sensei who trains the character).

The one trick with static encounters is that you must place them in spots that the player must pass through, or else they might as well not be there. If we take a look at the first floor of our dungeon, you'll realize that there are only a few spots where this is true. So, let's add a few more. Then, we can add Battle Processing events that look like so:

```
@>Battle Processing: Slime, Hill Orc
: If Win
   @>Control Self Switch: A =ON
   @>
: If Escape
   @>
: Branch End
@>
```

I have the troop we created in Chapter 3 here, but you can use any troop you prefer. As they are non-boss fights, we can toggle Can Escape. However, we do not want the players "cheating" the encounters, as it were. That is, we have to make sure that they defeat the encounter before being allowed to pass. So, we make it so that the encounter only disappears if self-switch A is turned on (via the use of a second blank event page with the appropriate conditional). I placed five events and circled them on the following screenshot. (See Figure 5-2).

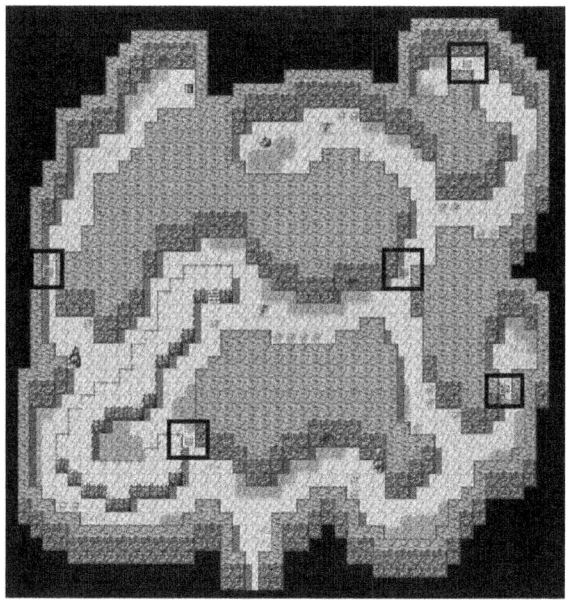

Figure 5-2. *The five static encounters on the first floor of this dungeon*

You can also see that I tweaked the terrain around some of those events, to make sure that the player had to interact with the encounters. Next, I will add five treasure chests to that floor as well. Can you guess where I'm going to place them? A good rule of game design is that the player should feel rewarded for going out of his/her way to explore a dungeon in its entirety. (See Figure 5-3).

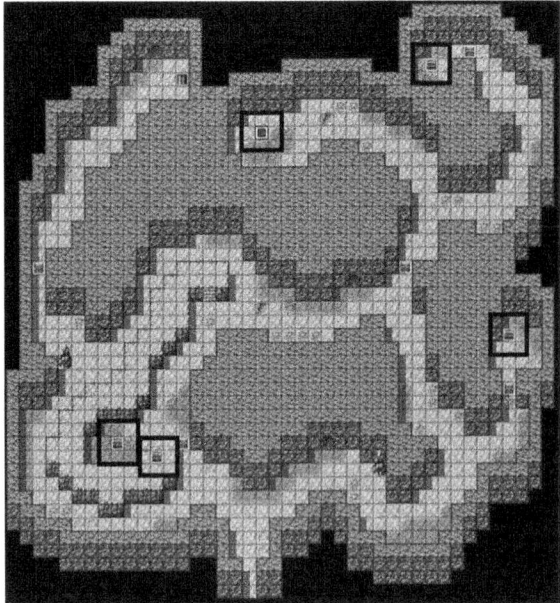

Figure 5-3. *The first floor of the dungeon, now with added treasure chests!*

I placed five treasure chests on the map (four of them are visible, while the fifth is a blank graphic placed atop the rock near the northern end of the floor). That hidden chest rewards players who interact with their surroundings. As we don't want random encounters to appear on the first floor, we won't use the Region tool. Instead, we'll use it for the basement and declare the random encounters that we want the player to find in the Map properties. Drawing in all of those region tiles seems daunting, doesn't it? I'm actually inclined to agree. There's another way to set it, so that we have no random encounters on the first floor and then have them in the basement.

The Change Encounter Event Command

Given that I've covered a fair number of the event commands already, you have probably seen Change Encounter under the System Settings section of the event command list. This simple command defaults to Enable. If you set it to Disable, then you will encounter no enemies until it is set back to Enable, even if the map in question has listed encounters. In this particular dungeon, it's as easy as setting up the Parallel Process transfer event as we have several times before and then just adding the Change Encounter command before the actual transition.

```
@>Control Variables: [0002:X] = Player's Map X
@>Control Variables: [0003:Y] = Player's Map Y
@>Conditional Branch: Variable [0002:X] == 15
   @>Conditional Branch: Variable [0003:Y] == 7
      @>Comment: This exit leads to the basement.
      @>Change Encounter: Enable
      @>Transfer Player:[005:Goblin CaveF1F] (061,041), Right
      @>
   : Branch End
   @>
```

```
: Branch End
@>Conditional Branch: Variable [0002:X] == 20
   @>Conditional Branch: Variable [0003:Y] == 45
      @>Comment: This exit leads to the world map.
      @>Change Encounter: Enable
      @>Transfer Player:[003:Field 3] (027,082), Left
      @>
   : Branch End
   @>
: Branch End
@>Conditional Branch: Variable [0002:X] == 60
   @>Conditional Branch: Variable [0003:Y] == 41
      @>Comment: This exit leads to the first floor.
      @>Change Encounter: Disable
      @>Transfer Player:[005:Goblin CaveF1F] (014,007), Left
      @>
   : Branch End
   @>
: Branch End
@>
```

■ **Note**   You'll want to tweak the relevant world map transfer event to disable encounters when you enter this dungeon as well.

Once you've set up the transfer events, the static encounters, and the first floor treasure chests, we have only the following to do:

1. Go to Map Properties and set up some random encounters for the player.

2. Add a few chests to the basement. We'll add three. That puts the event count at nine for those of you using Lite . . .

3. . . . which allows us to use the tenth event for the boss of the dungeon.

Given that the toughest enemies in the parts of the world map that the player can currently access are Wisps, we will want to include some troops here that are somewhat tougher. Wisps should be the weakest troop in the encounters list. Take a look at Figure 5-4 to see my own.

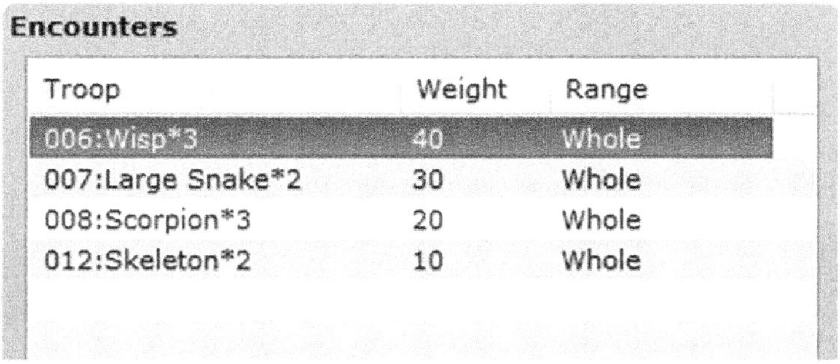

Encounters

Troop	Weight	Range
006:Wisp*3	40	Whole
007:Large Snake*2	30	Whole
008:Scorpion*3	20	Whole
012:Skeleton*2	10	Whole

Figure 5-4. *The encounter list for the Goblin Cave*

The player has a 4/10 chance of encountering three Wisps, a 3/10 chance of encountering a pair of Large Snakes, a 2/10 chance of encountering three Scorpions, and a 1/10 chance of encountering a pair of Skeletons. The Skeletons are particularly stronger than the rest of the possible troops, so they have the lowest appearance chance. After that is said and done, we can add some treasure chests to the basement and the boss enemy event. See Figure 5-5 for a view of the basement floor with the added events.

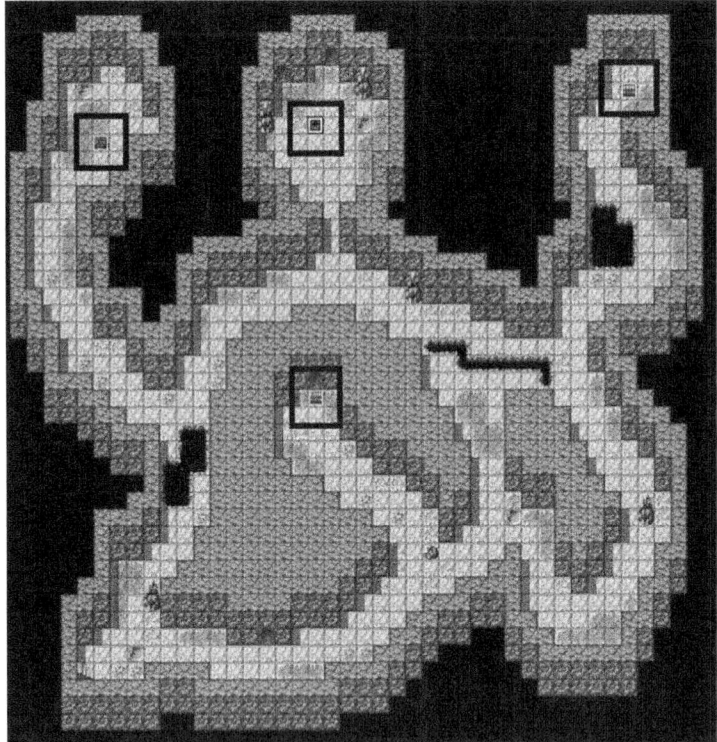

Figure 5-5. *The basement floor of the dungeon*

As you can see, we have two visible chests and an invisible chest on the upper-left corner. The player enters the map through the staircase on the lower-left corner and has to make his/her way up to the boss to the north of the southern treasure chest. Once the player speaks with the boss, he/she will be forced to fight them.

Our First Boss

A role-playing game (RPG) would be rather boring if all of the enemies had similar levels of power. That is one of the main reasons why bosses exist. As the name implies, a boss is the strongest enemy in a given area. If the area in question is plot-relevant, then the boss must usually be defeated, to progress in the game's story. See Figure 5-6 for the relevant boss data.

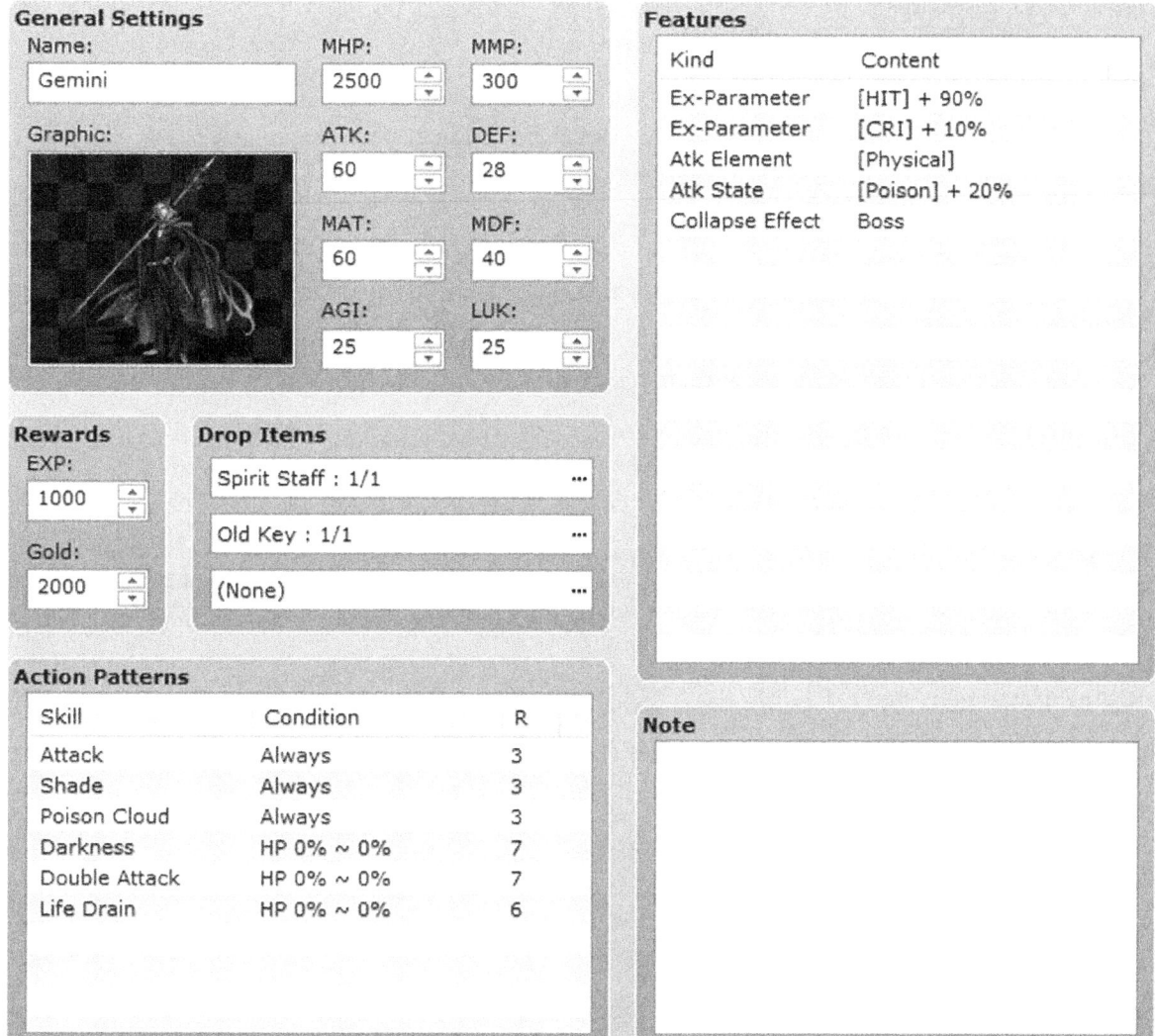

Figure 5-6. *Gemini, the first boss of the game*

Not pictured: I replaced monster #29 and renamed troop #29 to accommodate him. The conditionals for the second set of three boss skills are actually misleading. There's a text bug in RMVXA that doesn't display HP/MP conditionals correctly. While it reads HP 0% - 0%, it is actually set to HP 0% - 50% (meaning that the boss will add those skills to his pattern once he's at half HP or lower). For the first 50% of his health, Gemini will use normal attacks, a weaker darkness spell, and a cloud that can poison its targets. Once he is hurt, he will use a stronger darkness spell, attack twice, and use a life draining spell as well. When defeated, he is guaranteed to drop a Spirit Staff and the Key Item I created back at Chapter 3. (See, I didn't forget about it; now's the perfect time to give it to the player, though). Read on to see the boss event itself in all of its glory.

```
@>Text: 'Evil', 3, Normal, Bottom
:      : It has been far too long...brother.
@>Text: 'Actor5', 6, Normal, Bottom
:      : Gemini?
@>Text: 'Evil', 3, Normal, Bottom
:      : Yes, my brother. I have heard of your
:      : companion. Eric, is it not? The hero of
:      : old. My dark master has requested this
:      : boy's head.
@>Text: 'Actor4', 0, Normal, Bottom
:      : I am not a boy, and you may not have it!
@>Text: 'Evil', 3, Normal, Bottom
:      : Heh, think you can surpass the power
:      : that has been granted to me? Prepare to
:      : suffer!
@>Change Battle BGM: 'Dungeon9', 100, 100
@>Battle Processing: Gemini
@>
```

Page 1 of the boss event has an Action Button trigger, so the player has to walk up to the boss before it will act. Note that we change the battle background music to something else before the fight. Feel free to replace the one I used with another of your choosing (Battle5 and Battle9 are my favorites, although the latter is more for a final boss fight against a particularly malevolent foe).

```
@>Change Battle BGM: 'Battle1', 100, 100
@>Text: 'Evil', 3, Normal, Bottom
:      : Impossible. So, this is the power that the chosen one
:      : holds...
@>Text: 'Actor5', 6, Normal, Bottom
:      : It is a power greater than either of us
:      : will ever be able to bear. Your time is
:      : done, brother.
@>Fadeout Screen
@>Control Self Switch: A =ON
@>Wait: 120 frame(s)
@>Fadein Screen
```

Page 2 is an Autorun trigger with a switch conditional (BossDefeated = ON). That particular switch, as you will see in a few pages, will be toggled when Gemini is defeated by the player and before he dies. The last page has a conditional of Self Switch A = ON and is otherwise completely blank with an Action Button trigger. Last, look below to see the troop event for our first boss.

- Page 1 of 2

- Condition: Enemy [1. Gemini]'s HP 50% or below

- Span: Battle

```
@>Text: 'Evil', 3, Normal, Bottom
:     : The little brat and my misguided brother
:     : show their teeth. Very well. Feel the
:     : full extent of my power!
@>Change Enemy State: Entire Troop, + [Immortal]
@>
```

- Page 2 of 2

- Condition: Enemy [1. Gemini]'s HP 0% or below

- Span: Battle

```
@>Text: 'Evil', 3, Normal, Bottom
:     : This is not over. My master will avenge
:     : me!
@>Text: 'Actor4', 0, Normal, Bottom
:     : We will stop your master as well!
@>Control Switches: [0004:BossDefeated] = ON
@>Change Enemy State: Entire Troop, - [Immortal]
@>
```

I cut the Span setting to save some space, but both of them share the same Battle span, so that they will only trigger once per battle. I use the Immortal state to great effect here, to make sure that the boss does not die before giving his final speech. We add the Immortal state before he reaches 0% HP and then take it away once he's done speaking at 0% HP. We also make it so that the BossDefeated switch is turned on when he is defeated, which plays into the boss event mentioned on the previous pages.

That just about finishes our very first dungeon. Now, play-test the game and see if it is balanced or not. If you find that some of the enemies are too strong or too weak, feel free to increase or decrease their stats accordingly. Constant play-testing is most important when dealing with enemies, given that you may over- or underestimate their numbers. What seemed like a particularly difficult enemy troop on paper may be trivial for the player's party by the time it reaches the relevant area.

You'll want to add appropriate weapons and armor for Eric and Noah to become stronger. Among the chests of our first dungeon, I placed a Hard Leather, a Magic Staff, and a Battle Axe.

Additional Exercises

Here are some more exercises to make your dungeon a little more interactive.

1. **Create some interparty banter between Eric and Noah, if they are both present.**

We can cheat a little with this, given that Eric will always be in the party and given the layout of this dungeon's basement floor. Thus, we only need conditionals to check for Noah's presence and can use a single variable that is increased in value by 1 for each event triggered. This is one of those things that will make more sense if I just show you, so check the following code.

```
@>Conditional Branch: Variable [0002:X] == 70
  @>Conditional Branch: Variable [0003:Y] >= 40
    @>Conditional Branch: Variable [0003:Y] <= 41
      @>Conditional Branch: [Noah] is In the Party
        @>Conditional Branch: Variable [0005:Dungeon1Talk] == 0
        @>Control Variables: [0005:Dungeon1Talk] += 1
        @>Text: 'Actor5', 6, Normal, Bottom
```

```
       :      : ...
       @>Text: 'Actor4', 0, Normal, Bottom
       :      : Are you well, Noah?
       @>Text: 'Actor5', 6, Normal, Bottom
       :      : I have a strange feeling at the pit of
       :      : my stomach.
       @>Text: 'Actor4', 0, Normal, Bottom
       :      : You haven't eaten for a while.
       @>Text: 'Actor5', 6, Normal, Bottom
       :      : Hah! No, it's not that. Let's move on.
       @>
     : Branch End
   @>
  : Branch End
  @>
 : Branch End
@>
: Branch End
@>
: Branch End
```

This particular event triggers at the marked location shown in Figure 5-7.

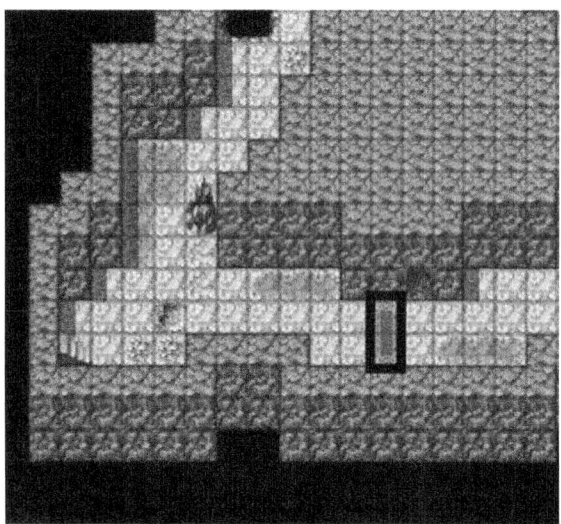

Figure 5-7. *The location where the previously mentioned event will trigger*

There's a whopping *five* conditional branches up there, but the first three are just location-checking, in the way we have usually done for our Parallel Process events so far. The fourth branch checks for Noah's presence, while the fifth makes sure that the relevant variable is set to 0. If everything checks out, the variable value is increased by one, and we get a short conversation between our two party members.

■ **Note**   An event, unless you use Jump Label, will always resolve from top to bottom, once it has been triggered. Thus, it doesn't matter if you increase the value of the variable directly after the branches or at the end of the conversation, so long as you do so after the event is triggered and before the end of that event as a whole.

You can add more of those conversations throughout the dungeon as the player gets closer and closer to the boss location. It's a nice little way to add some atmosphere to what would otherwise be a rather unassuming affair.

2. **Expand the boss event so that the square it occupies becomes a one-way exit from the dungeon after its defeat.**

- My favorite graphics to use from RMVXA's default set for this task are the hexagrams (!Hexagram) and crystals (!Crystal).

- Add the graphic of your choosing; use the Action Button trigger for the last page of the boss event; and then add the following content (replace crystal with hexagram, if applicable).

```
@>Text: -, -, Normal, Bottom
:       : A strange crystal stands on the spot that Gemini
:       : was slain. It appears that it will send you
:       : back to this dungeon's entrance. Touch it?
@>Show Choices: Yes, No
: When [Yes]
  @>Text: -, -, Normal, Bottom
  :       : You feel yourself being whisked away!
  @>Transfer Player:[003:Field 3] (027,082), Left
  @>
: When [No]
  @>Text: -, -, Normal, Bottom
  :       : You decide against touching the crystal.
  @>
: Branch End
@>
```

Summary

During the course of this chapter, we created our very first dungeon and populated it with treasure chests and enemy encounters, both of the static and random types. Additionally, we created our game's first boss to oppose the player. In the next chapter, we will work on our game's second dungeon, which will be somewhat more exciting than this one.

PART II

![marker]

Increasing the Complexity

Up to now, we have created a bare-bones game with a single town (with one map for the exterior, and another for the interior), a single dungeon, and a pair of starting area maps all connected by a world map. The Lite version of RMVXA has a twenty map limit (which personally baffles me as it means that it has a lighter cap on number of maps than on number of events), of which we are currently at six. During this part of the book we will be covering the following topics:

- Adding a second dungeon to the game that requires the key item we created in Chapter 2 to be opened.

- Adding an arena that makes ample use of eventing and allows the player to fight predetermined enemy encounters for fame and glory.

- Adding a treasure hunt system to the game with a Compass item that tells the player their X,Y coordinates and hiding treasure in certain parts of the world.

- And more!

We have just scratched the tip of the iceberg of RMVXA so far (which might come as a surprise given how we've only touched the Script Editor once for a relatively easy programming exercise). When I said at the start that RMVXA is robust, I meant it! So, enough babble. Let's keep on going!

CHAPTER 6

Your Second Dungeon

So, when last we left off our role-playing game (RPG) story, Eric and Noah defeated the latter's brother in (not-so) gruesome combat. What follows next? Well, as a longtime RPG player and overall gamer, my first reaction would be to return to Seaside and see what (if anything) has changed and then decide on my alter-ego's next course of action. That is the initial topic for this chapter. The first order of business is to update the Seaside nonplayer characters (NPCs), to reflect recent events.

Updating Our NPCs

In true RPG convention, our intrepid hero and his mysterious companion will find that news of their endeavors travels faster than they do. To update any NPC, all you need to do is make a new event page for it that requires the BossDefeated switch we created last chapter. Let's have the barkeeper tell the player of the new tidings. Here's a short setting blurb that you can use to tweak the barkeeper's conversation:

> *Ever since Eric and Noah's defeat of Gemini, the locals claim to hear a disturbing humming sound that fills the night air at Seaside. One of the locals believes that the strange sounds are coming from the ancient tower at the far end of the continent. The ancient tower, they are quick to add, has been sealed for the better part of a century and seemingly has no path of entry. The people of Seaside worry that perhaps the sounds portend some greater calamity . . .*

As in any good RPG story, we had previous events lead the player into new ones. In this case, and as you'll recall, Gemini gave away a plot hook after being defeated by Eric and Noah. He spoke of the dark master that would "avenge him," as it were. What better place to house a dark master than in another dungeon? Now you may be wondering why I would have two dungeons in a row. Well, I finished Part 1 with a dungeon, so it felt appropriate to start Part 2 with the same. With that said, it is also a good chance to show off some more advanced eventing than we've seen up to now. As a minor teaser, think about the following situation:

> *You have a majestic dragon statue that you want the player to look at (and possibly even interact with). The easiest way to set up the events is to have a single Same As Characters/Action Button event for every square that the statue occupies. However, that is highly wasteful of event slots. What if I told you that there was a way to have two events that could cover a theoretically infinite amount of places?*

Do the possibilities boggle the mind? Well then, let us hurry toward that particular exercise. First, however, we must create our dungeon maps. This time, we'll have three levels to our dungeon and each map occupy its own slot (if only to vary a bit from what we designed for the first one).

The First Two Floors of Our Second Dungeon

The map we're using is Tower of the Void F1F, with quite a few changes. First of all, I closed off the starting area, allowing the player to advance no farther unless he/she has the Old Key with which to open the tower's door. Players that fancy themselves explorers can see and enter the tower ahead of time but will be unable to get past that first room. If they do have the relevant item, they can open the door, which acts as a transfer event to the middle of the map. Take a look at Figure 6-1, to see the ground floor.

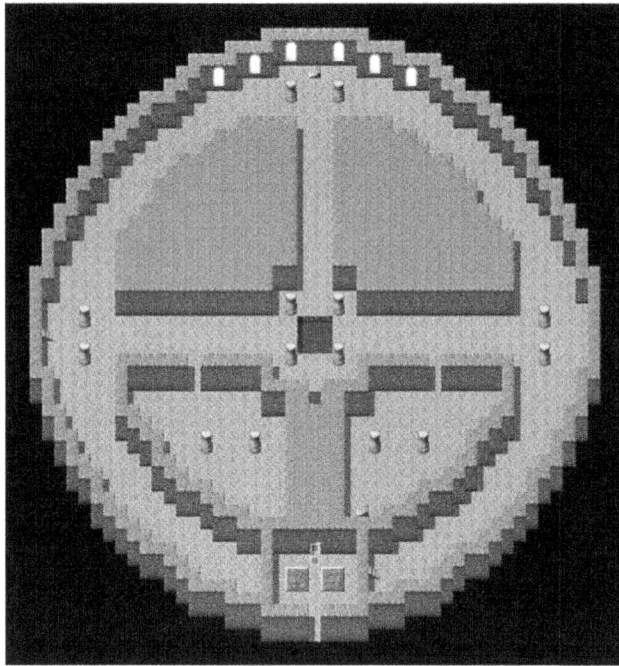

Figure 6-1. *The first floor of our second dungeon*

There's a little recessed area a few spaces below that sends the player back to the other side of the passage. (Trapping your players is usually a very bad idea, except when it's not, but that's something experience will teach you.)

I left the top and west stairs intact but removed the eastern stairs and placed a new set of stairs that can be seen from the dungeon entrance. I also removed all other stairs on the ground floor, save for the ones slightly to the northeast of the entrance, in addition to completely sealing off the top two wedges in the central part of the map. You can see the dungeon's second floor in all of its edited glory in Figure 6-2.

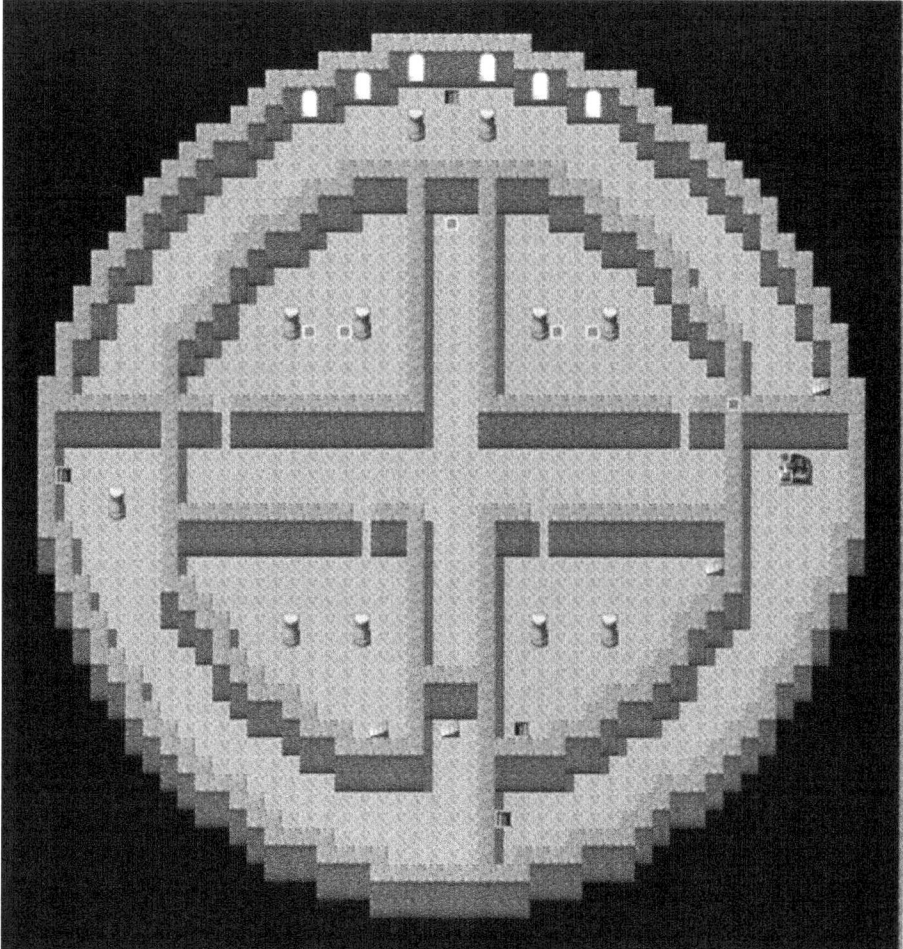

Figure 6-2. *The second floor of this dungeon*

This is Tower of the Void F4F. As I skipped F2F and F3F completely, I had to do quite some tweaking to the terrain. I removed stairs that didn't link appropriately to the ground floor and sealed off certain areas to change up how the player explores the dungeon. I placed treasure chests next to the four pillars located within the top two wedges of the central area, as well as a fifth chest in the gap to the south of the top staircase. As noted in the teaser a few pages preceding, there's a dragon statue here that I decided to use as fuel for our latest eventing exercise.

Interacting with the Dragon Statue

What we want to do here is make it so that the player can interact with the dragon statue from every adjacent square, using only two events. Doing this the wasteful way would spend two extra events (four in total). The larger the object in question, the more efficient these pairs of events will be, as compared to having one event per square.

As I tend to note, eventing is just like programming, which is all about problem-solving. So, we have a problem and want to solve it.

- We need an event to keep track of the player's position while he/she is around the dragon statue.

- We need the other event to act as the interaction event (this is, the one that will be Same As Characters/Action Button).

- We have to make sure that the player is actually looking at the statue. It wouldn't do for the player to be looking in the opposite direction and getting the dragon statue information when he/she presses the Action Button.

We actually have all that is called for in the preceding three bullet points, even if it does not appear to be so. We've used the first event several times already, but for transfer events. All we will do is change what we're going to use it for.

Drawing a Perimeter

Our first order of business is noting which squares are around the dragon statue. That will be our perimeter, if you will. Take a look at Figure 6-3.

Figure 6-3. *A zoomed-in picture of the dragon statue present on this floor of the dungeon*

Figure 6-3 is a highly zoomed-in screenshot of the dragon statue and its surrounding squares. You'll want the X and Y values to draw the effective perimeter. Check the following code to see what I did for that first part.

```
@>Control Variables: [0002:X] = Player's Map X
@>Control Variables: [0003:Y] = Player's Map Y
@>Conditional Branch: Variable [0002:X] >= 43
   @>Conditional Branch: Variable [0002:X] <= 46
      @>Conditional Branch: Variable [0003:Y] >= 25
         @>Conditional Branch: Variable [0003:Y] <= 27
            @>Jump to Label: Step 2
            @>
          : Branch End
         @>
       : Branch End
      @>
    : Branch End
   @>
: Branch End
```

So, as usual, we write the player's position into a pair of variables and then check against the current map coordinates to see if they are in the dragon statue's perimeter. If they aren't, nothing happens. If they are, we have a label called Step 2 that continues the event. Here's the next part of the event:

```
@>Conditional Branch: Variable [0078] >= 999
   @>Label: Step 2
   @>Conditional Branch: Variable [0002:X] == 43
      @>Conditional Branch: Variable [0003:Y] >= 25
         @>Conditional Branch: Variable [0003:Y] <= 26
            @>Control Variables [0002:X] += 1
            @>Set Event Location: [DragonTopic], Variable [0002][00003]
            @>Jump to Label: Done
            @>
          : Branch End
         @>
       : Branch End
      @>
    : Branch End
   @>
: Branch End
```

Moving Our Interaction Event

We have two new things in the perimeter-establishing event that are of interest.

- First, we have a dummy variable (that has a set value of 0), and we have the system try to resolve the branch if said variable is greater than or equal to 999. As we are not writing anything there, this branch will never be true. So, why have it at all? Remember: Events execute from top to bottom, unless prevented from doing so. We have this dummy branch here so that the rest of the event will only execute when we use the Jump to Label command to jump to Step 2 inside of the branch itself.

- Second, we have the engine of what will make this whole event work in the first place. In this portion of the event, we're checking to see if the player is standing on the two squares to the left of the dragon statue. If he/she is, we add one to the value of X and use a new event command.

- **Set Event Location** allows you to change the position of any event (including the triggering event itself, if you would want to do so for any reason) on the map. What we want to do is have the Action Button event used for the dragon statue move to meet the player's movement. It's a sneaky little trick that gets the job done in this case. See Figure 6-4 for a screenshot of what the command entails.

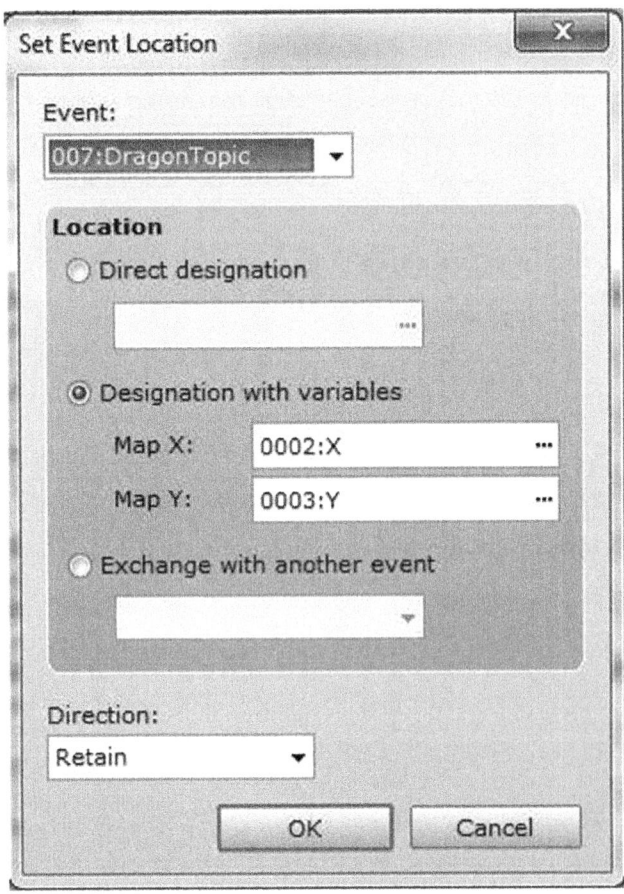

Figure 6-4. *The Set Event Location event command*

From here, you can select which event to move. Then you can choose to designate a specific location for the event, use variables to determine the location, or exchange it with another event's location. In the case of events with graphics, you can also determine whether they retain their former facing or change to a different direction. You can probably already tell what that +1 to X is about. Because the player is standing one space to the left of the statue, we have to move the event one space to the player's right, so that he/she can interact with it while facing eastward.

Now that you understand the logic behind this event, can you figure out how to do the other two? The northern squares are blocked by a wall, so you don't have to take them into consideration for the purposes of this exercise. To clarify, you need to account for the player being below the statue and to its right. If you think you have it (or otherwise need the help), here's the final part of the Parallel Process event:

```
@>Conditional Branch: Variable [0003:Y] == 27
   @>Conditional Branch: Variable [0002:X] >= 44
      @>Conditional Branch: Variable [0002:X] <= 45
         @>Control Variables: [0003:Y] -= 1
         @>Set Event Location: [DragonTopic], Variable [0002][00003]
         @>Jump to Label: Done
         @>
       : Branch End
      @>
    : Branch End
   @>
: Branch End
@>Conditional Branch: Variable [0002:X] == 46
   @>Conditional Branch: Variable [0003:Y] >= 25
      @>Conditional Branch: Variable [0003:Y] <= 26
         @>Control Variables: [0002:X] -= 1
         @>Set Event Location: [DragonTopic], Variable [0002][00003]
         @>Jump to Label: Done
         @>
       : Branch End
      @>
    : Branch End
   @>
: Branch End
@>Label: Done
@>
```

The first set of branches is called when the player is below the statue, and the second set is used when he/she is to the right side of the statue. You'll also see the Jump to Label that trigger once a single branch has been executed. They are there merely as an extra precaution to make sure nothing strange happens when the event runs. We're done with one-half of this exercise. Now we need the event that will actually trigger when the player attempts to interact with the statue. First, right-click any one of the squares that makes up the dragon statue and creates the event. Looking back at the zoomed picture, you'll note the following:

- The player may only interact with the top-left and top-right squares by facing right and left, respectively.

- For the lower two squares, the player has two possible facings.

Checking Our Player's Directional Facing

We need a way to make sure that the player is facing the right way. Enter the Conditional Branch once again. Up to now, we have been using conditional branches almost exclusively to check against variable and switch values. However, there are *three* more pages full of things that you can check against. If you click page 3 of the conditional branch command, you will find the Character X is Facing Y conditional. X defaults to the player but can also check for every single event on the current map, and Y is the direction the player or event in question is facing. Here's the first part of the relevant event from my end:

```
@>Conditional Branch: Player is Facing Right
   @>Conditional Branch: Variable [0002:X] == 44
      @>Text: -, -, Normal, Bottom
      :      : You see a majestic dragon statue. It hums with
      :      : power.
      @>Text: 'Actor5', 6, Normal, Bottom
      :      : I sense immense power emanating from this
      :      : statue. Be mindful. It would be best to
      :      : return at a later time.
      @>Text: -, -, Normal, Bottom
      :      : Touch the statue?
      @>Show Choices: Yes, No
      : When [Yes]
         @>
      : When [No]
         @>
         : Branch End
      @>
    : Branch End
   @>
: Branch End
```

We set up a conditional branch to ensure that the player is facing to his/her right. Afterward, we make sure that X is equal to 44 (which it will be, if the player is standing next to the statue's two left squares, which is assuming, of course, that you have not tweaked the size of that particular map). If both conditions check out, we display the relevant text and give the player a choice. As you can already tell, I have left both possible answers empty. I'll leave that as an exercise for you for now. We'll revisit this one much later in the book, as we put the finishing touches on our game. Anyway, take a look at Figure 6-5 for the tweaked third floor of our second dungeon. The base sample map used was Tower of the Void F5F.

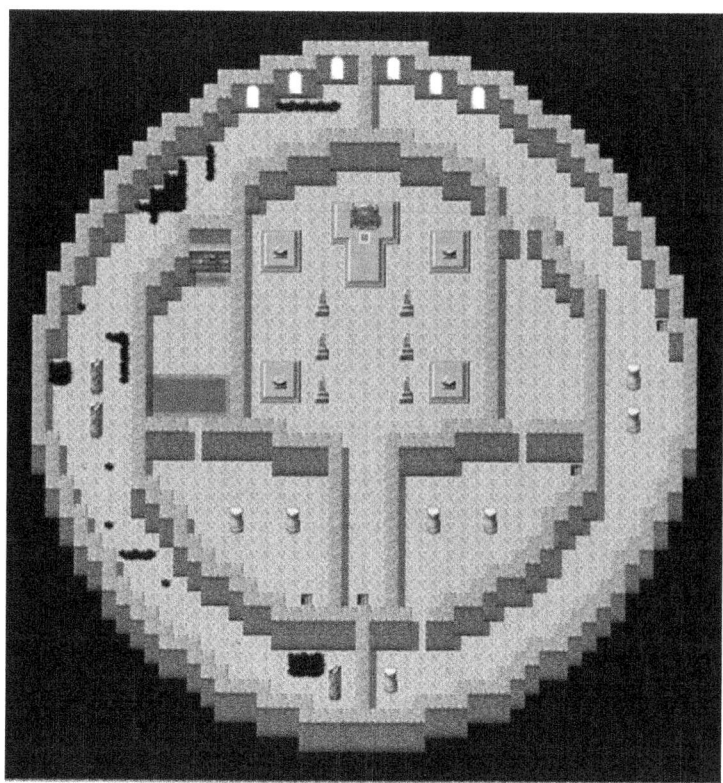

Figure 6-5. *The third floor of this dungeon*

From there, I split off the western half, changed the position of the staircase in the southwest wedge of the central area, opened some areas, and closed others. I decided to go with a deteriorated-structure feel for the top floor, with holes and such. The biggest change was adding a bookcase and some red carpet to that left area. I have a particular plan for that bookcase. But first, let's create this dungeon's boss. Given how we've been replacing monsters from the bottom up, that leaves the highest non-altered enemy at #28. I think the Demon could serve as a good second boss for our game. However, we have to tweak his stats. Take a look at Figure 6-6 for a comparison of the Demon's base stats and his adjusted stats.

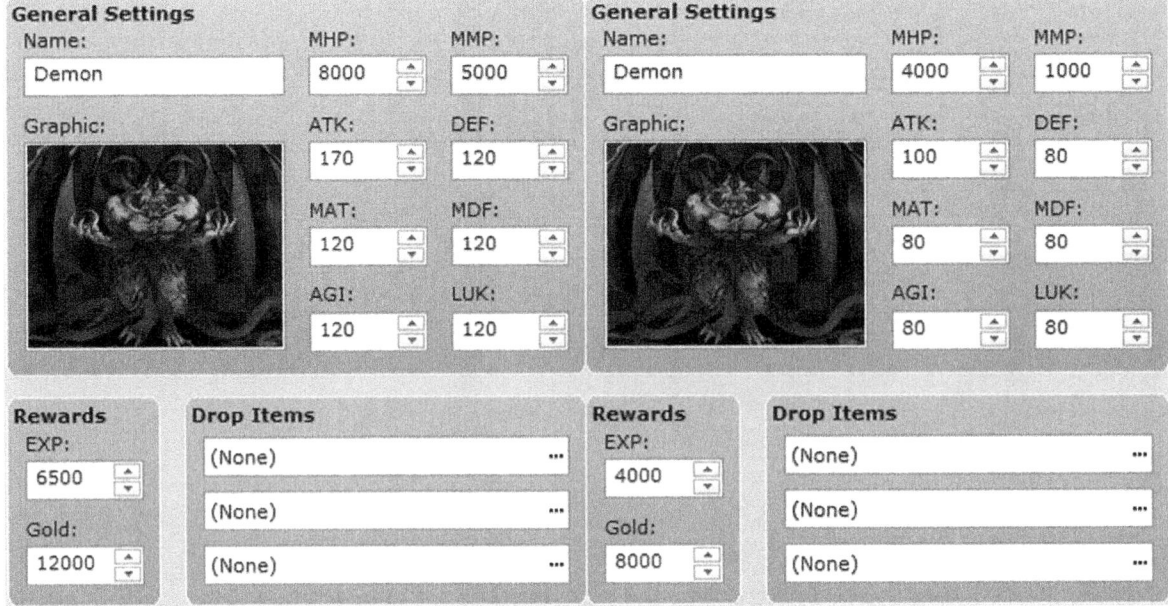

Figure 6-6. *A side-by-side comparison of the default Demon enemy and my tweaked version*

Our Second Boss

In Figure 6-6, the left side is unadjusted, while the right is the tweaked version for our game. It will probably be necessary to tweak the Demon even further, but that's something we can do when play-testing. Of note is the Demon's weakness to Holy.

Creating a Bookcase Interaction Event

Let's give Noah an item that allows him to capitalize on the Demon's weakness to Holy. There are two bookcases on the top floor, and we want the right-most one to grant the book. Let's use the same pair of events that we used for the dragon statue. This time, however, it will be a lot easier. See, the dragon statue is a 2×2 graphic. Our line of bookcases, on the other hand, is a straight line. Thus, all we have to do is make sure the relevant item is placed on the right bookcase, and we're set. Here's the event to set the book interaction:

```
@>Control Variables: [0002:X] = Player's Map X
@>Control Variables: [0003:Y] = Player's Map Y
@>Conditional Branch: Variable [0003:Y] == 18
   @>Conditional Branch: Variable [0002:X] >= 13
      @>Conditional Branch: Variable [0002:X] <= 15
         @>Control Variables: [0003:Y] -= 1
         @>Set Event Location: [BookTopic], Variable [0002][00003]
         @>
       : Branch End
      @>
    : Branch End
   @>
 : Branch End
@>
```

Much cleaner than the dragon statue equivalent, right? Here's the interaction event as well:

```
@>Conditional Branch: Player is Facing Up
   @>Conditional Branch: Variable [0002:X] >= 13
      @>Conditional Branch: Variable [0002:X] <= 15
         @>Text: -, -, Normal, Bottom
         :      : You see an ancient bookcase filled with old books.
         @>Conditional Branch: Variable [0002:X] == 15
            @>Conditional Branch: Self Switch A == OFF
               @>Text: -, -, Normal, Bottom
               :      : Noah appears to be lost in thought as he runs a
               :      : hand through the bookcase.
               @>Text: 'Actor5', 6, Normal, Bottom
               :      : I feel warm power coming from one of
               :      : these books.
               @>Text: -, -, Normal, Bottom
               :      : Noah passes a finger over each book, eventually
               :      : landing on an otherwise unassuming red book.
               @>Text: 'Actor5', 6, Normal, Bottom
               :      : I'll be taking this book. It feels like
               :      : we'll have a need for it soon.
            @>Play SE: 'Item3', 80, 100
            @>Change Armor: [Book of Light] + 1
            @>Text: -, -, Normal, Bottom
            :      : Obtained \C[2]Book of Light\C[0]!
            @>Control Self Switch: A =ON
```

Not noted: several branch ends that are ultimately irrelevant to the event. First, we make sure the player is facing the bookcases (in this particular case, merely a precaution, as there's only one way to face to actually interact with them). Then we make sure that the player is at the correct location. If so, we show a text box describing the bookcase. Additionally, if the player is interacting with the right-most bookcase for the first time, we have Noah find our new item. (I replaced armor #60 to create that Book of Light, which is equipped to the accessory slot.) While Noah has the Book of Light equipped, it gives him 5 MAT, 5 MDF, 10 MMP, and the ability to cast God's Will, a default skill in RMVXA that deals Holy damage to its targets. Of course, because we don't want this sequence of events to repeat more than once, we have the relevant self-switch flip on, so that the event skips through the self-switch conditional on subsequent interactions.

Creating Our Second Boss Event

Once we have created the bookcase event and the Book of Light item, all we have to do is create the boss event on the top floor and set up the area's random encounters. Because we already created an Action Button boss event, let's make this one rely on Autorun.

What we'll need:

- A Parallel Process event (You can use the transfer event for this, and you want to check for the player's x and y coordinates in any case.)

- An Autorun event that activates when a particular switch is flipped on. This switch would be toggled when the player walks near the boss.

- A graphic that represents the boss itself, to be used in a third event

Here are the commands I appended to the end of the Parallel Process transfer event.

```
@>Conditional Branch: Variable [0003:Y] == 29
   @>Conditional Branch: Variable [0002:X] >= 24
      @>Conditional Branch: Variable [0002:X] <= 26
         @>Conditional Branch: Self Switch A == OFF
            @>Control Self Switch: A =ON
            @>Control Switches: [0005:Boss2Encounter] = ON
```

As with the bookcase event, we only want this snippet to trigger once, so we set an extra conditional that only allows the branch to be executed if self-switch A is off and then turn it on. We then flip the aptly named *Boss2Encounter* switch.

Creating the Boss Encounter

Our second event is an Autorun that only triggers if that switch is on. It contains most of the meat of the boss encounter, hence the descriptive heading. Page 1 of this event looks like this:

```
@>Tint Screen: (-68,-68,-68,0), @60, Wait
@>Fadeout BGM: 3 sec.
@>Wait: 60 frame(s)
@>Text: 'Actor4', 0, Normal, Bottom
:       : What's going on?
@>Wait: 60 frame(s)
@>Text: -, -, Normal, Bottom
:       : A cackling sound pierces the strangely silent air.
@>Text: -, -, Normal, Bottom
:       : So, you are the two who defeated my servant.
@>Text: -, -, Normal, Bottom
:       : Eric and Noah advance to the source of the voice.
@>Conditional Branch: Variable [0002:X] == 24
   @>Set Move Route: Player (Wait)
   :                    : $>Move Right
   @>Jump to Label: Center
   @>
: Branch End
@>Conditional Branch: Variable [0002:X] == 26
   @>Set Move Route: Player (Wait)
   :                : $>Move Left
   @>Jump to Label: Center
   @>
: Branch End
@>Label: Center
@>Set Move Route: Player (Wait)
:                 : $>Move Up
:                 : $>Move Up
:                 : $>Move Up
:                 : $>Move Up
:                 : $>Move Up
:                 : $>Move Up
:                 : $>Move Up
```

```
:                    : $>Move Up
:                    : $>Move Up
:                    : $>Move Up
@>Text: 'Monster1', 3, Normal, Bottom
:     : Welcome humans. I am glad to make your
:     : acquaintance. I would have you join my
:     : cause.
@>Text: 'Actor4', 0, Normal, Bottom
:     : No.
@>Set Move Route: [Boss] (Wait)
:                    : $>Move Down
:                    : $>Move Down
:                    : $>Move Down
@>Text: 'Monster1', 3, Normal, Bottom
:     : Heh. Was worth a try.
@>Control Self Switch: A =ON
@>Change Battle BGM: 'Dungeon9', 100, 75
@>Battle Processing: Demon
@>
```

Take a look at Figure 6-7 to see the boss area of our second dungeon.

Figure 6-7. *The room of the dungeon in which the player will do battle with the second boss*

The Autorun starts with the screen being tinted using the Dark filter. Afterward, the background music fades out over the next three seconds. A one-second pause precedes Eric wondering what's happening, and another one-second pause is triggered afterward. Some flavor text is displayed, and then the player is told that the party advances toward the source of the voice. If he/she is not standing on the center square (the center part of that black rectangle in the preceding screenshot), we move him/her one space to the side, so that he/she is. Then we have the player move up a total of ten squares, to where the monster continues speaking. We have the event that represents the boss move three squares down (so that it is directly in front of the player), turn on self-switch A, change the battle music, and start the boss fight. Page 2 of the Autorun event has the "self-switch A equals on" conditional and is completely blank. (Make sure that the trigger for page 2 is *not* Autorun).

The Aftermath of the Boss Encounter

Page 3 of our second boss encounter event has a conditional that uses a switch that is toggled when the boss is defeated (I called that particular switch Boss2Defeated) and is another Autorun page.

```
@>Text: 'Monster1', 3, Normal, Bottom
:      : Tch. You two are messing with forces
:      : beyond your ken. I am but one of many
:      : pledged to the will of the All Master.
@>Text: 'Monster1', 3, Normal, Bottom
:      : Push farther then, fools. One of the
:      : Three awaits at a castle far to the
:      : north of here. Defeat him and see the
:      : truth of this world!
@>Fadeout Screen
@>Change Battle BGM: 'Battle1', 100, 100
@>Control Switches: [0007:PlotAdvance2] = ON
@>Control Self Switch: B =ON
@>Wait: 60 frame(s)
@>Fadein Screen
```

Once the monster has finished speaking, we fade out the screen, restore the battle music back to its default, and flip on two switches. The first one we will use to make the boss graphic event disappear, and the second one allows us to create the fourth and last page for this event. The last page will require self-switch B to be on and will be completely empty with an Action Button trigger (much like page 2 was). The third and final event is the boss graphic and is two pages long. The first page has the boss graphic and no conditional. The second page has no graphic and requires PlotAdvance2 to be switched on.

Summary of Our Second Boss Event

That will conclude our most recent boss event. To summarize, we used three events.

1. **A Parallel Process event to determine when the player walks into the boss' domain**. It used a self-switch conditional to make sure that it cannot trigger multiple times (really important when dealing with a Parallel Process event).

2. **An Autorun event that made up the meaty portion of this exercise**. It spans four pages, with the first one activating thanks to the switch flipped in the Parallel Process event. The second page has a conditional that is met right before the boss attacks the party, while the third requires that the boss be defeated to be automatically executed. Last, the fourth page is the one that remains after the boss is defeated.

3. **A simple event meant to hold the boss graphic and nothing else**. This exists until the boss has finished talking after the battle and then disappears.

There are three more things to cover before I end the chapter. The first is that we must set the random encounters for our second dungeon. We want the game's encounters to become progressively more difficult, so let's bump up the bar as compared to the previous dungeon. Second, we'll need to add our dungeon to the world map and create a relevant transfer event. Last, I need to list where each staircase leads in our tweaked dungeon.

The Second Dungeon's Random Encounters

On the first floor of the second dungeon, Wisps will appear half the time, while a pair of Jellyfish will appear 3/10ths of the time. A trio of Ghosts is the rare encounter on the first floor, with a 2-in-10 chance of being encountered (Figure 6-8).

Troop	Weight	Range
009:Jellyfish*2	30	Whole
011:Ghost*3	20	Whole
006:Wisp*3	50	Whole

Figure 6-8. *The encounters list for the first floor*

On the second floor, we have the encounter table as presented in Figure 6-9.

Troop	Weight	Range
012:Skeleton*2	30	Whole
011:Ghost*3	35	Whole
014:Imp*2	30	Whole
017:Zombie*3	5	Whole

Figure 6-9. *The encounters list for the second floor*

Wisps have been phased out completely, making Ghosts the common encounter on this floor. Skeletons are encountered with the same frequency as Imps, a new foe in this dungeon, while the rare encounter is a trio of Zombies, another new enemy type. I decided against having encounters on the top floor, but you could consider using the same encounter table as the second floor, but with altered weights to make the weaker monsters rarer and the stronger monsters more common. Last, but not least important, we want to keep Eric and Noah progressing nicely in terms of gear. I added the following gear to some of the treasure chests I placed in the dungeon: Bardiche, Bronze Plate, Crossbow, Runed Robe, and Spike Shield. You don't have to make every treasure chest item an upgrade, mind you. In fact, the Bronze Plate is a downgrade, compared to the Hard Leather we placed in the first dungeon.

Placing the Second Dungeon on the World Map

All of the work that has been done in this chapter is for naught if we don't actually allow the player to visit the dungeon, right? So, I'm going to add an appropriate tower graphic (the left-most Tower in tab B of the Field tileset) on the map. I'll place the base of the tower at 13,76. See Figure 6-10 for a screenshot of how it should look once placed.

Figure 6-10. *The world map, now with the tower graphic added at the northern end*

Once that is done, all that is left to do is create the transfer event, like so:

```
@>Conditional Branch: Variable [0002:X] == 13
  @>Conditional Branch: Variable [0003:Y] == 82
    @>Transfer Player: [007:Tower of the VoidF1F] (025,049), Up
    @>
  : Branch End
  @>
: Branch End
```

Place that code within your preexistent Parallel Process event and make sure to add an appropriate transfer event within the dungeon to allow the player to leave.

The Staircases of the Second Dungeon

The second dungeon has quite a few staircases, so it's a good idea to have a table that lists what staircase goes where. See Table 6-1 and note that, when you create the relevant transfer events, you need to move the destination location off of the staircase or you'll trap the game in an infinite loop.

Table 6-1. *The list of staircases within the second dungeon*

This Staircase	Connects With This Staircase
3,26 (1F)	3,26 (2F)
25,5 (1F)	25,5 (2F)
29,40 (1F)	29,40 (2F)
30,45 (1F)	28,45 (2F)
46,21 (2F)	46,21 (3F)
21,40 (2F)	21,40 (3F)
25,40 (2F)	25,40 (3F)
40,31 (2F)	40,31 (3F)

Summary

This chapter covered the creation and population of our game's second dungeon. We used RMVXA's Sample Maps to great effect once again to create a foreboding tower housing a powerful demon for our player to defeat. The dragon statue was the host of a particularly neat application of Parallel Process events to allow a single Action Button event to be used for interaction purposes. In the next chapter, we will have some fun with arenas and other such minigames!

CHAPTER 7

■ ■ ■

Arenas and Other Minigames

Eric and Noah's adventures in our world have been relatively gloom and doom up to now. While they're merely player-characters and don't mind their status as such, their alter egos (a.k.a. the players themselves) would probably appreciate a change of pace. Minigames are a classic video game tradition. To take a somewhat recent example, *Grinsia* (which had a mobile release and a recent rerelease on the Nintendo 3DS) has a shooting gallery minigame. Sometimes, the player just wants to explore off the beaten path and do something unrelated to the main plot at hand. Sidequests are a good way to do that, and I'll be talking about them in a later chapter. This particular chapter, however, is all about having fun within the fun that is a game. Meta, isn't it?

Why an Arena?

Well, while being nominally less of a minigame than most other concepts (given that arenas usually involve battling, which you already do in most role-playing games [RPGs]), arenas require a decent amount of eventing and afford the opportunity to introduce features we haven't talked about before. Besides, you get to beat up assorted baddies for fame, glory, and special prizes! What's not to like?

What If I Want Another Minigame?

I have a few more ideas lined up for this chapter, including using eventing to come up with a similar treasure chest game as the one in *The Legend of Zelda*. For now, though, let's press on with the arena.

Arena Overview

Just the mere mention of the word *arena* evokes gladiatorial combat, as in the times of ancient Rome. In an RPG, arenas can be loosely divided into two categories:

1. One in which the player and/or his/her allies fight against predetermined encounters.

2. One in which the player watches a group of combatants face each other and bets on the outcome.

The first type is much more common than the second, especially nowadays. You can look to *Dragon Warrior 3* for an example of the second. Here's a list of the things we'll need to have or know:

- A map in which we can host our arena. You can have both parts of the arena on one map, but we'll split them into two, to make things a little less cluttered.

- A nonplayer character (NPC) that allows the player to sign up for arena events

- Another NPC that allows the player to trade in his/her hard-earned arena currency for rare prizes

- A list of ranks to aspire to and battles to be fought, as well as the amount of special currency to award for each victory in a rank

- Whether the player will have to fight alone or with the companions he/she has recruited during his/her quest n

Outlining Our Arena

This is one of those bigger projects for which it is better to write down everything you can before you actually sit down and start trying to event it. Let's lay this out one step at a time.

1. Number of Arena Ranks: 4 (D, C, B, A)

2. Number of battles per rank: 3

3. Currency awarded for clearing a rank (D = 2, C = 4, B = 8, A = 16)

4. Rank D Battles

   - Slime*2

   - Bat*2

   - Wisp*3

5. Rank C Battles

   - Large Snake*2

   - Scorpion*3

   - Orc*3

6. Rank B Battles

   - Imp*2

   - Gazer*3

   - Puppet*2

7. Rank A Battles

   - Chimera

   - Werewolf*2

   - Gargoyle*2

So, that's the outline for the things we want to include within our arena.

Creating the Arena Exterior

So, how do we go about setting up the arena itself? First, we have to create the first map for the arena. This is where the player will land, upon accessing the location from the world map. Take a look at Figure 7-1 to see the layout of the first arena area.

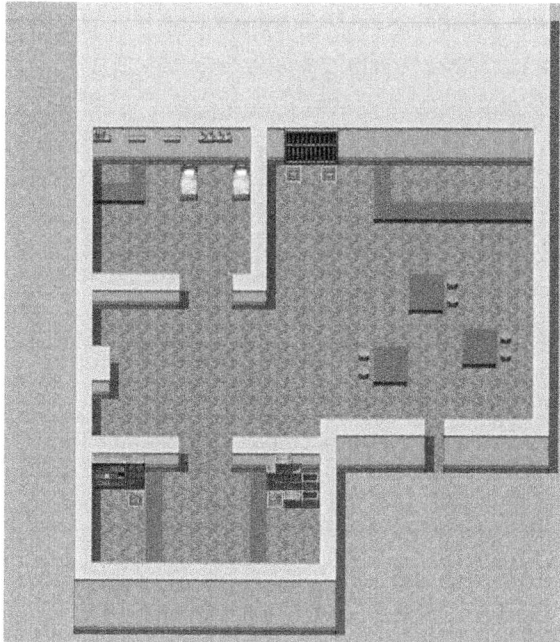

Figure 7-1. *The building that contains the arena*

The player enters the area from that opening near the southeastern end of the map. In front of him/her is the lobby that could be home to other arena fighters. The northwest corner of the map has an inn, if the player needs to recover from wounds, while the southwest holds the arena sign-up NPC (left) and the arena exchange NPC (right). Feel free to use this basic map idea and flesh it out to your heart's content. Be forewarned that creating the arena as I did was a task requiring many long hours of trial and error. As we work through this, you'll quickly see why.

Overview of the Arena Sign-up Event

The arena sign-up NPC (and the exchange NPC, for that matter) will have an Action Button trigger. The NPC will greet the player, welcoming him/her to the arena, and then ask what it can do for him/her. I use a Show Choices event command with three choices at this point. The choices are

- *Arena Battle*: As the choice suggests, this will bring up a list of ranks that the player can challenge. At the start of the player's arena career, he/she can only challenge the lowest rank (in this case, D).

- *How does this work?*: Perfect for the first-timer. This will prompt the NPC to explain exactly how the arena works.

- *Bye*: The player ends the conversation.

The preceding seems rather unassuming, but here's what happens in the event code when the player chooses Arena Battle:

- The game determines, via the analysis of various related switches, what ranks of the arena (if any) the player has cleared.

- A Show Choices prompt appears, based on said analysis.

    1. If the player has not cleared any ranks, the prompt will show Rank D and Nevermind.

    2. If the player has cleared Rank D, the prompt will show Rank D, Rank C, and Nevermind.

    3. If the player has cleared Rank C, the prompt will show Rank D, Rank C, Rank B, and Nevermind.

    4. If the player has cleared Rank B, there will be two prompts. The first will contain Rank D, Rank C, Next Page, and Nevermind. Clicking Next Page will reveal the second prompt, which contains Previous Page, Rank B, Rank A, and Nevermind.

    5. As Rank A is the highest rank, clearing it doesn't change anything.

- When the player chooses a rank to challenge, the arena NPC will charge the player a certain amount of gold (the higher the rank, the higher the cost). If he/she accepts the cost, it is deducted from the player's gold, and he/she is transferred to the proper arena map.

And that's only what's on the first map. There is an Autorun event that triggers, based on each separate rank, once the player reaches the second one, which serves out the relevant fights. If the player wins all three matches or is defeated, he/she is sent back to the first map, to speak with the arena NPC once again, which will either congratulate the player and give him/her a reward (in the case of a win) or urge him/her to do better next time (in the case of a loss).

Creating the Arena Sign-up

I'm going to make this slightly simpler than the version I came up with and disregard party members. Eric and Noah will be able to both participate in the arena at the same time. Even then, I have to note that a total of ten switches are used for this event. (You would need one more switch on top of that for every character you want to temporarily remove from the player's party.) Here's the first stage of our arena event.

```
@>Text: -, -, Normal, Bottom
:       : Welcome to the Arena, where battlers from
:       : all over existence come to do battle!
@>Label: MainMenu
@>Text: -, -, Normal, Bottom
:       : What can I do for you?
@>Show Choices: Arena Battle, How does this work?, Bye
: When [Arena Battle]
    @>
: When [How does this work?]
    @>Text: -, -, Normal, Bottom
    :       : I'm glad you asked, wanderer.
    @>Text: -, -, Normal, Bottom
    :       : Essentially, you start at the bottom of the ladder,
    :       : at Rank D. Win three matches in Rank D and you
    :       : will unlock Rank C, and so forth. It costs Gold to
    :       : compete in each rank, so mind your pocket.
```

```
   @>Text: -, -, Normal, Bottom
   :     : The top rank is Rank A, but none have ever
   :     : completed the three bouts at that level.
   @>Text: -, -, Normal, Bottom
   :     : You are completely healed at the end of
   :     : each match, and you can use items as need
   :     : be. However, be careful as we do not
   :     : refund the cost of items used in the Arena.
   @>Text: -, -, Normal, Bottom
   :     : Use them only if they will secure your victory in
   :     : battle.
   @>Jump to Label: MainMenu
   @>
: When [Bye]
   @>Text: -, -, Normal, Bottom
   :     : Later.
   @>
: Branch End
@>Label: EndPage
@>
```

The good news is that we're on our way. The bad news is that this is the simplest this event will rather be. Oh, boy, is it going to get extensive! We're going to want conditionals for each and every possibility. As already noted, a fresh player will have cleared no ranks. Each rank clear will be stored in a single appropriately named switch. We need to have a switch for each possible challenge as well. Last, we need a switch to flip when the player wins his/her matches and another to flip when the player loses his/her matches. What follows are a large series of conditional branches that will make perfect sense in hindsight. First, we have the conditional branch for when the player has not cleared Rank D. As you can see in the following code listing, we have a universal sentence that will show up before the event starts determining which branch will be executed. The sentence asks the player what rank he/she would like to challenge. As Rank D has not been cleared, the resulting prompt will only have two choices. Rank D has a cost of 100 Gold for the player, and if the player doesn't have the money, the game will return an error message and send him/her back to the initial three choices. If the player *does* have the Gold, it will be deducted, and the RankDChallenge switch will be flipped.

```
: When [Arena Battle]
   @>Text: -, -, Normal, Bottom
   :     : What rank would you like to challenge?
   @>Conditional Branch: Switch [0008:RankDClear] == OFF
      @>Show Choices: Rank D, Nevermind
      : When [Rank D]
         @>Label: RankDChallenge
         @>Text: -, -, Normal, Bottom
         :     : This will cost you 100 Gold. Are you sure?\$
         @>Show Choices: Yes, No
         : When [Yes]
            @>Conditional Branch: Gold is 100 or more
               @>Change Gold: -100
               @>Text: -, -, Normal, Bottom
               :     : Good luck!
               @>Fadeout Screen
               @>Play SE: 'Move', 80, 100
```

```
            @>Control Switches: [0014:RankDChallenge] = ON
            @>Transfer Player:[012:Arena] (008,008), Up
            @>Jump to Label: EndPage
            @>
          : Else
            @>Text: -, -, Normal, Bottom
            :       : You don't have enough Gold!
            @>Jump to Label: MainMenu
            @>
          : Branch End
        @>
      : When [No]
          @>Jump to Label: MainMenu
          @>
      : Branch End
```

You may notice the strange lack of Fadein Screen on this event. As we transfer the player to the other map, we use Fadein over there instead.

Creating the Arena Battle Event

Once the player has signed up to participate in the arena, he/she is transferred to the arena grounds. This section will walk you through creating the battle event that the player will have to face in the arena. Before talking about the event in question, take a look at Figure 7-2 for a screenshot of the arena grounds.

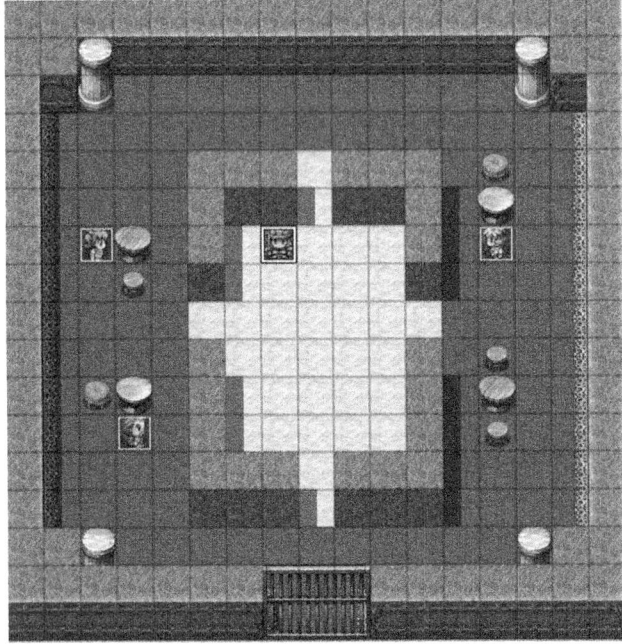

Figure 7-2. *The interior part of the arena, where the player battles assorted baddies for fame and glory*

We transfer the player to the center of that map, a few squares to the south of the armored NPC that we're using as the arena announcer. An RPG arena just isn't much of one if someone isn't announcing challengers and such. We can kill two birds with one stone, as it were, by making that particular NPC our Autorun event as well. He will have a total of four event pages. Each page has a conditional for each particular rank challenge switch. So, page 1 requires RankDChallenge to be on, page 2 requires RankCChallenge to be turned on, and so forth. The general format of the arena challenges is as follows:

- A short announcement of the player's party is made.

- A Battle Processing event in which the player can continue the game if he/she happens to lose the battle begins.

- If the player wins, the game loads up the second fight. If the player loses, he/she is sent back to the first map.

- The same process is repeated until the player wins three fights or loses.

- Take a look below for a large part of the Rank D Challenge Autorun event.

```
@>Fadein Screen
@>Wait: 60 frame(s)
@>Text: -, -, Normal, Bottom
:      : Welcome to the Rank D Arena Challenge!
:      : Are the challengers ready?
@>Text: 'Actor4', 0, Normal, Bottom
:      : I am.
@>Text: 'Actor5', 6, Normal, Bottom
:      : As am I.
@>Text: -, -, Normal, Bottom
:      : Let the games begin!
@>Battle Processing: Slime*2
: If Win
   @>Recover All: Entire Party
   @>Text: -, -, Normal, Bottom
   :      : Our challengers have won Round 1!
   @>Play SE: 'Applause1', 80, 100
   @>Text: -, -, Normal, Bottom
   :      : However, there are still two more rounds left!
   :      : Will our challengers rise to the challenge?!
   @>Text: -, -, Normal, Bottom
   :      : Round 2 is now!
   @>Battle Processing: Bat*2
   : If Win
      @>Recover All: Entire Party
      @>Text: -, -, Normal, Bottom
      :      : The challengers take the second win of the day
      :      : in Rank D!
      @>Play SE: 'Applause1', 80, 100
      @>Text: -, -, Normal, Bottom
      :      : This is the moment of truth!
      :      : Will our aspiring challengers take the
      :      : title? Or, will the final challenge of Rank D
      :      : prove too much to handle?!
```

```
@>Text: -, -, Normal, Bottom
:        : Let loose the monsters of war!!
@>Battle Processing: Wisp*3
: If Win
   @>Recover All: Entire Party
   @>Text: -, -, Normal, Bottom
   :        : They have done it!
   @>Control Switches: [0013:ArenaWin] = ON
   @>Jump to Label: Return
   @>
: If Lose
   @>Recover All: Entire Party
   @>Text: -, -, Normal, Bottom
   :        : Aww. So close, yet so far!
   :        : They have lost the final match!
   :        : Better luck next time!
   @>Control Switches: [0012:ArenaLoss] = ON
   @>Jump to Label: Return
   @>
 : Branch End
```

As noted before, the Autorun event on the second map starts with a Fadein Screen (if we didn't do this, the screen would stay black). When you toggle the *Continue When Loser* check box, the Battle Processing event command as displayed splits into *If Win* and *If Lose*. Note the differing switches that are flipped depending on whether the player wins or loses. We heal the player's party after every battle, win or lose. You can see the rest of the event, following.

```
 @>
 : If Lose
   @>Recover All: Entire Party
   @>Text: -, -, Normal, Bottom
   :        : Ouch. Well, at least they won 1 out of 3.
   :        : Better luck next time.
   @>Control Switches: [0012:ArenaLoss] = ON
   @>Jump to Label: Return
   @>
 : Branch End
 @>
: If Lose
  @>Recover All: Entire Party
  @>Text: -, -, Normal, Bottom
  :        : It appears they have been trounced in
  :        : their very first match!
  @>Text: 'Actor4', 0, Normal, Bottom
  :        : …
  @>Text: -, -, Normal, Bottom
  :        : Better luck next time!
  @>Control Switches: [0012:ArenaLoss] = ON
  @>Jump to Label: Return
  @>
```

```
  : Branch End
@>Label: Return
@>Fadeout Screen
@>Transfer Player:[011:Arena] (009,027), Left
@>
```

Here you can see where all of those Jump to Label: Return commands lead. As in several other cases previously, I used these solely as a precaution, given that there's no way for unwanted events to execute. The screen is faded out before we transfer the player back to the first map. The other three rank challenge events can be added to our announcer in the same way. All you have to change between each one are the chosen encounters and, if you desire, some of the text shown to the player.

Creating the Arena Result Event

Back at the first map, we need an Autorun event (I placed a blank graphic event behind the arena sign-up NPC) to handle the post-arena results. Because we have four possible challenges, and two possible outcomes for said challenges, this event will have eight total pages. Don't be daunted, as the pages are simple enough.

- Page 1 requires RankDChallenge and ArenaWin to be on.

- Page 2 requires RankDChallenge and ArenaLoss to be on.

- Every pair of pages after that will represent a different ranked challenge when the player wins and when the player loses.

```
@>Fadein Screen
@>Wait: 60 frame(s)
@>Conditional Branch: Switch [0008:RankDClear] == OFF
   @>Text: -, -, Normal, Bottom
   :     : Congratulations on clearing Rank D!
   :     : Greater challenges await you in Rank C,
   :     : whenever you are ready to face them!
   @>Play SE: 'Item3', 80, 100
   @>Text: -, -, Normal, Bottom
   :     : You have earned 2 Arena Tokens!
   @>Change Items: [Arena Token], + 2
   @>Control Switches: [0014:RankDChallenge] = OFF
   @>Control Switches: [0014:ArenaWin] = OFF
   @>Control Switches: [0014:RankDClear] = ON
   @>Jump to Label: Done
   @>
 : Branch End
@>Conditional Branch: Switch [0008:RankDClear] == ON
   @>Text: -, -, Normal, Bottom
   :     : Way to beat Rank D there!
   :     : However, you've done this already, right?
   :     : Come on, take a risk or two and take
   :     : a harder challenge, would you?!
   @>Play SE: 'Item3', 80, 100
   @>Text: -, -, Normal, Bottom
   :     : You have earned 2 Arena Tokens!
```

```
    @>Change Items: [Arena Token], + 2
    @>Control Switches: [0014:RankDChallenge] = OFF
    @>Control Switches: [0014:ArenaWin] = OFF
    @>Jump to Label: Done
    @>
 : Branch End
@>Label: Done
@>Recover All: Entire Party
@>
```

This is the first half of the pair of events for Rank D challenges. As the pair of conditional branches and their contained text will imply, this is the page that requires that the player clear his/her challenge. We start with a `Fadein` (as the event on the other map ended with a Fadeout) and a one-second wait time after the screen fades in. Afterward, what executes next depends on whether the player has cleared Rank D before or not. If he/she has not, the first branch triggers, and the player is congratulated on the first-time win and earns two Arena Tokens. (I replaced item #14 to add them to the game; they are a Key Item that cannot be consumed, used, or sold from the player's inventory.) Afterward, because the player is through competing for the moment, we flip off the pair of switches that have been flipped on (in this case, RankDChallenge and ArenaWin) and flip on the RankDClear switch. That `Jump to Label` is *not* superfluous. Because the player now has RankDClear switched on, the next branch will execute automatically, unless we skip it via a label jump. That branch, incidentally, is what executes when the player has already beaten Rank D before and is just repeating the challenge. After a minor berating by the NPC, the player earns his/her reward, and the two relevant switches flip off. On the other hand, here's the loss event for Rank D challenges:

```
@>Fadein Screen
@>Wait: 60 frame(s)
@>Text: -, -, Normal, Bottom
 :      : Don't sweat it. It happens to the best of
 :      : us. Get a bit stronger and come back fighting!
@>Recover All: Entire Party
@>Control Switches: [0014:RankDChallenge] = OFF
@>Control Switches: [0012:ArenaLoss] = OFF
@>
```

As you can see, it's pretty much a little fluff, then the party is healed, and then the challenge and arena loss switches are flipped off. Rather simple compared to the win event, isn't it? Now, win or lose, we're back at our starting location. The player can choose to attempt another challenge (including taking the Rank C challenge, if he/she beats Rank D on his/her first attempt) or go do something else.

Miscellaneous Arena Considerations

There are only two things left to cover with the arena. First, let's include the code of the Arena Battle event when the player has beaten Rank D.

```
@>Conditional Branch: Switch [0008:RankDClear] == ON
    @>Conditional Branch: Switch [0009:RankCClear] == OFF
        @>Show Choices: Rank D, Rank C, Nevermind
        : When [Rank D]
            @>Jump to Label: RankDChallenge
            @>
        : When [Rank C]
```

```
@>Label: RankCChallenge
@>Text: -, -, Normal, Bottom
:      : This will cost you 500 Gold. Are you sure?\$
@>Show Choices: Yes, No
: When [Yes]
  @>Conditional Branch: Gold is 500 or more
    @>Change Gold: -500
    @>Text: -, -, Normal, Bottom
    :      : Good luck!
    @>Fadeout Screen
    @>Play SE: 'Move', 80, 100
    @>Control Switches: [0015:RankCChallenge] = ON
    @>Transfer Player:[012:Arena] (008,008), Up
    @>Jump to Label: EndPage
    @>
  : Else
    @>Text: -, -, Normal, Bottom
    :      : You don't have enough Gold!
    @>Jump to Label: MainMenu
    @>
  : Branch End
  @>
: When [No]
  @>Jump to Label: MainMenu
  @>
: Branch End
```

What we see here will be consistent in every conditional branch from here to the end of the arena sign-up event. We check to see if the previous rank in the list was cleared. If so, we make sure that the next one has not been cleared yet. If it has, we'd be skipping to the next branch in the line. In this case, as the player has only beaten Rank D, he/she should be challenging Rank C next. Note the Jump to Label if the player picks Rank D. Redundancy is fine for some fields of work, but in game design, you usually only want to write the same code once, if possible. Then, you call back to that code when you need it. I'll be touching upon common events in a later chapter, to tidy up some of our previous code. For now, it will suffice to know that we have already written out the Rank D challenge in a previous conditional branch, so we just jump back to it, instead of repeating the same code a second time.

I'll leave the rest of the eventing of these already mentioned events up to you, as it is pretty much identical to what we have done so far. What you would need to fill out follows:

- *Pages 2 to 4 of the announcer Autorun event*: As already mentioned, each page will have a conditional based on the rank that is being challenged. You would have to create Ranks C through A.

- *Pages 3 to 8 of the post-challenge Autorun event placed behind the arena sign-up NPC*: Remember to have one page for a win and another for a loss, in each particular rank.

- *The remaining conditional branches in the arena sign-up event*: We need one when the player has beaten Rank C and another when the player has beaten Rank B.

Creating Our Arena Shop

Now we have most of the events set up; however, we have not done anything with the NPC that will exchange tokens for items. Let's remedy that. There are two ways to set up a token shop.

1. You award special key items that serve as currency. Then, you set up a special shop that, in reality, is a series of Show Choices that each costs a differing amount of tokens.

2. You award arena currency by adding value to a variable. Then, by clever use of currency swapping, you make it so that you can use the default shop with the currency you have earned. I'll provide a template for the latter later on.

I'll show both possibilities, but the second is definitely easier than the first. Following, you'll find a listing of half of the first arena shop possibility.

```
@>Text: -, -, Normal, Bottom
:      : Hello there! This is the Arena Exchange! I can trade
:      : you special items for any tokens you may have
:      : earned from your Arena participation.
@>Text: -, -, Normal, Bottom
:      : Here's what I have available.
@>Control Variables: [0006:arenacurrency] = [Arena Token] in Inventory
@>Show Choices: Elixir - 5 Tokens, Defense Piece - 15 Tokens, Solomon's Ring - 30 Tokens, Bye
: When [Elixir - 5 Tokens]
   @>Text: -, -, Normal, Bottom
   :      : To confirm, an Elixir will cost you 5 Tokens.
   @>Text: -, -, Normal, Bottom
   :      : You currently have \V[6] Arena Tokens. Will you
   :      : purchase an Elixir?
   @>Show Choices: Yes, No
   : When [Yes]
      @>Conditional Branch: Variable [0006:arenacurrency] >= 5
         @>Change Items: [Elixir], +1
         @>Change Items: [Arena Token], -5
         @>Text: -, -, Normal, Bottom
         :      : Enjoy!
         @>
         : Else
         @>Text: -, -, Normal, Bottom
         :      : You don't have enough Tokens!
         @>
         : Branch End
      @>
   : When [No]
      @>Text: -, -, Normal, Bottom
      :      : Okay. See you later!
      @>
   : Branch End
```

We have the NPC greet the player, as is usual. Then, we have a new variable to hold the number of Arena Tokens that the player has in his/her inventory. A Show Choices prompt appears with three possible item purchases and Bye as the last option. When the player clicks an item choice, the NPC confirms the cost, tells the player how many Arena Tokens he/she currently has, and asks if he/she wishes to purchase the item, bringing up a Yes/No choice prompt. In what is perhaps one of the few times I'll ever use *Set handling when conditions do not apply*, we make sure that the player has the Arena Tokens to purchase the item in question. If the player doesn't, we return an error message; otherwise, we add the item to the player's inventory and remove the appropriate number of tokens.

```
: When [Defense Piece - 15 Tokens]
   @>Text: -, -, Normal, Bottom
   :     : You currently have \V[6] Arena Tokens. Will you
   :     : purchase a Defense Piece?
   @>Show Choices: Yes, No
   : When [Yes]
     @>Conditional Branch: Variable [0006:arenacurrency] >= 15
        @>Change Items: [Defense Piece], +1
        @>Change Items: [Arena Token], -15
        @>Text: -, -, Normal, Bottom
        :     : Enjoy!
        @>
        : Else
        @>Text: -, -, Normal, Bottom
        :     : You don't have enough Tokens!
        @>
        : Branch End
     @>
   : When [No]
     @>Text: -, -, Normal, Bottom
     :     : Okay. See you later!
     @>
: When [Solomon's Ring - 30 Tokens]
   @>Text: -, -, Normal, Bottom
   :     : You currently have \V[6] Arena Tokens. Will you
   :     : purchase a Solomon's Ring?
   @>Show Choices: Yes, No
   : When [Yes]
     @>Conditional Branch: Variable [0006:arenacurrency] >= 15
        @>Change Items: [Defense Piece], +1
        @>Change Items: [Arena Token], -15
        @>Text: -, -, Normal, Bottom
        :     : Enjoy!
        @>
        : Else
        @>Text: -, -, Normal, Bottom
        :     : You don't have enough Tokens!
        @>
        : Branch End
     @>
   : When [No]
     @>Text: -, -, Normal, Bottom
     :     : Okay. See you later!
```

```
      @>
   : Branch End
: When [Bye]
  @>Text: -, -, Normal, Bottom
   :     : Later.
  @>
   : Branch End
@>
```

This type of arena shop, as you can see, is simple enough. Unfortunately, it becomes less and less useful the more items you want to add to the shop. The Show Choices event command can only hold a total of four choices, so you would be required to add options merely to switch between Choice branches.

The second way is much easier and has only one quirk that will require scripting to address. However, as the quirk is graphical in nature, it doesn't affect the event's functionality, so have at it! Take a look at the following:

```
@>Text: -, -, Normal, Bottom
:       : Hello there! This is the Arena Exchange! I can trade
:       : you special items for any tokens you may have
:       : earned from your Arena participation.
@>Text: -, -, Normal, Bottom
:       : Here's what I have available.
@>Control Variables: [0007:PartyGold] = Gold
@>Change Gold: - 9999999
@>Change Gold: + Variable [0006:arenacurrency]
@>Shop Processing: [Elixir]
:                              : [Defense Piece]
:                              : [Solomon's Ring]
@>Control Variables: [0006:arenacurrency] = Gold
@>Change Gold: -9999999
@>Change Gold: + Variable [0007:PartyGold]
@>
```

In the second type of arena shop, we save the player's Gold in a variable appropriately named PartyGold. In this setup, you would have the player receive his/her arena currency in a variable instead of in the form of items. Then, we zero out the player's Gold and add his/her arena currency to his/her Gold value. We make sure that the *Purchase Only* check box is toggled and then add any items we wish the player to be able to purchase. Set the price of Elixirs to 5, the price of Defense Pieces to 15, and the price of Solomon's Rings to 30. After the player closes the shop, we restore his/her Gold and arena currency to their original places. Figure 7-3 is a screenshot of the arena shop in all of its glory.

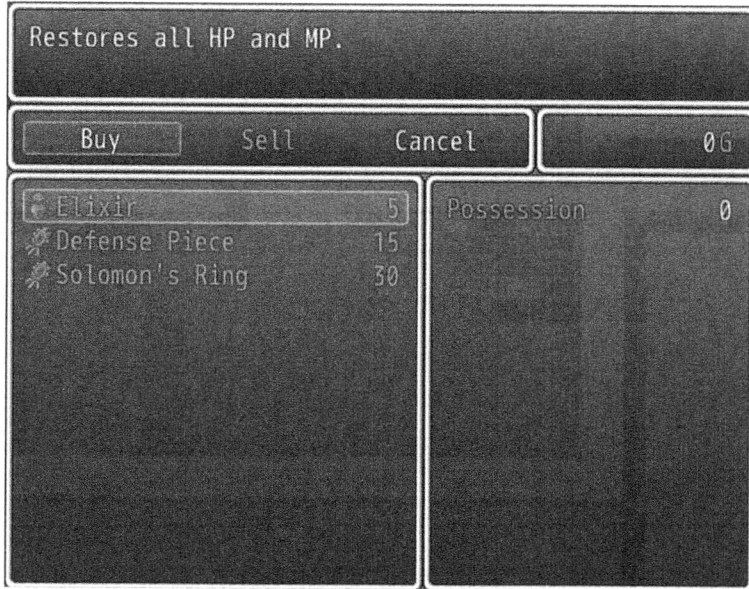

Figure 7-3. *The arena shop*

As you can already tell, despite the fact that we switched from Gold to arena currency, it is still using G (to represent Gold). A small amount of scripting can be used to change the currency symbol, as desired. I'll link to a short script created for that purpose by Tsukihime in the Appendix, so go take a look, if you wish to do that now.

■ **Note**   Keep in mind that you will not be able to use the above mentioned script (or any others, for that matter) if you are working with the Lite version of RMVXA.

With that said and done, we have finally completed this part of Chapter 7, a whopping 15 pages after we started! Here are some exercises to do before we move on to another minigame.

1. Add extra rewards that are earned by the player the first time he/she clears a certain rank.

2. Use Battle Processing: Same As Encounter in tandem with an encounter table on the map, to add some random possibilities to arena battles at Rank A.

As the player doesn't move while on the second map, you could leave the default Range on the possible encounters. Just to be safe, you could make it so that random encounters only appear on that map within a specific Region.

The Treasure Chest Game

This is a game in which the player opens a certain number of chests in the designated playing area. Will the player receive riches or scraps? During the course of this section, I'll be creating a seven-chest game. Take a look at Figure 7-4 to see what the area looks like when complete.

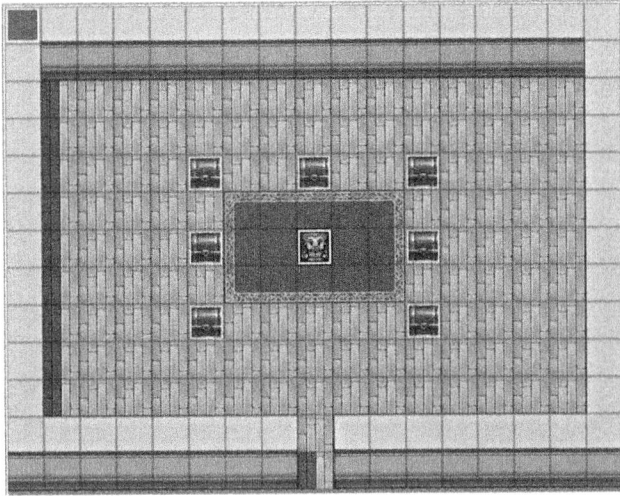

Figure 7-4. *The treasure chest room*

We have the game host in the center of the map, surrounded by his seven chests. Here's what we need to do to make our treasure chest game:

- Come up with a list of rewards that can be obtained. I'll list my seven, but feel free to come up with your own.

  1. Potion

  2. 1 Gold

  3. Elixir

  4. 1 Gold (Yes, the player has two chances to get 1 Gold).

  5. Hi-Potion

  6. 200 Gold

  7. 500 Gold

     - Add a variable that will store the current "seed" for the treasure chests. We want to make it so that the contents of a particular chest are one of those seven, on a random basis. Otherwise, the player can just open the same chest and get the same reward consistently. A chest's contents will change, based upon the seed value.

     - Add a switch that will be flipped on while the minigame is in progress and turned off once it is completed.

     - Make it so that, once opened, a chest disappears for the duration of the minigame and reappears afterward.

     - Have a variable that decreases every time the player opens a chest. We'll set this to two at the start of the minigame, meaning that the player can open two of the seven chests present.

     - Once two chests have been opened, announce that the game is over and reset the initial starting conditions, so that the player can play again, if he/she so chooses.

To pull this off with eventing, we'll have to set up each treasure chest individually, as well as create the NPC and the Parallel Process event that triggers when the game is over. I'm going to start with the chest in the upper-left corner. Let's call that chest the master, as the rewards listed previously will be placed into the event in the same order. As the chests will be present even while the game is not active, we have to make sure that the player cannot open them. Each chest will be a two-page event, in which page 1 has a treasure chest graphic and *Direction Fix* has been toggled. (This makes it so that the chest does not appear to open slightly if the player interacts with it from certain angles). If the player tries to interact with the chest, the event will show a text box declaring that it is locked. Page 2 has the TreasureChestStart switch conditional, meaning that it will not trigger unless the minigame is currently active. As with page 1, this page will have an Action Button trigger.

```
@>Set Move Route: This event (Wait)
:                    : $>Direction Fix OFF
:                    : $>Turn Left
:                    : $>Wait: 3 frame(s)
:                    : $>Turn Right
:                    : $>Wait: 3 frame(s)
@>Conditional Branch: Variable [0009:TreasureChestSeed] == 1
   @>Change Items: [Potion], + 1
   @>Text: -, -, Normal, Bottom
   :      : Got a Potion!
   @>
: Branch End
@>Conditional Branch: Variable [0009:TreasureChestSeed] == 2
   @>Change Gold: + 1
   @>Text: -, -, Normal, Bottom
   :      : Got a single Gold piece!
   @>
: Branch End
@>Conditional Branch: Variable [0009:TreasureChestSeed] == 3
   @>Change Items: [Elixir], + 1
   @>Text: -, -, Normal, Bottom
   :      : Got an Elixir!
   @>
: Branch End
@>Conditional Branch: Variable [0009:TreasureChestSeed] == 4
   @>Change Gold: + 1
   @>Text: -, -, Normal, Bottom
   :      : Got a single Gold piece!
   @>
: Branch End
@>Conditional Branch: Variable [0009:TreasureChestSeed] == 5
   @>Change Items: [Hi-Potion], + 1
   @>Text: -, -, Normal, Bottom
   :      : Got a Hi-Potion!
   @>
: Branch End
@>Conditional Branch: Variable [0009:TreasureChestSeed] == 6
   @>Change Gold: + 200
   @>Text: -, -, Normal, Bottom
   :      : Got 200 Gold!
   @>
: Branch End
```

```
@>Conditional Branch: Variable [0009:TreasureChestSeed] == 7
   @>Change Gold: + 500
   @>Text: -, -, Normal, Bottom
   :      : Got 500 Gold!
   @>
: Branch End
@>Wait: 30 frame(s)
@>Control Variables: [0010:ChestsToOpen] -= 1
@>Erase Event
@>
```

The first part of the event was copy-pasted from RPG Maker VX Ace's (RMVXA's) Treasure Chest quick event. It displays the animation that the player sees when opening a treasure chest. Afterward, we have the seven different possible chest contents, based on the value of the TreasureChestSeed variable. The player will earn the appropriate item and be apprised of the fact via text box, and after a half-second pause, the value of ChestsToOpen will drop by 1, informing the game that the player has opened a chest. Erase Event is an event command I have not covered up to now, but it is as simple as can be. When an event processes Erase Event, it effectively ceases to exist until the player leaves the map. As you might have inferred, this could cause problems in the execution of the minigame. This will definitely be addressed in the Parallel Process event, when we get it to it.

Populating the Chests of the Treasure Chest Game

So, if we want to have randomized results and have all seven rewards represented with every seed, each chest has to give different items for the same seed value. For example, if the chest in the upper-left corner gives a Potion when the seed is 1, another chest could give the single Gold piece in that case. Think of the list of items in a numerical sense. That first chest has its items in the order 1234567. My second chest (the one to the right; let's go in a clockwise rotation) has the items in the order 6412753. When the seed is 1, the player will receive 200 Gold, if he/she opens the second chest. The idea is that two chests not give the same item (except in the case of the pair of 1 Gold chests). This is rather hard to figure out mentally, given the large number of possibilities (many of which actually don't apply, as they would cause two or more chests to give the same item). I personally used random.org's (specifically, www.random.org/lists) list shuffler. I wrote down 1234567 and then let the site do its work. A lot of the shuffled lists will not be valid, but it will give you a good idea of what item combinations you need, especially as you get closer to the last chest. Check Table 7-1 to see the seven-number lists I came up with.

Table 7-1. *The Seven-Number Lists That Determine What Chest Has What Item in the Treasure Chest Game*

1	6	2	7	4	3	5
2	4	7	3	5	1	6
3	1	6	2	7	5	4
4	2	1	5	6	7	3
5	7	4	1	3	6	2
6	5	3	4	1	2	7
7	3	5	6	2	4	1

As you can see, our master list is the left-most column. Each column corresponds to a different chest from top to bottom. Take a moment to look at the numbers and note that no numbers repeat when reading from left to right. For example, the first row is 1627435, which has no numerical repeats. If your rows aren't repeating, chances are that the slot in question is fine. To prove the point, if the minigame rolls a 1 for the seed, here's what you can expect from each chest:

1.   Potion

2.   200 Gold

3.   1 Gold

4.   500 Gold

5.   1 Gold

6.   Elixir

7.   Hi-Potion

Pretty neat, isn't it? As crunching permutations is rather secondary to the point of this book, feel free to use the grid that I came up with for your own chests. What you can do is copy-paste page 2 of the master chest event. Then, depending on the chest number, you move around the various items in the event page, so that the item order matches the ordered list that you want. Once you have done that, you renumber the conditional branches such that they go from 1 to 7, as in the master chest: same items, different seed order. For additional context, check the eventing of the second treasure chest on the following page, so that you can get a visual of what I mean. I'll leave the rest of the chests to you, as this involves more of the same, as already has been noted.

```
@>Set Move Route: This event (Wait)
:                 : $>Direction Fix OFF
:                 : $>Turn Left
:                 : $>Wait: 3 frame(s)
:                 : $>Turn Right
:                 : $>Wait: 3 frame(s)
@>Conditional Branch: Variable [0009:TreasureChestSeed] == 1
   @>Change Gold: + 200
   @>Text: -, -, Normal, Bottom
   :     : Got 200 Gold!
   @>
: Branch End
@>Conditional Branch: Variable [0009:TreasureChestSeed] == 2
   @>Change Gold: + 1
   @>Text: -, -, Normal, Bottom
   :     : Got a single Gold piece!
   @>
: Branch End
@>Conditional Branch: Variable [0009:TreasureChestSeed] == 3
   @>Change Items: [Potion], + 1
   @>Text: -, -, Normal, Bottom
   :     : Got a Potion!
   @>
: Branch End
```

```
@>Conditional Branch: Variable [0009:TreasureChestSeed] == 4
   @>Change Gold: + 1
   @>Text: -, -, Normal, Bottom
   :      : Got a single Gold piece!
   @>
: Branch End
@>Conditional Branch: Variable [0009:TreasureChestSeed] == 5
   @>Change Gold: + 500
   @>Text: -, -, Normal, Bottom
   :      : Got 500 Gold!
   @>
: Branch End
@>Conditional Branch: Variable [0009:TreasureChestSeed] == 6
   @>Change Items: [Hi-Potion], + 1
   @>Text: -, -, Normal, Bottom
   :      : Got a Hi-Potion!
   @>
: Branch End
@>Conditional Branch: Variable [0009:TreasureChestSeed] == 7
   @>Change Items: [Elixir], + 1
   @>Text: -, -, Normal, Bottom
   :      : Got an Elixir!
   @>
: Branch End
@>Wait: 30 frame(s)
@>Control Variables: [0010:ChestsToOpen] -= 1
@>Erase Event
@>
```

That is a large part of the treasure chest minigame.

Creating the Treasure Chest Game NPC

Next, let's create the NPC. He's going to get straight to the point and begin with the all-important question: Want to play the Treasure Chest game? The player will get three choices at that time. He/She can answer yes, at which point the NPC will note that it costs 500 Gold to play and ask the player to confirm. We have the usual processing to make sure that the player can't play if he or she doesn't have the Gold and have the NPC say good-bye if he/she says no. The second choice is humorously named "Huh?" and prompts the NPC to explain what the game is actually about. The last choice allows the player to say no from the first question and not have to initially say yes. If the player says yes and has the Gold to play, the NPC will deduct 500 Gold from the player, say a little line, and the screen will fade out. After the fade-out, we set the value of ChestsToOpen to 2, set the value of TreasureChestSeed to a random value between 1 and 7, and flip the TreasureChestStart to the on state. One second later, the screen fades back in, and the fun can begin. We add a simple second page to the NPC that gives him a witty one-liner urging the player to "Get to opening!" the chests, as it were, but only when TreasureChestStart is on. A listing of the first page of the NPC event follows.

```
@>Label: Main
@>Text: -, -, Normal, Bottom
 :      : Want to play the Treasure Chest game?
@>Show Choices: Yes, Huh?, No
: When [Yes]
```

```
@>Text: -, -, Normal, Bottom
:      : That will be 500 Gold, if you will.\$
@>Show Choices: Yes, No
: When [Yes]
   @>Conditional Branch: Gold is 500 or more
      @>Change Gold: - 500
      @>Text: -, -, Normal, Bottom
      :       : Let the game begin!
      @>Fadeout Screen
      @>Wait: 60 frame(s)
      @>Control Variables: [0010:ChestsToOpen] = 2
      @>Control Variables: [0009:TreasureChestSeed] = Random No. (1...7)
      @>Control Switches: [0019: TreasureChestStart] = ON
      @>Fadein Screen
      @>
    : Else
      @>Text: -, -, Normal, Bottom
      :       : Come back when you have enough Gold!
      @>
    : Branch End
      @>
  : When [No]
     @>Text: -, -, Normal, Bottom
     :       : See you later, then.
     @>
   : Branch End
   @>
: When [Huh?]
   @>Text: -, -, Normal, Bottom
   :       : Guess I should explain. These seven chests around
   :       : me contain either an item, some Gold, or a single
   :       : gold piece. The catch, of course, is that you may
   :       : only open two of them.
   @>Text: -, -, Normal, Bottom
   :       : Oh, and it costs you 500 Gold to play.
   @>Jump to Label: Main
   @>
: When [No]
    @>Text: -, -, Normal, Bottom
    :       : See you later, then.
   @>
   Branch End
@>
```

▓ **Note**   It's as good a time as any to mention that \$ causes the game to display the party's current Gold when used within a text box. We've used it several times already for precisely that purpose.

Completing the Treasure Chest Game

Last, but definitely not least, we have the Parallel Process event. We have to make sure that we end the game right when the player has opened the second chest, lest he/she get greedy and open all seven of them. Also, we have to make it so that the player is temporarily removed from the map, so that the chosen chests can reappear for future play-throughs of the minigame. We can do this via the clever use of a switch that I'll call Intermission. The Parallel Process event is one page long and needs to have a condition of TreasureChestStart is ON (otherwise the player will loop infinitely between the two maps). The Parallel Process event starts with a conditional branch that requires that ChestsToOpen be equal to 0. Then, it checks for Intermission to be off (which it should be). The NPC will say "That's it!" and the screen will fade out. The player will be transferred to a nearly blank map that contains a small Autorun event that flips on the Intermission switch and sends the player back to the Treasure Chest game map (specifically, one square to the south of the NPC and facing the player).

Back at the game map, the Parallel Process event has a second conditional branch that only triggers when Intermission has been turned on. We take a one-second pause and turn off the TreasureChestStart and Intermission switches, effectively resetting the minigame state so that the player can play again. Here's the Parallel Process event:

```
@>Conditional Branch: Variable [0010:ChestsToOpen] == 0
   @>Conditional Branch: Switch [0020:Intermission] == OFF
      @>Text: -, -, Normal, Bottom
      :     : That's it!
      @>Fadeout Screen
      @>Transfer Player:[014:Intermission] (007,006), Up, None
      @>
    : Branch End
   @>
: Branch End
 @>Conditional Branch: Switch [0020:Intermission] == ON
   @>Wait: 60 frame(s)
   @>Control Switches: [0019:TreasureChestStart] = OFF
   @>Control Switches: [0020:Intermission] = OFF
   @>Fadein Screen
   @>
: Branch End
```

The Autorun event on the intermission map is made up of two little lines:

```
@>Control Switches: [0020:Intermission] = ON
@>Transfer Player:[013:TreasureChestGame] (008,007), Up, None
```

Related Exercises

With that done, you have just completed your very own treasure chest game in the vein of some of the *Zelda* games. Here are some neat exercises for you to try out that are related to this particular minigame.

1. Using the "Item exists" conditional of an event, make it so that the player can see the item that a particular minigame chest contains.

    - The inspiration for this one comes from *Ocarina of Time*. In that particular *Zelda* entry, the player can see the contents of chests in a minigame, by using an item found at the bottom of a well.

- You could duplicate page 2 of each of your chests for this purpose and have a text box that allows the player to decide whether or not to open the chest, based on what it contains. Just make sure that said page is 3 and not 2; otherwise, it will never trigger. (Never forget that events attempt to execute from right to left; the right-most page will always be executed, if possible).

2. Make it so that an opened chest remains visible until the minigame ends.

    - It's as simple as having for each chest one switch (you could name them TreasureChest1, TreasureChest2, and so forth) that is flipped on when its related chest is opened and including another event page that requires that switch to be flipped on and has a graphic of the open treasure chest. Grant bonus points for telling the player that the chest has already been opened, if they examine it.

    - You'll have to toggle off those switches to reset the minigame conditions. Incidentally, that's the reason why I don't use self-switches for the same purpose. A self-switch can only be affected at a local level, which means that if you flip Chest 5's A switch, for example, you would have to flip it off via Chest 5's event specifically.

3. Have items that can only be received once per play-through.

    - Say you wanted to have a rare medallion as one of the seven possible rewards. What you could do is use a switch that flips on when the player finds the item for the first time, then have a conditional branch that changes the item found in a chest in subsequent minigames.

    - It might be tempting to use an *Item exists* conditional branch here, but that will only work if the rare item in question cannot be obtained elsewhere. Otherwise, weird things will happen. Mainly, the player will not be able to obtain the item if he/she already has it (even if the player has never gotten one from the minigame) and can get it multiple times if it has a sell price (by selling the one he/she has before replaying the minigame).

Other Minigames

The mark of a great minigame is one that makes the player want to play it even more than the actual game. I'm a personal fan of card games and have to admit that the ninth version of *Final Fantasy* and *Xenosaga Episode 1* have card games that hooked me for dozens of hours. That's not bad for what is supposed to be a diversion from the main plot. Following, I'll list some other ideas for minigames and offer tips and tricks on how I would start tackling them within RMVXA.

1. A sequence where the player has limited time to escape a certain area

    - For the sake of having an example, let's say the player is in a space station that is being overrun by baddies. If the player does not reach the escape pod within 1000 steps, he/she gets a game over.

    - There's no direct way to determine via eventing when a player has taken a step in RMVXA. The easiest workaround is to use three variables. One variable checks the player's total steps at the start of the escape minigame. The second saves the player's current steps every time he/she moves, while the last variable is the difference between the first and second variables. We'll need a Parallel Process event to cover those interactions.

    - The Parallel Process event would have a conditional branch that requires the difference between the two variables to be 1000 or more. Once that is met, you employ the Game Over command for its sole use.

- Of course, if the player makes it out in time, all is well.

- To add to the tension of the situation, you can make it so that certain doors and elevators become inoperable at certain step milestones (such as 700 steps left, 300 steps left, and so on).

2. A matching-pair memory game involving NPCs or symbols

- Each pair of identical events should have its own variable. There should also be a variable equal to the number of total pairs at the start of the game.

- Another variable should be set to 2 and drop each time the player selects a spot. When a member of a pair is spotted, its variable should be increased by 1.

- When two spots have been uncovered, the counting variable will be at 0. The game should check to see if any pair variables are at 2. If they are, we remove them and award the player a point.

- We can have another variable for Lives. The player loses a life every time he or she fails to match a pair. If the player is out of lives, the minigame ends prematurely, and we reward him/her based on points received.

- If a pair has not been matched, we hide the two uncovered spots. If a pair has been matched, we use Erase Event on it.

Adding the Minigame Areas to Our World Map

That just about concludes our chapter, but for one last thing: we haven't added our new locations to the world map! Take a look at Figure 7-5.

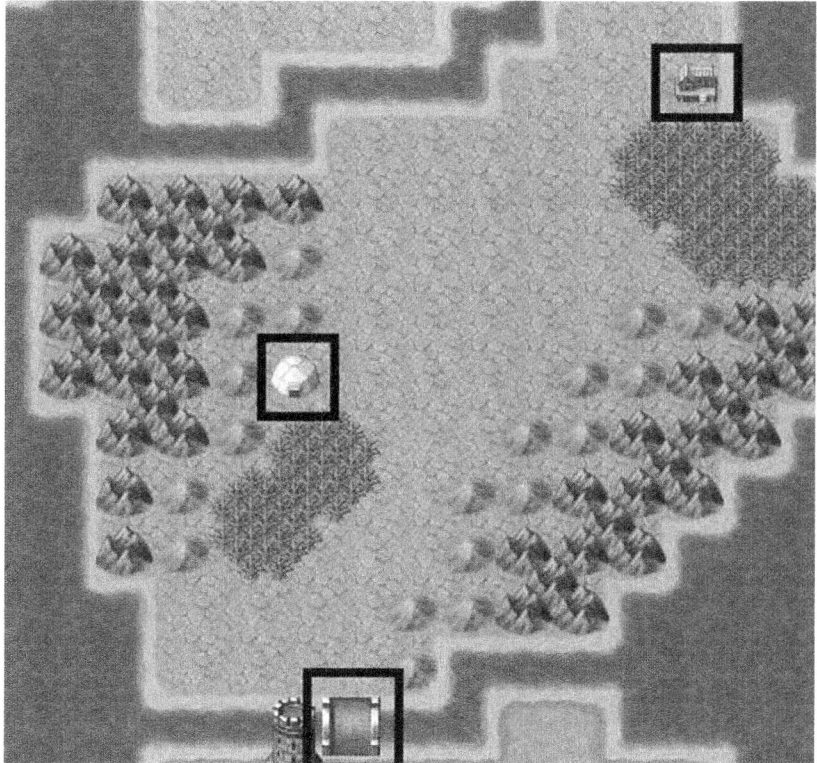

Figure 7-5. *Another part of our world map that has been populated with locations*

The tent is the arena and is located at (13,69). The treasure chest game is located at the small building at (20,64). The bridge directly to the east of the tower is locked until you beat the tower's boss. You can do that by placing a conditional branch that triggers when the player steps on the bridge and has not beaten the boss yet. Give a short message (I have the game display "A horrible force blocks the way!"), and then have the player take a step back, putting him/her back on the first small continent.

Summary

This chapter covered how to create an arena in which the player can battle predetermined enemies to earn points toward rare and special items. In addition, I covered how to make a treasure chest game in the spirit of some of the *Legend of Zelda* games. Last, I gave ideas for other possible minigames. In the next chapter, I will be covering optional quests (also called sidequests).

CHAPTER 8

Sidequests

In the previous chapter, we took a break from working on our game's main narrative. In this chapter, we're going to extend that break some more! Sidequests serve a similar purpose as minigames, in that they allow the player to walk off the beaten path and receive rewards for things that do not directly advance the narrative. I would loosely classify sidequests into two major categories.

1. **Permanent.** These sidequests become available at a certain point of the game and can be completed at any time before the player beats the final boss. Is the player one step away from entering the final dungeon? He or she can go kill the giant boar terrorizing the village halfway across the world.

2. **Time-sensitive.** A sidequest that is active only for a certain part of the game. While not an actual given sidequest, Excalibur in *Final Fantasy* 9 is a perfect example of a time-sensitive quest. Excalibur is a sword located within a chest in a late-game dungeon. The catch? You must reach the chest within 24 hours of starting the game. It's basically an extra reward for players trying to speedrun (beat the game as fast as possible). However, perhaps there's an old man sick with a horrible disease. A sidequest could be to go get the cure. If you keep advancing in the game while disregarding that sidequest, the old man may perish.

During the course of this chapter, we'll be making a sidequest from both of the preceding categories. However, let's take a moment for an important intermission.

End of the Line for Lite

For those of you following along with the Lite version, I have gone as far as I can go. Up to now, I have been using RMVXA Lite to work on the game and will now transfer the project to the full version. So, if you have both versions of RPG Maker VX Ace (RMVXA) installed on your computer, you may think it is as easy as just going into the full version of Ace and opening your Lite project. (See Figure 8-1).

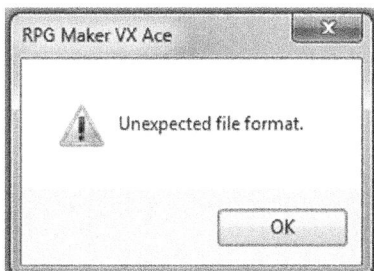

Figure 8-1. *The Unexpected file format error that appears if you try to open a Lite project with the full version of RMVXA*

As Figure 8-1 shows, you would be wrong. But, don't fret, as the solution to this problem is relatively painless.

- Create a new project in the full version of RMVXA (name it whatever you like).

- Take the `Game.rvproj2` file from your new project and copy it into the folder containing your Lite project.

- Overwrite the Lite project's game file with the full project's game file.

▪ **Note** If you're using default directory paths for your projects, both your Lite game and your new project should be contained within `My Documents/RPGVXAce`, if you're using Windows 7.

After that is done, you can now use the full version of RMVXA to edit what was your Lite project! However, it's important to point out that you will still only have the Lite resources (music, sounds, etc.) available to use. If you want to copy over the full RMVXA set, you'll want to do the following:

1. Download (if you do not already have it available) RMVXA's Run-Time Package from `www.rpgmakerweb.com/download/additional/run-time-packages` (make sure that RPG Maker VX Ace is selected).

2. Once that is done, open the compressed archive and run `Setup.exe`. Follow the onscreen instructions and extract the RTP to the chosen folder. The default directory path in Windows 7 is `Program Files(x86)/Common Files/Enterbrain/RGSS3/RPGVXAce`.

3. Copy-paste the Audio and Graphic Folders from the RTP to your game project (located in `My Documents/RPGVXAce/<yourprojectname>`, if you did not use a custom path) and overwrite any applicable files in your project's Audio and Graphic folders.

Mission accomplished!

Let's Create a Permanent Sidequest!

We now return to our regularly scheduled programming. As promised, we're going to create a pair of sidequests for our game. The first one will be a permanent sidequest that can be done at any time, once it is unlocked. We'll make it so that the nonplayer character (NPC) appears after the player clears out of the first dungeon. As to where the NPC will be, there's only one place it could realistically be! Take a look at Figure 8-2 for a screenshot of the eastern part of our port town.

Figure 8-2. *The eastern part of the port town*

We're going to have a sidequest involving the well, because quests involving a well are a role-playing game (RPG) classic. For this exercise, we'll need the following things:

- An NPC that appears after the player has defeated Gemini at the first dungeon. It (in my case, the NPC is a little girl) will mention strange sounds coming from within the well. Noah will ask Eric if they should investigate, which prompts a yes/no choice. If the player says no, Eric will say that "It is too dangerous" and end the event. If the player says yes, the sidequest switch will be flipped.

- Page 2 of the quest NPC will be processed if the sidequest start switch is on and causes the NPC to warn the player to be careful. If the player has completed the sidequest, page 3 of the NPC's event will be triggered. The player will be able to talk to the NPC, who will ask what was inside of the well. Upon receiving an answer, the NPC will leave the area (via the use of a Fadeout screen and flipping self-switch A; we then require self-switch A to be flipped on for the fourth and last blank page).

- A Same As Characters/Action Button blank graphic event placed on the well. The first page will have no conditional and will display "You see Seaside's well." The second page will require that the sidequest switch be flipped on and will display the message but then continue to a choice asking if the player wishes to enter the well.

- A map of the well area that the player will enter upon climbing in.

- Some enemies to populate the well's innards.

- A boss to fight at the end, along with a special drop.

Creating the Sidequest NPC

Let's go in order. First, let's create the sidequest giver. Here is the sidequest giver's event pages:

- Page 1: Switch `BossDefeated` must be on.

```
@>Comment: Page 1
@>Text: -, -, Normal, Bottom
:     : Hello mister. I've been hearing strange sounds
:     : coming from the well.
@>Text: -, -, Normal, Bottom
:     : Noah looks at Eric.
@>Text: 'Actor5', 6, Normal, Bottom
:     : Should we investigate?
@>Show Choices: Yes, No
: When [Yes]
   @>Text: 'Actor4', 0, Normal, Bottom
   :     : Let's do it!
   @>Text: 'Actor5', 6, Normal, Bottom
   :     : Indeed. Let us investigate.
   @>Control Switches: [0021:SQ1Start] = ON
   @>
: When [No]
   @>Text: 'Actor4', 0, Normal, Bottom
   :     : Sounds too dangerous.
   @>
: Branch End
@>
```

- Page 2: Switch `SQ1Start` must be on.

```
@>Comment: Page 2
@>Text: -, -, Normal, Bottom
:     : Be careful, mister!
```

- Page 3: Switch `SQ1Completed` (flipped when the sidequest boss has been defeated) must be on.

```
@>Comment: Page 3
@>Text: -, -, Normal, Bottom
:     : What was down there?
@>Text: 'Actor4', 0, Normal, Bottom
:     : Some monsters. They won't be making
:     : noise anymore.
@>Fadeout Screen
@>Wait: 60 frame(s)
@>Text: -, -, Normal, Bottom
:     : The girl runs off into the distance.
@>Control Self Switch: A =ON
@>Fadein Screen
@>
```

- Page 4: Self-switch A must be on. It is a blank page with no NPC graphic.

Creating the Well (Event)

Of course, this won't be much of a sidequest if the player can't interact with the well. So, have a well event.

- Page 1: Has no conditions. Blank graphic with Same As Characters priority.

```
@>Text: -, -, Normal, Bottom
:       : You see Seaside's well.
```

- Page 2: Requires SQ1Start to be on.

```
@>Text: -, -, Normal, Bottom
:       : You see Seaside's well. Do you wish to climb in?
@>Show Choices: Yes, No
: When [Yes]
    @>Transfer Player:[010:Inside the Well] (011,002), Down
    @>
: When [No]
    @>
: Branch End
@>
```

That's the extent of our sidequest eventing on top.

Creating the Area Below the Well

Now, let us make our way into the bowels of the earth and continue. Take a look at Figure 8-3 for a screenshot of the well map that I created. Keep in mind that the first half of the picture is the top of the area, while the second represents the lower half.

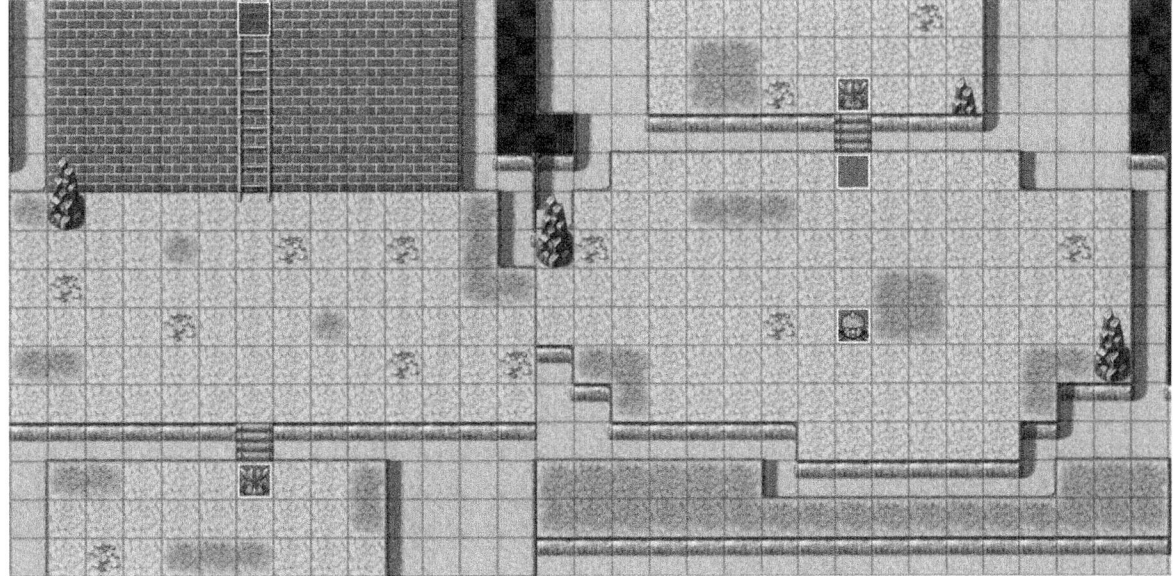

Figure 8-3. *The area below the town well*

The player appears two squares south of the transfer event that leads back to the surface. The area, instead of having random encounters, has three static encounters. The first two are against a single Sahagin, while the last is against an Ogre. Discerning eyes will notice that the Ogre event is displaying only a head. Some of RMVXA's largest stock monsters have 2×2-sized sprites contained in the $BigMonster1 and $BigMonster2 graphic sets. The Ogre is one of them. So, while it appears that way in the editor, here's how it looks in-game (Figure 8-4).

Figure 8-4. *An in-game picture of the Ogre sprite*

I placed an Autorun event one square below the second bridge, which will cause the player to fight the Ogre. For large enemies represented on the game map, I prefer to do it that way, as their sprites act weird if forced to move (with good reason: large enemies only have a forward-facing sprite). Thus, the Ogre itself is a two-page event with a page 1 that has a graphic and a page 2 that does not (page 2 requires that SQ1Completed be on). The trigger event, on the other hand, has a little more meat to it.

- Page 1: Has no conditionals. Has a Below Characters Priority and a Player Touch Trigger.

```
@>Text: 'Actor4', 0, Normal, Bottom
:      : What is THAT thing?
@>Text: -, -, Normal, Bottom
:      : Eric points to a nearby giant.
@>Text: 'Actor5', 6, Normal, Bottom
:      : That appears to be an Ogre.
@>Text: -, -, Normal, Bottom
:      : A rumbling sound makes itself heard.
@>Text: 'Actor5', 6, Normal, Bottom
:      : The Ogre appears to know we're here.
:      : Ready yourself, Eric!
@>Change Battle BGM: 'Battle2', 100, 100
@>Battle Processing: Ogre
@>
```

As is standard for boss fights, we change the Battle BGM to reflect the fact that the player is facing a particularly strong foe. This Ogre is a tweaked version. Its adjusted stats are shown in Figure 8-5. (I left its Attack Patterns and Features in their default settings).

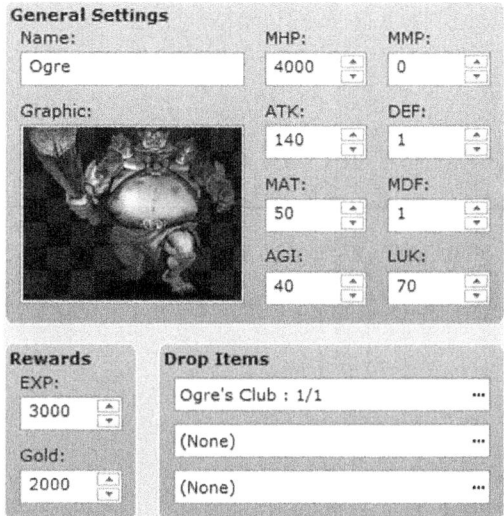

General Settings

Name:	MHP:	MMP:
Ogre	4000	0
Graphic:	ATK:	DEF:
	140	1
	MAT:	MDF:
	50	1
	AGI:	LUK:
	40	70

Rewards

EXP:
3000

Gold:
2000

Drop Items

Ogre's Club : 1/1 ...

(None) ...

(None) ...

Figure 8-5. *Tweaked stats for the Ogre enemy*

The Ogre's Club is a weapon that has identical ATK to the Crimson Axe in the default database but gives its user a 25% penalty to his/her HIT and -10 DEF. In exchange, it gives the user 20% CRI.

▪ **Tip**   As the player cannot escape from the Ogre battle, you can flip the SQ1Completed switch as soon as the battle begins. No need to make the Ogre Immortal, as we did with Gemini, unless you want to have the party (or the boss) talk at the end of the fight.

▪ **Note**   Make sure you change the Battle BGM back after the Ogre is defeated. Given the fact that the well has no random encounters, you could "cheat" and add a Change Battle BGM command to the map's transfer event. A conditional branch requiring SQ1Completed to be on should be enough to ensure you don't get boss music against the Sahagins.

Page 2 of the boss trigger event requires that SQ1Completed be toggled (alternatively, you could have the event flip a self-switch and then require said switch to be on instead), is Below Characters/Action Button, and has no event commands. If we don't have a page 2, the player will not be able to leave the area (as he/she would keep getting turned around and forced to fight another Ogre).

Last, but not least, we have the Sahagin encounters, which are standard-fare static battles, as described in Chapter 5. For the sake of completeness, here's the relevant eventing:

```
@>Text: -, -, Normal, Bottom
:     : The fishman makes a slurping noise and attacks!
@>Battle Processing: Sahagin
: If Win
  @>Control Self Switch: A =ON
  @>
```

```
: If Escape
   @>
: Branch End
@>
```

There you have it! The player now has an extra quest that he/she can go on that is not strictly tied in to the main plot.

Additional Exercises

Here are some exercises for you to flesh out this sidequest.

1. Suppose we did want to tie this to the main plot. After the Ogre has been defeated, have Eric and Noah talk about the possible relation between the Ogre's appearance and the sounds the villagers have been hearing ever since Gemini was defeated.

   - You can use an Autorun event that requires SQ1Completed to be on. Just make sure the event has a page 2 that does *not* Autorun.

   - For greater consistency, you could have a switch flip on when the player talks to a villager who mentions the strange nighttime sounds. Then, the party should only speak about the relation *if* they have heard about the happenings. Otherwise, you could just skip the chat altogether.

2. Change the Ogre encounter from its current state to one in which the player has to withstand the monster's assault for a few turns. At the end of the final turn, the **SQ1Completed** switch is flipped, and the Ogre leaves the battle of its own volition, with the Escape skill.

   - The easiest way to make sure that a certain level of damage output is kept up is to have a completely static attack pattern. That way, the boss fight doesn't have random elements, such as the enemy using its strongest attack four times in a row.

3. Have Seaside's shopkeepers give the player a permanent discount for defeating the Ogre.

   - This is as simple as having a conditional branch in each of the town's shops. If SQ1Completed is on, then you charge a lesser price for every item in the shop. (You'll have to specify the lower price of each item manually).

We have completed one of the sidequests we set out to make. Now, on to the second one!

Let's Create a Time-Sensitive Quest!

We have already made a quest that can be completed whenever the player chooses. However, time-sensitive quests are useful for giving the player a sense of the world moving on its own. So, let's make a second quest that is active from the start of the game *until* Gemini has been defeated. The quest will involve a man who wants five rat tails and is willing to give the player a monetary reward for getting them for him. We want this quest to have three possible outcomes.

1. **Quest forfeited.** Occurs if the player doesn't talk to the NPC at all until Gemini has been defeated. The man will reference the work of a third party to get him his rat tails and drop a hint that the player missed a possible quest.

2. **Quest failed.** Occurs if the player starts the quest but does not finish it before defeating Gemini. The man will chastise the player for not delivering on his/her word, while mentioning that another person came through for him.

3. **Quest successful.** The player accepted the quest and got the five rat tails, as requested, receiving a reward for his/her troubles.

This quest only needs some troop eventing and the quest-giving NPC event. First, let's place the quest-giver event. (See Figure 8-6.)

***Figure 8-6.** The location of our time-sensitive NPC*

The lower-left home on the northern part of town has a nice one-square gap that allows the NPC to be all hidden and shady.

Creating the Sidequest NPC

For once, I'm going to work backward with this NPC. Create a total of five event pages for our quest-giver's event. We are going to fill them out from 5 to 1. Why? Recall that I mentioned that we want to have three possible outcomes. Pages 3 through 5 will contain those outcomes. On page 5, we'll require that SQ2Completed be on and have the NPC say some words of thanks for the player's earlier help.

```
@>Text: -, -, Normal, Bottom
:       : Thank you for the help, lad!
@>
```

Page 4 will contain the quest failed message. This requires both BossDefeated and SQ2Start to be turned on. The player has taken too long to turn in the rat tails (or didn't even bother to do anything after accepting the quest). Here's what the NPC has to say about that.

```
@>Text: -, -, Normal, Bottom
:       : Oh, hello there...
@>Text: -, -, Normal, Bottom
:       : Guess you didn't want the gold so badly. I got an
```

```
:        : ambitious lass to do me the favor. Next time, don't
:        : say you'll do something and then not do it.
@>
```

Harsh, eh? Serves the player right for not bending to a NPC's will! Page 3 will require that `BossDefeated` is on (`SQ2Start` must be off). This will be the quest forfeited message. That is, the player didn't speak to the NPC at all before going on to defeat Gemini. The player didn't even know about the quest, so the NPC makes reference to it.

```
@>Text: -, -, Normal, Bottom
:        : Hello lad. I just recently procured some Rat Tails
:        : to make my special potion. Shame you didn't talk
:        : to me earlier. I paid a lass 500 Gold for her
:        : efforts.
@>
```

That leaves only the first two pages. Page 1 will have no conditionals and consist of the NPC attempting to task the player with the quest that he/she can accept or refuse.

```
@>Text: -, -, Normal, Bottom
:        : Hello there, lad. Could I interest you in a business
:        : proposition?
@>Show Choices: Yes, No
: When [Yes]
   @>Text: -, -, Normal, Bottom
   :        : Awesome! I need 5 Rat Tails. I'm not particularly
   :        : picky about the rats you get them from.
   @>Text: 'Actor4', 0, Normal, Bottom
   :        : What do you need them for?
   @>Text: -, -, Normal, Bottom
   :        : It's for a special brew I make this time every year.
   :        : You needn't concern yourself with the details.
   @>Text: -, -, Normal, Bottom
   :        : Come talk to me again when you have all five.
   @>Control Switches: [0022:SQ2Start] = ON
   @>
: When [No]
   @>Text: -, -, Normal, Bottom
   :        : A shame, that. I'll be here waiting if you change
   :        : your mind. I can only wait so long, though, so don't
   :        : tarry overmuch.
   @>
: Branch End
@>
```

Accepting the quest will flip `SQ2Start`, allowing page 2 to be processed, so long as the player has not defeated Gemini or actually completed the quest already. Here's page 2:

```
@>Conditional Branch: Variable [0008:RatTails] < 5
   @>Text: -, -, Normal, Bottom
   :        : Do you have my Rat Tails, lad?
   @>Text: 'Actor4', 0, Normal, Bottom
   :        : I'm working on it.
```

```
    @>Text:-, -, Normal, Bottom
    :      : Ah. Fair enough. Do deliver them as soon as you can.
    @>
: Branch End
@>Conditional Branch: Variable [0008:RatTails] >= 5
    @>Text: -, -, Normal, Bottom
    :      : Do you have my Rat Tails, lad?
    @>Text: 'Actor4', 0, Normal, Bottom
    :      : Here they are.
    @>Text: -, -, Normal, Bottom
    :      : The man counts them.
    @>Wait: 60 frame(s)
    @>Text: -, -, Normal, Bottom
    :      : ...and 5. That'll do it, lad. Much obliged.
    @>Change Gold: + 500
    @>Text: -, -, Normal, Bottom
    :      : Got 500 Gold!
    @>Text: -, -, Normal, Bottom
    :      : This should tide me over for the rest of the year.
    @>Text: 'Actor4', 0, Normal, Bottom
    :      : Glad I could help!
    @>Control Switches: [0023:SQ2Complete] = ON
    @>
: Branch End
@>
```

Page 2 has a pair of conditional branches that trigger, depending on whether the player has five rat tails or not. If he/she doesn't, the NPC will ask if the player has his/her rat tails, and the player will say that he/she is working on it. If the player does have five rat tails, the man will count them and give the player 500 Gold. Last, SQ2Complete will be flipped.

Of Rats and Their Tails

Now, you may be wondering how to make the rats drop their tails on defeat. That's as simple as some troop eventing. Make your way to the Troops tab at the Database and find the Rat*3 (or Rate*3, if you've left the typo as is) troop. As with the arena currency in the last chapter, you can have the rat tails be an actual item or a variable that is increased. In the case of the former, I would have the rat tail be an item that can be sold for a little gold, and then make it so that a rat will drop one at a 1/1 or 1/2 chance. I've always found it silly in RPGs when a monster doesn't drop a relevant body part when you can see it on their graphic! With that said, let's use the variable approach for our ratty friends. Given that we want a rat to drop its tail on death, recall that death in RMVXA is prioritized over every other possible event. If we don't use the Immortal approach, the third rat to fall in a fight will never drop its tail. Of course, if we're using a variable to keep track of their tails, we only want Immortal to be added to the enemies while we're doing the quest. Here's page 1 of the Rat*3 troop:

- Condition: Turn No. 0

- Span: Battle

```
    @>Conditional Branch: Switch [0022:SQ2Start] == ON
        @>Conditional Branch: Switch [0023:SQ2Complete] == OFF
            @>Change Enemy State: Entire Troop, + [Immortal]
            @>
        : Branch End
        @>
    : Branch End
```

Turn 0 is the very start of a battle, before anyone has acted. We only want the event to trigger once per battle, and we only want it to trigger at all if the player has accepted the subquest and not yet completed it. In addition to what is displayed in the preceding code, you could add another conditional branch to that nest that requires BossDefeated to be off as well (remember that the player fails the quest if he or she defeats Gemini before turning in the rat tails). Following, I'll give the code for page 2, which is essentially identical to that for pages 3 and 4. The only difference is the rat that is considered for the condition and the loss of its Immortal state. You'll want to tweak the subsequent pages as relevant to ensure that all three rats have their own event page, such as the one following:

- Condition: Enemy [1. Rat]'s HP 0% or below

- Span: Battle

```
@>Conditional Branch: Switch [0022:SQ2Start] == ON
   @>Conditional Branch: Variable [0008:RatTails] < 5
      @>Control Variables: [0008:RatTails] += 1
      @>Text: -, -, Normal, Bottom
      :      : You got a Rat's Tail!
      @>
    : Branch End
   @>
 : Branch End
@>Change Enemy State: [1. Rat], - [Immortal]
```

When the first rat's HP drops to 0% or below, we check to see if the player is currently on this subquest. If he/she is, we check to see if he/she has five rat tails already. If he/she doesn't, we add one to the value of the RatTails variable and inform the player that he/she received a rat tail. At the very bottom of the battle event, we remove the rat's immortality.

■ **Note**   It doesn't matter much either way, but if you want a little more efficiency, you can have a conditional branch that checks first to see if that rat has the Immortal state, rather than attempting to remove a state it might not even have.

■ **Caution**   To be clear, page 3 should involve [2. Rat] and page 4 should involve [3. Rat]. Make sure you're removing Immortal from the right rat!

There you have it! And it only took us four pages to create this quest as well.

Additional Exercises

Here are some extra exercises with which to flex your mental muscles.

1.   Have an Autorun event on the world map that triggers when the player has five rat tails and forces them to fight a stronger rat (a sort of Rat King, if you will).

- As with every Autorun, make sure you have some way of escaping the page, or your game will loop it endlessly. Flipping a self-switch is as good a solution as any.

- I would make it so that the player cannot escape that fight.

2. Allow the NPC to sell his special brew to the player.

- It could be a special potion that both restores HP and removes some negative status effects. The man could sell the potion to the player via Shop Processing.

- Alternately, it could be a one-time gift that boosts the stats of the character who drinks it.

Other Sidequest Ideas

As promised, we have come up with one sidequest that the player can go on at any time, once it is active, and another that has to be completed before a certain point in the game. Here are some other cool ideas that you can add to your own game.

1. A chest that works like *Final Fantasy* 9's Excalibur.

- Steps Taken or Play Time both work equally well for this. You could have a conditional branch for the treasure chest that requires Steps Taken or Play Time to be below a certain value. If the branch is true, then the chest will open; otherwise, a cryptic message will tell the player that the chest is sealed until the end of time.

2. A multistaged time-sensitive quest.

- The *Tales* series of RPGs (developed by Namco Bandai) are notorious for this. You have a quest that has five stages, but you have to finish the first stage before you beat the first boss, the second stage before you set sail to a new continent. On the new continent, you can start stage 3. Stage 4 requires that you not have uncovered the artifact of doom, while the last stage is permanently unlocked once you're on your way to the final dungeon.

- I'm not a huge fan of such types of quests, but they're not much harder to event than a regular time-sensitive quest. You just have to have each subsequent stage of the multi-quest check for the completion of the previous stage. If the player ever skips/misses a stage, he/she cannot reach the quest's conclusion.

3. A permanent sidequest that allows progression throughout the entire game.

- For this particular idea, I'm thinking about *Dragon Quest*'s Tiny Medals and *Grinsia*'s Old Glass Bottles. An NPC with a particular obsession wants you to collect all of the items of a certain type in the world. Each time you reach a milestone of items collected, it will give you a special item as a reward. It's something neat to do and look out for while traveling the world, and you can turn in the last collectible right before you end the game (or otherwise reach a point of no return).

In Chapter 10, I will be touching on a cool idea that could qualify as #3. But, given the eventing involved and what you can do with it, I think it deserves a whole chapter's worth of material. The next chapter will be dedicated to the functionality that will make it possible.

Summary

In this chapter, I covered the concept of sidequests in RPGs, and we added a permanent sidequest to our game that could be done at any time, as well as a time-sensitive quest that must be completed before the player defeats Gemini. In the next chapter, we will be discussing common events.

CHAPTER 9

■ ■ ■

All About Common Events

This chapter is going to cover common events. You have probably seen the relevant tab within the RPG Maker VX Ace (RMVXA) Database already and are probably wondering what it's about. Well, here's the summary:

- A common event can be called using the *Call Common Event* command from any other event.

- It is useful for eventing things that you will repeat many times over during the course of your game. You can probably already think of two or three occasions on which this is true in the game we've been making throughout this book.

- A common event can have an Autorun or Parallel Process trigger, contingent on a certain conditional switch being on, as defined in the Common Events tab.

- Common events have a limit of one page—no more, no less.

- Common events are the only way to trigger events on item and skill use.

The final point is most important to what we want to do in the next chapter. Of course, this is as good a time as any to show off the Common Events tab itself. (See Figure 9-1.)

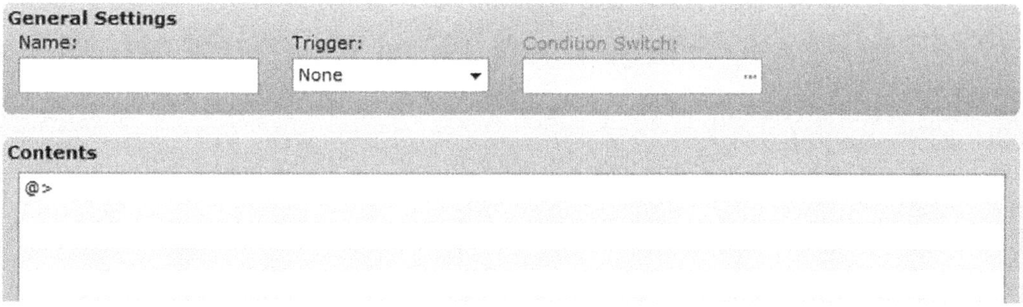

General Settings

Name:

Trigger: None

Condition Switch:

Contents

@>

Figure 9-1. The Common Events tab of the RMVXA Database

Not much to it, literally. That should not come as a surprise, given that common events are just another type of event. A common event can have a trigger of None (in which case, it will always trigger when called), Autorun, or Parallel Process. In the latter two cases, the conditional switch has to be on for the common event to trigger. We could have a two-line common event that contains the two Control Variable commands we use for our Parallel Process transfer events. There's a particularly neat item concept I learned how to event some time ago that I'm going to share in this chapter. Do you want to *Escape* from a dungeon automatically?

The Exit Item/Skill

Envision this scenario: The player has gotten through a particularly long dungeon and defeated the boss at the end. His/Her resources were sorely diminished, and he/she needs to get back to town. Most role-playing games (RPGs) include a skill that automatically returns the player to the entrance to the dungeon, thereby bypassing the trip back.

To create an item or skill that will allow the player to exit a dungeon automatically, we'll need the following:

- A common event that checks to see which dungeon the player is currently in. If the player is not inside a dungeon, the event will return an error message. (You can also make it so that you can't escape from certain dungeons.)

- We have to update the world map's transfer event, so that it writes the dungeon location to a variable.

- We have to update our dungeons' relevant transfer events, so that, in the case of the player exiting to the world map manually, the dungeon location variable is set to its default value.

- Last, we must actually create the item or skill that will hold this event.

Updating Our Transfer Events

First of all, we currently have two dungeons. (Given that the subquest well is right in town, let's not count it for the sake of this exercise.) The dungeon where the player finds Gemini will be 1, and the tower will be 2. I'm going to call the variable in question DungeonLocation, for the sake of clarity. In the world map's transfer events, you'll want to find the two that lead to our dungeons and insert the appropriate Control Variable command, like so:

```
@>Conditional Branch: Variable [0002:X] == 28
  @>Conditional Branch: Variable [0003:Y] == 82
    @>Control Variables: [0011:DungeonLocation] = 1
    @>Transfer Player:[005:Goblin CaveF1F] (020,043), Up
    @>
  : Branch End
  @>
: Branch End
@>Conditional Branch: Variable [0002:X] == 13
  @>Conditional Branch: Variable [0003:Y] == 76
    @>Control Variables: [0011:DungeonLocation] = 2
    @>Transfer Player:[007:Tower of the VoidF1F] (025,049), Up
    @>
  : Branch End
  @>
```

Then, in both of the dungeons, we find the transfer event that leads the player to the world map and have DungeonLocation set itself to 0 in those.

Creating the Exit Scroll

Next, let's create the item that will call the common event we want to make. Take a look at Figure 9-2 for details.

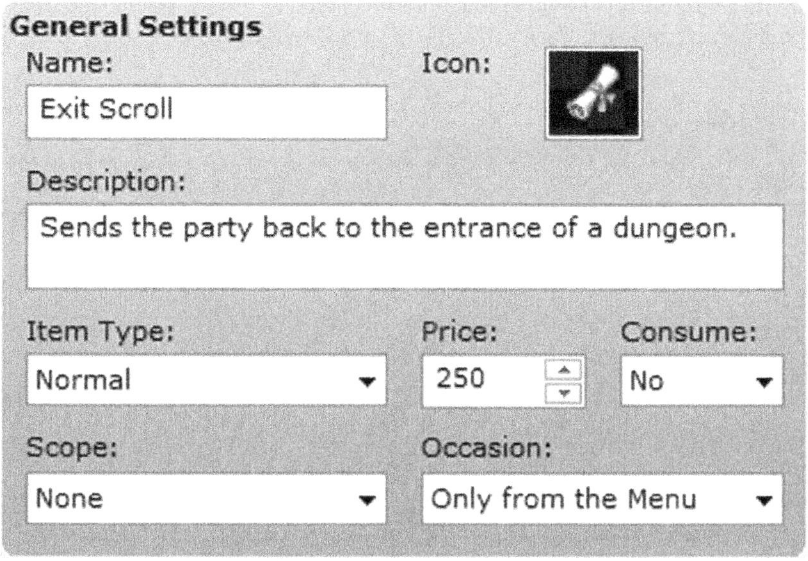

General Settings
Name: Exit Scroll
Icon:
Description: Sends the party back to the entrance of a dungeon.
Item Type: Normal   Price: 250   Consume: No
Scope: None   Occasion: Only from the Menu

Figure 9-2. The Exit Scroll's general settings

The Exit Scroll is occupying slot 17 in the Database (hurray for lifting those Lite version restrictions). We have it set so that it can only be used from the menu and is not consumed when used. Why? It's easier to handle item consumption within the event itself. Instead of just having the item consume itself, it will prompt a choice when used. It asks the player if he/she wants to leave the dungeon. If the player says no, then the item is left intact. On the other hand, when the player says yes, the event determines what dungeon the player is currently in and transfers the player to its entrance, consuming one Exit Scroll in the process.

Creating the Exit Event Logic with Common Events

I use two common events for the exit event logic. Here's the first common event:

- Name: ExitEvent

- Trigger: None

```
@>Text: -, -, Normal, Bottom
:      : Would you like to leave the dungeon?
@>Show Choices: Yes, No
: When [Yes]
   @>Call Common Event: [ExitEventBranches]
   @>
: When [No]
   @>
: Branch End
```

It's nice and simple. We ask the player if he/she would like to leave the dungeon. If the player says no, we exit out of the event. If the player says yes, we call the second common event. I do it this way to reduce the clutter within one event. You could have a chain of common events, each calling the next one. The rest of the current common event is executed as applicable. For example, if you were to add a Control Variables command directly below the common event call, it would be processed before switching events. If you're using Autorun or Parallel Process events, you have to be particularly careful of chaining common events in that way, as it could get messy really fast. Here's the second common event called by the first:

```
@>Conditional Branch: Variable [0011:DungeonLocation] == 0
   @>Text: -, -, Normal, Bottom
   :       : You cannot use that here!
   @>
 : Branch End
@>Conditional Branch: Variable [0011:DungeonLocation] == 1
   @>Change Items: [Exit Scroll], -1
   @>Control Variables: [0011:DungeonLocation] = 0
   @>Transfer Player:[003:Field 3] (027,082), Left
   @>
  : Branch End
@>Conditional Branch: Variable [0011:DungeonLocation] == 2
   @>Change Items: [Exit Scroll], -1
   @>Control Variables: [0011:DungeonLocation] = 0
   @>Transfer Player:[003:Field 3] (013,077), Down
   @>
  : Branch End
@>
```

DungeonLocation is equal to 0 at any time that the player is not within an applicable dungeon. If that is the case, then the player will get an error message, and the event will end without consuming an item. When DungeonLocation has a value, the player is transferred to the entrance of the dungeon equal to that value, but not before consuming an Exit Scroll and setting DungeonLocation to 0. What if we wanted an item to allow the player to return to the last visited town? We could have another variable to store the value of the last town visited by the player and then transport him/her directly inside when the item is used. You could even combine the DungeonLocation and TownLocation variables to make it so that you can only teleport to town if you are not inside a dungeon. That pretty much covers the use of common events, but this wouldn't be much of a chapter if I ended it this quickly, right? Instead, I'm going to write up some other ideas that I've created over time that involve the use of common events. But first, have a skill version of Exit (Figure 9-3).

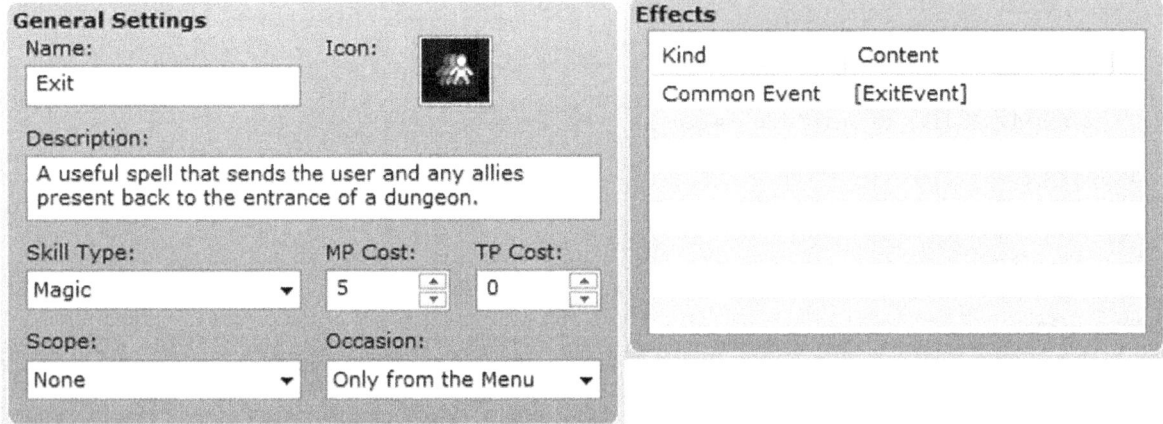

Figure 9-3. *The Exit skill uses the same common event as the Exit item*

Creating an Enemy with a Shifting Anti-element Barrier

Some of the most classic RPG battles involve a boss that has the ability to become immune to a certain element. That is as easy as creating a skill that grants an appropriate state. However, what happens if we want a *shifting* barrier? That's where common eventing comes in. Here's what we'll need:

- *Creating the skill*: It will have no other effects besides executing a common event.

- *A monster to use the skill*: We'll want it to begin battle with an anti-element barrier already, as the shifting skill *changes* the barrier that the user already has.

- *Three states that represent the elemental barriers*: Taking a look at Noah, we see that he has relatively easy access to Earth, Thunder, and Water magic, so let's have states for a barrier for each of those types.

- *The common event to govern the skill itself*

- *A small troop event for the monster that will use the barrier change skill*

I have future plans for the monster we're creating. (They'll be added as an encounter in Chapter 10.) For now, let's complete this exercise. Check Figure 9-4, to see our Barrier Change skill.

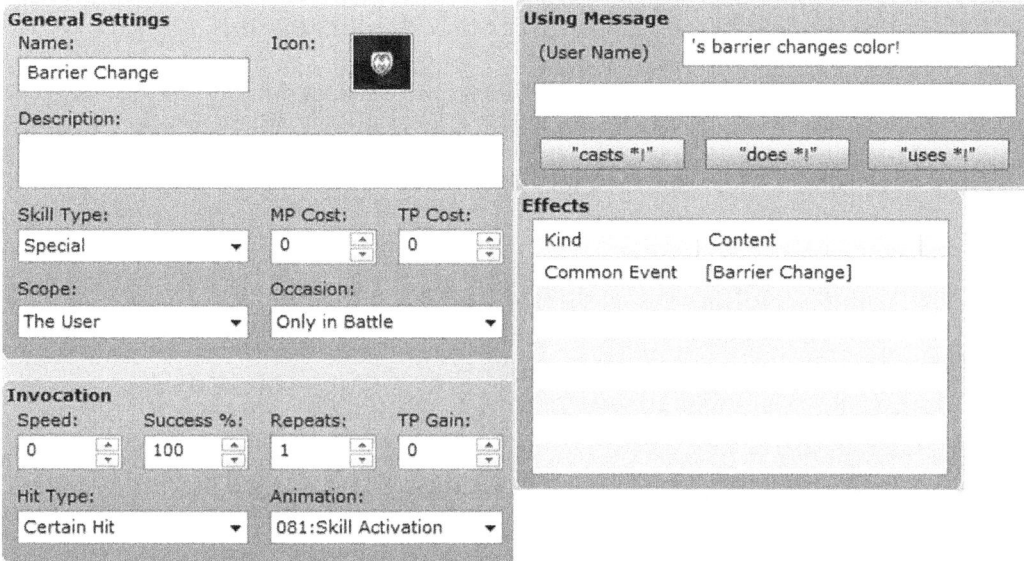

Figure 9-4. *The Barrier Change skill details*

Besides a simple message being displayed when someone uses the skill and calling the Barrier Change common event, the skill does nothing else. Check Figure 9-5 to see the monster that will use the Barrier Change skill.

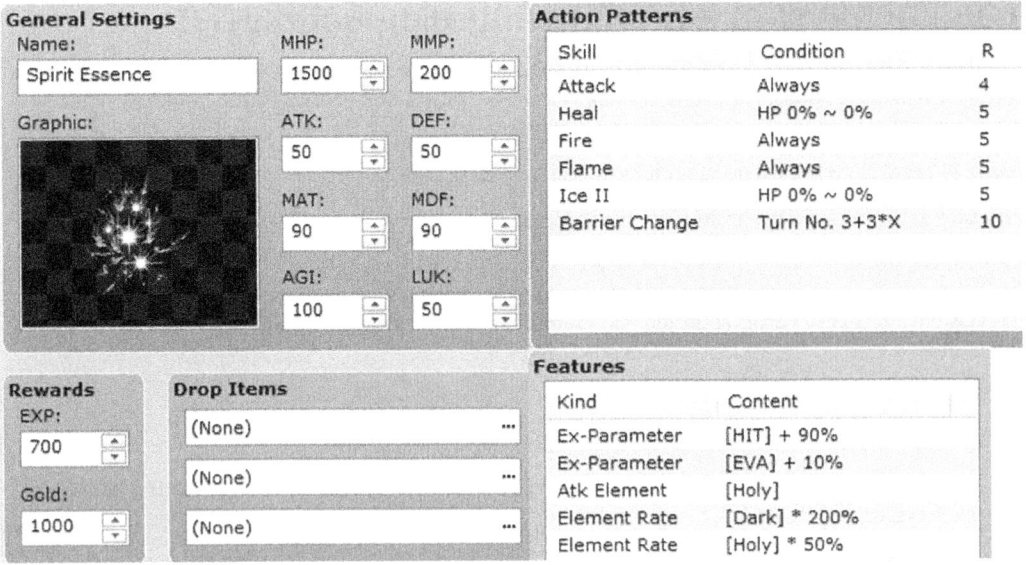

Figure 9-5. *The Spirit Essence, a new enemy that will use our associated new Barrier Change skill*

As you can see, we have it so that the Spirit Essence will use Barrier Change starting on turn 3 and will recast it every third turn after that. Heal is used when the monster is at 40% HP or less, and Ice II will be used when it is at 50% HP or lower. Next, let's create the appropriate states for our Barrier Change skill. I'll show off the first one and leave the other two to you. Take a look at Figure 9-6, to see the first state.

General Settings

Name: Anti-Earth Barrier

Icon:

Restriction: None

Priority: 50

Removal Conditions

☑ Remove at Battle End ☐ Remove by Restriction

Auto-removal Timing: Turn End

Duration in Turns: 5 ~ 1

Features

Kind	Content
Element Rate	[Earth] * 0%

Message when an actor fell in the state

(Target Name) put up a barrier!

Message when an enemy fell in the state

(Target Name) put up a barrier!

Message when the state remains

(Target Name)

Message when the state removes

(Target Name) 's barrier has changed!

Figure 9-6. *Anti-Earth Barrier, one of three states affected by Barrier Change*

The Anti-Earth barrier is automatically removed at the end of a battle but will also auto-remove itself if five turns have passed. As per its name, someone affected by this state will sustain no damage from Earth-based attacks. You can copy this state to do the same for Anti-Thunder and Anti-Water. The common event isn't much more of a hassle, to be honest. We want the skill, when used, to change the monster's active barrier, as previously noted. The relevant listing follows. You'll quickly notice the Jump to Label command used to great effect. A cursory look at the common event will show that Anti-Water Barrier would be up pretty much permanently, if we did not have those label jumps, as the conditions for each branch are met in the branch preceding it. The blank 1 in Change Enemy State represents the first enemy placed in a particular troop. For ease of use, we'll have our Spirit Essence be an army of one.

```
@>Conditional Branch: [1. ] is [Anti-Earth Barrier] Inflicted
    @>Change Enemy State: [1. ], - [Anti-Earth Barrier]
    @>Change Enemy State: [1. ], + [Anti-Thunder Barrier]
    @>Jump to Label: Done
    @>
: Branch End
@>Conditional Branch: [1. ] is [Anti-Thunder Barrier] Inflicted
    @>Change Enemy State: [1. ], - [Anti-Thunder Barrier]
    @>Change Enemy State: [1. ], + [Anti-Water Barrier]
    @>Jump to Label: Done
    @>
: Branch End
@>Conditional Branch: [1. ] is [Anti-Water Barrier] Inflicted
    @>Change Enemy State: [1. ], - [Anti-Water Barrier]
    @>Change Enemy State: [1. ], + [Anti-Earth Barrier]
    @>Jump to Label: Done
    @>
: Branch End
@>Label: Done
```

Last, let's create a troop containing a single Spirit Essence and then add the following troop event:

```
Condition: Turn No. 0
Span: Battle
@>Change Enemy State: [1. Spirit Essence], + [Anti-Water Barrier]
@>Force Action: [1. Spirit Essence], [Barrier Change], Random
@>
```

We want the initial barrier to be Anti-Earth. However, if we apply the state without using the Barrier Change skill, we won't get the skill use message. So, we intentionally start one step away at Anti-Water and then force the Spirit Essence to use Barrier Change as the battle starts, setting it on the correct state. You can Battle Test this new troop with a Noah at level 15 or so (so that he has access to the elements that the Spirit Essence can block) and then use the elemental spells, to make sure that the monster is shifting barriers correctly. It's time for something a little more complicated.

Sneaky Like Ninjas: Creating the Smoke Bomb

I once had occasion to want to create an item that allows the player to escape combat without fail. My initial attempts were functional but overly complex. After getting quite a bit of help, I learned of a solution that requires only a tiny bit of scripting. Suffice it to say that using the Escape effect available for items and skills is actually a bad idea. See, that will allow the player to flee *any* battle. Fighting the final boss? I'd rather not. Let's just Smoke Bomb out of there like ninjas. As you can already see, that's a terrible idea. We want the player to be able to use the Smoke Bomb at any time he/she would be able to select the normal Escape command in the battle menu. As already noted, if you give an item the special

Escape effect (you'll want to give the item itself a scope of User), the player will be able to retreat from any battle. To counter that, we need a way to make sure that the player is allowed to escape the battle. Make your way to the Script Editor and take a look at the BattleManager module. Near the top of the page, you'll see a particular variable named @can_escape. That variable shows up within the can_escape? method in BattleManager and determines whether or not the player can escape from a particular battle. By default, the player can escape from every randomly generated battle and all event-created (Battle Processing) battles that have the Can Escape check box toggled. Conversely, escape from an event battle with Can Escape untoggled is impossible. Now, let's create the common event that will handle the Smoke Bomb logic. Of particular note is the fact that you can use script code within conditional branches to the same effect as the more standard uses I have covered up to now. To call a method using a script, you use the format Module.method. That's why we have BattleManager.can_escape? in the following code.

```
@>Conditional Branch: Script: BattleManager.can_escape? == true
   @>Comment: Escape = TRUE
   @>Change Items: [Smoke Bomb], -1
   @>Text: -, -, Normal, Bottom
   :       : You distract the enemy with the Smoke Bomb and
   :       : escape!
   @>Abort Battle
   @>
: Else
   @>Comment: Escape = FALSE
   @>Text: -, -, Normal, Bottom
   :       : You can't escape from this fight!
   @>
: Branch End
@>
```

When the player uses a Smoke Bomb, we check to see if he/she can escape the fight in question. If the @can_escape variable returns true, the player can escape. In that case, we consume one Smoke Bomb, display a message, and abort the battle. If the player cannot, he/she will receive an error message saying as much, and the item will not be consumed. I'll leave the creation of the item up to you. Now, there are two more things to discuss before the end of this chapter. Thing the first . . .

Making Specific Random Battles Inescapable

We have created an item that can be used to escape from a battle with no fail rate, so long as the player is allowed to escape it normally. Now, that brings up an interesting question: What happens if we want to make certain random battles inescapable? It's as easy as creating a new method within the BattleManager module.

```
module BattleManager
  def self.set_can_escape(bool)
    @can_escape = bool
  end
end
```

> ■ **Note** As you'll find out later in the book when I delve ever deeper into scripting, I'm not the biggest fan of adding things to preexistent RMVXA code. It is preferable to create a new script page (by right-clicking under the Materials section of the Script Editor and clicking Insert) and write up your new code on it. The preceding code assumes that you'll be using a new script page.

The preceding method is a simple one-liner. The `bool` inside the parentheses is a method parameter (recall our use of these back in Chapter 3 with the custom damage formulas). Because `@can_escape` is meant to be either true or false (an assertion that you can verify by seeing how it is used within `BattleManager`), those are the values you should use for the method parameter. How do you use that new method? The easiest way is to have a troop event that triggers on Turn 0 and uses a script call for the new method. So, if you want to make it so that the player cannot escape from Slimes (for whatever reason), all you have to do is structure the troop event as follows:

```
Condition: Turn 0
Span: Battle
@>Script: BattleManager.set_can_escape(false)
```

Once the battle begins, you'll notice that it is impossible to escape, whether via the Escape command or the use of Smoke Bombs. In this way, it is possible to make troops that prevent the player from escaping when encountered.

Additional Exercises

Before we end this chapter, I'll leave some more exercises for you to tackle concerning common events.

1. **Create a note that someone would write before embarking on a long journey. Leave it on a table for the player to find and add to his/her inventory.**

   - You can have the note display its text when the player grabs it. Then, you make it a key item that cannot be consumed and have the common event, if the player ever wants to read its text again.

2. **Make a troop with three enemies, in which one enemy gives a random anti-elemental barrier to its allies.**

   - You can cover random with a variable similar to the seed we used for the treasure chest minigame. Just have the variable roll from 1 to 3.

   - Create one skill for each type of anti-elemental barrier.

   - The common event would have conditional branches for the three possible results. When the enemy with the skill uses it, the common event will trigger. The type of barrier will depend on the value of the variable and will be applied by means of Force Action. (Make sure you're applying Force Action to the skill user; it will be best if you only have one enemy that can use this skill.) Following is some sample code:

```
@>Control Variables: [0018:BarrierUp] = Random No. (1...3)
@>Conditional Branch: Variable [0018:BarrierUp] == 1
  @>Force Action: [1. ], [Anti-Earth Barrier], Last Target
  @>
: Branch End
@>Conditional Branch: Variable [0018:BarrierUp] == 2
  @>Force Action: [1. ], [Anti-Thunder Barrier], Last Target
```

```
    @>
: Branch End
@>Conditional Branch: Variable [0018:BarrierUp] == 3
    @>Force Action: [1. ], [Anti-Water Barrier], Last Target
    @>
: Branch End
@>
```

Summary

In this chapter, I covered common events and several applications related to them. Among these applications are creating a Smoke Bomb item that allows guaranteed escape from non-forced encounters and a shifting barrier skill. In the next chapter, I will cover all sorts of hidden things, such as treasures and passages.

■ ■ ■

## CHAPTER 10

Treasure Hunting and Other Hidden Things

Who doesn't like finding hidden things and ancient treasure? This chapter will be all about finding hidden treasure with the help of special items provided by nonplayer characters (NPCs) or found in different locations. We'll apply what you have learned in the previous chapter to come up with all sorts of relevant things for the aspiring explorer and treasure hunter. First of all, we have to create a new establishment in Seaside. A treasure hunter is coming to town! You can see the treasure hunter's shop in Figure 10-1.

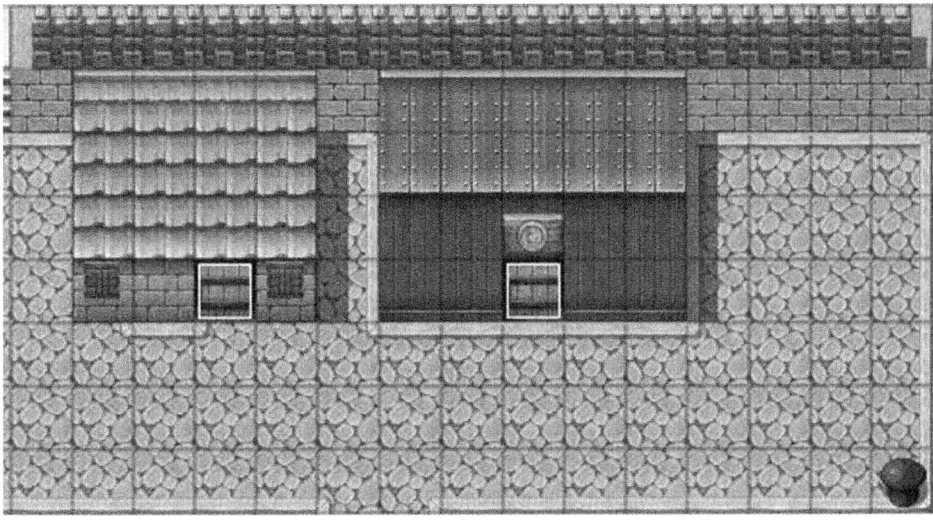

Figure 10-1.   *The treasure hunter's shop is the building on the right*

I reworked the last building on the lower end of the port town to reflect its special status. The interior map is a tweaked premade Item Shop. We want the door to remain locked until Gemini has been defeated. Inside, behind the counter, we have the treasure hunter, who urges the player to pick up the sack at the nearby table when spoken to. The sack will contain this chapter's first item: The Compass.

The Compass

This item will be used to determine the player's current location, as well as enable the player to find hidden treasure chests in dungeons. The former can be accomplished with a three-line common event, while the latter will rely on the hidden chest events to require that the player possess the Compass (Item exists conditional). You can see the Compass item in Figure 10-2 and its associated common event immediately thereafter.

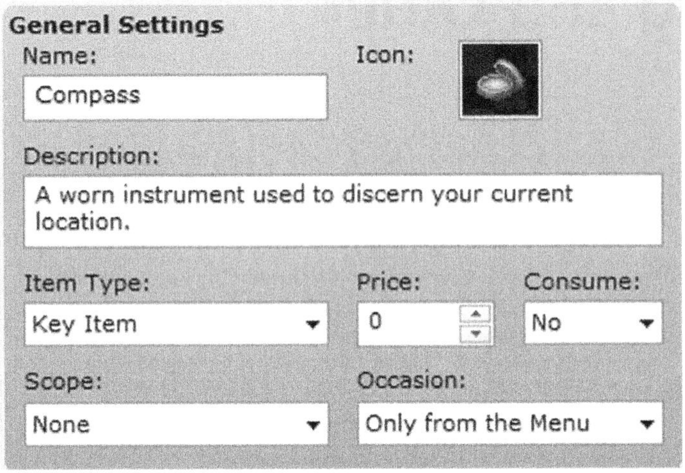

Figure 10-2. *The Compass Key Item to be used for treasure hunts*

- Name: Compass

- Trigger: None

```
@>Control Variables: [0002:X] = Player's Map X
@>Control Variables: [0003:Y] = Player's Map Y
@>Text: -, -, Normal, Bottom
:      : Your current position is \V[2], \V[3].
@>
```

When the player uses the Compass from the menu, the game will poll the player's current X and Y position and display it in a text box. How will the player know where those chests are? The simplest way, and the one I'll be covering, is to have treasure notes that give the exact location of hidden chests, which makes it so that the player only needs to use the Compass to find them. That, of course, leaves the question of how the player will find those treasure notes. We can have the treasure hunter sell them! Or, rather, we can have him sell most of them, and make it so that the player can find certain notes from other treasure chests. As already established in Chapter 7, eventing a shop with Show Choices is a pain, at best. Yet, we know that we want the treasure hunter to sell treasure notes that will lead the player to special loot. I have an alternate solution to our little quandary. We're going to use an event command we have not touched up to now: *Input Number*. First, let's come up with five hidden treasure locations. (See Figure 10-3).

Figure 10-3. *The locations for the hidden treasure we are going to add to our game*

The ones listed in Figure 10-3 will do. I have marked the precise treasure locations with Region #5. From top left to bottom right, they are as follows:

- (75,7) at the first dungeon's basement

- (85,25) at the first dungeon's basement

- (10,14) at Tower of the Void F1F

- (18,35) at Tower of the Void F4F. Southwestern pair of pillars

- (31,17) at Tower of the Void F5F

How to Change Whether a Map Displays Its Name

For the sake of this exercise, it's time to give our dungeons proper names, so I'll call the first dungeon the Dark Cave. The second dungeon will be the Dark Spire. Unoriginal, I know, but it serves our purposes. You can make it so that the game displays a location's name once and then no more (good for the first time a player reaches a new location). Displaying it is as easy as giving the location a name (by default, an RPG Maker VX Ace [RMVXA] game will display a location's name every time the player arrives at the area). I'll leave this as an exercise for you; however, if you decide to go through with this, you'll need switches for each location you would like to do this for. Additionally, you will have to have conditionals to make sure that the map name display is disabled on subsequent visits. Here's the example eventing for the first dungeon:

```
@>Conditional Branch: Variable [0002:X] == 28
  @>Conditional Branch: Variable [0003:Y] == 82
    @>Control Variables: [0011:DungeonLocation] = 1
    @>Conditional Branch: Switch [0024:Dungeon1Visit] == ON
      @>Change Map Name Display: $s
      @>
    : Branch End
```

```
    @>Conditional Branch: Switch [0024:Dungeon1Visit] == OFF
        @>Control Switches: [0024:Dungeon1Visit] = ON
        @>
      : Branch End
      @>Transfer Player:[005:Goblin CaveF1F] (020,043), Up
      @>
    : Branch End
    @>
: Branch End
```

I expanded the relevant transfer event to include the new content. If Dungeon1Visit is on, we disable the map name display. This event command is victim to the same text bug that HP/MP conditionals suffer from in RMVXA. Instead of actually seeing Enable or Disable, you see $s. Rest assured that it will work as intended, despite the textual hiccup. If Dungeon1Visit is off, we flip it on. This allows the dungeon's name to be displayed one time. You'll want to make sure you have an Enable Map Name Display command for any transfer events leading out of that dungeon. Personally, I feel this is more of a hassle than it is worth and would rather either leave the map name blank or just let it display, no matter what. In any case, now you know, and learning is why you're here!

Creating Hidden Treasure Chests That Require the Compass to Be Found

So, back to the topic at hand. We want to make hidden treasure chests that require the player to have the Compass. Once the player does have the Compass, he/she can press the Action Button while standing directly over the spot in question and uncover hidden loot! I'll write out how the actual event should look like shortly, but I'll summarize it first.

- We can start from the Quick Treasure Chest Event template. From there, remove the chest graphic from page 1 of the event. We want to fade out the screen, give the player a message that he/she is digging, and then have the player take a step back. That last part is arguably the most important. If you don't move the player's character out of the chest's square, he or she will be stuck once the chest is dug up.

- Before we fade the screen back in, use Set Move Route to change the chest graphic from None to our desired sprite set. I chose the wooden chest graphic located below the default red chest set.

- We fade in the screen and announce that the player has found a hidden chest. The rest of the event plays out normally.

With that said and done, here's the promised code:

```
@>Fadeout Screen
@>Text: -, -, Normal, Bottom
:      : You dig under your feet.
@>Set Move Route: Player (Wait)
:               : $>1 Step Backward
@>Set Move Route: This event (Wait)
:               : $>Graphic: '!Chest', 4
@>Wait: 30 frame(s)
@>Fadein Screen
@>Text: -, -, Normal, Bottom
:      : You found a hidden chest!
```

```
@>Play SE: 'Chest', 80, 100
@>Set Move Route: This event (Wait)
:                 : $>Direction Fix OFF
:                 : $>Turn Left
:                 : $>Wait: 3 frame(s)
:                 : $>Turn Right
:                 : $>Wait: 3 frame(s)
@>Control Self Switch: A =ON
@>Change Items: [Elixir], + 1
@>Text: -, -, Normal, Bottom
:      : Elixir was found!
```

You can copy-paste that same event for all of your hidden treasure needs.

The Treasure Hunter

Next, let's head back to Seaside and set up the treasure hunter NPC. We want him to do the following:

- Greet the player when talked to for the first time. He will tell him/her to check the sack on the nearby table.

- Once the player has grabbed the Compass, talking to the NPC again will prompt the character to talk about the shop that he has set up for aspiring treasure hunters. He will sell treasure notes.

- We run a common event to see which treasure notes the player already has. Then, if the player is still missing notes from the shop, the NPC will offer to sell treasure notes.

- If the player says yes, we call the common event for the treasure note shop.

Here's page 1 of the treasure hunter event:

```
@>Conditional Branch: [Compass] in Inventory
   @>Text: -, -, Normal, Bottom
   :      : Neat little instrument, that Compass. Follow it
   :      : and you'll never be lost again.
   @>Text: -, -, Normal, Bottom
   :      : Okay, fine. You still have to mind your
   :      : surroundings. But, it will help you find hidden
   :      : treasure. Isn't that exciting?
   @>Show Choices: Yes, No
   : When [Yes]
      @>Text: -, -, Normal, Bottom
      :      : I knew you'd say yes!
      @>Jump to Label: Continue
      @>
   : When [No]
      @>Text: -, -, Normal, Bottom
      :      : You only say that because you haven't done it before.
      @>Jump to Label: Continue
      @>
   : Branch End
```

```
   @>Label: Continue
   @>Text: -, -, Normal, Bottom
   :      : I'm running a Treasure Note shop. It will tell you
   :      : where to dig for treasure. Use that Compass to find
   :      : out your current location.
   @>Text: -, -, Normal, Bottom
   :      : Talk to me again if you want to buy Treasure Notes.
   @>Control Self Switch: A =ON
   @>
 : Else
   @>Text: -, -, Normal, Bottom
   :      : Hello there! I have never seen you before, traveler
   :      : Do you wish to embrace the path of the explorer?
   :      : Sure you do! Take a look at the sack over there.
   @>Control Switches: [0025:THunterTalk] = ON
   @>
 : Branch End
@>
```

As is usually the case for item-based conditionals, I leave "Set handling when conditions do not apply" on, so that I can use that Else. In this case, we want to see if the player has the Compass in his/her inventory. If the player does not, the text box at the very end of the event will be shown, along with a switch being flipped on that we'll use later for the sack that contains the Compass. If the player does have the key item, the treasure hunter will talk a little and give the player a false choice (as in, it doesn't matter what is answered). Then, he'll talk about his treasure note shop and urge the player to talk to him again, if he/she wants to buy treasure notes. We flip self-switch A, which allows page 2 of this NPC event to be processed. Page 2 contains a greeting for the player and immediately calls a common event. As there are a few things to process for the shop we wish to make, it's better to use common events to reduce clutter.

The Treasure Hunter's Treasure Note Shop

For the first common event, we start by checking if the player has any treasure notes sold by the NPC already. To do that, we create a new variable called TreasureNotesForSale and set it to 5 within the common event (as the NPC will have five notes for sale). Then, we create a conditional branch to check if the player has each of the treasure notes. For each note in the player's inventory, the value of TreasureNotesForSale is reduced by 1. If the player has all five treasure notes sold by the NPC, he will say as much via a message: "I don't have any treasure notes for sale!" Otherwise, he will say that he has X treasure notes for sale, where X is equal to the value of TreasureNotesForSale. Then, he will ask the player if he/she wishes to buy a treasure note. If the player says yes, we call the second common event. If he/she says no, we end the conversation.

Here's the event code for the first common event:

- Name: Treasure Note Check

- Trigger: None

```
@>Control Variables: [0015:TreasureNotesForSale] = 5
@>Conditional Branch: [Treasure Note 1] in Inventory
   @>Control Variables: [0015:TreasureNotesForSale] -= 1
   @>
 : Branch End
```

```
@>Conditional Branch: [Treasure Note 2] in Inventory
   @>Control Variables: [0015:TreasureNotesForSale] -= 1
   @>
: Branch End
@>Conditional Branch: [Treasure Note 3] in Inventory
   @>Control Variables: [0015:TreasureNotesForSale] -= 1
   @>
: Branch End
@>Conditional Branch: [Treasure Note 4] in Inventory
   @>Control Variables: [0015:TreasureNotesForSale] -= 1
   @>
: Branch End
@>Conditional Branch: [Treasure Note 5] in Inventory
   @>Control Variables: [0015:TreasureNotesForSale] -= 1
   @>
: Branch End
@>Conditional Branch: Variable [0015:TreasureNotesForSale] == 0
   @>Text: -, -, Normal, Bottom
   :      : I don't have any Treasure Notes for sale!
   @>
: Else
   @>Text: -, -, Normal, Bottom
   :      : I have \V[15] Treasure Notes for sale. Would you
   :      : like to purchase one?
   @>Show Choices: Yes, No
   : When [Yes]
      @>Call Common Event: [Treasure Note Purchase]
      @>
   : When [No]
      @>Text: -, -, Normal, Bottom
      :      : Take care!
      @>
   : Branch End
   @>
: Branch End
@>
```

For the second event, we have the player input a number from 1 to 5. If the NPC has that particular treasure note in stock, he'll give his price and ask if the player wants it. If the player already has that treasure note, the NPC will say as much. Check the following code to see the framework for the second common event:

```
@>Text: -, -, Normal, Bottom
:      : \C[3]Please input the Treasure Note number you would
:      : like to purchase (1-5 are valid). Input 0 to cancel.
@>Input Number: [0014:TreasureNoteNumber], 1 digit(s)
@>Conditional Branch: Variable [0014:TreasureNoteNumber] == 0
   @>
: Branch End
```

```
@>Conditional Branch: Variable [0014: TreasureNoteNumber] == 1
   @>Conditional Branch: [Treasure Note 1] in Inventory
      @>Text: -, -, Normal, Bottom
      :     : You already own that Treasure Note!
      @>
   : Else
         @>Text: -, -, Normal, Bottom
         :     : That'll be 200 Gold, if you will.
      @>Show Choices: Yes, No
      : When [Yes]
         @>Conditional Branch: Gold is 200 or more
            @>Change Gold: - 200
            @>Change Items: [Treasure Note 1], +1
               @>Text: -, -, Normal, Bottom
               :     : Thank you for your custom!
            @>Play SE: 'Item1', 80, 100
            @>Text: -, -, Normal, Bottom
            :     : Received \C[2]Treasure Note 1\C[0]!
            @>
         : Else
            @>Text: -, -, Normal, Bottom
            :     : You don't have enough gold!
            @>
            : Branch End
            @>
      : When [No]
            @>
      : Branch End
   @>
   : Branch End
@>
: Branch End
@>Conditional Branch: Variable [0014:TreasureNoteNumber] == 2
   @>
: Branch End
@>Conditional Branch: Variable [0014:TreasureNoteNumber] == 3
   @>
: Branch End
@>Conditional Branch: Variable [0014:TreasureNoteNumber] == 4
   @>
: Branch End
@>Conditional Branch: Variable [0014:TreasureNoteNumber] == 5
   @>
: Branch End
@>Conditional Branch: Variable [0014:TreasureNoteNumber] > 5
   @>Text: -, -, Normal, Bottom
   :     : I don't have a Treasure Note of so high a number!
   @>
: Branch End
@>
```

I left the branches for treasure notes 2 through 5 empty, to save space, but they should also follow the structure laid out in treasure note 1.

■ **Note**   \C[n] is one of the various modifiers you can apply to text. It changes the color of text placed after the modifier when used. \C[0] is white. The colors I have used in the preceding event are two of my favorite available in RMVXA. (I've already used \C[2] quite a few times in this book).

Following is a list of the colors I've most used in RMVXA:

- \C[2] is orange. I like to use this for important/key items.

- \C[3] is green. I prefer to use this color when I'm writing messages that break the fourth wall, as it were. Because the initial message tells the player directly how to use the input box, it makes sense to differentiate it from what the NPC would say in-game.

- \C[18] is red. If you want to draw the player's attention to a particular word or phrase, you can't get much more emphatic than red.

- Incidentally, \C[32] and above are also white.

Giving the Player the Compass

That, of course, leaves us with creating the sack event that will give the player a Compass and actually add the treasure note items to the Database. As we need the Compass to actually access the shop in-game, let's make that event first.

```
@>Conditional Branch: Switch [0025:THunterTalk] == OFF
   @>Text: -, -, Normal, Bottom
   :      : Oh, does that sack on the table intrigue you?
   :      : It used to belong to an old treasure hunter, but
   :      : he retired recently. Why don't you take it?
   @>
: Branch End
@>Conditional Branch: Switch [0025:THunterTalk] == ON
  @>Text: -, -, Normal, Bottom
  :      : There you go. Take it!
  @>
: Branch End
@>Text: -, -, Normal, Bottom
:      : Will you take it?
@>Show Choices: Yes, No
: When [Yes]
  @>Text: -, -, Normal, Bottom
  :      : Take a look inside. It's not the sack that's
  :      : important!
  @>Text: -, -, Normal, Bottom
  :      : You open the sack.
  @>Play SE: 'Item1', 80, 100
  @>Text: -, -, Normal, Bottom
  :      : Eric finds a \C[2]Compass\C[0]!
```

```
    @>Change Items: [Compass], + 1
    @>
: When [No]
    @>
: Branch End
@>
```

We check to see if the player has talked to the treasure hunter before. If he/she has, the NPC will urge him/her to take the sack. If not, he will give a little backstory to the sack and then urge the player to take it all the same. When the player does, he/she receives the Compass.

Creating the Treasure Notes

As for the treasure notes, there are two ways to make them. Both ways are easy, but one of them is more efficient than the other.

- We can put the relevant treasure information in the Item description box.

- We can use a short common event to use Show Text commands for the same effect.

One way requires the additional use of common events, while the other requires only the item itself, so we'll be using the first option. See Figure 10-4 for the treasure notes, with their respective descriptions. As they share the same general settings, I copied the settings box once and just have screenshots of the different descriptions.

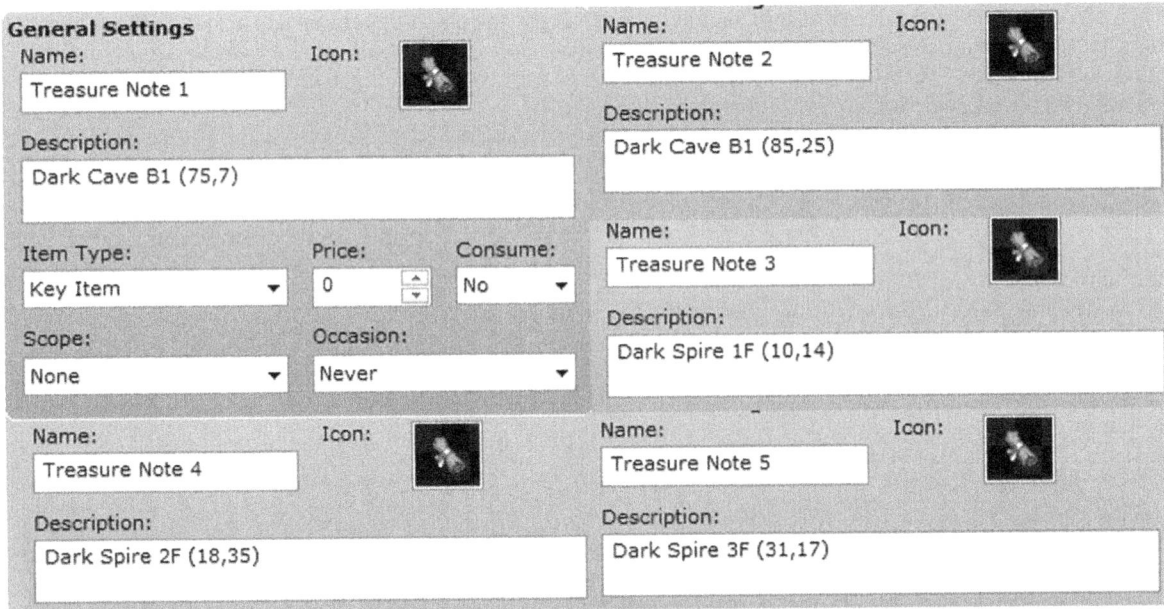

Figure 10-4. *The five treasure notes, with their location descriptions*

That just about sums up hidden treasure chests and how we can have the player find them. Of course, we can hide all sorts of things besides treasure. When the second boss was defeated by Eric and Noah back in Chapter 6, we had him mention a dark castle far to the north. We have already added a bridge that the player can cross after defeating the first boss. However, to get the player from the second landmass to the third, let's make a hidden dungeon that requires the player to have the Compass to find. Instead of using a treasure note to hide the location, we can have an NPC at the arena tell the player about it.

A Hidden Location

We'll have our new NPC require the player to have cleared out Rank C before she'll tell them the exact location of the dungeon. Since different players have different play styles, we have to accommodate both of the following possibilities:

- The player talks to the NPC as soon as he/she notices her on a first visit to the arena.

- The player talks to the NPC for the first time after having cleared out Rank C of the arena.

A Page of Evented Plot

While we're at it, we might as well have her drop some plot tidbits. (Seems like so long ago that we last had something relevant to the main plot, right?) On that note, here's the first part of page 1 of the new NPC's event, full of juicy plot:

```
@>Text: -, -, Normal, Bottom
:      : Oh, hello there. Haven't seen either of you before!
@>Text: 'Actor4', 0, Normal, Bottom
:      : My name is Eric.
@>Text: 'Actor5', 6, Normal, Bottom
:      : I am Noah.
@>Text: -, -, Normal, Bottom
:      : Nice to meet you! I'm Amanda. I've been here
:      : for the better part of two years, honing my skills
:      : to be able to protect the villagers of Rocksdale.
@>Text: 'Actor4', 0, Normal, Bottom
:      : Rocksdale?
@>Text: -, -, Normal, Bottom
:      : It's a hidden mountain town on the small continent
:      : to the north of here. Where are you two from,
:      : anyway?
@>Text: 'Actor5', 6, Normal, Bottom
:      : We hail from Seaside.
@>Text: -, -, Normal, Bottom
:      : Wait, isn't that the port town to the far south?
@>Text: 'Actor4', 0, Normal, Bottom
:      : Not THAT far south, but yes.
@>Text: -, -, Normal, Bottom
:      : Amanda ponders her choice of words carefully.
@>Text: -, -, Normal, Bottom
:      : I do not wish to call you two liars, but no one has
:      : left the southern continent in over fifteen years.
```

```
@>Show Balloon Icon: Player, Exclamation, Wait
@>Text: 'Actor5', 6, Normal, Bottom
:      : Truly?
@>Text: -, -, Normal, Bottom
:      : I'm afraid so.
@>Text: -, -, Normal, Bottom
:      : Noah thinks on Amanda's words.
@>Text: 'Actor5', 6, Normal, Bottom
:      : Both continents are connected by a stone bridge.
@>Text: -, -, Normal, Bottom
:      : Which no one could cross. A strange force would repel all attempts.
@>Text: 'Actor4', 0, Normal, Bottom
:      : I think we stopped the source of that.
@>Text: -, -, Normal, Bottom
:      : So it would seem.
```

Not much to say here. Plot is plot. Check the next page to see the final parts of page 1.

```
@>Conditional Branch: Switch [0009:RankCClear] == OFF
   @>Text: -, -, Normal, Bottom
   :      : Tell you what: If you can clear Rank C of the Arena,
   :      : I'll tell you where the entrance to the forest maze
   :      : lies. You can reach the northern continent through
   :      : there.
   @>
: Branch End
@>Conditional Branch: Switch [0009:RankCClear] == ON
   @>Text: -, -, Normal, Bottom
   :      : You two have already cleared Rank C, so I think
   :      : it's safe to trust you.
   @>Text: -, -, Normal, Bottom
   :      : Go to (21,66) and examine the area. You should find
   :      : a secret entrance. You'll need a Compass. So, if you
   :      : don't already have one, you'd better find one.
@>Conditional Branch: Self Switch B == OFF
   @>Control Self Switch: B =ON
   @>Text: 'Actor4', 0, Normal, Bottom
   :      : Many thanks!
   @>Text: 'Actor5', 6, Normal, Bottom
   :      : Your assistance is appreciated.
   @>Text: -, -, Normal, Bottom
   :      : No problem. Just do me a single favor.
   @>Text: 'Actor4', 0, Normal, Bottom
   :      : Sure. What do you need?
   @>Text: -, -, Normal, Bottom
   :      : Stay safe. A nefarious monster lives in the castle
   :      : past the mountain range.
   @>
   : Branch End
   @>
: Branch End
@>Control Self Switch: A =ON
@>
```

Making Sure That the Player Has Progressed in the Arena

Here, we have the NPC check if the player has already cleared out Rank C of the arena. If he/she has, then the NPC will give the location of the hidden location on the world map. Eric and Noah will thank the NPC and self-switch B will be flipped on. Self-switch A is flipped at the end of page 1, regardless of what happens. Page 2 requires that self-switch A be flipped. If the player talked to Amanda for the first time before completing Rank C, page 2 is where he/she will land when he/she talks to her again (otherwise, the player will skip to page 3).

```
@>Conditional Branch: Switch [0009:RankCClear] == OFF
   @>Text: -, -, Normal, Bottom
   :      : Oh hi there! Go clear Rank C, would ya?
   @>
: Branch End
@>Conditional Branch: Switch [0009:RankCClear] == ON
   @>Text: -, -, Normal, Bottom
   :      : Congratulations on clearing Rank C!
   :      : I think it's safe to trust you two.
   @>Text: -, -, Normal, Bottom
   :      : Go to (21,66) and examine the area. You should find
   :      : a secret entrance. You'll need a Compass. So, if you
   :      : don't already have one, you'd better find one.
@>Conditional Branch: Self Switch B == OFF
   @>Control Self Switch: B =ON
   @>Text: 'Actor4', 0, Normal, Bottom
   :      : Many thanks!
   @>Text: 'Actor5', 6, Normal, Bottom
   :      : Your assistance is appreciated.
   @>Text: -, -, Normal, Bottom
   :      : No problem. Just do me a single favor.
   @>Text: 'Actor4', 0, Normal, Bottom
   :      : Sure. What do you need?
   @>Text: -, -, Normal, Bottom
   :      : Stay safe. A nefarious monster lives in the castle
   :      : past the mountain range.
   @>
   : Branch End
  @>
: Branch End
@>
```

If the player has yet to clear Rank C when he/she talks to Amanda again, she'll urge him/her to go do so. If the player has cleared Rank C, we have a similar sequence play out, in which Amanda tells the player where to press the Action Button to find the hidden dungeon. Page 3 is processed when self-switch B has been turned on and consists of Amanda asking if the party needs her to repeat her directions. If they say yes, she will do so.

▒ **Note** In lieu of having page 3 work in this manner, you could have Amanda give the party a note that repeats her words via calling a common event. In that case, you could just have her say some form of greeting when self-switch B is on instead.

```
@>Text: -, -, Normal, Bottom
:      : Hello there! Do you need me to repeat my directions?
@>Show Choices: Yes, No
: When [Yes]
   @>Text: -, -, Normal, Bottom
   :      : Go to (21,66) and examine the area. You should find
   :      : a secret entrance, so long as you have a Compass.
   @>
: When [No]
   @>Text: -, -, Normal, Bottom
   :      : Ok. Stay safe, you two!
   @>
: Branch End
@>
```

The player now knows to look at 21,66 in the world map to find a hidden dungeon.

Creating Our Hidden Location

Using Load Sample Map, add Cave Entrance to our map list. Then, let's place an event triggered by the Action Button at that location that leads to that new area. We want to make sure that the player cannot find the location without having the Compass, so you'll want to set the *Item: Compass Exists* condition on page 1 of the event. As for the transfer event, it looks like this:

```
@>Text: -, -, Normal, Bottom
:      : You found a hidden location!
@>Transfer Player:[015:Cave Entrance] (008,026), Up
@>
```

On that map, you'll want to set up the appropriate transfer events. The player arrives at the area on the left picture in Figure 10-5.

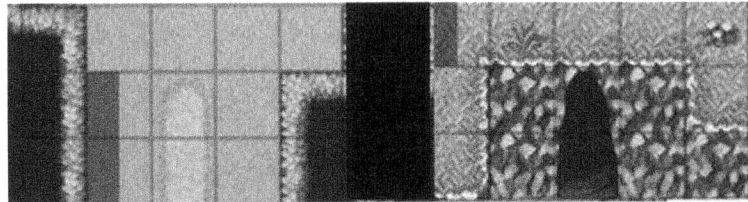

Figure 10-5. *Pictures of the exit to the world map and the entrance into the third dungeon*

You'll want a Parallel Process event to cover the transfer locations behind that area. They should lead back to the world map. The cave entrance displayed on the right should lead into our third dungeon, where I will take the time to talk about the last type of hidden thing that I will cover in this chapter.

Hidden Passages

For those times when you want players to explore off the beaten path or otherwise flex their minds to figure out how to reach the end of the dungeon, hidden passages do the trick. For this exercise, we will require the following:

1. Go to the Tilesets tab in the Database. Then, find the Dungeon tileset and add Dungeon_A4 to slot D. This will allow us to use certain tiles from tileset A for eventing purposes.

2. Click over to tileset A in Dungeon, making sure that Passage is selected on the right-hand side of the page, and set the Transparent tile to passable. *Passable tiles have a circle instead of an x.*

3. Add the three Abandoned Mine levels to your project. Make it so that the cave entrance transfers the player to Abandoned Mine F1F.

I used a screenshot (Figure 10-6) to show the greater extent of the changes that we will be making to the stock dungeon. Mainly, we want to seal off most of the side passages, such that the player has to find and use the secret passages to progress through the floor. Additionally, I completely removed the left-most stairs on this floor.

Figure 10-6. *The first floor of the Abandoned Mines, tweaked to include various secret passages*

You can probably see sequences of blocks right on top of the secret passages. Those are specific events used to hide the passages from plain sight. Let me zoom in on the first passage the player will probably find. (See Figure 10-7).

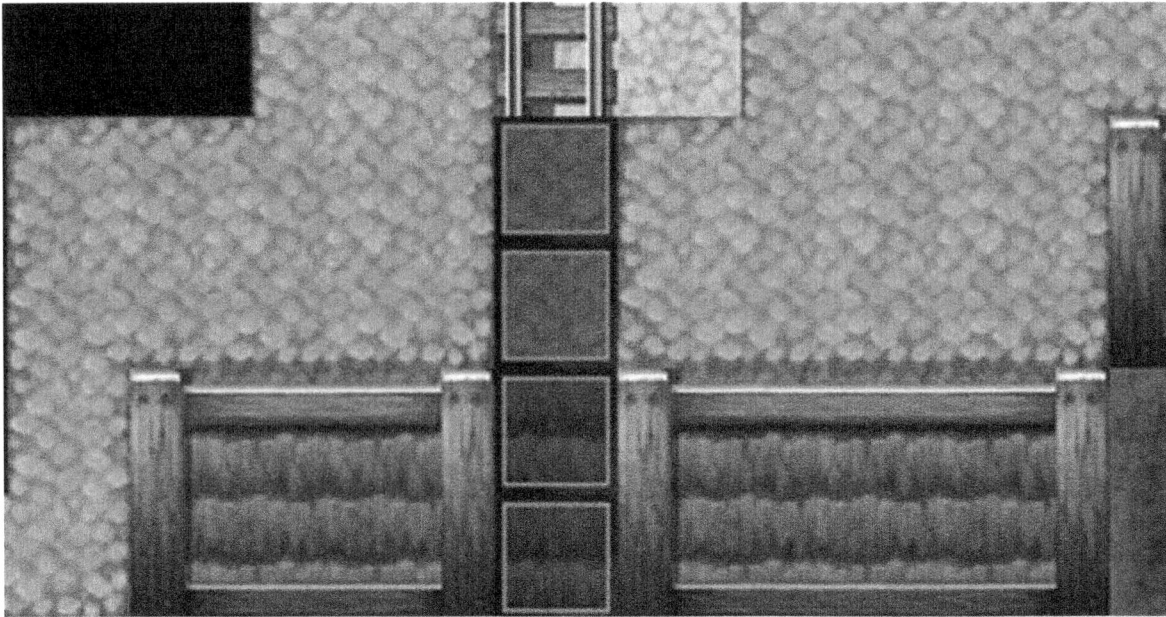

Figure 10-7. *One of the secret passages in the first floor of the dungeon*

Once you have Dungeon_A4 in Dungeon's D tileset, you can use wall and roof tiles to complement your event graphics. Here, we have four individual events. From top to bottom, they are as follows:

- The two roof tiles are Above Characters. That means that the player will walk under them in the game.

- The first wall tile is also Above Characters.

- The second wall tile is Same As Characters. You can have it so that the player effortlessly passes through the tile by checking Through in that event. What I do is ever so slightly more involved.

```
@>Text: -, -, Normal, Bottom
:      : You find a secret passage!
@>Control Self Switch: A =ON
@>
```

Mainly, I have a two-page event, in which page 1 announces that the player has found a secret passage. Then, I flip on self-switch A, which causes the tile to disappear, leaving behind a transparent tile (which appears black in-game) that allows the player to continue forth. On that note, you'll want to make sure that there are transparent tiles beneath each of the secret passage events. That will allow the player to actually walk through one side to reach the next. For side-facing secret passages, such as the one in Figure 10-8, you can assign a Same As Characters priority to the tile connecting the passage to the dungeon.

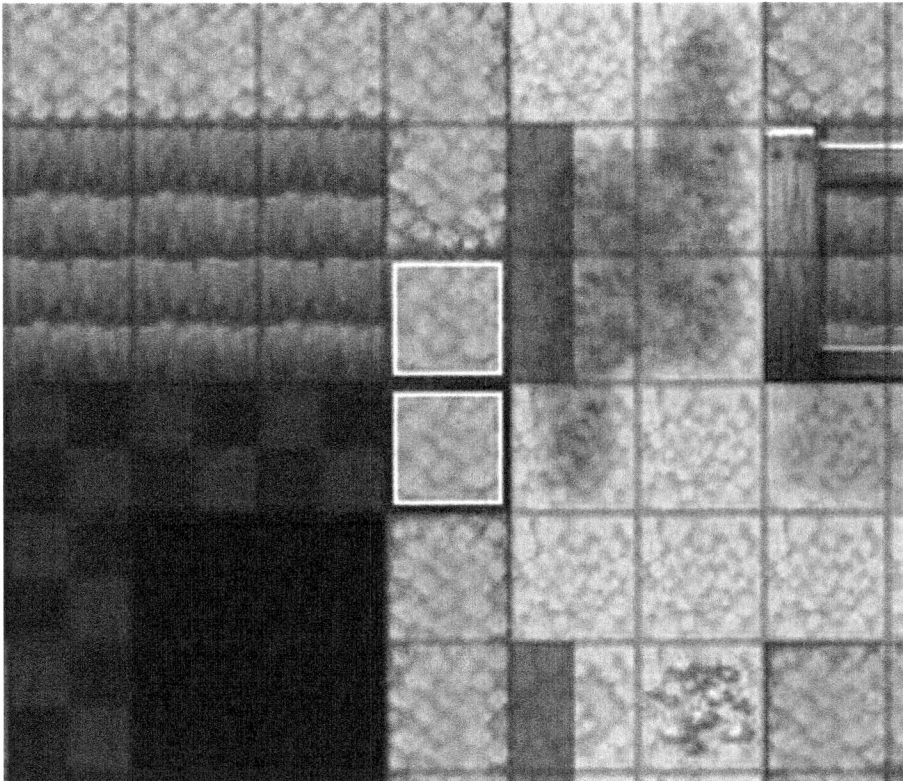

Figure 10-8. A side-facing secret passage

When the player presses the Action Button, we can display the same text message as in the previous event and change that event's priority to Above Characters. In any case, it's a good time to note that you will notice small graphical discrepancies, as RMVXA won't try to meld the roof and wall event graphics as it would if you had drawn them with the Map Editor. Figure 10-9 is an example of what I mean. Notice the vertical lines on either side of the secret passage.

Figure 10-9. A picture of the visible discrepancy when terrain tiles are used as event graphics

Given that we have to use a bare minimum of two events (you can get away with a single roof for the side-facing passages) per passage created in this way (one roof and one wall), this is highly taxing on the map event cap. It's best to use this type of eventing sparingly.

■ **Tip** Another cool use of passable transparent tiles in Darkness is to make areas without illumination. You could just have corridors that end into nothingness and start into new areas unexpectedly.

Additional Exercises

That just about concludes this chapter. As is typical, however, here are a few exercises to apply your learned knowledge:

1. Create a new item that can be used to detect secret passages.

   - You could have secret passage events require the player to have said item in his/her inventory to actually find it, much like we had the hidden location require the Compass.

2. Make it so that the player must learn of the dungeon's location from Amanda before he/she can go find it.

   - You would want to do this to stop *sequence breaking* (that is, players doing things out of an intended order). I don't mind sequence breaking at all, but I'm sure there are people out there who do.

   - All you would have to do is have a switch that is flipped on when Amanda's self-switch B is on. Then, you require the player to have the Compass and to have flipped on that switch to progress.

Summary

This chapter covered hidden things that can be implemented throughout the course of a game, such as treasure and passages. The knowledge of common events gained in Chapter 9 was used to great effect for the hidden treasure. In addition, we have placed the foundation for our third dungeon. In the next chapter, we will be discussing puzzles and how to create them within RMVXA.

PART III

The Finishing Touches

We have come a long way from the start of the book, wouldn't you agree? In that time, we have done the following with our game:

- Created two dungeons and started working on a third

- Made two fun minigames for our players to distract themselves from the main narrative

- Created a pair of sidequests for much the same purpose

- Created a town and an overarching plot for the player to follow

Our player learned that a great evil lies in a castle to the northeast of the second continent. So, he/she set off to the hidden dungeon to find a way to reach the dark castle. This last part of the book will be dedicated to finishing up our game. But, don't fret! I still have some neat things lined up in what's left!

## CHAPTER 11

Puzzles

A common mainstay of most role-playing games (RPGs), both new and old, is the puzzle. Defeating monsters and other assorted baddies to get through dungeons can be fun for quite a while, but puzzles break the monotony and make it so that the players have to flex their mental muscles as well as their alter egos' physical muscles. During the course of this chapter, I will be covering three puzzles that I have devised in my time working with RPG Maker VX Ace (RMVXA). Without further ado, let us begin with the first one.

Slippery Floors!

Perhaps the bane of any gamer who has played RPGs for even a short amount of time, slippery floors prevent you from controlling your character until it slams face-first into an obstacle. Making slippery floors is actually a very nuanced process in RMVXA eventing, as there are many things you have to take in consideration. For example:

- You have to prevent the player from inputting actions as he or she is slipping.

- You have to define what constitutes a slippery floor, unless you have an entire floor full of such tiles.

- You want the game to auto-input movement commands in the same direction, until the player gets stuck against an obstacle.

- You have to determine when the player has been stopped by an obstacle, so that he or she can move manually again.

The good news is that, once you understand what you need to do, you only require a single Parallel Process event to handle everything.

Creating Our Staging Area

First, however, I'm going to unveil the tweaked version of Abandoned Mine FB1, which is where I'll have the icy area that the player can slide on. Take a look at Figure 11-1 to see the area map. I segmented the large central area and separated the westernmost part of the floor into its own little section. Besides that, I added secret passages that connect the eastern sections. I placed a new staircase at the northern end of the western corridor. So, how does the top floor connect with this lower floor of the mines?

- The staircase at (23,15) on F1F leads to the ice section staircase located at (24,44).

- The stairs at (48,5) on F1F lead to (49,34) on FB1.

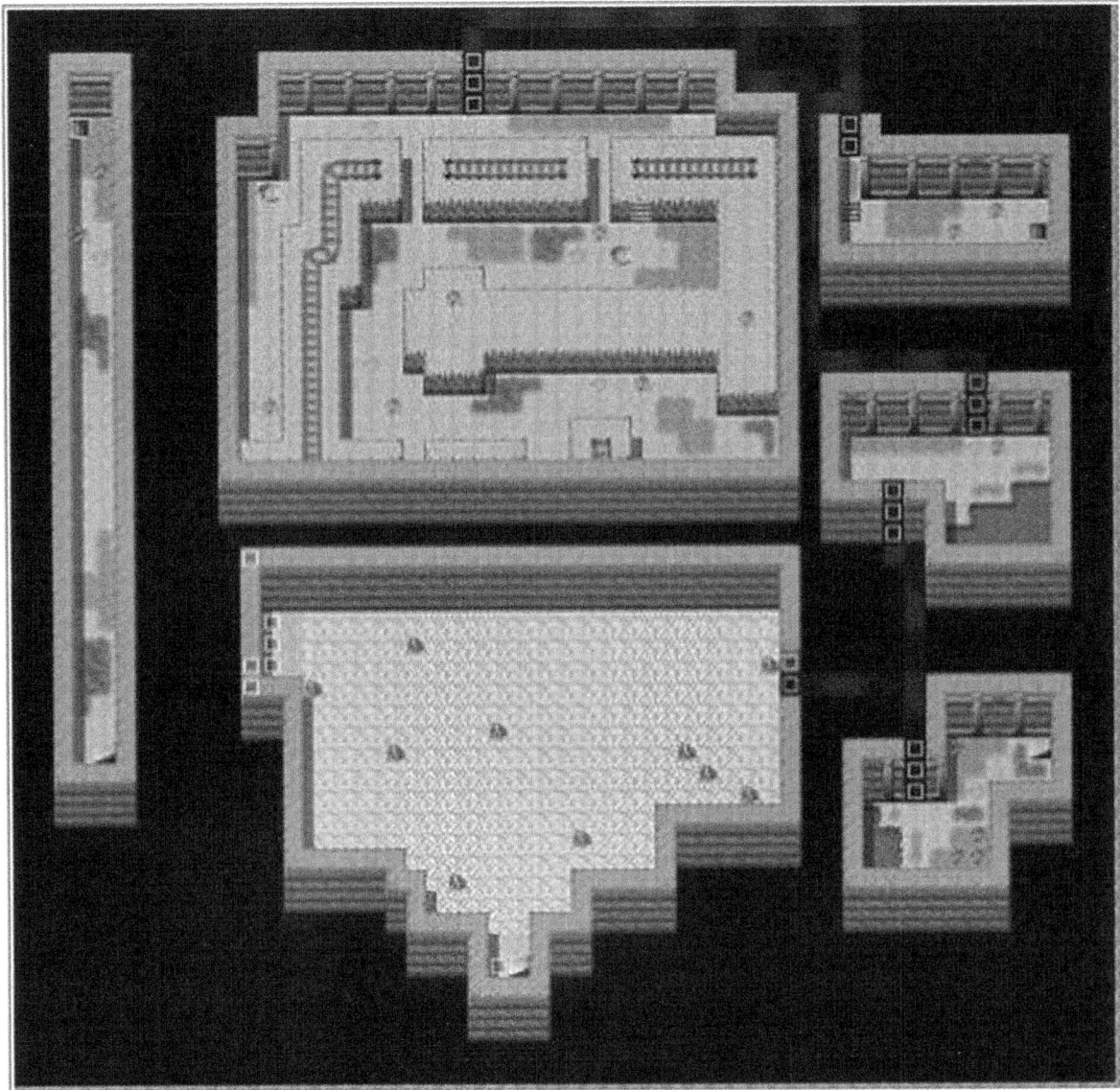

Figure 11-1. *A screenshot of the first basement floor of the mines*

That leaves the two staircases at the western corridor and a third near the northeastern corner of FB1 (at 49,10). We'll set up those transfer events, once we work with the last level of this dungeon. For now, let's work on our sliding puzzle!

Eventing Our Sliding Puzzle

We'll begin by defining the icy floor as slippery, through the use of terrain tags. You could use Regions as well. The particular tile I'm using is Ground (Crystal), located within the A tab of the Dungeon tileset. Once that is done, we create a Parallel Process event to hold our slippery floor logic. I'll break this down into parts.

```
@>Control Variables: [0002:X] = Player's Map X
@>Control Variables: [0003:Y] = Player's Map Y
@>Get Location Info: [0017], Terrain Tag, Variable [0002][0003]
@>Conditional Branch: Variable [0017:TerrainTag] == 1
@>Loop
      @>Set Move Route: Player (Skip, Wait)
       :                 : $>Walking Animation OFF
       :                 : $>Change Speed: 5
       :                 : $>Change Freq: 5
      @>Label: Repeat
```

As is standard with most of our Parallel Process events, we have it write the player's current location to a pair of variables and then fetch the location info for the tile that the player character is standing on at that precise moment. Next, we have a conditional branch that only triggers if the Terrain Tag is equal to 1. If it is, we use the *Loop* event command. As per its name, event commands within a Loop will repeat endlessly until you use a Jump To Label to escape the loop. In essence, an Autorun event is a loop (which is the reason why it is so easy to accidentally hang your game using one, if you forget to use a self-switch or some other method to break out of the event page).

The first order of action when the event enters its loop is to make it so that the player appears as if he/she is sliding on air. As mentioned near the start of the book, turning off a character's walking animation will accomplish precisely that. We can increase the speed at which the player slips on ice by using Change Speed and increasing its value. I set it to 5. Change Frequency does nothing in this particular exercise, but I kept it there for testing purposes. You'll see why it does nothing, as I reveal more of the event. The last thing I placed in that sample code was Label: Repeat. That was not a coincidence. Everything after that label will be repeated until a certain condition is met (more on that later). Here's the second part of the event:

```
@>Control Switches: [0026:WalkMovement] = OFF
@>Set Move Route: Player (Skip, Wait)
:                  : $>1 Step Forward
@>Control Variables: [0019:X'] = Player's Map X
@>Control Variables: [0020:Y'] = Player's Map Y
@>Conditional Branch: Variable [0019:X'] == Variable [0002:X]
   @>Conditional Branch: Variable [0020:Y'] == Variable [0003:Y]
      @>Jump to Label: GoToNext
      @>
   : Else
      @>Control Variables: [0002:X] = Player's Map X
      @>Control Variables: [0003:Y] = Player's Map Y
      @>Jump to Label: Repeat
      @>
   : Branch End
   @>
: Else
   @>Control Variables: [0002:X] = Player's Map X
   @>Control Variables: [0003:Y] = Player's Map Y
   @>Jump to Label: Repeat
   @>
: Branch End
```

As of this time, the player character has no walking animation. We want to have a dedicated switch that is off when the player cannot move and is flipped on when he/she can. (You could invert the states so that the switch is on when the player cannot move. Just make sure you keep track of the fact.) WalkMovement will be that switch. We'll have a conditional branch after this loop that checks to see if WalkMovement is off. If it is, we restore the player's walking animation and normalize his/her speed. But, I'm getting ahead of myself.

When the player is found to be on slippery ground, he/she will slip uncontrollably in his/her current direction. It is extremely important that you make sure that you toggle both the "Skip if cannot move" and "Wait for completion" check boxes. If the former is untoggled, the game will hang as soon as the player reaches an obstacle. If the latter is untoggled, the event will not work. (Give it a try and note how the character moves on the icy terrain.) Next, I assign a new pair of variables to store the player's current x and y coordinates after moving one space. Why? Well, recall the last bullet point in the summary list at the start of the chapter. We need to check to see if the player has been stopped by an obstacle.

We can figure that out by comparing the values of X' and Y' with the values of X and Y. The only time X' and X (and Y' and Y) will be identical is when the player is stationary. How can I guarantee this? It all comes down to the event flow. At the very top of the event, we write the player's location to X and Y. After moving a single space (or failing to, if the character is already adjacent to an obstacle), we write his/her location to X' and Y'.

We escape the loop if the values of X' and Y' are equal to the values of X and Y; otherwise, we loop back to the top of the sequence.

A Note About Redundant Code

As it turns out, you may have already noticed that we don't actually require that Loop command. That's something really important to learn in programming in general and RMVXA specifically: *Don't do in ten lines what you can do in nine or fewer*. In other words, make your events as efficient as possible. As you gain proficiency with RMVXA, you'll probably find cases in which you created an event that has some fat that can be trimmed with no negative effects. In this case, the Loop command doesn't take anything away from the slippery floor event, but you can use labels to achieve the same effect.

Eventing Our Sliding Puzzle (continued)

Here's the last part of the slippery floor event:

```
    @>
: Branch End
@>Label: GoToNext
@>Conditional Branch: Switch [0026:WalkMovement] == OFF
    @>Set Move Route: Player (Skip, Wait)
    :                    : $>Walking Animation ON
    :                    : $>Change Speed: 4
    :                    : $>Change Freq: 3
    @>Control Switches: [0026:WalkMovement] = ON
    @>
: Branch End
@>
```

This is where we go if the player is stationary from having bumped into an obstacle. We check to make sure that WalkMovement is off and restore the player character's walking animation and set its speed back to 4. We set WalkMovement to ON and we're all set. Of course, the event still isn't as clean as it could be. Think hard on what the event is doing, and see if you can trim it down some more.

Creating the Icy Area

Of course, we've gone through all the trouble of creating this event. It wouldn't be proper to just have it there doing nothing. Hence, let's make a little ice maze. You can already see it in a zoomed-out state in the full-map screenshot, but Figure 11-2 shows a zoomed-in picture of the relevant area.

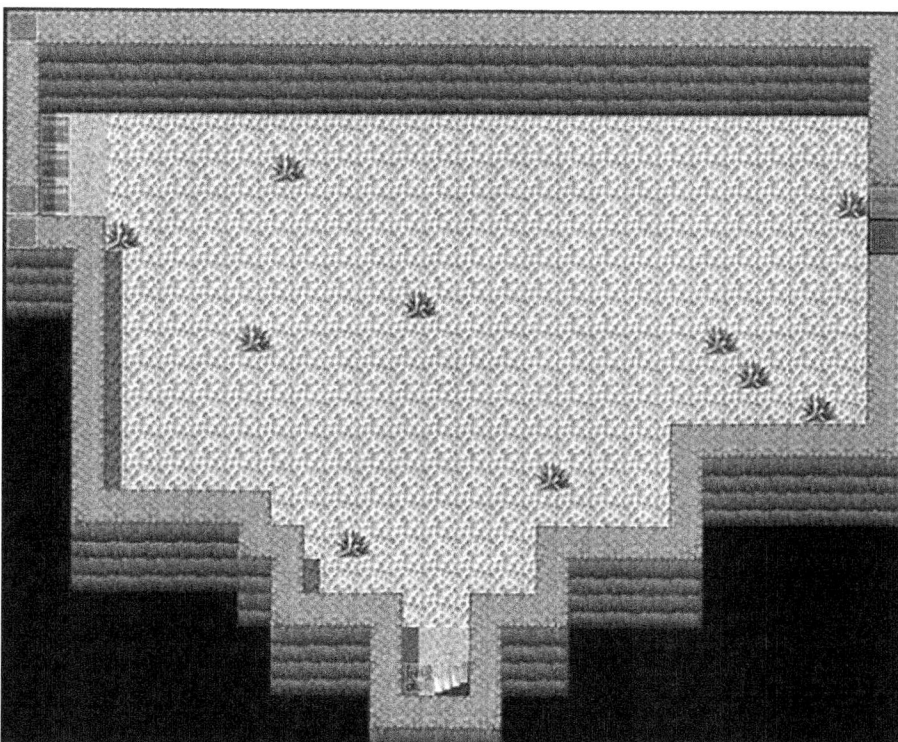

Figure 11-2. *The ice area in the first basement floor*

Note the secret passage on the right-hand side of the ice maze. We have a small section at the northwest corner of the room with three chests to reward exploration. You can add or remove obstacles, as wanted, to make it easier or harder to reach the chests or the entrance to the passage.

A Treasured Intermission

Speaking of chests, I scattered Mithril gear throughout the dungeon, to serve as the party's possible upgrades. The first floor contains the Mithril Rod, which is actually a downgrade for Noah, but as good as any item to sell for gold. It also contains a Mithril Axe that will work wonderfully as an upgrade for Eric. The second floor has a Mithril Bow and a Mithril Shield. Finally, the third floor that I'm going to add in a few moments will contain Mithril Armour (RMVXA uses British English for item names, for some odd reason, considering that most of the rest of the engine uses American English) and a Mithril Circlet. Now then, let's add the third and final floor to our dungeon, so I can talk about the second puzzle of this chapter. (See Figure 11-3.)

Figure 11-3. *The bottom floor of the abandoned mines*

For the final floor, I added a staircase in the left room, covered the hallway linking the two other rooms with debris, used a secret passage to connect them via an alternate route, and sealed off the entrance with a door.

- The staircase at (3,41) of this level connects with the stairs at (49,10) on FB1.

- The newly added staircase at (6,15) of this level connects with the other new staircase at (3,5) of FB1.

The door is the protagonist of our next puzzle.

Riddles!

Riddles are one of my favorite ways of flexing my gray matter. Quite a few RPGs have one quest or another that involves having to solve a riddle. For this exercise, we'll have that locked door pose a riddle to the player when he/she interacts with it. If the player can answer the riddle correctly, the door will open; otherwise, it will remain shut, patiently waiting.

Overview

How do we begin? We have two ways of handling a riddle.

- We could use Show Choices to display three possible answers and a Cancel option. Alternatively, we could have Show Choices display four answers and set the "When Cancel" option to Disallow (forcing the player to choose an answer) or Branch (and then have a Continue/Cancel branch pop up if the player would rather not try to answer).

- We can use Name Input Processing to have the player write his/her answer to the riddle in question and then have a conditional branch that triggers if the answer is correct.

I'll be showing off the second method, as it is a little more involved eventing-wise.

Our Riddle of Choice

The first order of business is to figure out what riddle we want the player to solve. I'll be using a classic riddle solved by Oedipus. Here it is (well, one translation of it, anyway): "What is that which has one voice and yet becomes four-footed and two-footed and three-footed?" (The traditional answer for that, by the way, is man. For the purposes of this exercise, we'll make *human* the answer.) As the correct answer has five letters, we want the input box generated by the Name Input Processing command to have a limit of five characters. As you may have already noticed, we are using this event command in quite an unconventional way. It is intended as the means of changing a character's name. For example, you could have a Name Input Processing event that allows the player to change Eric's name to something else. Here, we want to use the command, to allow the player to answer a riddle.

Creating Our Riddle Event

To begin, you'll want to make your way to the Actors tab of the Database and increase the maximum number of actors from ten to eleven. Once you do that, you'll get a blank actor on the new slot. That's exactly what we want. You could have a portrait for the riddle giver in this way, if you so desire. Because the player is talking to a door, we'll skip that. Next, we have to write the player's input into a variable. This is where we call upon scripting once again to come to our aid. Thankfully, the scripting required is not nearly as elaborate as that for the Smoke Bombs in Chapter 9. We need scripting for four small things.

1. Placing the blank actor's name into a variable. We need to find out where RMVXA stores actor names.

2. Using a Ruby method to make the player's answer case insensitive.

3. Using the Script option in the Conditional Branch command to write out the conditional we need.

4. For subsequent attempts, we want to clear out the blank actor's name before the player tries again.

You might wonder why at all we have to do this. After all, Conditional Branch also has an option on page 2 to check for a particular actor's name. Well, let's follow that thought process and work out a simple riddle event. In theory, your riddle event could look as simple as this.

```
@>Text: -, -, Normal, Bottom
:      : What is that which has one voice and yet becomes
:      : four-footed and two-footed and three-footed?
@>Name Input Processing:   , 5 characters
@>Conditional Branch: [] is Name 'human' Applied
   @>Text: -, -, Normal, Bottom
   :      : Correct.
   @>
: Else
   @>Text: -, -, Normal, Bottom
   :      : Wrong.
   @>
: Branch End
@>
```

We have a single text box giving the riddle to be solved, and then a screen comes up, so that the player can write in his/her answer. The screen in question is displayed in Figure 11-4.

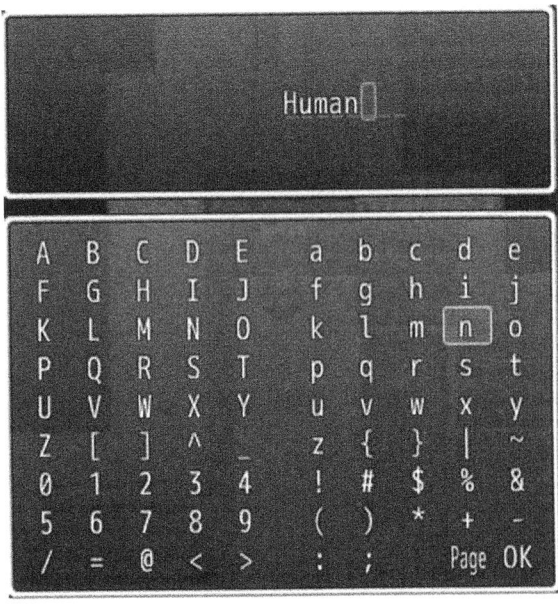

Figure 11-4. *The Name Input Processing event command in action*

However, as you'll quickly find, if you do not write *human* exactly as I did in the relevant sentence, you will receive an error message. After all, the conditional branch is looking for "human," not "hUmAn" or "HUMAN." It also doesn't solve the minor problem that the blank actor's name will not be cleared if the player writes an incorrect answer. So, let us begin with our small snippets of Ruby script.

Finding How RMVXA Handles Actor Names Within Its Code

First, we have to find out how RMVXA handles actor names within the code. A good place to start our search is the code that governs the Conditional Branch command. After all, one of the possible conditionals involves inputted names. Running a search in the Script Editor for "conditional branch" returns a single result. Click it and scroll down until you find this part of the code.

```
when 4  # Actor
    actor = $game_actors[@params[1]]
    if actor
      case @params[2]
      when 0  # in party
         result = ($game_party.members.include?(actor))
      when 1  # name
         result = (actor.name == @params[3])
```

From here, we learn that, whatever our end result looks like, it has to involve $game_actors in some capacity. As it turns out, that is correct. There *is* a Game_Actors class within the Script Editor, but checking it out is largely fruitless, save for one single tidbit: *This is a wrapper for an actor array.* An *array* in programming is a list of items. In this case, Game_Actors combines all of the relevant actor information into a single array. What we want is a specific actor's name, so let's head on over to Game_Actor, where we're almost immediately greeted by the information following:

```
attr_accessor :name                    # Name
attr_accessor :nickname                # Nickname
attr_reader   :character_name          # character graphic filename
attr_reader   :character_index         # character graphic index
attr_reader   :face_name               # face graphic filename
attr_reader   :face_index              # face graphic index
attr_reader   :class_id                # class ID
attr_reader   :level                   # level
attr_reader   :action_input_index      # action number being input
attr_reader   :last_skill              # For cursor memorization:  Skill
```

attr_accessor, attr_reader, and attr_writer (not present in Game_Actor) are a trio of Ruby modules that allows for instance variables to be used outside of the classes in which they normally exist. For the purposes of this exercise, all you have to know is that the listed attributes are contained within the array created by $game_actors. This is what you would need to write in the Script box of Control Variables to fetch an actor's name: $game_actors[n].name (where n is equal to the actor's ID in the Database).

▪ **Note**   You can also grab the other attributes in the same way. Just replace *name* with the attribute in question. Level, in particular, could be pretty useful in creating areas that can only be accessed if a player is of a certain level or higher.

How to Use the Script Option to Store and Modify Text in a Variable

To be precise, we'll be storing an actor name within the Riddle1 variable, but this can be applied to any other type of text you can think of. While the most common use of variables in RMVXA is to store numbers, text can fit in there just fine. In any case, now that we know how to call for a specific actor's name, we can write that value into a variable by using the Script option.

```
@>Control Variables: [0016:Riddle1] = $game_actors[11].name
```

That's what the event command should look like, once you're done (11 being the database ID of the new blank actor for this specific exercise). Next, we have to make sure that the player receives a positive response for a correct answer, no matter how it is written. There is a class within Ruby called String that contains various methods we can use to modify text. You can check the appropriate help page within RMVXA for additional details, but the two we're interested in are upcase and downcase. Suppose the player writes "Human" in the name input screen. If we modified it with upcase, it would become "HUMAN." On the other hand, downcase would turn it into "human." For this exercise, I'll be using downcase. What we want to do is modify the contents of the Riddle1 variable after the previously pictured event command has been processed. It's as simple as doing the following:

- Finding Script on page 3 of the event command list

- Writing in $game_variables[16] = $game_variables[16].downcase (or whichever variable ID you are using for your riddle)

▪ **Note**   Make sure that you don't split a single expression in twain while scripting. In the following lines of script, the first example is correct; the second is incorrect.

```
@>Script: $game_variables[16] =
:        : $game_variables[16].downcase

@>Script: $game_variables[16] = $game_variables
:        : [16].downcase
```

It's easier if you think of the preceding as three separate expressions. $game_variables[16] is the first one, the equal sign is the second, and applying the downcase method to $game_variables is the third. RMVXA reads the second example as four expressions, as you're cutting the third into two halves.

Finishing Up Our Riddle Event

Next, we need a conditional branch, to check if the value of our riddle variable is equal to human (if you used upcase instead of downcase, you'll want to check for HUMAN instead). We use the script option and write out $game_variables[16] = "human" (make sure you include the quotation marks). In this particular case, you can either check "Set handling when conditions do not apply" or have another conditional branch for $game_variables[16] != "human" (!= is "not equal" in Ruby). In either case, the last thing that requires scripting is emptying out the actor name. To do this, we have another line of script: $game_actors[11].name = ""

The quotation marks are important here as well. If you leave the method assignment completely empty, the game will crash with an error. Here's what the skeleton of the completed event looks like:

```
@>Text: -, -, Normal, Bottom
:      : What is that which has one voice and yet becomes
:      : four-footed and two-footed and three-footed?
@>Name Input Processing:  , 5 characters
@>Control Variables: [0016:Riddle1] = $game_actors[11].name
@>Script: $game_variables[16] =
:        : $game_variables[16].downcase
```

```
@>Conditional Branch: Script: $game_variables[16] == "human"
   @>Text: -, -, Normal, Bottom
   :       : Correct.
   @>
: Else
   @>Text: -, -, Normal, Bottom
   :       : Wrong.
   @>
: Branch End
@>Script: $game_actors[11].name = ""
@>
```

Because we want the door to open on a correct answer, you'll want to flip a self-switch after the door announces "Correct." Next, you display a message stating that the door opens and then switch to a second event page that is completely blank. There are areas of opportunity to tweak this event as well. Here are some tips if you choose to do so:

- You can directly modify an actor's name, as already noted in the last line of the completed event. Turns out you don't even have to have a variable to store the name given the fact. You could just apply downcase to $game_actors[11].name instead.

- You could use the Name Applied conditional in the Conditional Branch command.

One of the beauties of programming (and working with RMVXA events) is that there can be multiple correct solutions to a problem. Some may even be equally efficient! I have one more puzzle to discuss in this chapter, so let's get to it!

Remote Statue Manipulation!

I left the most nuanced of the three puzzles for last. Manipulating objects from a distance has been a mechanic used in many video game genres throughout the years. For this exercise, the player will be sent to a distant snowy mountain to move two statues to their respective pedestals. Figure 11-5 is a screenshot of the area in question. The map is 27×23 and uses the Exterior tileset.

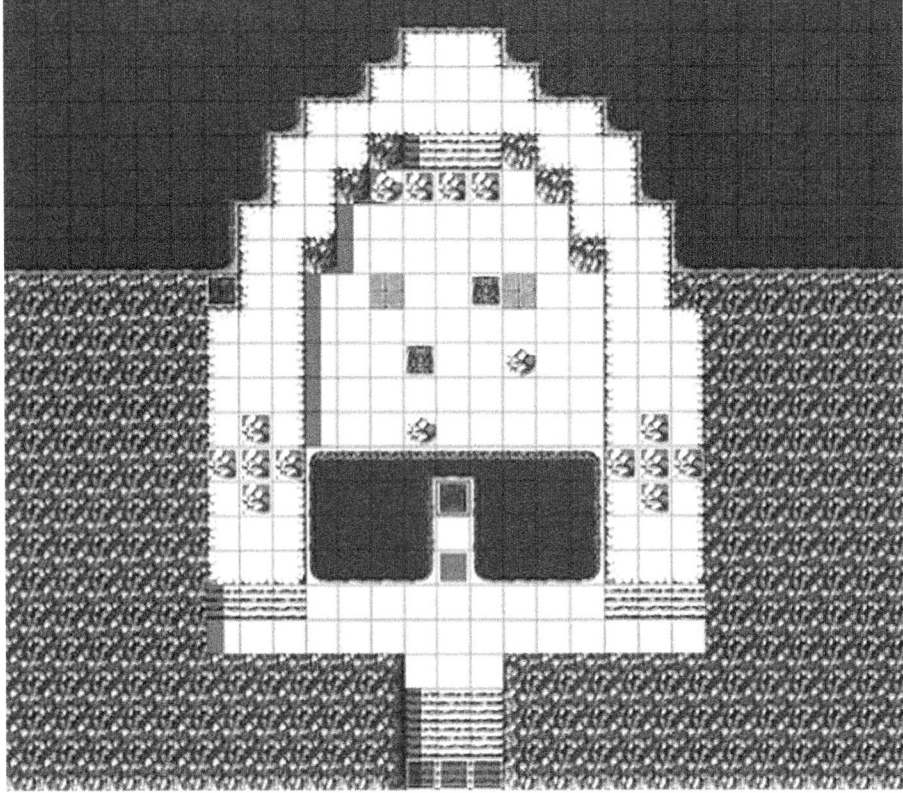

Figure 11-5. *The map where the statue manipulation puzzle takes place*

We have a pair of dragons that will be our statues for this exercise. The rock crosses on either side of the area are actually events that will disappear once the puzzle has been completed. The same goes for the three rocks blocking the staircase at the northern end of the area.

Overview

Here are the things that we need, in no particular order:

- Have an event that allows the player to start the puzzle (we'll place it on the gravestone).

- Once the puzzle has started, we freeze the player character in place and scroll the map up a few squares, so that the statues are at the center of the player's vision.

- Set up an event that translates the player's arrow keys presses into statue movement. This event could also allow the player to press a button to cancel out of the puzzle (if the player would rather go do something else, for example) without completing it.

- Make the extra rocks disappear once the puzzle has been solved.

- After each move, check to see if the statues are on their pedestals. If they are, we flip a switch confirming that the puzzle has been solved. Otherwise, we allow the player to move the statues again.

- The two events that will represent the statues

- An invisible event that blocks the player from moving while the puzzle is in progress

First, place the assorted rocks that will prevent the player from passing to the other side of the area until he/she completes the puzzle. Next, place a green dragon event at (12,10) and a red dragon event at (14,8). I specified color to differentiate the two statues. This will be important, as we want the green dragon to go on the left pedestal and the red dragon to go on the right pedestal. The pedestals are at (11,8) and (15,8) and are the golden cobblestone tiles present in tab A of the Exterior tileset.

Creating the Puzzle Trigger (Interaction) Event

The first event we're going to fill out is the first one that the player will interact with, namely, the gravestone event. When the player interacts with the gravestone, we want a message to be displayed, then the game will ask if the player wants to touch the gravestone. If he/she does, we scroll the map up to center the player's vision on the statues. We need to differentiate between when the puzzle is active and when it is not. For that, we can have a switch called StatuePuzzleStart. When it is off, the puzzle is inactive. When it is on, the puzzle is active. Check the following code to see the gravestone event in its entirety and note the extra things that it has. Some of it may not make sense currently, but it should by the end of this exercise.

```
@>Conditional Branch: Switch [0029:StatuePuzzleDone] == OFF
   @>Conditional Branch: Switch [0030:StatuePuzzleStart] == OFF
      @>Text: -, -, Normal, Bottom
      :       : The gravestone says: Place the statues
      :       : on their pedestals to open the way forward.
      @>Text: -, -, Normal, Bottom
      :       : Will you touch the gravestone?
      @>Show Choices: Yes, No
      : When [Yes]
         @>Scroll Map: Up, 5, 4
         @>Set Move Route: Player (Wait)
         :                 : $>Direction Fix ON
         @>Text: -, -, Normal, Bottom
         :       : Press A to reset the statues.
         :       : Press a directional key to move the statues.
         @>Control Switches: [0031:ButtonPressOFF] = ON
         @>Jump to Label: PuzzleStart
         @>
      : When [No]
         @>
      : Branch End
      @>
   : Branch End
@>Label: PuzzleStart
@>Control Switches: [0030:StatuePuzzleStart] = ON
@>
: Branch End
```

```
@>Conditional Branch: Switch [0029:StatuePuzzleDone] == ON
   @>Text: -, -, Normal, Bottom
   :        : This gravestone no longer serves any purpose.
   @>
: Branch End
@>
```

So, the player has touched the gravestone and is now looking at the statues. We have to make it so that he/she can actually move them. That's a job worthy of a Parallel Process event. First, however, two squares south of the gravestone, you'll want to place a blank event that requires StatuePuzzleStart to be flipped on and has a Same As Characters priority. This ensures that the player is locked into one location for the duration of the puzzle. Given that we're going to be using arrow key conditionals, we don't want the player's character to suddenly run off mid-puzzle.

Creating the Puzzle Logic Event

The Parallel Process event will have two pages. The first page will cover button presses, while the second page will check to see if the statues are at their desired destinations. Here's the first part of page 1 of the Parallel Process event:

```
@>Conditional Branch: The Down Button is Being Pressed
   @>Set Move Route: [LeftStatue] (Skip)
   :                : $>Move Down
   @>Set Move Route: [RightStatue] (Skip, Wait)
   :                : $>Move Down
   @>Jump to Label: SpotCheck
   @>
: Branch End
@>Conditional Branch: The Left Button is Being Pressed
   @>Set Move Route: [LeftStatue] (Skip)
   :                : $>Move Left
   @>Set Move Route: [RightStatue] (Skip, Wait)
   :                : $>Move Right
   @>Jump to Label: SpotCheck
   @>
: Branch End
@>Conditional Branch: The Right Button is Being Pressed
   @>Set Move Route: [LeftStatue] (Skip)
   :                : $>Move Right
   @>Set Move Route: [RightStatue] (Skip, Wait)
   :                : $>Move Left
   @>Jump to Label: SpotCheck
   @>
: Branch End
@>Conditional Branch: The Up Button is Being Pressed
   @>Set Move Route: [LeftStatue] (Skip)
   :                : $>Move Up
   @>Set Move Route: [RightStatue] (Skip, Wait)
   :                : $>Move Up
   @>Jump to Label: SpotCheck
   @>
: Branch End
```

We have a conditional branch for each separate direction. Of course, it wouldn't be much of a puzzle if both statues moved identically, so we make it so that the right statue (that would be the red one) moves on an inverted horizontal axis. In simpler terms, the red statue will move left when the player presses right and right when the player presses left. Notice how I only use the wait command once per branch. There's nothing wrong with having a wait command on the left statue's movement as well, but it just makes the puzzle take longer. When you set it up as I have, both of the statues will move in response to the key press, and the puzzle flows faster. Here's the second half of page 1:

```
@>Conditional Branch: The X Button is Being Pressed
   @>Text: -, -, Normal, Bottom
   :      : Reset the statues?
   @>Show Choices: Yes, No
   : When [Yes]
      @>Set Event Location: [LeftStatue], (012,010)
      @>Set Move Route: [LeftStatue]
      :                 : $>Turn toward Player
      @>Set Event Location: [RightStatue], (014,008)
      @>Set Move Route: [RightStatue] (Wait)
      :                 : $>Turn toward Player
      @>Scroll Map: Down, 5, 4
      @>Set Move Route: Player (Wait)
      :                 : $>Direction Fix OFF
      @>Control Switches: [0030:StatuePuzzleStart] = OFF
      @>
   : When [No]
      @>
   : Branch End
   @>
: Branch End
@>Label: SpotCheck
@>Control Switches: [0031:ButtonPressOFF] = OFF
@>Control Switches: [0032:ButtonPress] = ON
@>
```

As mentioned before, we want the player to have a way to stop the puzzle if he or she would rather do something else. RMVXA has three otherwise functionless buttons named X, Y, and Z that tie into the A, S, and D keys of a keyboard, respectively. So, when the player presses A during the puzzle, the game will ask if he or she wishes to reset the statues. Saying no does nothing, but saying yes returns both statues to their initial positions. We scroll the map down the number of squares that we had moved it up previously and turn off the Direction Fix that we had imposed on the character.

At the very bottom of page 1, we have the SpotCheck label referenced in the quartet of directional conditional branches. The pair of button press switches is used for flow control. In essence, we want the following sequence:

- The player presses one of the arrow keys. The relevant actions are processed and switches are flipped, causing the Parallel Process page to execute page 2.

- Page 2 of the event checks to see if both statues reached their respective pedestals in that particular button press.

- If they didn't, we toggle switches such that page 1 is now ready to be executed once again.

It is functionally a two-page loop that can be broken by puzzle completion or the player pressing A and selecting Yes. With that said, page 1 requires that StatuePuzzleStart and ButtonPressOFF be on. Page 2, on the other hand, requires that StatuePuzzleStart and ButtonPress be on. Don't let the minor switch name differences trip you up!

If they do, feel free to differentiate them a little more. Check the following code for the first part of page 2 of the Parallel Process event.

```
@>Control Variables: [0023:LeftStatueX] = [LeftStatue]'s Map X
@>Control Variables: [0024:LeftStatueY] = [LeftStatue]'s Map Y
@>Control Variables: [0025:RightStatueX] = [RightStatue]'s Map X
@>Control Variables: [0026:RightStatueY] = [RightStatue]'s Map Y
@>Conditional Branch: Variable [0023:LeftStatueX] == 11
   @>Conditional Branch: Variable [0024:LeftStatueY] == 8
      @>Conditional Branch: Variable [0025:RightStatueX] == 15
         @>Conditional Branch: Variable [0026:RightStatueY] == 8
            @>Text: -, -, Normal, Bottom
             :                  : About time!
            @>Fadeout Screen
            @>Play SE: 'Push', 80, 100
            @>Set Event Location: [LeftStatue], (011,008)
            @>Set Event Location: [RightStatue], (015,008)
            @>Control Switches: [0029:StatuePuzzleDone] = ON
            @>Scroll Map: Down, 5, 4
            @>Fadein Screen
            @>Control Switches: [0030:StatuePuzzleStart] = OFF
            @>Set Move Route: Player (Wait)
             :                          : $>Direction Fix OFF
            @>
          : Else
            @>Jump to Label: DirectionCheck
            @>
          : Branch End
         @>
       : Else
         @>Jump to Label: DirectionCheck
         @>
       : Branch End
      @>
   : Else
     @>Jump to Label: DirectionCheck
     @>
   : Branch End
  @>
: Else
  @>Jump to Label: DirectionCheck
```

Dissecting the Statue Manipulation Puzzle Logic

Now, don't run off just yet. This might seem a bit overwhelming, but it's actually very simple. Here's a play-by-play of what the preceding event does:

- We create a whopping four new variables to store the values of X and Y for both of the statues.

- Once adequately stored, we check said values against the pedestal positions, as defined earlier in this section.

- If *all* four of the variables check out, it means that both statues are in their rightful places. We have Eric say a short remark and then fade out the screen.

- A sound effect is played, and the event locations of both statues are moved to the pedestal location. If you do not do this, the statues will move back to their original locations after the player leaves the map. For our game's purposes, this is actually unimportant (this will be a location visited only once), but it can be, if you want to make puzzles of this type in locations that the player would want to visit multiple times.

- We set StatuePuzzleDone to on, scroll the map back down the same number of steps we scrolled it up before, and fade in.

- The rest of the event has the same logic used when the player presses A to cancel out of the puzzle.

- On the other hand, if *any* of the four variables are off, we jump to the DirectionCheck label near the bottom of the page.

```
    @>
: Branch End
@>Label: DirectionCheck
@>Control Switches: [0032:ButtonPress] = OFF
@>Control Switches: [0031:ButtonPressOFF] = ON
@>
```

By swapping which of the button press switches is toggled, we can switch between the two pages of the Parallel Process event as needed. On that note, we have concluded our third and final puzzle for the chapter!

Creating the Second Town

All that remains is adding a relevant location that will lead us to the snowy statue puzzle mountain area. Use Load Sample Map to add Mountain Village to your project's map list. We're going to be tweaking the bottom part of the village to serve our needs. Take a peek at Figure 11-6, to see the changes.

209

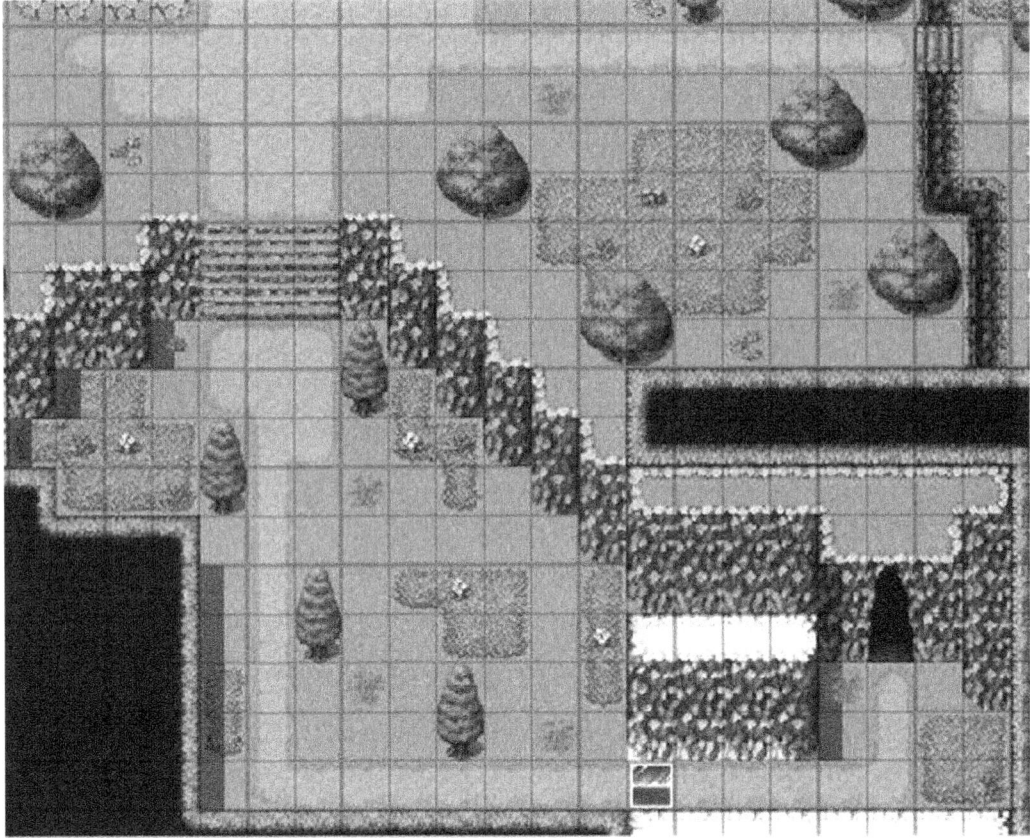

Figure 11-6. *The tweaked part of the Mountain Village. The rest of the terrain remains the same as normal*

That cavern entrance connects with the one staircase in the Abandoned Mines we have not touched until now. For the sake of clarity, I'm talking about the stairs at (4,34) of FB1. The block impeding entry into the village is actually an event (the graphic is from !Door2) that transfers the player to our statue puzzle area. This block disappears once StatuePuzzleDone is turned on by completing the statue puzzle.

Additional Exercises

As is tradition, I'll close out the chapter by giving you some exercises to work on.

1. **Create a crate-pushing puzzle that involves three buttons that need weight to stay pushed down. When all three buttons are pressed, open a door.**

    -   If you want to have a crate that can be both pushed and pulled, you could have a Show Choices command that disallows being canceled. Then, the player could choose whether to push or pull the crate.

    -   Be mindful of the order of your movement events. You want the crate to move first when pushed, but you want the player to move first when it is pulled. Doing it backward is self-defeating at best and can hang your game at worst (if you don't set the relevant move commands to skip, if they cannot be executed).

2. **Make some ice blocks that slide in one direction until they collide with an obstacle.**

- This is as simple as applying the same sliding logic to the blocks that we assign to the player.

- The blocks can have an Action Button trigger. Given that they can be pushed from all directions, you'll need to have a conditional branch for each of the player's facings, to handle the block's movement.

Summary

This chapter covered three puzzles that I have devised in the time that I've used RMVXA. We made a door that could only be opened by correctly answering a riddle, a movement puzzle involving slippery ice, and a manipulation puzzle involving a pair of dragon statues. In the next chapter, we'll be populating our newly added town.

CHAPTER 12

Final Preparations

We are fast approaching the end of this book. Our game, short as it may be, is nearly complete. All that is left is to populate the mountain town of Rocksdale, connecting it with the world map, and create the game's final dungeon. Well, all that and filling out the random encounter tables for our third dungeon and finishing the dragon statue event we started back in Chapter 6. I'll be covering the final dungeon in Chapter 13. When last we saw our heroes, they were busy solving a statue puzzle to gain entry into Rocksdale. Make sure that you have a Transfer Event set up within the puzzle area, so that the player can return to the mountain village after he or she is done. With that ready, let's get started!

Populating Rocksdale

A town isn't much of one without nonplayer characters (NPCs) and building interiors. As with Seaside, here's some setting flavor for Rocksdale.

> *The quiet town of Rocksdale has always been a favorite destination for travelers seeking to settle down and otherwise retire from the outside world. In recent times, monsters have started to threaten the townsfolk's safety, prompting a few of the villagers to leave their seclusion and train themselves for the day when the foul creatures decide to do more than just harass. The village elder is a wise man who knows of a secret passage that leads to the other side of the mountain ridge, where a solitary castle and its dark master await the chosen one of legend . . .*

Riveting, I know! As compared to the Port Town sample map, that for the mountain village is more spacious but has fewer amenities. Only an inn and an item shop can be found there. You may decide to repurpose one or more of the houses to add weapon and armor shops, but there's nothing wrong with compensating only for the fact that we have but one of each of those shops in the entire game by adding more relevant loot to the dungeons we already have. It wouldn't be the first game in which most of a party's equipment has to be found outside of town shops. (See Figure 12-1.)

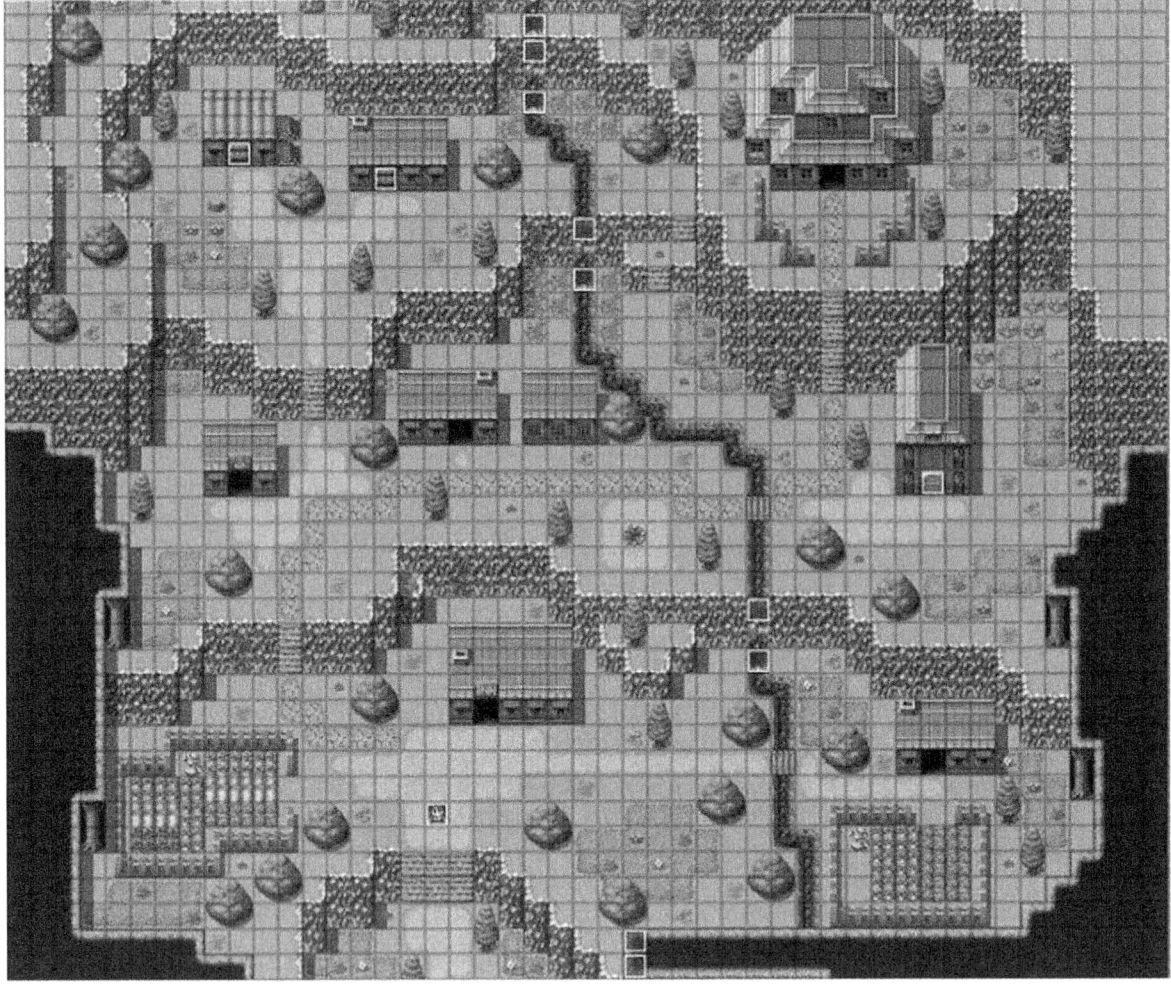

Figure 12-1. *The mountain village of Rocksdale. The top two houses are sealed off*

Here's a list of the main plot events that I will be covering within Rocksdale:

- When the player goes up the steps into the village, the town greeter will inform the player that he/she should make his/her way to the large house in the northeastern part of the village.

- The player reaches the dwelling and finds the village elder, named Wren. Wren has been waiting for Eric's arrival for nearly two decades. He speaks of a malevolent being that lives within a castle in the middle of a dark swamp and of the sword that only the chosen one may wield.

- Wren tells the player that a secret passage exists within the village. He further explains that it leads to the far side of the mountain ridge. More important, the passage puts the adventuring party within reach of the villain's castle.

The Town Greeter

Our first order of business will be to place the town greeter on the map. Let's place our relevant NPC at (17,34). While I'm going to have the greeter give the bulk of his conversation via an Autorun, I'll still have him say a few words when talked to a second time.

```
@>Text: -, -, Normal, Bottom
:     : Welcome to Rocksdale, adventurers. We don't have
:     : much, but I hope you enjoy your stay.
```

First, here's the Parallel Process event that we'll use to flip the switch for the Autorun to trigger.

```
@>Control Variables: [0002:X] = Player's Map X
@>Control Variables: [0003:Y] = Player's Map Y
@>Conditional Branch: Variable [0003:Y] == 36
   @>Conditional Branch: Variable [0002:X] >= 16
      @>Conditional Branch: Variable [0002:X] <= 18
         @>Control Switches: [0033:MountainArrival] = ON
```

There's nothing in the above code that we haven't already performed many times before. We want to trigger the Autorun in this way to prevent the game from hanging. Check the following code to see the Autorun event in all of its glory.

```
@>Show Balloon Icon: [Villager], Exclamation, Wait
@>Text: -, -, Normal, Bottom
:     : Did you two reach this place through the mines?
@>Text: 'Actor5', 6, Normal, Bottom
:     : We did.
@>Text: -, -, Normal, Bottom
:     : The villager's eyes widen in disbelief.
@>Text: -, -, Normal, Bottom
:     : You must go visit Wren. He lives in the large
:     : dwelling at the northeastern part of town. He has
:     : been waiting for a long time.
@>Text: 'Actor4', 0, Normal, Bottom
:     : For us?
@>Text: -, -, Normal, Bottom
:     : I believe it would be best for him to speak of it
:     : himself.
@>Text: 'Actor5', 6, Normal, Bottom
:     : Very well.
@>Control Self Switch: A =ON
@>
```

An exclamation balloon will be displayed over the villager's head when the Autorun starts. After the short conversation, we switch on self-switch A. We make page 2 of the event have a non-Autorun trigger, and that completes our first task of the chapter.

Creating the Village Elder and His Home

Next, we need a worthy interior for the village elder. We'll use the Village Headman's House F1F sample map for our purposes. I removed the staircase, changed the dirt floor in one of the rooms to wood, and added a single bed to that same room. (See Figure 12-2.)

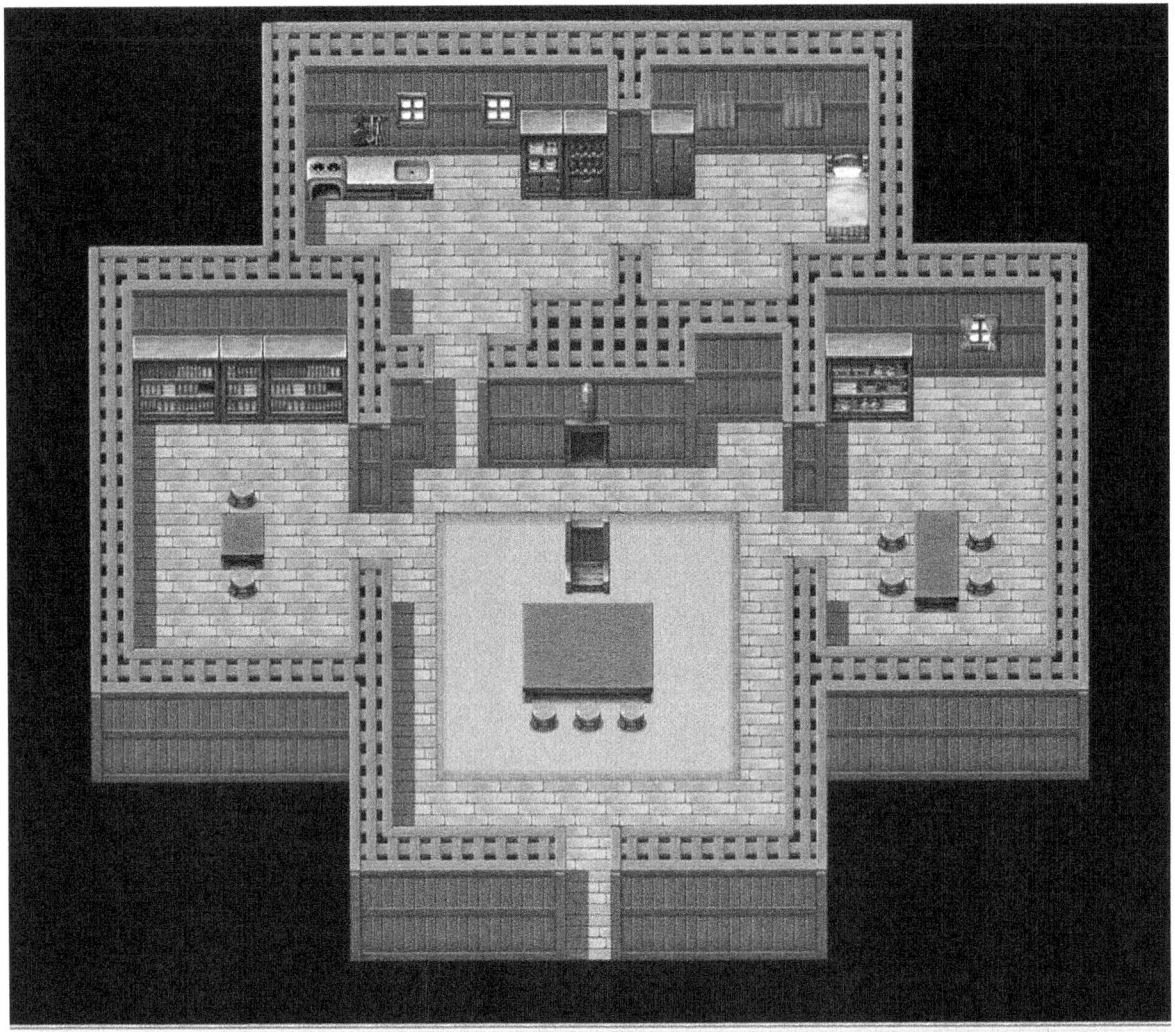

Figure 12-2. *Screenshot of the tweaked Village Headman's House sample map available in RMVXA*

We'll place the village elder himself at (13,14). This event is essentially plot exposition for the player. He/She gets to learn a little more about the game world and then receives his/her next main objective. Take a look at the following for the event code.

```
@>Show Balloon Icon: This event, Exclamation, Wait
@>Text: 'Actor4', 0, Normal, Bottom
:      : I'm Eric.
@>Text: 'Actor5', 6, Normal, Bottom
:      : And I am Noah.
@>Text: -, -, Normal, Bottom
:      : I am Wren, the leader of this small village. It
:      : was the father of my father's father, king of the
:      : western lands, who said that you would return.
@>Text: 'Actor4', 0, Normal, Bottom
:      : You're not making any sense, Wren.
@>Text: -, -, Normal, Bottom
:      : Noah clears his throat.
@>Text: 'Actor5', 6, Normal, Bottom
:      : Perhaps it would be best to allow him to
:      : speak.
@>Text: -, -, Normal, Bottom
:      : My ancestor claimed that the chosen one would return
:      : to the world in its time of greatest need. I beseech
:      : your aid to defeat the dark master.
@>Text: 'Actor4', 0, Normal, Bottom
:      : It is what we're here for.
@>Show Balloon Icon: This event, Music Note, Wait
@>Text: -, -, Normal, Bottom
:      : Wonderful! There is an orb of power that will aid
:      : you in your quest. My ancestor claimed that it
:      : is hidden within the lowest level of the castle.
@>Text: 'Actor5', 6, Normal, Bottom
:      : How did he know that?
@>Wait: 30 frame(s)
@>Show Balloon Icon: This event, Silence, Wait
@>Text: -, -, Normal, Bottom
:      : Isn't it obvious? The castle where the evil
:      : enveloping our land resides was the king's home
:      : in times past.
@>Text: 'Actor5', 6, Normal, Bottom
:      : In hindsight, it all makes sense. How do
:      : we get there?
@>Text: -, -, Normal, Bottom
:      : There is a secret passage inside of the village
:      : temple. Tap the wall three paces north of the
:      : northeastern pillar.
@>Text: 'Actor4', 0, Normal, Bottom
:      : Thank you, Wren!
@>Text: -, -, Normal, Bottom
:      : On the contrary, thank you.
@>Control Switches: [0034:ElderTalk] = ON
@>Control Self Switch: A =ON
```

As with most plot-advancing events, this one is important, not for what it does internally, but for the information that it gives the player. Thanks to the village elder, the player learns that the castle inhabited by the mysterious dark master used to be home to the king of the western lands. At the end of the conversation, we flip on the `ElderTalk` switch, which allows the player to find the secret passage within the temple.

The Temple of Rocksdale

I used the Temple sample map to create the area in question. I erased the side sections, leaving only the central portion. In addition, I changed the style of the temple walls and the pillars to give a rustic feel. The secret passage is visible in Figure 12-3, but there's another event that may not be as easy to see. I placed a Same As Characters/Action Button event on the statue's lower half. If the player interacts with the statue, he/she will be teleported to Seaside. Where exactly? Take a look at Figure 12-4, to see.

Figure 12-3. *A screenshot of the upper half of the temple*

Figure 12-4. *A screenshot of where the player lands if he or she touches Rocksdale's statue*

Because this statue is two squares tall, we need a pair of events to draw it. The top half has a priority of Above Characters and no commands. The lower half has a priority of Same As Characters and returns the player to the mountain village if he/she touches it.

■ **Tip** If you want to make it so that the statue at Seaside is only visible after the player has used Rocksdale's statue, you can add an appropriate condition to both of the events. ElderTalk will work, as will creating a new switch that is flipped the first time that the player uses Rocksdale's statue.

Leaving Rocksdale

The secret passage event is three pages long. To use the appropriate wall graphic for the first two pages of the event, you'll need to add Inside_A4 to tab D of the Exterior tileset in the Database. Because we don't want the player to find the passage ahead of time, the first page will have no conditionals and no event commands. The only thing that the first page will have is the wall graphic. Page 2 will require that ElderTalk is switched on and shares the same graphic as page 1. However, if the player interacts with the wall using the Action Button, the event in the following code is triggered.

```
@>Text: 'Actor4', 0, Normal, Bottom
:    : This should be the place.
@>Text: -, -, Normal, Bottom
:    : Eric taps the wall with his knuckles.
@>Wait: 60 frame(s)
@>Fadeout Screen
@>Play SE: 'Push', 80, 100
@>Text: -, -, Normal, Bottom
:    : You have found a secret staircase!
@>Control Self Switch: A =ON
@>Fadein Screen
```

The use of Fadeout/Fadein Screen in page 2 is so that we can switch to page 3's event graphic off-camera via the usual self-switch toggle. Figure 12-5 shows a visual of what it looks like in-game.

Figure 12-5. *Eric finds himself staring at a staircase*

Page 3 of the secret passage event has a Below Characters priority and a Player Touch trigger. It requires self-switch A to be on. The first time that the player takes this passage, we want to display some extra text. Thus, we start page 3 with a conditional branch requiring self-switch B to be off. If it is, we display the additional text; otherwise, we skip straight to the transfer event.

```
@>Conditional Branch: Self Switch B == OFF
   @>Control Self Switch: B =ON
   @>Fadeout Screen
   @>Text: -, -, Normal, Bottom
   :      : Eric and Noah walk down the steps and find
   :      : themselves in a rocky passage.
   @>Text: -, -, Normal, Bottom
   :      : Several minutes later, they find themselves at a
   :      : new location...
   @>Play SE: 'Move', 80, 100
   @>Wait: 60 frame(s)
   @>
: Branch End
@>Transfer Player:[003:Field 3] (017,054), Up
```

If you were to play-test the game after adding that specific event, you would find a considerable lack of screen after being transferred back to the world map. We could add in the Fadein Screen command directly before Transfer Player, but that would look somewhat sloppy in execution. Instead, go to the world map's Parallel Process transfer event and add the following to it:

```
@>Conditional Branch: Variable [0003:Y] == 54
   @>Conditional Branch: Self Switch A == OFF
      @>Fadein Screen
      @>Control Self Switch: A =ON
      @>
   : Branch End
   @>
: Branch End
@>
```

We use a self-switch conditional branch within the coordinate conditional, as we only require this to trigger once (to match the fading-out sequence caused at Rocksdale's temple). We use Y == 54, as the player has no chance of reaching that coordinate on the world map before this point in the game.

■ **Caution**   Be very careful with the preceding example when applying it to your own games. In a more open world map, your players might cross your declared coordinate(s) prematurely during the course of their adventures. When they get around to triggering the area transition, the fade-in is functionally nonexistent, and the game will hang.

With all that said and done, Eric and Noah will find themselves near the dark villain's castle, as shown in Figure 12-6.

Figure 12-6. *Surrounded by poison swamps, the final dungeon awaits!*

Before closing out this section, here are some ideas to flesh out Rocksdale.

- Have one of the villagers give the player a sidequest involving the two scarecrows in town. You could have them attack the player, when examined. When both are defeated, the player is attacked by a puppet-master. Defeating the mini-boss completes the sidequest.

- We originally had most of the default items in RPG Maker VX Ace (RMVXA) available for sale in Seaside. Create some items specifically for sale in Rocksdale and move the Elixir from Seaside to the mountain village.

- Add several NPCs, to liven up the village. The locals should talk mostly about the monsters threatening to attack. Have one of them make reference to Amanda.

Next, we should populate the world map's Regions and the mines with enemies. As of now, only the landmass containing Seaside includes random encounters. Afterward, we'll start working on the game's final dungeon.

Enemies of the World

To be fair, I could have covered this earlier in the book (arguably much earlier, in the case of the second landmass), but I figured it'd be better to clump them all here, away from the central ideas they would have otherwise cluttered. After all, I also have the dragon statue event back at the Dark Spire that I still have to complete. It's as good a time as any to go off on this tangent.

First, take a look at Figure 12-7, for the full encounter list that we'll be using for the world map.

Troop	Weight	Range
001:Slime*2	30	1
002:Bat*2	20	1, 2
003:Hornet*2	15	2
004:Spider*3	10	2
005:Rate*3	20	1, 2, 3
006:Wisp*3	5	3, 4
010:Man-Eating Plant*3	5	4
008:Scorpion*3	10	4
012:Skeleton*2	20	5, 6
017:Zombie*3	10	5, 6
024:Gargoyle*2	10	6

Figure 12-7. *The encounters list for our game's world map*

We'll be using Regions 3 and 4 for the second landmass and 5 and 6 for the area surrounding the castle. Check Figure 12-8 to see just how I laid out the relevant Regions.

Figure 12-8. *A screenshot of the world map, now updated with Regions*

Next, we need some encounters for the mines (Figure 12-9). I will use the same troops for both of the top levels of the mines. Much like the Dark Spire, I'll leave the last floor encounter-free.

Troop	Weight	Range
014:Imp*2	35	Whole
017:Zombie*3	25	Whole
018:Cockatrice*2	30	Whole
033:Living Metal	9	Whole
034:Living Metal*2	1	Whole

Figure 12-9. *Random encounter list for the Abandoned Mines*

A perceptive eye will notice that the weights add up to exactly 100, and we have a pair of encounters that account for a mere 10 of that. I created that monster as a little tribute to a classic enemy archetype in RPGs. You can see him (her? it?) in Figure 12-10.

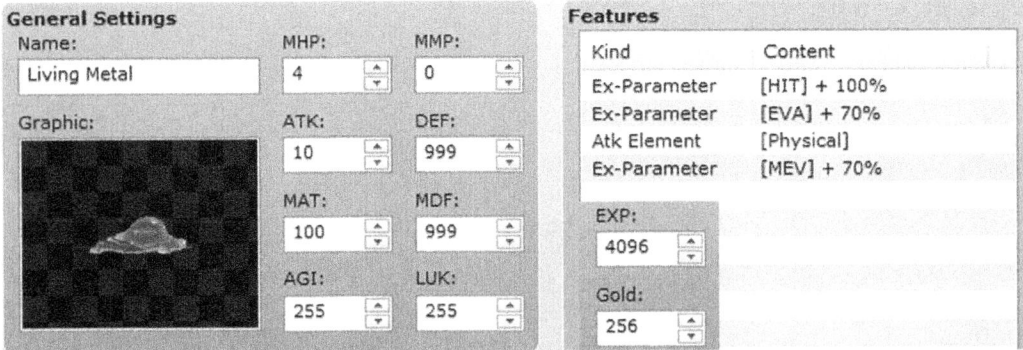

Figure 12-10. *Screenshot of the Living Metal enemy*

It has merely 4 HP, but so much DEF and MDF that it is functionally impossible to damage it, if you can even get past its 70% EVA and MEV. The only thing that would be able to stop a Living Metal is an attack that ignores defense or does fixed damage. I personally find it fun when an RPG throws curveballs like this, forcing me to think outside the box for ways to defeat an enemy, especially when the rewards are worth it. The bombs we created all the way back in Part 1 could be useful, but they're considered physical attacks, so they only have a 30% chance of actually connecting. You could always fill some dungeon treasure chests with a damage item that hits for only 5 HP but is a Certain Hit. Alternatively, you could sell them at Rocksdale's item shop for a lot of gold and make players decide whether the 4096 EXP is worth the inflated price for what is otherwise a worthless item.

With both the mines and the world map fully populated, let's turn our attention to the dragon statue in the Dark Spire. I had originally left the event incomplete in Chapter 6, because I wanted to make an optional boss fight—a superboss fight, to be exact.

A Discussion on Superbosses

The general flow of an RPG involves defeating bosses, until you reach a final boss. Superbosses are located outside of that continuity and exist solely as a form of challenge for the player. If the player can beat a superboss, he/she is more than ready to beat the final boss and, by extension, the game itself. The monster that I created for this precise purpose can be seen in Figure 12-11.

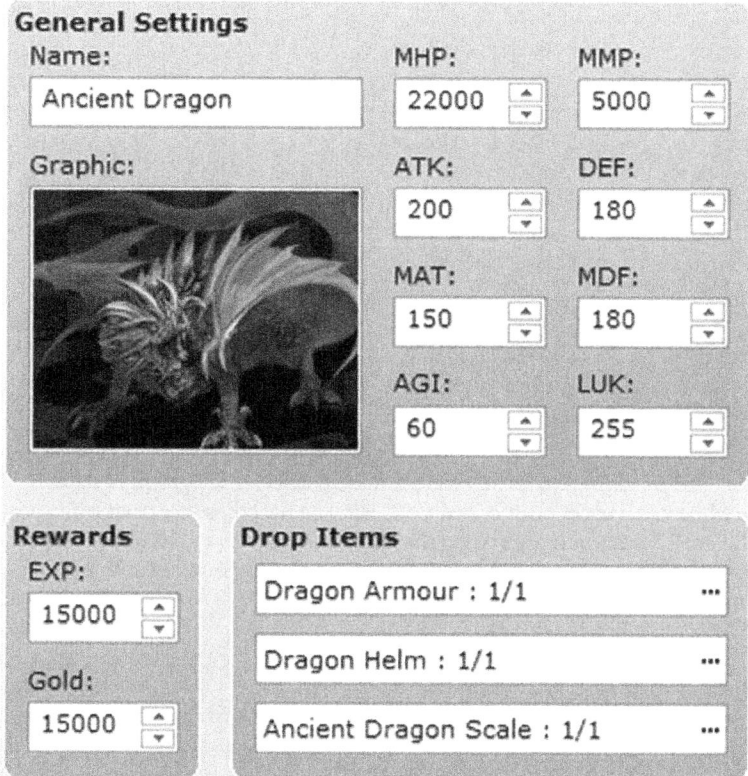

General Settings

Name:

Ancient Dragon

Graphic:

MHP: 22000
MMP: 5000
ATK: 200
DEF: 180
MAT: 150
MDF: 180
AGI: 60
LUK: 255

Rewards

EXP: 15000

Gold: 15000

Drop Items

Dragon Armour : 1/1 ...

Dragon Helm : 1/1 ...

Ancient Dragon Scale : 1/1 ...

Figure 12-11. *Screenshot of the Ancient Dragon. It gives the highest experience and gold gains of any monster in the game*

The Ancient Dragon boasts higher stats than the game's final boss. Eric and Noah will most likely not be ready to take this beast on until they have gotten the gear from the final dungeon and perhaps some extra level-ups as well. Defeating the Ancient Dragon gives the player a whopping 15,000 experience and gold. More important, it gives the player the best armor and helmet available in the default RMVXA armor list. That third item is an accessory I created. It grants +10 to all eight of a character's main stats, +5 EVA, +5 CRI, 20% Fire Resistance (expressed in the Database as [Fire]*80%) and 5 Attack Speed (AGI only applied during attacks). You can see the Ancient Dragon's Features and Action Pattern lists in Figure 12-12.

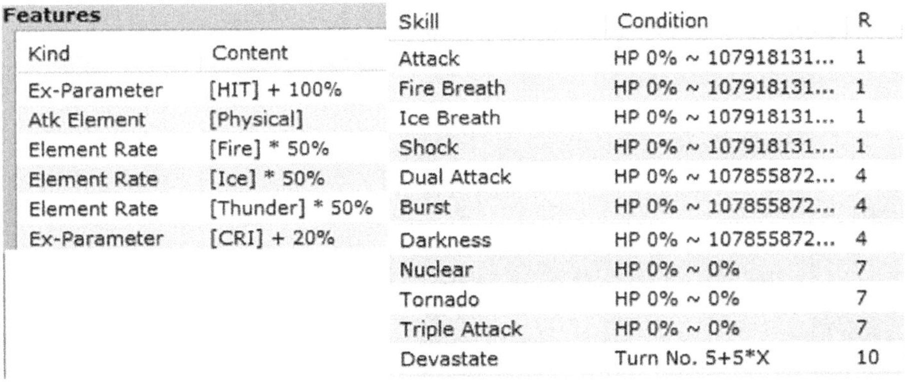

Features			Skill	Condition	R
Kind	**Content**		Attack	HP 0% ~ 107918131...	1
Ex-Parameter	[HIT] + 100%		Fire Breath	HP 0% ~ 107918131...	1
Atk Element	[Physical]		Ice Breath	HP 0% ~ 107918131...	1
Element Rate	[Fire] * 50%		Shock	HP 0% ~ 107918131...	1
Element Rate	[Ice] * 50%		Dual Attack	HP 0% ~ 107855872...	4
Element Rate	[Thunder] * 50%		Burst	HP 0% ~ 107855872...	4
Ex-Parameter	[CRI] + 20%		Darkness	HP 0% ~ 107855872...	4
			Nuclear	HP 0% ~ 0%	7
			Tornado	HP 0% ~ 0%	7
			Triple Attack	HP 0% ~ 0%	7
			Devastate	Turn No. 5+5*X	10

Figure 12-12. *Screenshot of the Ancient Dragon's feature and action pattern lists*

The infamous text bug strikes again, so I used the ratings to further differentiate between each group of skills. The Ancient Dragon uses the first four skills while it has between 76% and 100% HP. The next three are used when it is between 51% HP and 75% HP. The three skills with 7 rating are used when the Ancient Dragon is at 50% HP or lower. Last, Devastate is a special skill I created that the Ancient Dragon uses every five turns, starting from the fifth turn. It has the special property of doing more damage the later in the fight that it is used. Figure 12-13 contains the damage formula box for Devastate.

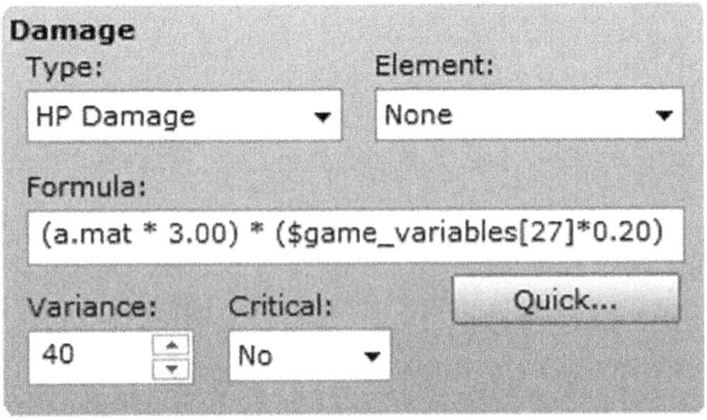

Damage

Type:
HP Damage ▼

Element:
None ▼

Formula:
(a.mat * 3.00) * ($game_variables[27]*0.20)

Variance:
40

Critical:
No ▼

Quick...

Figure 12-13. *A screenshot of Devastate's damage formula box*

We set it up so that the value of $game_variables[27] (I call it turncount) is multiplied by 0.20 and factored in to the first part of the formula. To have a turn count variable, all we have to do is go into the Ancient Dragon's troop (after creating it, of course) and add a troop event page with a "When the end of the turn" conditional that has a Turn span (so it triggers once per turn). Then we use Control Variables to increase the value of turncount by 1. So, every five turns, Devastate causes extra damage equal to three times the Ancient Dragon's MAT (so, 450). Basically, the battle is a race to defeat the superboss before it can wipe out the party with a casting of Devastate. Of course, the less HP the Ancient Dragon has, the stronger the skills that it uses.

Completing the Dragon Statue Event

Now that we have created our superboss and given it a robust set of skills to use against our player, let's complete the dragon statue event. As you'll recall, we set up the dragon statue event so that the player could inspect it from different angles. The interaction event has three conditional branches. Following is a refresher for part of the event:

```
@>Conditional Branch: Player is Facing Right
    @>Conditional Branch: Variable [0002:X] == 44
        @>Text: -, -, Normal, Bottom
        :       : You see a majestic dragon statue. It hums with
        :       : power.
        @>Text: 'Actor5', 6, Normal, Bottom
        :       : I sense immense power emanating from this
        :       : statue. Be mindful. It would be best to
        :       : return at a later time.
        @>Text: -, -, Normal, Bottom
        :       : Touch the statue?
        @>Show Choices: Yes, No
        : When [Yes]
            @>Jump to Label: DragonStatue
            @>
        : When [No]
            @>
        : Branch End
        @>
    : Branch End
    @>
: Branch End
```

The preceding code covers what happens if the player is facing right, but the three branches are used for the same purpose. At each [Yes] present within the interaction event, you'll want to place the Jump to Label event command as shown above. Then, at the very end of the event, you'll want to add the following:

```
@>Conditional Branch: Switch [0100] == ON
    @>Label: DragonStatue
    @>Text: -, -, Normal, Bottom
    :       : You place a hand on the statue.
    @>Text: -, -, Normal, Bottom
    :       : You feel yourself being whisked away!
    @>Change Battle BGM: 'Battle6', 100, 100
    @>Control Self Switch: A =ON
    @>Battle Processing: Ancient Dragon
    @>
: Branch End
@>
```

That is a dummy switch, a strategy we've used in previous chapters to make sure this part of the event can only execute when jumped into. When the player decides to touch the statue, we change the battle BGM and set self-switch A to on. Then, we send the player into the superboss battle. If the player triumphs, the interaction event flips to a second page that displays only the first bit of descriptive text. Look at the following code:

```
@>Conditional Branch: Player is Facing Right
   @>Conditional Branch: Variable [0002:X] == 44
      @>Text: -, -, Normal, Bottom
       :    : You see a majestic dragon statue. It hums with
       :    : power.
      @>
   : Branch End
```

With that said, we have one thing left to do.

Setting Up the Use of the Exit Skill/Item Inside a Dungeon with Two Exits

We have set up all of our relevant transfer events for the mines, but we have yet to update them with appropriate changes to the DungeonLocation variable. More important, we also need to update the common event that is tied to our Exit Scroll. As noted in this section's heading, the mines are peculiar in that they have two exits. We have the cave entrance hidden within the forest, and we have the entrance in Rocksdale. So, we have to have one value of DungeonLocation for each of the two entrances. We'll set them in the order that the player finds them, so that the entrance to the mines from the hidden location will set DungeonLocation to 3, while the entrance in Rocksdale will set its value to 4. Let's get started.

```
@>Control Variables: [0002:X] = Player's Map X
@>Control Variables: [0003:Y] = Player's Map Y
@>Conditional Branch: Variable [0002:X] == 29
   @>Conditional Branch: Variable [0003:Y] == 4
      @>Control Variables: [0011:DungeonLocation] = 3
      @>Transfer Player:[017:Abandoned MineF1F] (024,049), Up
      @>
   : Branch End
   @>
: Branch End
```

We have this event on the cave entrance map. Directly inside, at Abandoned Mines F1F, we tweak that event, so that DungeonLocation will become 0 if the player steps back out.

■ **Note** In what is another difference between this dungeon exit and the two previous locales, you can set Dungeon Location to 0 when the player leaves the mines, or when he/she steps back into the world map. I decided to set the value back to 0 as soon as the player breaks free of the mines, as the cave entrance is not part of the dungeon.

```
@>Control Variables: [0002:X] = Player's Map X
@>Control Variables: [0003:Y] = Player's Map Y
@>Conditional Branch: Variable [0002:X] == 24
   @>Conditional Branch: Variable [0003:Y] == 51
      @>Control Variables: [0011:DungeonLocation] = 0
      @>Transfer Player:[015:Cave Entrance] (029,005), Down
      @>
   : Branch End
   @>
: Branch End
@>
```

Next, we have to handle the other possible dungeon exit. The following code belongs to the transfer event in Rocksdale:

```
@>Control Variables: [0002:X] = Player's Map X
@>Control Variables: [0003:Y] = Player's Map Y
@>Conditional Branch: Variable [0002:X] == 30
   @>Conditional Branch: Variable [0003:Y] == 44
      @>Control Variables: [0011:DungeonLocation] = 4
      @>Transfer Player:[016:Abandoned MineFB1] (003,034), Up
      @>
   : Branch End
   @>
: Branch End
@>
```

Note how we set DungeonLocation to 4 here instead of 3. The last transfer event to be tweaked is the one that leads from the staircase at Abandoned Mine FB1 to the mountain village.

```
@>Control Variables: [0002:X] = Player's Map X
@>Control Variables: [0003:Y] = Player's Map Y
@>Conditional Branch: Variable [0002:X] == 4
   @>Conditional Branch: Variable [0003:Y] == 34
      @>Control Variables: [0011:DungeonLocation] = 0
      @>Transfer Player:[019:Mountain Village] (030,045), Down
      @>
   : Branch End
   @>
: Branch End
@>
```

With that said and done, we have only to tweak the common event that governs our exit code, and we're all set, like so:

```
@>Conditional Branch: Variable [0011:DungeonLocation] == 3
   @>Change Items: [Exit Scroll], -1
   @>Control Variables: [0011:DungeonLocation] = 0
   @>Transfer Player:[003:Field 3] (021,067), Down
   @>
: Branch End
```

```
@>Conditional Branch: Variable [0011:DungeonLocation] == 4
   @>Change Items: [Exit Scroll], -1
   @>Control Variables: [0011:DungeonLocation] = 0
   @>Transfer Player:[019:Mountain Village] (030,045), Down
   @>
: Branch End
@>
```

Summary

During the course of this chapter, I covered our preparations leading up to the final dungeon of the game. We populated Rocksdale with a few essential NPCs that drive the main narrative forward. Adding other buildings and NPCs to the town was left as an exercise for you. In addition, we completed the dragon statue event that had been started all the way back in Chapter 6, introducing our game's superboss in that way. Last, but not least, we updated the transfer events of our latest dungeon to include the DungeonLocation variable and did the same for the common event that governs our Exit skill/item. In the next chapter, we will be creating and populating our game's final dungeon.

CHAPTER 13

▤ ▤ ▤

The Final Dungeon

It has been 12 chapters, and I hope you have enjoyed the journey up to now. While I will be covering a few more things before I conclude this book, this will be the last chapter that's directly related to the game we've been developing together. The final dungeon is perhaps the most important part of a role-playing game (RPG). The player has gone through countless tribulations and obstacles, and he/she is finally at the doorstep of whoever, or whatever, is causing the game's central conflict. In our game, Eric and Noah find themselves in front of an ancient castle that used to house the kings of the western lands. It has been corrupted by a malevolent being known by many names but who we'll call the Dark Master. During the course of this chapter, we will be developing our game's final dungeon.

The Beginning of the End—The First Floor

For our game's final dungeon, I will be using the Devil's Castle series of sample maps. They will all be used, although not all of them will be used as the developers of RPG Maker VX Ace (RMVXA) possibly intended. The first order of business is to add the first floor to our project. Once that has been done, you'll want to connect it with the world map.

▤ **Note**   The DungeonLocation value of the final dungeon should be 5. Keep in mind that the castle we placed on the world map has a single tile that is considered passable (namely, the lower-middle tile).

The Teleportation Puzzle

Once we have our first floor added, we are going to create a little puzzle. It's only logical that a final boss is going to do everything in his power to stop the player from reaching it. Similarly, a final dungeon isn't much of one if the player can just walk up to the final boss as easy as saying it. What I'm going to add is a teleportation puzzle. To make this puzzle, we'll need the following:

- The use of Region Mode, to paint in the areas that will teleport the unwary player when he/she steps on it

- A Parallel Process event to handle the transfer events when the player steps on a Region

- A crystal that can be destroyed to flip on a switch. When the switch is flipped on, the Parallel Process event is skipped, allowing the player to progress in the dungeon.

For the sake of convenience, I painted the destination of each teleport Region trap on the map, using the same Region number. For example, the line made up of Region 63 will teleport the player to the square marked as 63. Check Figure 13-1 for most of the area involved in the teleportation puzzle. (The destination for Region 61 will be covered in Figure 13-2).

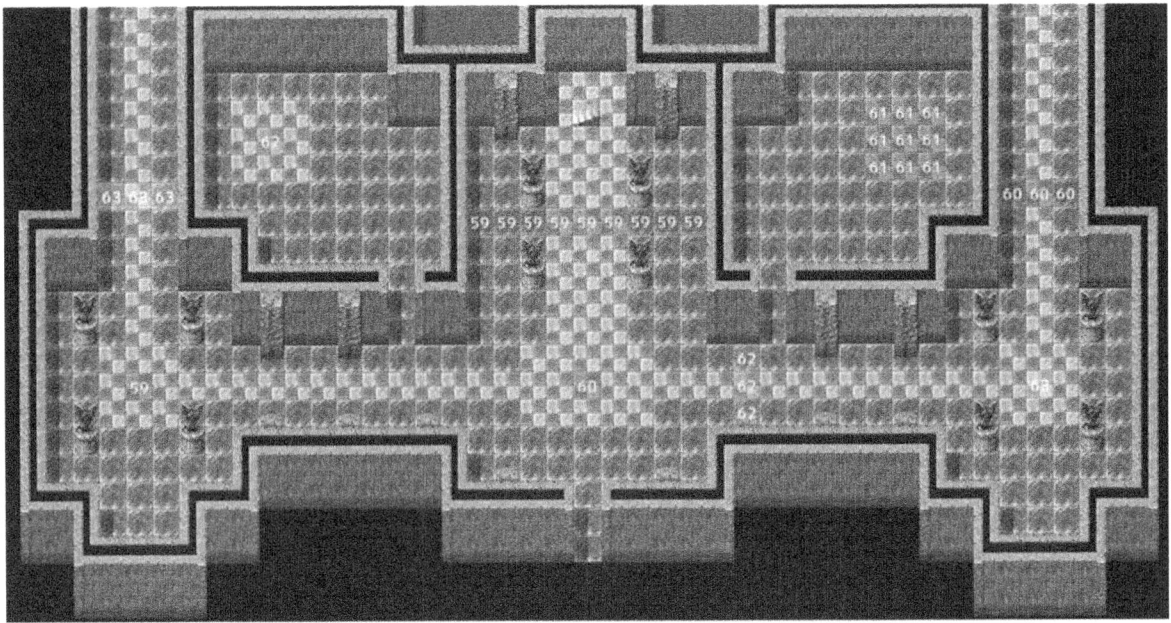

Figure 13-1. *A screenshot of the Regions that will be used to create our teleportation puzzle. The player wants to step on the area marked 61 to reach the crystal that will destroy the traps*

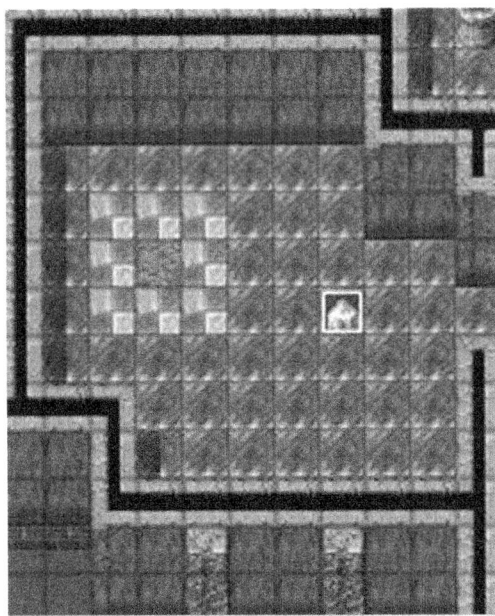

Figure 13-2. *A screenshot of the destination for Region 61 (represented by a grass tile). The nearby crystal event is what the player needs to interact with to disable the teleportation puzzle*

■ **Note**   Don't forget to erase the Regions at your intended destination. The reason for this will become obvious when we work on the Parallel Process event.

As promised, the player's two possible routes to leave the floor are blocked by teleportation Regions. Region 61 leads to another part of the map, as covered in Figure 13-2.

Creating the Puzzle Logic

We have defined where each particular Region leads within the floor, so let's work on the Parallel Process event now. The first part of our Parallel Process will check the player's x and y coordinates and then use the Get Location Info event command to get the Region ID from his/her current location. Whenever the player steps into a Region, he/she is teleported to the appropriate destination. Once the player shatters the crystal powering the teleportation traps, he/she can advance.

```
@>Control Variables: [0002:X] = Player's Map X
@>Control Variables: [0003:Y] = Player's Map Y
@>Get Location Info: [0028], Region ID, Variable [0002][0003]
@>Conditional Branch: Switch [0036:TeleportTrapOFF] == ON
   @>Jump to Label: Skip
   @>
: Branch End
@>Conditional Branch: Variable [0028:teleportspot] == 63
   @>Transfer Player:[024:Devil's CastleF1F] (040,042)
   @>
: Branch End
@>Conditional Branch: Variable [0028:teleportspot] == 62
   @>Transfer Player:[024:Devil's CastleF1F] (011,033)
   @>
: Branch End
@>Conditional Branch: Variable [0028:teleportspot] == 61
   @>Transfer Player:[024:Devil's CastleF1F] (031,017)
   @>
: Branch End
@>Conditional Branch: Variable [0028:teleportspot] == 60
   @>Transfer Player:[024:Devil's CastleF1F] (023,042)
   @>
: Branch End
@>Conditional Branch: Variable [0028:teleportspot] == 59
   @>Transfer Player:[024:Devil's CastleF1F] (006,042)
   @>
: Branch End
@>Label: Skip
```

Here you can see why you need to erase the Region squares I used to mark each destination (save for Region 61). The event is set up so that the player will be moved if he/she steps upon a Region.

■ **Caution** If you didn't heed my previous warning, you'll trap the player in an infinite loop, once he/she is teleported, given that his/her destination also contains the same Region ID used to get there in the first place!

Creating the Crystal That Controls the Puzzle

The last thing left to do for this puzzle is to set up the crystal event, which will have two pages. Page 1 will contain the lion's share of the total code, and page 2 will exist solely to inform the player that the crystal has been shattered. The graphic I'm using for page 1 of the crystal event is the very first one in the !Crystals graphic set. While the crystal appears cut off in the map editor, it will display correctly in-game.

```
@>Text: -, -, Normal, Bottom
:      : A glowing crystal floats in place.
@>Text: 'Actor5', 6, Normal, Bottom
:      : This crystal is probably what is stopping
:      : us from getting anywhere. We should
:      : shatter it.
@>Text: -, -, Normal, Bottom
:      : Will you destroy it?
@>Show Choices: Yes, No
: When [Yes]
   @>Fadeout Screen
   @>Play SE: 'Crash', 80, 100
   @>Text: -, -, Normal, Bottom
   :      : The crystal shatters!
   @>Control Self Switch: A =ON
   @>Fadein Screen
   @>
: When [No]
   @>
: Branch End
@>
```

When the player decides to shatter the crystal, we fade out the screen, play an appropriate sound effect, and display a message. We flip on a self-switch and then fade the screen back in, allowing the event to process page 2. Page 2 of the crystal event uses the Gravel (Crystal) tile as its graphic, requires self-switch A to be on, and displays a single message. The message is: "Where once the glowing crystal stood, only shards remain."

Encounters of the First Floor

Next, we must add a list of encounters for the player to potentially face in battle. You can see it in Figure 13-3.

Troop	Weight	Range
021:Werewolf*2	10	Whole
022:Sahagin*2	10	Whole
024:Gargoyle*2	10	Whole
039:Dragon	5	Whole

Figure 13-3. *The encounter list for the first floor of the Devil's Castle*

The first three enemy types are unchanged from their default forms. Dragons, on the other hand, are an entirely new monster type. I figured that, if we were going to have a Dragon superboss, it would only be proper to have lesser Dragons appear as an enemy type at some point before the end of the game. Ladies and gentlemen, I present to you the Dragon (Figure 13-4).

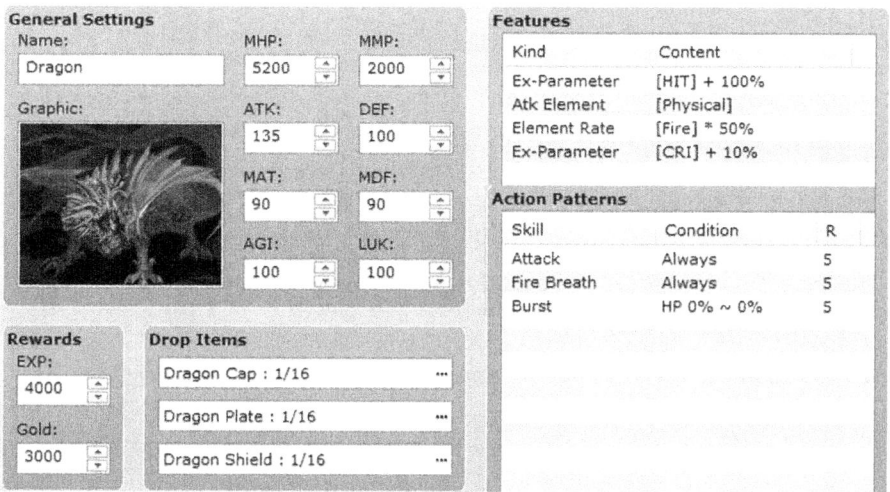

Figure 13-4. *Screenshot of the Dragon enemy created for the final dungeon. The Dragon adds Burst to its repertoire when it is at 50% HP or less*

The Dragon stands head and shoulders above every other normal (non-boss) enemy in our game. Nothing, save for the bosses in this dungeon (and the superboss, of course) is as strong as a Dragon. This enemy is a worthy addition to this game's final dungeon. They are notable in that they have a 1 in 16 chance of dropping some of the best default armor in RMVXA. All three drops are for Eric, as Noah does not have the ability to use Light Armor (Dragon Cap), Heavy Armor (Dragon Plate), or Shields. Now you may be wondering, if the mines dropped Mithril-quality gear, and Dragons have a chance to drop their self-named level of gear, what type of gear will we find in chests within this final dungeon? That will be something to cover a little later. For now, let's add two more levels to our project. We want Devil's Castle F2F and FB1. Of the two, the more significant is definitely FB1.

The Basement

We had the village elder of Rocksdale reference that an orb of great power was hidden beneath the castle. More important, the orb will be necessary to defeat the final boss. This makes the basement the most important floor for the player to visit during his/her time in the final dungeon. The layout of Devil's Castle FB1 can be seen in Figure 13-5.

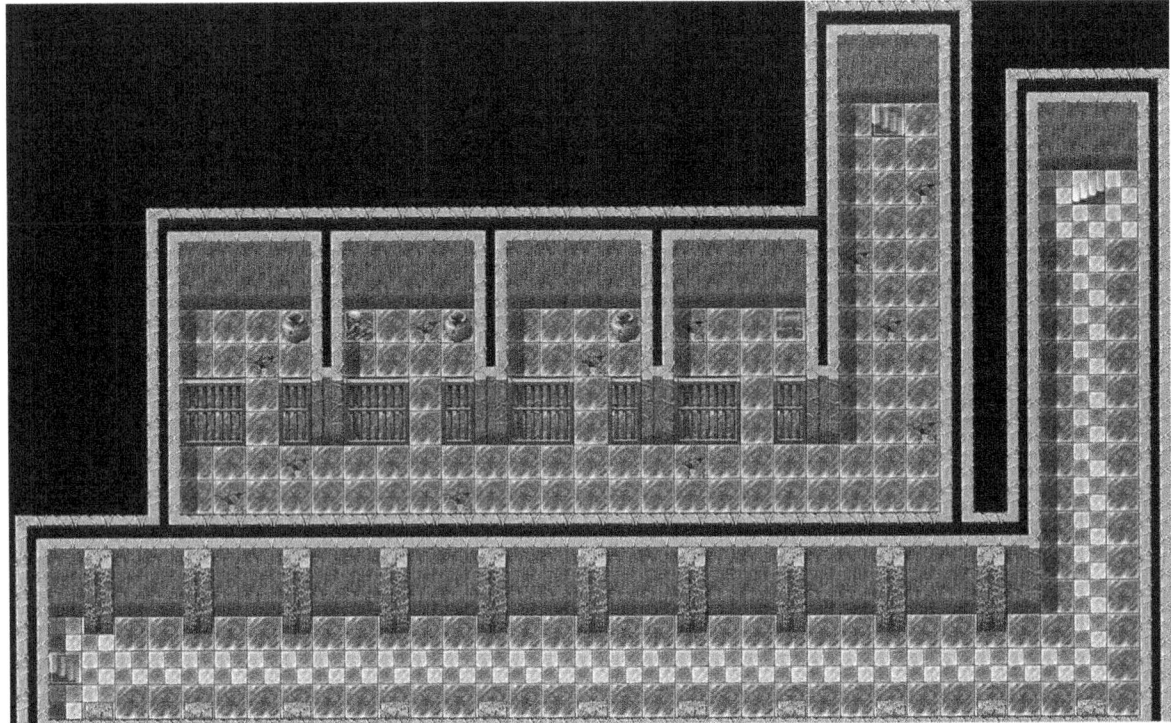

Figure 13-5. *A screenshot of Devil Castle's basement*

So, you're probably thinking that the chest contains the orb. You'd be wrong. The orb is in the hands of the skeleton in the second prison cell. The chest contains a piece of the armor that I created for this dungeon. Before I unveil it, let me show the code for the event related to the skeleton.

```
@>Text: -, -, Normal, Bottom
:    : The skeleton lets off a faint glow. Will you touch
:    : it?
@>Show Choices: Yes, No
: When [Yes]
   @>Text: -, -, Normal, Bottom
   :    : Light envelops your body!
   @>Change Items: [Orb of Light], + 1
   @>Play ME: 'Fanfare1', 100, 100
   @>Text: -, -, Normal, Bottom
   :    : You have found the \C[2]Orb of Light\C[0]!
   @>Change Items: [Orb of Light], + 1
   @>Text: 'Actor5', 6, Normal, Bottom
   :    : Such power! Keep it safe, Eric.
   @>Control Self Switch: A =ON
   @>
: When [No]
   @>
: Branch End
@>
```

The skeleton event is blank, with a Same As Characters priority and an Action Button trigger. If the player touches the skeleton, he/she will receive the Orb of Light, the item needed to be able to have a fighting chance against the final boss.

■ **Note**   Alternatively, you could remove the skeleton graphic from the map and add it to the event itself. The overall result is the same.

The Orb of Light is a Key Item in the same vein as the Old Key we created in Chapter 5. That is to say, it cannot be used from the inventory at any time. It will be automatically used by Eric when the party faces down the final boss. Now, let's reveal the first piece of armor that I created for this dungeon. (See Figure 13-6.)

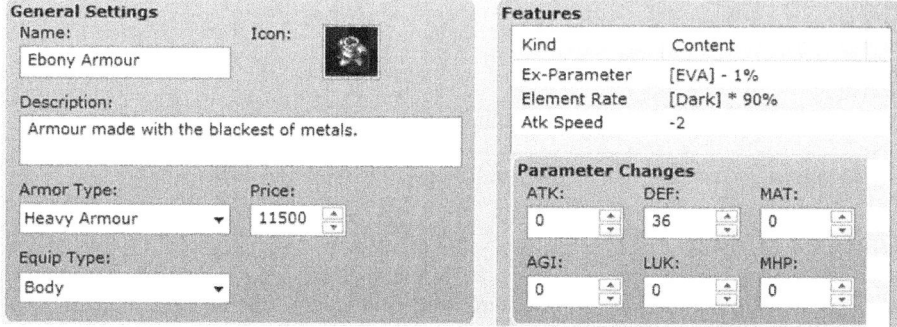

Figure 13-6.   *A screenshot of the Ebony Armour. Not pictured are the parameter changes for MDF and MMP, both of which are 0*

This is one of four pieces of Ebony gear that I made. They all follow the same formula. Basically, I took the average of the top two items in a specific set of armor (Heavy Armour, in this case) and averaged out their parameters and price. I added 10% Dark resistance to this armor, much like Dragon Armour has 20% Fire resistance. This armor is between Mithril Armour and Dragon Armour, in terms of the protection that it gives Eric. Use transfer events to connect the stairs near the prison cells with the staircase at (34,10) on the first floor. In addition, couple the basement staircase at (3,21) with the first floor stairs at (9,26). Last, link the remaining basement stairs at (34,7) with the first floor staircase at (40,12). With that set up, take a look at Figure 13-7 containing the basement's encounter list, before moving on to the next section.

Troop	Weight	Range
021:Werewolf*2	5	Whole
022:Sahagin*2	15	Whole
024:Gargoyle*2	10	Whole
025:Lamia	10	Whole
026:Vampire	10	Whole

Figure 13-7.   *The list of encounters for the Devil's Castle's basement*

I altered the Vampire's parameters to put it more in line with the other area encounters. You can see its altered stats later on in Figure 13-8.

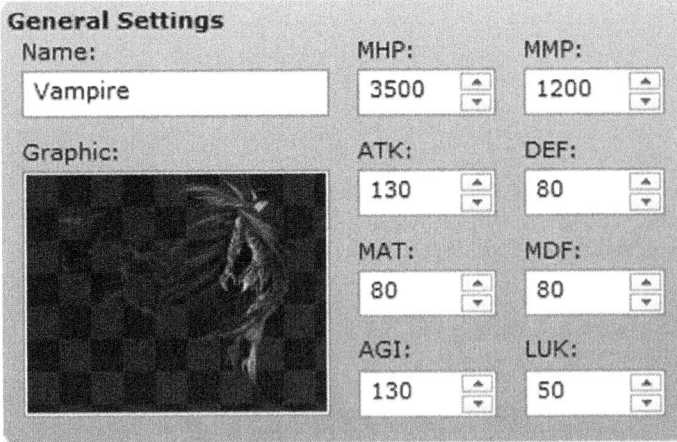

Figure 13-8. *A screenshot of the Vampire, weakened to fit my purposes of having it as a regular encounter*

The Second Floor

We used the first floor for a teleportation puzzle, so let's use the second floor for something a little more mundane. We have made three dungeons and filled up countless chests, but what happens when the chest contains an enemy? Then, the player has to defeat the enemy to get the treasure! I'm placing a total of five treasure chests on the second floor (Figure 13-9). The top two chests contain pieces of Ebony gear. Those will be guarded by Vampires.

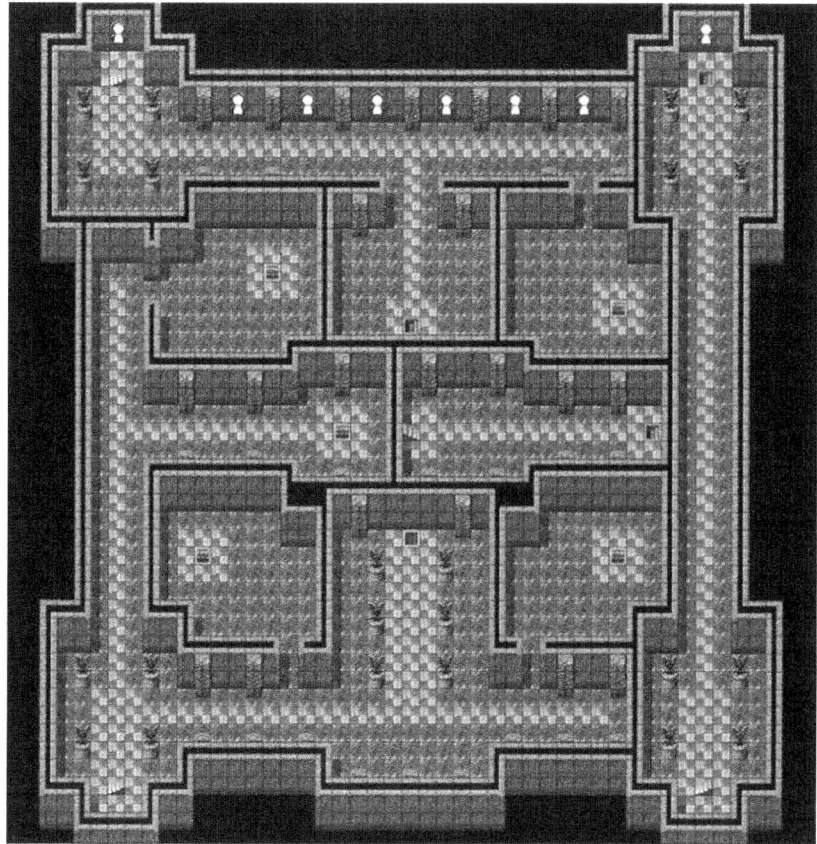

Figure 13-9. *Screenshot of the second floor of the Devil's Castle. Note the five treasure chests present on the level*

So, how do you make a chest that contains an enemy? It is incredibly simple. All you have to do is add the following two lines to a treasure chest event:

```
@>Text: -, -, Normal, Bottom
:      : You are attacked by a monster in a box!
@>Battle Processing: Vampire
```

■ **Note**   You can insert that code into any part of the default treasure chest event's first page, and the end result will be the same. The game interrupts event processing to do battle processing, so that the event will functionally "freeze in place" until the player defeats the forced encounter.

As promised, Figure 13-8 is an image of what my Vampire entry looks like now. As I only tweaked this enemy's parameters, that's all that the picture contains. Everything else is at their default settings.

This stat-block makes the Vampire the second strongest regular encounter in our game.

For reference to our altered treasure chests, take a look at the following event code for the northwestern chest at (15,17):

```
@>Control Self Switch: A =ON
@>Play SE: 'Chest', 80, 100
@>Set Move Route: This event (Wait)
:                 : $>Direction Fix OFF
:                 : $>Turn Left
:                 : $>Wait: 3 frame(s)
:                 : $>Turn Right
:                 : $>Wait: 3 frame(s)
@>Text: -, -, Normal, Bottom
:       : You are attacked by a monster in a box!
@>Battle Processing: Vampire
@>Change Armor: [Ebony Circlet] + 1
@>Text: -, -, Normal, Bottom
:       : Ebony Circlet was found!
@>
```

The Ebony Circlet is halfway between the Mithril Circlet and the Magi's Crown in terms of protection. The chest at (35,19) contains the Ebony Helm, which is between the Mithril Helm and the Dragon Helm in terms of protection (like the Ebony Armour, it grants 10% Dark resistance). The other chests contain lesser items, such as elixirs and gold. There's not much else to say about the second floor. As there are a whopping eight staircases on the second floor, I decided to write up in the form of a table (Table 13-1) where each of them connects to.

Table 13-1. *A List of Stairs on the Second Floor and Where They Connect to Within the Final Dungeon*

Stairs on 2F	Connecting Stairs
6,6	6,6(3F)
23,20	23,20(1F)
40,6	40,6(1F)
40,46	40,46(3F)
23,32	23,32(1F)
6,46	6,46(3F)
23,26	23,26(3F)
37,26	37,26(1F)

▪ **Caution**   As with the teleportation puzzle back on the first floor, be careful you don't create a situation in which you trap your player in an infinite loop! The actual transfer events should land adjacent to the destination staircase, not *on* them.

The last thing to do for this floor is to reveal the encounter list (Figure 13-10).

Troop	Weight	Range
021:Werewolf*2	5	Whole
022:Sahagin*2	15	Whole
024:Gargoyle*2	10	Whole
025:Lamia	10	Whole
039:Dragon	10	Whole

Figure 13-10. A screenshot of the encounter list for the second floor of the Devil's Castle

The general idea behind my encounter lists for this dungeon is that the player will have a greater chance of encountering harder enemies the farther away he/she gets from the entrance. This ramps up the tension in anticipation of the fated encounter with the final boss.

The Third Floor

While the first two floors of the Devil's Castle are fairly plain (in terms of layout, at least), the third floor is rather interesting. There's a dead-end area in the southwestern corner of the floor, as well as a large open space near the center that is most likely intended to be a treasure room. Given that I plan to have the final boss on the next floor, it is appropriate that we honor one of the most classic RPG conventions on this one. Let's have a boss rush!

A Boss Rush Overview

In some RPGs (and games of other genres, for that matter), the push toward the final boss is punctuated by having to re-fight all of the bosses that were previously battled. In our game, the player only has to fight two bosses (Gemini, at the Dark Cave, and the Demon, at the Dark Spire), so our boss rush will be two enemies long. You could loosely classify boss rushes into two broad categories.

1. **Consecutive boss rush**. The player has to fight each of the bosses without having a chance to recuperate, rest, or otherwise replenish his/her resources.

2. **Nonconsecutive boss rush**. The player gets a chance to restore him-/herself after each of the individual boss fights.

We'll be making a boss rush of the second type.

Locales of the Third Floor

Remember how I said at the beginning of the chapter that not all floors of the final dungeon would be used as intended? I'll be connecting Devil's Castle F5F to the entrance present within the third floor. Take a look at Figure 13-11 for reference.

Figure 13-11. *A screenshot of the area containing the entrance (6,18) that will take the player to the Devil's Castle F5F map*

Devil's Castle F5F will be the site of our boss rush. To make sure that the player has to defeat the bosses to progress, we can place a barrier much like the one that blocked the bridge on the world map before the player defeated the second boss. We'll use the same eventing strategy that we did for the teleportation puzzle on the first floor. Figure 13-12 has a screenshot of the area that is unblocked when the player completes the boss rush.

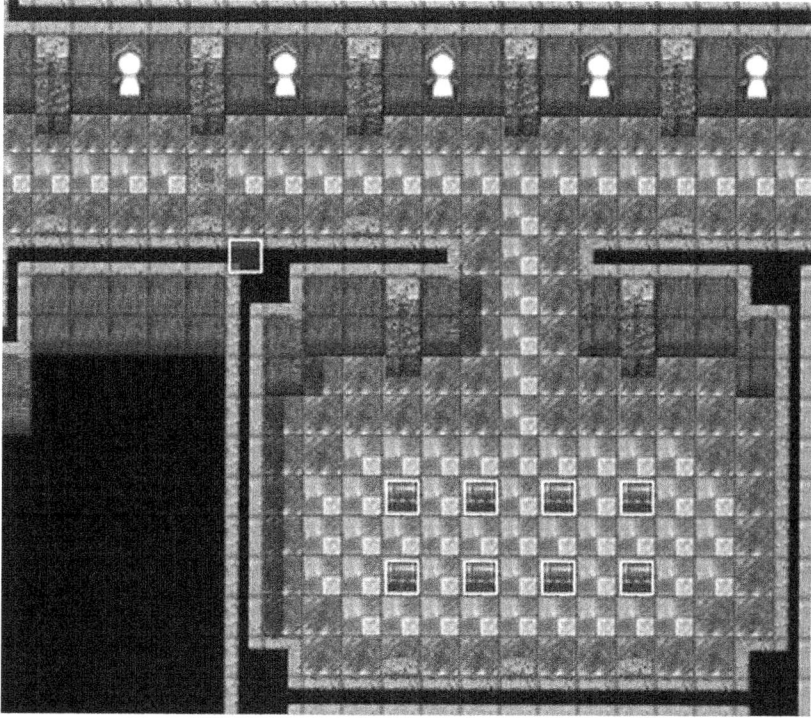

Figure 13-12. *A screenshot of the area to be blocked off by our event. I used one of the Rug tiles to mark the specific square that would be impassable*

Creating the Blocking Event

The square marked with a rug in Figure 13-12 is occupied by Region 63. Until the player completes the boss rush, he/she will be pushed back every time an attempt is made to try to pass that specific square. We'll talk about that treasure room in a bit. Here's the barrier event that requires the player to complete the boss rush:

```
@>Control Variables: [0002:X] = Player's Map X
@>Control Variables: [0003:Y] = Player's Map Y
@>Get Location Info: [0028], Region ID, Variable [0002][0003]
@>Conditional Branch: Switch [0035:CastleBarrierOFF] == ON
   @>Jump to Label: Skip
   @>
: Branch End
@>Conditional Branch: Variable [0028:teleportspot] == 63
   @>Text: -, -, Normal, Bottom
   :    : A strange force blocks the way!
   @>Set Move Route: Player (Wait)
   :              : $>1 Step Backward
   @>Conditional Branch: Self Switch A == OFF
     @>Text: 'Actor5', 6, Normal, Bottom
     :      : It appears we are blocked by another
     :      : sort of power, much like the one back
     :      : at the first floor. Let's try to find
     :      : the source.
```

```
    @>Control Self Switch: A =ON
    @>
  : Branch End
 @>
: Branch End
@>Label: Skip
```

As you can see, we can copy-paste the teleportation puzzle event to the point where we can even have the same variable to handle both. The first time that the player triggers this event, we have Noah reference that the situation is similar to what has happened once already and urge the player to find the source of the barrier. As you may have already inferred, the switch that will be flipped on when the player destroys the next crystal will be `CastleBarrierOFF`. So, the player cannot progress past that point and decides to walk through the entrance below the stairs, at a loss for where else to go. (The way the dungeon is laid out, there is no way to reach the final boss but through the blocked passage). Where does the player end up?

The Boss Rush

The player ends up at a long hallway that ends in a room with a single platform (Figure 13-13). That platform is where the player will find the crystal blocking the way. This room will have no random encounters.

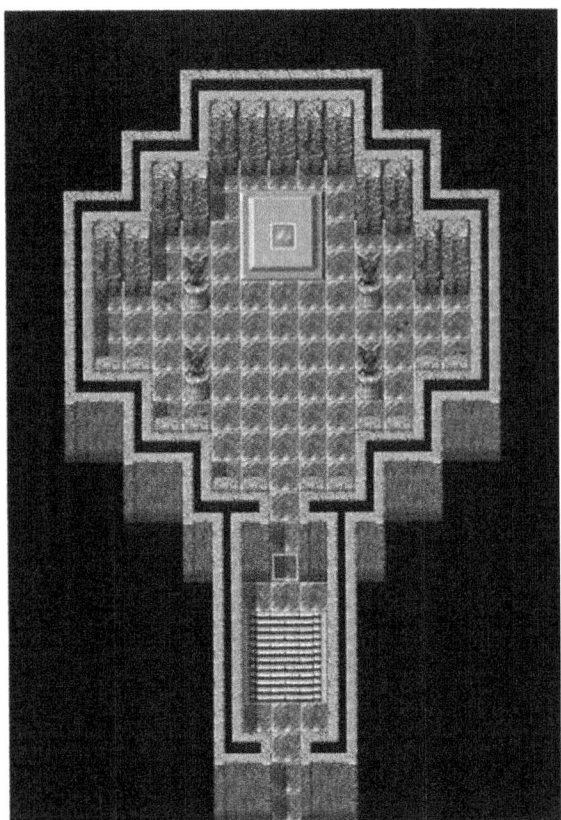

Figure 13-13. *A screenshot of Devil's Castle F5F. The stairs leading to the previous level have been replaced with an open entrance, and the long series of steps have been shortened*

I placed a Below Characters/Player Touch event at the doorway on top of the ornate staircase. When the player steps on the event, he/she has a rematch with a stronger version of Gemini, the first boss of the game.

```
@>Text: 'Actor5', 6, Normal, Bottom
:     : Brother?
@>Text: -, -, Normal, Bottom
:     : Yes, Noah. I have been resurrected by the will of
:     : the Dark Master. He decrees that none shall reach
:     : his inner sanctum! Fall before my power!
@>Change Battle BGM: 'Battle4', 100, 100
@>Battle Processing: Neo Gemini
@>Control Self Switch: A =ON
@>
```

We could leave Gemini and the Demon at their initial strength, and they would serve as a marker of just how far the player has progressed (seriously, the Demon has less HP than the Dragons the player can face here). Really, it's up to you. However, I'm going to improve their stats. Look at Figure 13-14 to see Neo Gemini's new and improved stats.

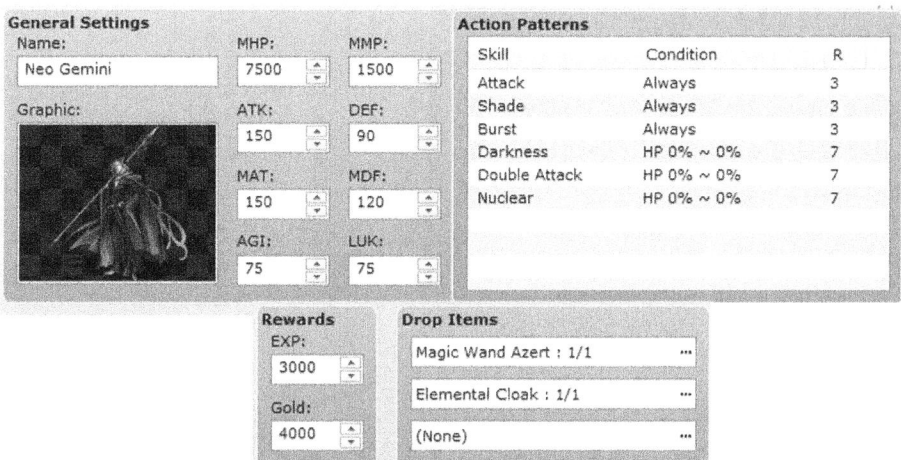

Figure 13-14. *A screenshot of Neo Gemini's stats and features. I changed his graphic color as well, because why not?*

Neo Gemini's action patterns are roughly identical to the first time Eric and Noah fought him. He replaces Poison Cloud with Burst and Life Drain with Nuclear. You can see the new pattern in Figure 13-15.

Action Patterns		
Skill	Condition	R
Attack	Always	3
Shade	Always	3
Burst	Always	3
Darkness	HP 0% ~ 0%	7
Double Attack	HP 0% ~ 0%	7
Nuclear	HP 0% ~ 0%	7

Figure 13-15. *A screenshot of Neo Gemini's action patterns*

Once the player defeats Neo Gemini, he/she can advance to the crystal forming the barrier blocking the path deeper into the castle. The crystal event will have three pages, as we want to cover the following:

- On Page 1, we want to tell the player that the crystal is emanating some sort of power and should be destroyed. If the player tries to destroy it, he/she is attacked by a stronger version of the game's second boss. A self-switch is flipped, and page 2 becomes active.

- If the player defeats the stronger Demon, he/she can interact with the crystal again and destroy it for real.

- Once the crystal is destroyed, the player receives a similar message about "shards being all that remain of the crystal."

```
@>Text: -, -, Normal, Bottom
:     : A dark crystal floats in place.
@>Text: 'Actor5', 6, Normal, Bottom
:     : I feel a terrible power coming from this
:     : crystal. We should destroy it.
@>Text: -, -, Normal, Bottom
:     : Will you destroy it?
@>Show Choices: Yes, No
: When [Yes]
  @>Text: -, -, Normal, Bottom
  :     : You will do no such thing!
  @>Text: -, -, Normal, Bottom
  :     : The party is interrupted by an enemy!
  @>Change Battle BGM: 'Battle4', 100, 100
  @>Battle Processing: Demon Lord
  @>Control Self Switch: A =ON
  @>
: When [No]
  @>
: Branch End
@>
```

Before I show the second page of the crystal event, take a look at Figure 13-16, to see a screenshot of the Demon Lord, a stronger version of the Demon the player had to face back at the Dark Spire.

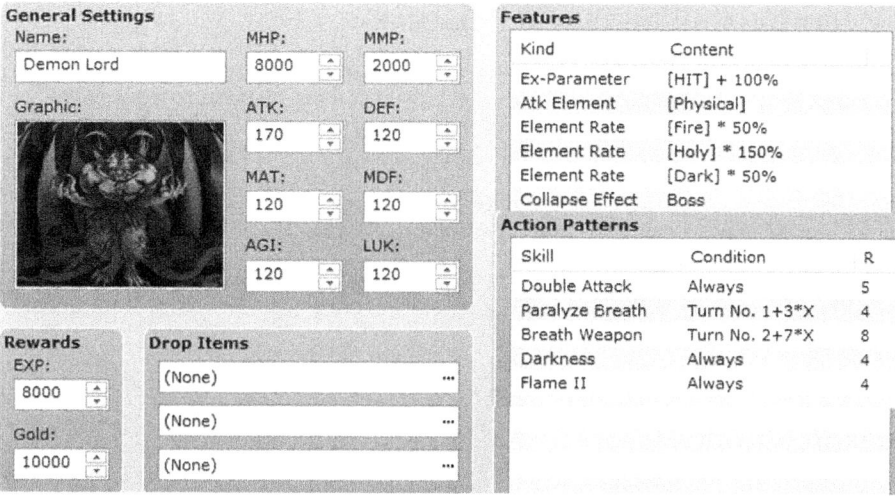

Figure 13-16. A screenshot of the Demon Lord, a stronger version of the second boss of our game. It switches Blind for Paralyze Breath and Shade for Darkness

The Demon Lord doesn't get as much of a power-up (relatively speaking) as Neo Gemini did, but that's mainly because Eric and Noah encounter the Demon later on. Thus, the difference in the player's overall power is lower in this case than it was for Gemini.

```
@>Text: -, -, Normal, Bottom
:        : The shadow crystal floats in place.
:        : Will you destroy it?
@>Show Choices: Yes, No
: When [Yes]
   @>Fadeout Screen
   @>Play SE: 'Crash', 80, 100
   @>Wait: 60 frame(s)
   @>Text: -, -, Normal, Bottom
   :        : The crystal has been destroyed!
   @>Control Switches: [0035:CastleBarrierOFF] = ON
   @>Control Self Switch: B =ON
   @>Fadein Screen
   @>
: When [No]
   @>
: Branch End
@>
```

Once the player defeats the Demon Lord, he/she can interact with the crystal again and destroy it for real. That will flip on the CastleBarrierOFF switch, allowing the player to get past the barrier blocking his/her way to the Dark Master's location.

Considerations Concerning the Boss Rush Room

Note that I glossed over changing the Battle BGM back to normal after the boss fights. The easiest way to do this is to have the transfer event leading back to the third floor have a Change Battle BGM command. Because this area will not have random encounters, the player will be none the wiser. However, if the player uses an Exit Scroll, you'll have a problem. You have two choices in that case.

1. Change the value of DungeonLocation to 0 while the player is in that room. (You can change it back to 5 when the player triggers the transfer event to leave the room.)

2. Add the Change Battle BGM command to the relevant conditional branch in the Exit Scroll common event.

The first option is cleaner, in my opinion.

Populating the Treasure Room

The next order of business is to populate the treasure room. (You can see a zoomed-in version of it in Figure 13-17.) Of course, a final boss does not merely leave its ill-gained loot out to be taken without a fight. In a similar vein as the previous floor, some of the chests will have encounters. The twist here is that the chests themselves will be the encounter!

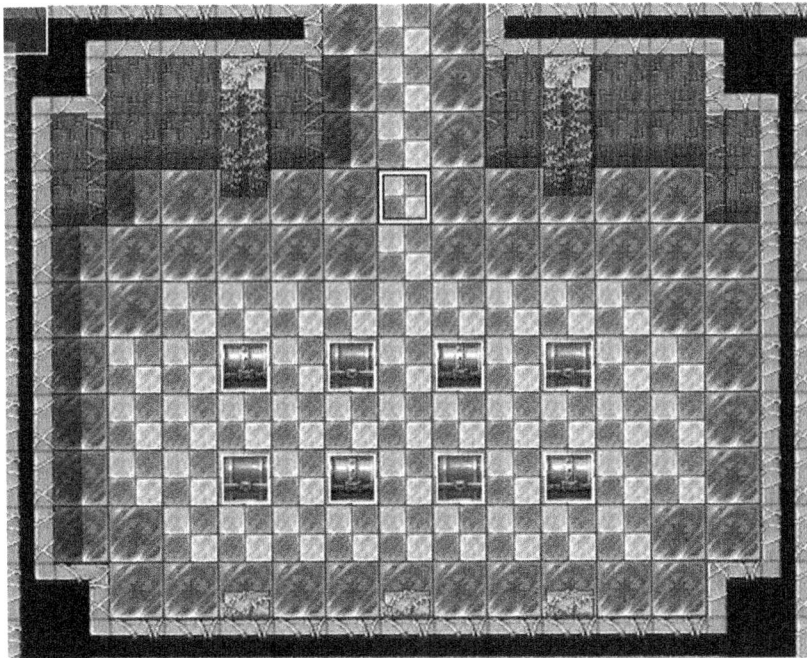

Figure 13-17. *A screenshot of Devil's Castle's treasure room. For the purposes of clarity, I used a different graphic to mark the chests that will be enemies*

The first and third chests on the top row and the second and fourth chests on the bottom row will be Mimics.

When Chests Attack

What's a Mimic, you might ask? Peeking at Figure 13-18 will give you an answer.

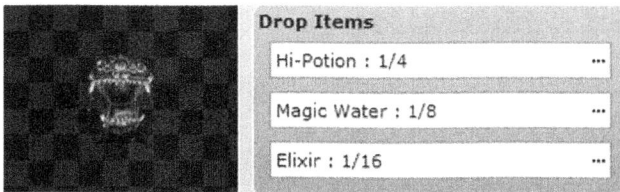

Figure 13-18. *Screenshot of a Mimic, the 20th default monster available in RMVXA*

I only placed a screenshot of the Mimic's item drop list, as I left everything else about this enemy at its default settings. It's only logical that a monster that acts like a chest should still have something to drop. The treasure chest event we use is nearly identical to the Vampire encounters I showed in Figure 13-14. Take a look.

```
@>Play SE: 'Chest', 80, 100
@>Set Move Route: This event (Wait)
:                  : $>Direction Fix OFF
:                  : $>Turn Left
:                  : $>Wait: 3 frame(s)
:                  : $>Turn Right
:                  : $>Wait: 3 frame(s)
@>Text: -, -, Normal, Bottom
:     : The chest was actually a Mimic!
@>Battle Processing: Mimic
@>Control Self Switch: A =ON
```

As for the four chests that *do* contain treasure, I placed the last piece of Ebony gear (the Ebony Robe) in the fourth chest of the top row. It provides protection between the Hermit Robe and the Elemental Cloak (70% protection vs. the elements listed in the other two armors). But wait, you might say. Noah got a better robe not more than five minutes prior! Yes, that is true. You could shuffle some of the Ebony gear, such that Noah can use the weaker robe until he gets the better one. Alternatively, you could swap out the Ebony Robe altogether for an accessory of some sort. The third chest on the bottom row contains the Gigantes Axe, which is the strongest axe available by default in the RMVXA database and will serve as a final upgrade for Eric. The other two chests contain an elixir and gold, respectively.

Miscellaneous Odds and Ends

With that done, the battle with the final boss is nigh! I have but three more things to cover in this section, and then we can move on to the floor containing the final boss. Thing #1: The secluded room (as displayed in the lower-left corner of Figure 13-19).

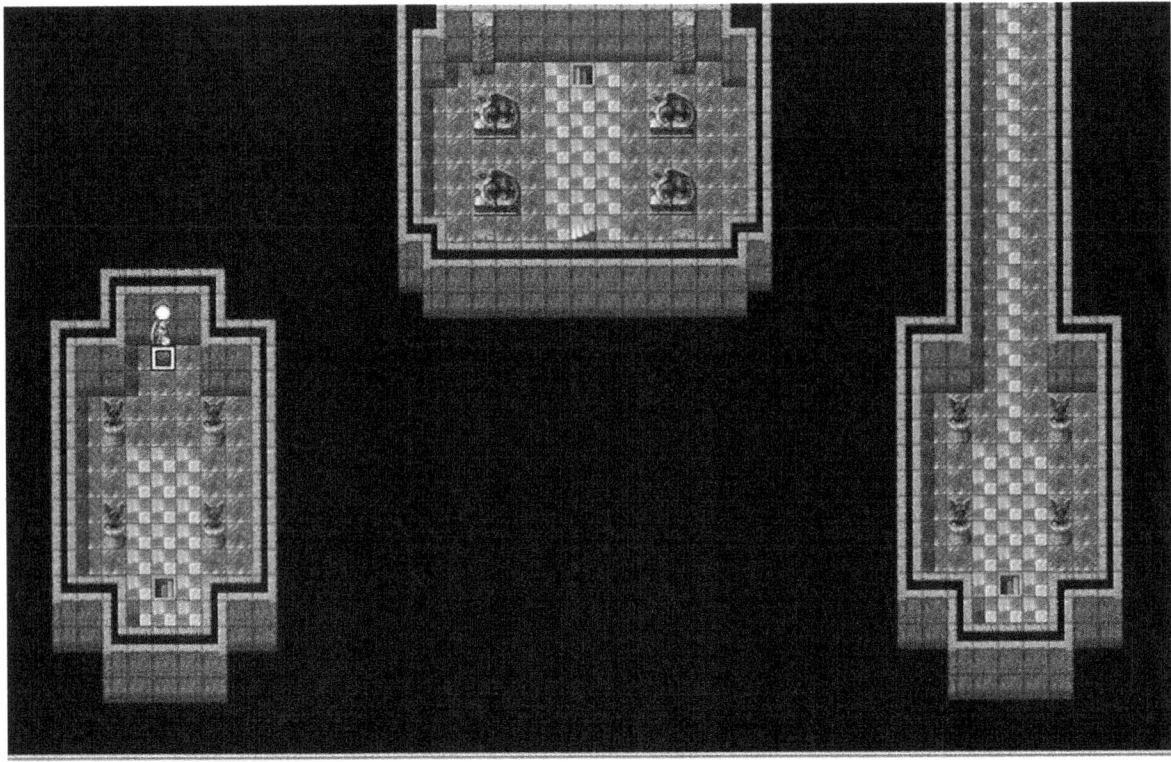

Figure 13-19. *A screenshot of the lower half of the third floor of the Devil's Castle*

Here's the rest (save for the reverse-L hallway connecting the two staircases) of the third floor, for context.

For the final dungeon's dead end, I decided to add a statue in front of the window. On the lower half of the statue, I placed an event with Same As Characters priority and an Action Button trigger. This statue will heal Eric and Noah when they touch it.

```
@>Text: -, -, Normal, Bottom
:     : A single statue stands defiant amidst the others.
:     : Will you touch it?
@>Show Choices: Yes, No
: When [Yes]
   @>Play SE: 'Heal1', 80, 100
   @>Recover All: Entire Party
   @>Text: -, -, Normal, Bottom
   :     : The party's HP and MP are restored!
   @>
: When [No]
   @>
: Branch End
@>
```

If you decide to make the final dungeon a point of no return (as in, the player cannot leave the dungeon once he/she enters), you'll want the player to have some way of recovering his/her HP and MP. Otherwise, a prolonged stay will drain his/her recovery items to the point that he/she may not be able to finish the game. This also allows the player to gain levels safely, that is, defeating the enemies in the area by staying near the statue. The second thing to cover is this floor's encounter list (Figure 13-20).

Troop	Weight	Range
026:Vampire	3	Whole
039:Dragon	2	Whole

Figure 13-20. *Screenshot of the encounter list for Devil's Castle 3F*

As the final dungeon level before the final boss, we have the two strongest enemy types of our game appear as the sole encounters in the area. Vampires have a 60% chance of appearing, while Dragons have a 40% appearance chance. The third and last thing is to point out that the staircase at (23,32) leads to the fourth floor, where the player will battle the final boss. Every other staircase has been accounted for already in previous sections. Are you excited? I am! It's time for . . .

The Final Boss

The player has fought tooth and nail through the entirety of the final dungeon to reach his/her foe. As is standard in RPGs, the final boss in our game is in the last possible place that Eric and Noah would think of looking. The route to the boss room takes the player up to the third floor, all the way down into the basement, and all the way up once again to the fourth floor. Once there, they are greeted by the sight of the Dark Master. Check Figure 13-21 to see the floor layout (of which I removed the rear staircase that would have led up to the fifth floor; the room that I repurposed for our boss rush in the previous section).

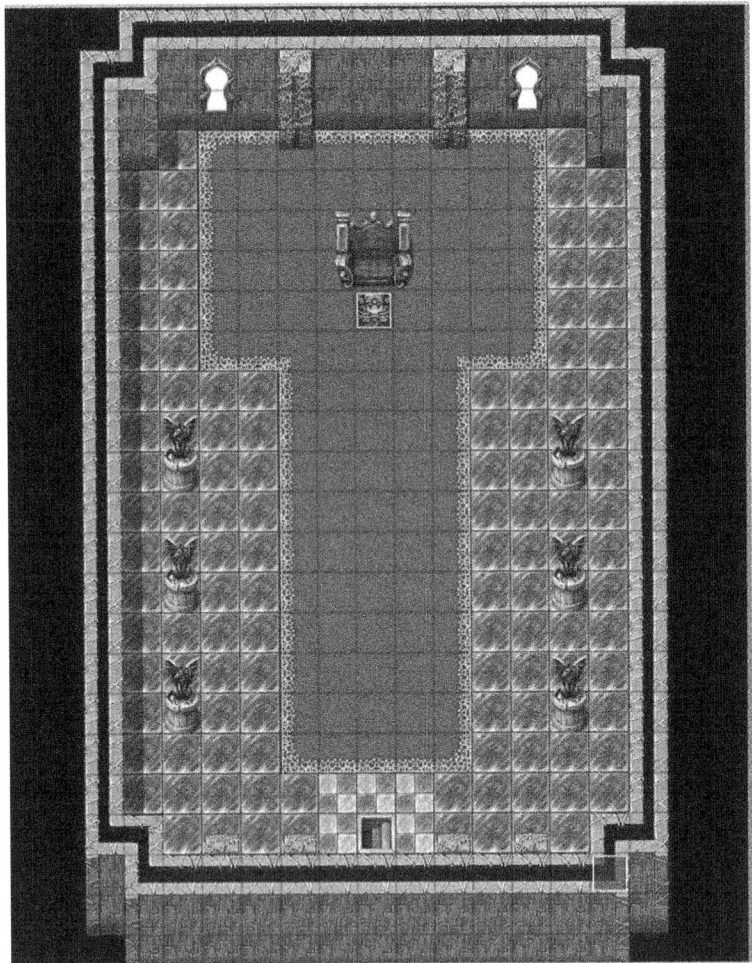

Figure 13-21. Screenshot of Devil's Castle 4F. The staircase at the back of the room has been removed and the wall patched up

Creating the Pre-Battle Autorun Event

When the player arrives at the fourth floor, an Autorun event will take over, tinting the screen. The player will walk toward the final boss as the tint slowly fades. Once there, the final boss will exchange some banter with the player's party before starting combat.

```
@>Tint Screen: (-68,-68,-68,0), @60, Wait
@>Text: -, -, Normal, Bottom
:      : Oho! So, you two have finally made it. Pity that
:      : this is where your quest ends.
@>Set Move Route: Player (Wait)
:                : $>1 Step Forward
:                : $>1 Step Forward
:                : $>1 Step Forward
```

```
@>Tint Screen: (-51,-51,-51,0), @60
@>Text: -, -, Normal, Bottom
:      : It's truly fascinating what humans will do for the
:      : sake of such petty things like justice and hope.
@>Set Move Route: Player (Wait)
:                 : $>1 Step Forward
:                 : $>1 Step Forward
:                 : $>1 Step Forward
@>Tint Screen: (-34,-34,-34,0), @60
@>Text: -, -, Normal, Bottom
:      : So, what would you like your gravestones to read?
@>Set Move Route: Player (Wait)
:                 : $>1 Step Forward
:                 : $>1 Step Forward
:                 : $>1 Step Forward
@>Tint Screen: (-17,-17,-17,0), @60
@>Set Move Route: Player (Wait)
:                 : $>1 Step Forward
:                 : $>1 Step Forward
@>Tint Screen: (0,0,0,0), @60
@>Text: 'Actor4', 0, Normal, Bottom
:      : The only one who's going to need a
:      : gravestone here is you!
```

■ **Caution**   If you overestimate the number of movement commands needed, the lack of a Skip at the end of the movement sequence will cause the game to hang.

```
@>Text: 'Actor5', 6, Normal, Bottom
:      : I concur. It is past time that you be
:      : dethroned!
@>Text: -, -, Normal, Bottom
:      : Ah, Gemini's brother. You already know the truth of
:      : the world. Or, at the least, you suspect it. So
:      : foolish are you that you would subject the people
:      : of the west to the truth?
@>Text: 'Actor5', 6, Normal, Bottom
:      : It serves no one to live in lies!
@>Text: 'Actor4', 0, Normal, Bottom
:      : What are you talking about, Noah?
@>Text: -, -, Normal, Bottom
:      : Ohoho! You haven't even told your traveling
:      : companion. Riveting! That'll be something to talk
:      : about. For sure. In the afterlife!
@>Change Battle BGM: 'Battle9', 100, 100
@>Control Self Switch: A =ON
@>Battle Processing: Dark Master
```

At the end of it all, the player realizes that Noah knows something he/she does not. However, there's a boss to defeat!

The Dark Master and the Final Battle

We want to use a troop event that triggers as soon as the battle starts to check and see if the player has the Orb of Light in his/her inventory. If the player does, we apply a state to the Dark Master that lowers all of his stats except AGI, MHP, and MMP by 50%. If he/she doesn't, the player has the unenviable task of somehow beating an enemy that has nearly twice the power as the game's superboss. See Figure 13-22 for the Dark Master's relevant information.

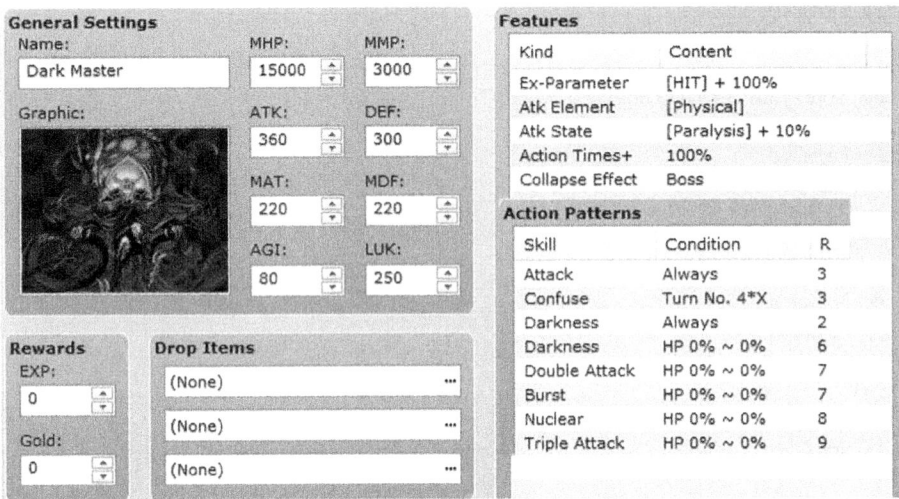

Figure 13-22. *Screenshot of the Dark Master's relevant information. Darkness, Double Attack, and Burst are used when he is below 50% HP. Nuclear and Triple Attack are added when he drops below 25% HP*

You will notice that defeating the Dark Master awards no EXP, gold, or items. Given that the game will end after defeating the final boss, there isn't much of a point in the player earning any of that. Action Times+ is a special feature that increases the number of actions that an enemy can take in a single turn. Each instance of Action Times+ allows an extra action at X%, where X is the percentage probability of using the extra action on any given turn. So, if an enemy has three Action Times+ entries, it can potentially act four times each turn.

■ **Note** This is not to be confused with Atk Times+, which influences how many extra times the enemy attacks when it uses the normal Attack skill.

Following, you will find the first page of the final boss's troop event:

```
Condition: Turn No. 0
Span: Battle
@>Change Enemy State: [1. Dark Master], + [Immortal]
@>Conditional Branch: [Orb of Light] in Inventory
   @>Text: -, -, Normal, Bottom
   :     : The Orb of Light shines bright!
   @>Change Enemy State: Entire Troop, + [Orb Debuff]
   @>Text: -, -, Normal, Top
   :     : Accursed light!
```

```
   @>Text: -, -, Normal, Top
   :     : The Dark Master's power is weakened!
   @>
: Else
   @>Text: -, -, Normal, Top
   :     : You dared to face me without the aid of the Orb?
   :     : Hahaha!
   @>
: Branch End
@>
```

We make the Dark Master immortal at the start of the fight, so that we can trigger a troop event when he drops to 0% HP or less. Orb Debuff is the name of the negative state applied to the Dark Master. When the player manages to defeat the Dark Master, the other troop event page is triggered.

- Condition: Enemy [1. Dark Master]'s HP 0% or below

- Span: Battle

```
@>Text: -, -, Normal, Top
:     : Guh! Impressive...
@>Control Switches: [0037:FinalBossDefeated] = ON
@>Change Enemy State: [1. Dark Master], - [Immortal]
```

After the player defeats the final boss, we should have an Autorun event that leads into the credits. However, let's entertain a "What if?" situation first. Mainly, what if the final boss had a second form?

Transform!

A hallmark of many classic RPGs is a final boss with multiple forms. Let's give our Dark Master a second form (you can see its information in Figure 13-23). We'll use the EvilGod battle sprite. The final form of the final boss deserves a special attack. So, I took Darkness as the base and made a new spell called Black Hole. It costs 80 MP and has a damage formula of [250 + a.mat * 3 - b.mdf * 2] with 40 Variance. Much like Darkness, it is a Dark element spell. Now, how do we switch our final boss to his second form? We can use the Enemy Transform command on page 3 of the event command list. In this case, when the player drops the Dark Master to 0 HP, we want him to transform into his second form. You can also use Enemy Transform for several other neat enemy archetypes, such as an unhatched egg that could turn into a dragon if you don't destroy it fast enough, or a jack-in-a-box-type monster that randomly morphs into one of several others when a certain condition is met.

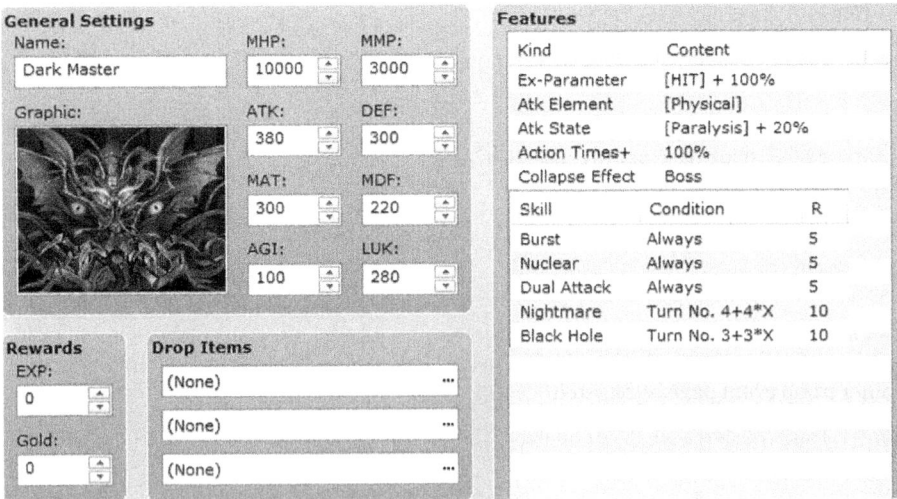

General Settings

Name: Dark Master

MHP: 10000   MMP: 3000

Graphic:

ATK: 380   DEF: 300

MAT: 300   MDF: 220

AGI: 100   LUK: 280

Rewards

EXP: 0

Gold: 0

Drop Items

(None)

(None)

(None)

Features

Kind	Content	
Ex-Parameter	[HIT] + 100%	
Atk Element	[Physical]	
Atk State	[Paralysis] + 20%	
Action Times+	100%	
Collapse Effect	Boss	

Skill	Condition	R
Burst	Always	5
Nuclear	Always	5
Dual Attack	Always	5
Nightmare	Turn No. 4+4*X	10
Black Hole	Turn No. 3+3*X	10

Figure 13-23. A screenshot of the Dark Master's second form. He uses skills from the last section of the first form's action patterns and Nightmare and Black Hole every few turns

■ **Note**   Transformed enemies count as a new foe. Make sure that the second form of the Dark Master makes the same check for the Orb of Light in its troop event as the first form! The previously listed stats are for a Dark Master who has not had its stats reduced.

The End (of the Game)

After a journey spanning four dungeons, three area bosses, two towns, and one Dark Master, this RPG has been completed! Of course, that only refers to the scope of this book concerning the subject. There is no reason that you have to stop working on the game. After all, we left a lot of things in the air. For example:

- What is the truth that the Dark Master (and the Demon, for that matter) hinted at? Noah seems to have known what was going on, but he kept his companion in the dark.

- What happens next, plot-wise? Perhaps there is more than one Dark Master.

- Amanda ended up a loose end, in terms of characterization. Maybe she joins Eric and Noah after they defeat the Dark Master.

- No one had been able to leave Seaside and return for the past few years. The defeat of the Dark Master may give the player an opportunity to understand why.

There's some food for thought for you. As for me, let me finish up the event involving the final boss. The FinalBossDefeated switch is flipped on when the Dark Master is finally defeated. (You could also flip it on at the start of the fight, as the player cannot escape the battle.) Page 3 of the event that started with an Autorun will end with an Autorun as well.

```
@>Fadeout BGM: 5 sec.
@>Text: 'Actor4', 0, Normal, Bottom
:      : It is over!
@>Text: -, -, Normal, Bottom
:      : Noah smiles wistfully at Eric.
@>Text: 'Actor5', 6, Normal, Bottom
:      : No, my friend. It has only begun.
@>Text: 'Actor4', 0, Normal, Bottom
:      : Huh? What are you talking about?
@>Text: 'Actor5', 6, Normal, Bottom
:      : Well, it goes like this...
@>Fadeout Screen
@>Play BGM: 'Field4', 100, 100
@>Text(S): Speed 2
:        : What Noah next tells Eric leaves the young hero in
:        : disbelief. A world in ruins...controlled by two
:        : other Dark Masters. Why had the west alone been
:        : spared? To that question, all Noah did was smile
:        : and point at Eric cryptically.
:        :
:        : So many questions unanswered. What path will our
:        : heroes' journey take next? What new companions will
:        : they find? Does humanity yet live in the rest of the
:        : world?
```

We fade out the background music in preparation for the ending. After a small chat between the two party members, the screen is faded out, we play some different background music, and some scrolling text is displayed. Unlike Show Text, Show Scrolling Text should only be used on a black screen (this event command displays only text, no text boxes).

```
@>Fadeout BGM: 2 sec.
@>Wait: 120 frame(s)
@>Play BGM: 'Theme1', 100, 100
@>Text(S): Speed 2
:        : CREDITS:
:        :
:        : Me - For making this game.
:        :
:        : You - For playing it.
:        :
:        : Enterbrain - For making RPG Maker VX Ace.
:        : Without it, this game would not exist.
:        :
:        : THANKS FOR PLAYING!!!
@>Return to Title Screen
```

Once we have displayed the epilogue text, we fade out the BGM once again and then start the music that's played by default at the title screen. Some short credits later, we send the player back to the title screen.

More Tips and Tricks for Final Dungeons

While this chapter is as good as done, there are so many more things that you can do with a final dungeon. RPGs have had all types of final dungeons, ranging from the one-room final dungeon (justified by the difficulty of getting into that one room; the player usually needs a series of keys or artifacts to open the path) to a sprawling mega-fortress that dwarfs the Devil's Castle many times over. Here's a list of other things you can add to the final dungeons of your future games.

- *Uncontrollable movement puzzle*: You could either use the ice puzzle we created before or make a new type of puzzle in which the player is forced in a certain direction, based on where he/she has stepped. Much like the teleportation puzzle we used on the first floor, this can be used to force the player to figure out how exactly he/she can get past that particular area.

- *The escape*: Once the player defeats the final boss, instead of ending the game right then and there, you can make it so that a countdown begins. (You can use the *Control Timer* event command for this purpose.) If the player has not escaped the castle when the timer hits zero, you can either give him/her a Game Over (probably a jerk move, considering that the player had to defeat the final boss even to get that far and probably has not even saved) or send him/her back to the throne room to try and escape again. On a related note, you might make it so that the timer doesn't start until the player starts trying to escape, so that he/she has a chance to save the game beforehand.

- *An alternate take on the boss rush*: Besides creating a boss rush as we have, you can also stagger its appearance. For example, if your game has four main bosses and you want them to reappear in the final dungeon that also has four floors, you can block each floor with a single boss. The player has to defeat the boss to advance upward (or downward).

- *An alternative to the final boss fight*: Perhaps the final boss gets its power from a crystal nexus or some other arcane artifact. Destroying the artifact could provide the player another way of winning the game while avoiding confrontation. It didn't seem appropriate for our game, but an RPG that wants to reward differing play styles could benefit from such an approach.

- Make it so that the final boss is weakened according to the number of sidequests the player has carried out. This is a neat way of rewarding the player for taking the time to explore beyond the beaten path.

Summary

During the course of this chapter, we created our game's final dungeon and populated it. We used a teleportation puzzle on the dungeon's first floor that would stop the player from progressing until he/she had destroyed the crystal powering the traps. On the second floor, chests containing Ebony gear were guarded by Vampires. The third floor was blocked by an invisible barrier that required our player to defeat stronger versions of bosses already faced. The treasure room on the same floor revealed that some chests can actually be monsters. Finally, we created a final boss (with a second alternate form) that, when defeated, triggered the end credits. In the next chapter, we will tackle some basic scripting exercises in RMVXA.

CHAPTER 14

Basic Scripting Exercises in RMVXA

We have now finished our game. All that is left is to cover a few things that I didn't cover in earlier chapters. While an in-depth look into Ruby scripting within RPG Maker VX Ace (RMVXA) is outside of the scope of this book, in this chapter, it would still be a good idea to cover the basics. Chapter 15 will cover other miscellanea that I did not feel fit within the overall narrative of our game and the book so far.

What Is Ruby?

Ruby is an object-oriented programming language that was created by Yukihiro Matsumoto in 1993. It is used within RMVXA in the form of the RGSS (Ruby Game Scripting System) and serves as the driving force behind this game-development engine. It is praised by programmers worldwide for its ease of use. The best part of all is that Ruby is open source (and thus costs the grand total of nothing to get; it can be downloaded freely). Learning how to use Ruby will help you greatly whenever you decide to start customizing your games with scripts.

What Is Object-Oriented Programming?

In a sentence: it is programming that uses code organized into objects as the building blocks for a desired result. We've been seeing examples of how Ruby (and, thus, object-oriented programming) works, in the few scripting exercises we tackled for our game. Here's what we've actually touched upon already.

- $ represents a global variable. That is, a value denoted with $ can be used anywhere within a project (e.g., our game).

- @ denotes an instanced variable (also known as an object variable). Instanced variables are used within classes (such as Game_Interpreter).

- $game_actors[n] (where n is the actor ID) is an array that contains several defining aspects of Actors in RMVXA, such as name, level, and nickname. You can reference any of the variables listed under the header Public Instance Variables in the Game_Actor class by using the format $game_actors[n].x (where x is the variable name).

- An array is an ordered collection of objects.

- You can call methods defined within the Script Editor in the damage formula box for items and skills.

As you can see, there are quite a few things we already know. During the course of this chapter, we'll be tackling other simple things that we can do with only the most basic of Ruby experience. The first exercise will be changing how critical hits are calculated, so that they are influenced by the Luck stat of the attacker and the defender.

Critically Coded

As robust as RMVXA is right out of the box, it has a few quirks that bug me. Thankfully, you can tweak and edit such things within the Script Editor. This first exercise is very nearly a one-liner. All we need to do is find the code that governs critical hit rates. Let's go to the Script Editor and run a search for "critical." Quite a few results will pop up, but we're interested in the entry that says "Game_Battler (487): * Calculate Critical Rate of Skill/Item." Clicking it takes us to the following method:

```
#--------------------------------------------------------------------------
# * Calculate Critical Rate of Skill/Item
#--------------------------------------------------------------------------
def item_cri(user, item)
  item.damage.critical ? user.cri * (1 - cev) : 0
end
```

What we see here is a method (item_cri) that accepts two parameters when run. For the curious, user is defined in Scene_ItemBase, while item is defined in Game_BaseItem. As you may recall from earlier in the book, what we're looking at right now is a ternary expression. The preceding text is equivalent to the following code. The question mark takes the place of the then, while the colon does the same for the else.

```
if item.damage.critical
then user.cri * (1-cev)
else 0
```

That's the extent of this particular method. Basically, if the skill or item is capable of landing criticals, then the chance to land a critical is equal to the user's critical hit chance multiplied by 1, minus the enemy's critical evasion rate (the result is a percentage). Let's create a new page in the Materials section of the Script Editor to hold the altered version of our item_cri method. Here's the altered result:

```
class Game_Battler
def item_cri(user, item)
  item.damage.critical ? (user.cri + (user.luk * 0.002)) - (luk * 0.002) \
    * (1 - cev) : 0
  end
end
```

In my version, I made it so that the luck of both the user and the target influence the ability to land a critical hit. The backward slash after (luk * 0.002) is used to tell RMVXA to read the next line as part of the previous one.

▮ **Note**   Recall that weird things happen when we split a single expression over multiple lines, if the game decides to run at all. The backward slash tells RMVXA to run the next line as a direct continuation of the previous one, which, of course, helps prevent such weirdness.

For every 5 LUK that the user has, he/she gains 1% to his/her CRI. For every 5 LUK that the target has, the user loses 1% to his/her CRI. So, how can I be so certain that we are working with percentages? There are two good ways to prove it.

1. Change the multiplier on `user.luk` to 1. You will notice that the attacker always lands critical hits, no matter how low its LUK is. If we were working with whole numbers, the attacker's CRI would be equal to its LUK and not a guaranteed 100%.

2. Note that CEV is expressed in the Database as a percentage, yet it is subtracted from 1 here. If we were working with whole numbers, you would have to subtract from 100 instead. 10% CEV will result in (1 - 0.10) and not (1 - 10), for example.

To be honest, it also helps that I tested this while initially attempting to figure it out and noticed how the attacker would land guaranteed critical hits when I had whole numbers for multipliers within the formula. So, another thing that I wanted to fix within RMVXA was the way that battle messages were expressed. Mainly, the ones that appear when damage is dealt or healing is performed. You've probably noticed that the default messages are a bit clunky, to put it mildly. How do we go about this? Welcome to the next section!

Coded Messages (in a Bottle)

What I seek to change is the messages that are displayed after an actor or an enemy performs a skill that has a damaging or healing effect. As those are possible results of actions taken, we can skim the list of classes and methods within the Script Editor, to see if that is covered by anything. As it turns out, this is covered in its very own class called `Game_ActionResult`. Now that we know that, we can head over there to take a look. As circumstances would have it, the three methods we are looking for are the very last ones of the entire class. Here's the first of them:

```
#--------------------------------------------------------------------------
# * Get Text for HP Damage
#--------------------------------------------------------------------------
def hp_damage_text
  if @hp_drain > 0
    fmt = @battler.actor? ? Vocab::ActorDrain : Vocab::EnemyDrain
    sprintf(fmt, @battler.name, Vocab::hp, @hp_drain)
  elsif @hp_damage > 0
    fmt = @battler.actor? ? Vocab::ActorDamage : Vocab::EnemyDamage
    sprintf(fmt, @battler.name, @hp_damage)
  elsif @hp_damage < 0
    fmt = @battler.actor? ? Vocab::ActorRecovery : Vocab::EnemyRecovery
    sprintf(fmt, @battler.name, Vocab::hp, -hp_damage)
  else
    fmt = @battler.actor? ? Vocab::ActorNoDamage : Vocab::EnemyNoDamage
    sprintf(fmt, @battler.name)
  end
end
```

Dissecting the hp_damage_text Method

Although the larger parts of the method may look like alphabet soup at the moment, we can deduce the four action results handled by this method, based on the code expressions.

- The initial if statement displays a message when the attacker uses a skill that drains HP. A draining attack heals the user for the same amount of HP that it deals to its target.

- The first elsif statement is called when the attacker uses a skill that does HP damage.

- The second elsif statement is relevant when the character uses a skill that heals HP.

- The else statement is used for the niche case in which the attacker uses a skill that does no damage to its target.

With that established, let's dissect the first statement. It is two lines long and says the following:

```
fmt = @battler.actor? ? Vocab::ActorDrain : Vocab::EnemyDrain
sprintf(fmt, @battler.name, Vocab::hp, @hp_drain)
```

■ **Note** Before you start working on this section, don't forget to insert a new page in Materials at the Script Editor and copy-paste the relevant methods as we require them. Direct alteration of code should always be avoided, if possible.

Our variable assignment in the first line (fmt) is a perfect example of a local variable. As its name implies, a local variable is only used wherever it is called. Thus, whatever is plugged into fmt is used only for this particular statement and then scrapped. @battler.actor? is an instance variable that returns true if the battler is an Actor. If he/she is an enemy, it will return false. If @battler.actor? is true, the ActorDrain text will be displayed; otherwise, the EnemyDrain text will be displayed. The second line uses a special method called sprintf. RMVXA's help file has a very useful write-up on the method. In layman's terms, you can use sprintf to fill in a predetermined sentence of text. Let's go to the Vocab module and find ActorDrain. You'll find it along with several other terms, so here are lines 51 through 67 of the Vocab module:

```
# Results for Actions on Actors
ActorDamage     = "%s took %s damage!"
ActorRecovery   = "%s recovered %s %s!"
ActorGain       = "%s gained %s %s!"
ActorLoss       = "%s lost %s %s!"
ActorDrain      = "%s was drained of %s %s!"
ActorNoDamage   = "%s took no damage!"
ActorNoHit      = "Miss! %s took no damage!"
# Results for Actions on Enemies
EnemyDamage     = "%s took %s damage!"
EnemyRecovery   = "%s recovered %s %s!"
EnemyGain       = "%s gained %s %s!"
EnemyLoss       = "%s lost %s %s!"
EnemyDrain      = "Drained %s %s from %s!"
EnemyNoDamage   = "%s took no damage!"
EnemyNoHit      = "Missed! %s took no damage!"
```

The preceding code has `ActorDrain` *and* `EnemyDrain` (kill two birds with one stone and all that). `%s` is used as an indicator within the `sprintf` method. To quote the help file for the `%s` indicator: *Character strings are output.* The `sprintf` method for our first statement uses three parameters (`fmt` is the sentence to be formatted and not a parameter per se). As you can see, both `ActorDrain` and `EnemyDrain` have three instances of `%s`. The method plugs in the value of its parameters, from left to right. So, the first `%s` in `ActorDrain` would be filled with `@battler.name` (the name of the actor or enemy, as appropriate); the second `%s` would house the current name of the HP stat (remember that you can switch the name of quite a few terms from the self-named tab in the Database); and the third `%s` would display `@hp_drain` (the amount of HP drained by the skill or item).

`ActorDrain` is used when an Actor is affected by a draining attack, whereas `EnemyDrain` is used when an enemy is hit by the same. Suppose Eric is hit with a draining attack that takes away 37 HP. The `ActorDrain` string would read as follows:

```
Eric was drained of HP 37.
```

Not the clunkiest statement, but we should invert the number and the HP term for sure. The `EnemyDrain` string, on the other hand, is terrible. Here's a sample line from a Slime drained of 11 HP.

```
Drained Slime 11 from HP.
```

There's a reason why I made it a point to figure out how to fix this. Your first instinct may be to just swap the location of the HP value and the number, as I noted in the previous paragraph. The problem in this initial `if` statement is that, if we do that, we still get the following for the `EnemyDrain` sentence:

```
Drained Slime HP from 11.
```

Closer, but still clunky. What we actually have to do is split both possibilities, such that RMVXA fills in the sentence, depending on whether it is `ActorDrain` or `EnemyDrain`. After all, the `%s` should not be filled out in the same order for both.

Tweaking the hp_damage_text Method

Without further ado, let's tweak this method. Here is what the code for `if @hp_drain > 0` should look like when tweaked:

```
def hp_damage_text
    if @hp_drain > 0
      fmt = @battler.actor? ? Vocab::ActorDrain : Vocab::EnemyDrain
      if fmt = Vocab::ActorDrain
        sprintf(fmt, @battler.name, @hp_drain, Vocab::hp)
      else
        sprintf(fmt, @hp_drain, Vocab::hp, @battler.name)
    end
```

As you can see, we split the single `sprintf` argument in two, based on whether the Vocab used is `ActorDrain` or `EnemyDrain`. In the first case, we flip the `@hp_drain` and `Vocab::hp` parameters. In the alternate case, we switch it all around. The previous example should now read like the following:

```
Drained 11 HP from Slime.
```

Victory! We have three more statements to go for this method. The next one uses the ActorDamage and EnemyDamage Vocabs. My copy-paste of part of the Vocab module (back on pages 4 and 5) is universally useful for what we'll be doing here, so take a peek at the relevant variables.

```
ActorDamage = "%s took %s damage!"
EnemyDamage = "%s took %s damage!"
```

As you can see, both ActorDamage and EnemyDamage use the same sentence structure. The only thing that would change is the origin of @battler.name. Incidentally, that particular elsif statement is fine. It requires no alterations. The next elsif statement uses ActorRecovery and EnemyRecovery, which read as such:

```
ActorRecovery = %s recovered %s %s!"
EnemyRecovery = "%s recovered %s %s!"
```

Much like the previous case, both variables share the same sentence structure. Thus, they share the same textual hiccup. Let's take the ActorRecovery sentence for example. The sprintf method passes @battler.name, Vocab::hp, and -hp_damage, in that order. If Eric is the Actor in question, and the value of -hp_damage is 20, it would read like this.

```
Eric recovered HP 20.
```

Thankfully, that statement *is* as easily fixed as swapping the order in which the parameters are plugged into the sentence, unlike the similar case back at the initial if statement. As the else statement is also correctly expressed, here's the completely tweaked version of hp_damage_text:

```
class Game_ActionResult
  #--------------------------------------------------------------------------
  # * Get Text for HP Damage
  #--------------------------------------------------------------------------
  def hp_damage_text
    if @hp_drain > 0
      fmt = @battler.actor? ? Vocab::ActorDrain : Vocab::EnemyDrain
      if fmt = Vocab::ActorDrain
        sprintf(fmt, @battler.name, @hp_drain, Vocab::hp)
      else
        sprintf(fmt, @hp_drain, Vocab::hp, @battler.name)
      end
    elsif @hp_damage > 0
      fmt = @battler.actor? ? Vocab::ActorDamage : Vocab::EnemyDamage
      sprintf(fmt, @battler.name, @hp_damage)
    elsif @hp_damage < 0
      fmt = @battler.actor? ? Vocab::ActorRecovery : Vocab::EnemyRecovery
      sprintf(fmt, @battler.name, -hp_damage, Vocab::hp)
    else
      fmt = @battler.actor? ? Vocab::ActorNoDamage : Vocab::EnemyNoDamage
      sprintf(fmt, @battler.name)
    end
  end
end
```

■ **Caution**   Don't forget the class definition at the very top of your script page!

One down, two more to go!

Dissecting the mp_damage_text Method

The second of the three action result display methods is mp_damage_text. You can see the relevant method code at the end of this page. The first thing to notice is that, with the sole difference of the specific parameters being passed, we have the same text issues that we had in the previous method. For example, the if statement will display the following text, we'll use Eric, a Slime, and the number value of 50 for this.

```
When ActorDrain: Eric was drained of MP 50
When EnemyDrain: Drained Slime of 50 from MP.
```

■ **Tip** Finding patterns in code will help you understand how things in RMVXA work. For everything else, RMVXA has a robust Ruby reference in the help file.

```
#--------------------------------------------------------------------------
# * Get Text for MP Damage
#--------------------------------------------------------------------------
def mp_damage_text
  if @mp_drain > 0
    fmt = @battler.actor? ? Vocab::ActorDrain : Vocab::EnemyDrain
    sprintf(fmt, @battler.name, Vocab::mp, @mp_drain)
  elsif @mp_damage > 0
    fmt = @battler.actor? ? Vocab::ActorLoss : Vocab::EnemyLoss
    sprintf(fmt, @battler.name, Vocab::mp, @mp_damage)
  elsif @mp_damage < 0
    fmt = @battler.actor? ? Vocab::ActorRecovery : Vocab::EnemyRecovery
    sprintf(fmt, @battler.name, Vocab::mp, -@mp_damage)
  else
    ""
  end
end
```

The only real difference between this method and the previous one, besides the changes in parameter names and the use of the ActorLoss and EnemyLoss vocabs, is the fact that the else statement has a pair of quotation marks instead of actual content. The reasoning behind this is actually very simple: hp_damage_text already covers the text displayed when a skill or item does no damage. Writing it out a second time in this method would be redundant.

Tweaking the mp_damage_text Method

Take a stab at tweaking this method, given what we have discussed up to now. Whenever you're ready, check the following code to see the tweaked version.

```
#--------------------------------------------------------------------------
# * Get Text for MP Damage
#--------------------------------------------------------------------------
def mp_damage_text
  if @mp_drain > 0
    fmt = @battler.actor? ? Vocab::ActorDrain : Vocab::EnemyDrain
    if fmt = Vocab::ActorDrain
      sprintf(fmt, @battler.name, @mp_drain, Vocab::mp)
```

```
    else
        sprintf(fmt, @mp_drain, Vocab::mp, @battler.name)
    end
  elsif @mp_damage > 0
    fmt = @battler.actor? ? Vocab::ActorLoss : Vocab::EnemyLoss
    sprintf(fmt, @battler.name, @mp_damage, Vocab::mp)
  elsif @mp_damage < 0
    fmt = @battler.actor? ? Vocab::ActorRecovery : Vocab::EnemyRecovery
    sprintf(fmt, @battler.name, -@mp_damage, Vocab::mp)
  else
    ""
  end
end
```

The tp_damage_text Method

The final method is tp_damage_text, which covers what happens when a skill or item lowers or increases the TP of an actor or enemy. All we have to do here is flip the two latter parameters once again.

```
#---------------------------------------------------------------------------
# * Get Text for TP Damage
#---------------------------------------------------------------------------
def tp_damage_text
  if @tp_damage > 0
    fmt = @battler.actor? ? Vocab::ActorLoss : Vocab::EnemyLoss
    sprintf(fmt, @battler.name, Vocab::tp, @tp_damage)
  elsif @tp_damage < 0
    fmt = @battler.actor? ? Vocab::ActorGain : Vocab::EnemyGain
    sprintf(fmt, @battler.name, Vocab::tp, -@tp_damage)
  else
    ""
  end
end
end
```

Once flipped, we get the following result:

```
#---------------------------------------------------------------------------
# * Get Text for TP Damage
#---------------------------------------------------------------------------
def tp_damage_text
  if @tp_damage > 0
    fmt = @battler.actor? ? Vocab::ActorLoss : Vocab::EnemyLoss
    sprintf(fmt, @battler.name, @tp_damage, Vocab::tp)
  elsif @tp_damage < 0
    fmt = @battler.actor? ? Vocab::ActorGain : Vocab::EnemyGain
    sprintf(fmt, @battler.name, -@tp_damage, Vocab::tp)
  else
    ""
  end
end
end
```

Again, the else statement contains quotation marks, as the no damage situation is handled in hp_damage_text. Once you have all three of the tweaked methods set up in a script page in the Materials section, you are done! Let's work on a much simpler exercise now.

Of TP and Their Preservation

I have to start this section by noting that it is bizarre that TP is never spelled out within RMVXA. I assume that TP is short for *Technique Points* (or Tech Points). Given that most default skills that require TP are weapons skills or empowered physical attacks, this seems to be a valid assumption. In any case, TP are different from MP in the following ways:

- Each party member starts each battle with between 0 and 25 TP.

- A character can gain TP from taking damage and skills that grant TP.

- After each battle, the party's TP is reset.

- TP as a stat is not displayed anywhere in the default RMVXA game menu, only in battle. You would have to use a script to add a visible TP stat into the game's menu.

But what if you want TP in your game to act like the Limit Break bar in *Final Fantasy* VII? Making TP a persistent resource is actually extremely easy but requires code tweaking, so it's a perfect exercise for this chapter. As usual, we have to find where and how RMVXA handles TP. We know that TP is set at the start of battle and reset at the end of combat.

Searching for TP

Let's run a search in the Script Editor for TP. Among the first sets of results that pop in, we can see the TP display messages that we tweaked in the previous exercise. Of particular interest is Game_BattlerBase (line 42), where we can see that Preserve TP is a special flag that can be set. Where? In weapons and armor. You can create pieces of equipment that grant their users the ability to carry over their TP values from battle to battle. Of course, that's not what we came here for, so let's scroll down some more in the search results.

The next item of interest is also in Game_BattlerBase (line 449). A click on that result leads us to the following snippet.

```
def preserve_tp?
  special_flag(FLAG_ID_PRESERVE_TP)
```

This is a method that allows us to set the flag to preserve TP. If you get the sudden urge to search for preserve_tp?, I applaud you. It is definitely the right way to go. Running a search for that particular term returns a mere three results. The latter two are in Game_Battler and are exactly what we're looking for. The first of them is the on_battle_start method (line 785), which initializes a player's TP at the start of each battle, unless the flag has been set.

```
def on_battle_start
  init_tp unless preserve_tp?
```

■ **Note** You should always try not to edit the default code and use script pages for that purpose. That way, if your changes break something, you can just erase the offending code, and all is well.

The other result is the on_battle_end method, which covers things that are resolved at the end of a battle, such as states that expire on battle end.

```
def on_battle_end
  @result.clear
  remove_battle_states
  remove_all_buffs
  clear_actions
  clear_tp unless preserve_tp?
  appear
```

Tweaking the TP Preserve Methods

Now, after that is said and done, take a look at the following code for the tweaked methods that should be present within a new script page. I commented out the lines of code that need to be removed.

```
class Game_Battler

  def on_battle_start
    # init_tp unless preserve_tp?
  end

  def on_battle_end
    @result.clear
    remove_battle_states
    remove_all_buffs
    clear_actions
    # clear_tp unless preserve_tp?
    appear
  end
end
```

Play-test the game afterward and note the following:

- Your party members start their first battle with 0 TP (init_tp handles the randomization of TP, but we removed it from on_battle_start).

- More important, your party members should now be able to carry over their TP from battle to battle (as we removed clear_tp, which handles the removal of TP at the end of battle).

Pretty awesome, isn't it?

Other TP Considerations

While we're on the subject of TP, we also have the max_tp method in line 494 of Game_BattlerBase. You can increase or decrease the maximum amount of TP that a player can stockpile. You could have skills that require more than 100 TP to use, in theory. In practice, the Database enforces the cap on TP cost of skills and TP gain from skills.

■ **Note**   Play-testing an altered TP cap will promptly reveal that the bar still fills up as if the party member had a cap of 100 TP. To correct this graphical hiccup, you'll want to take a look at `tp_rate` (line 529 of `Game_Battler`) and change the denominator in the expression to the same value as your maximum TP cap.

Also, if you increase the TP cap and then try to use the TP Gain effect, you'll find that you still get the same amount of TP, despite the fact that the amount should change, based on the new cap. How can we rectify this? Go to the Script Editor and run a search for "effects." The fifth entry should read as follows:

```
Game_Battler(10): # * Constants (Effects)
```

Clicking it will take you to a list of effects, as used in the Database and defined by RMVXA. The TP Gain effect is governed by `EFFECT_GAIN_TP`. Let's keep going down this rabbit hole. Run another search using `EFFECT_GAIN_TP` as the term to find. This time, the second result is the one we want. It takes us to line 550 of `Game_Battler`, where we see that `EFFECT_GAIN_TP` calls a method named `item_effect_gain_tp`. Guess what we're searching for next?

■ **Note**   This process of tracking down code may seem silly and/or inefficient, but it's an awesome way to figure out how RMVXA handles the many things that make it tick.

A search for `item_effect_gain_tp` returns only two results. The first one is the very code we're looking at right now. As it so happens, the other is the method code for `item_effect_gain_tp`.

```
#--------------------------------------------------------------------------
# * [TP Gain] Effect
#--------------------------------------------------------------------------
def item_effect_gain_tp(user, item, effect)
  value = effect.value1.to_i
  @result.tp_damage -= value
  @result.success = true if value != 0
  self.tp += value
end
```

The first line defines the recovery value gained through the TP Gain effect. Value will always be a number between 1 and 100. You'll want to apply a multiplier to the variable assignment, so that it correlates correctly with your newly changed cap. Following are three examples. Keep in mind that we are working with values expressed in percentages.

```
(effect.value1.to_i)*0.5
(effect.value1.to_i)*2
(effect.value1.to_i)*10
```

The first expression is appropriate for a TP cap of 50. The second expression is appropriate for a cap of 200; the last is used for a cap of 1000.

Damage Floors Revisited

I covered damage floors all the way back in Chapter 4. There, I discussed that you can change the damage that such terrain causes, based on Regions. Terrain tags work even better, and you can differentiate between types of floor damage in that way as well. However, what happens if you have (to give a hyperbolic example) more than 20 different types of floor damage? First, have a flash from the past (Chapter 4, to be exact).

```
#-------------------------------------------------------------------------
# * Get Base Value for Floor Damage
#-------------------------------------------------------------------------
def basic_floor_damage
return 2 if $game_variables[3] == 1
return 5 if $game_variables[3] == 2
return 10 if $game_variables[3] == 3
return 25 if $game_variables[3] == 4
end
```

I gave a list of four values of $game_variables[3] (the variable used to hold the Region ID in the exercise). You would have to write 16 more expressions in the form return x if $game_variables[3] = y to meet our lofty goal. However, Ruby provides a neater way of handling such a situation. Enter the case method. Here's what the RMVXA Ruby reference has to say on case: *case expressions execute branching for a single expression via matching*. While we're on the subject of bringing back older exercises to expand upon, let's repackage this one into a module. We'll call the module FloorDamage. It will contain a method called value that will return a certain damage number, based on the value of our Region ID variable. Look at the following code to see case in action.

```
module FloorDamage
  module_function

  def value
    case $game_variables[3]
    when 1
      2
    when 2
      5
    when 3
      10
    when 4
      25
    else
      0
    end
  end
end
```

We declare a case parameter (in this case, our variable) and then stipulate various conditions, as necessary. I won't actually expand this to 20 values of our variable, but you can probably already see that this can save a lot of time and space when used in the right situations.

> ▪ **Note** Instead of typing in `module_function`, an alternative way to declare module functionality is by using `self` for each of the methods contained within. So, you would have `def self.value`, were you to apply it to the preceding module. You do need to do one or the other, however, or your game will crash and return an error.

Game Over by Incapacitation

By default, the only way that a player will receive a game over is if his/her entire party is dead. However, not every role-playing game (RPG) throughout the years has followed such a system. Take the *Final Fantasy* games, for example. If the entire party is unable to act, that will result in a game over, even if the party is otherwise still alive. Petrification and Paralysis are two of the most common status effects that can cause this alternate game over. A look at the States tab reveals that none of the default movement-blocking states has infinite duration. Perhaps it was something that the designers thought of but decided against implementing. In any case, all we have to do is find the code that governs game overs and work from there. Running a search in the Script Editor for "game over" returns a few results. The third one (the only result that takes us to `Scene_Base`) is the one we're looking for. Take a look at the code below.

```
#--------------------------------------------------------------------------
# * Determine if Game Is Over
#   Transition to the game over screen if the entire party is dead.
#--------------------------------------------------------------------------
def check_gameover
  SceneManager.goto(Scene_Gameover) if $game_party.all_dead?
end
end
```

This method is where our rabbit hole starts. Our next step is to find the `all_dead?` method in `Game_Party` and see what that entails. Running a search for that method turns up a rather curious result (see Figure 14-1).

```
Game_Unit (122):    def all_dead?
Game_Party (300):    def all_dead?
```

Figure 14-1. *A screenshot of the third and fourth results returned after running a search for* `all_dead?`

Namely, `all_dead?` is defined in two places. Actually, that's not strictly true, as I'll promptly explain. Clicking the `Game_Unit` result reveals the following method:

```
def all_dead?
alive_members.empty?
```

Now, let's take a look at the `Game_Party` equivalent.

```
def all_dead?
super && ($game_party.in_battle || members.size > 0)
```

Why are they different? If you look at how the two classes are expressed within the Script Editor, they should look like this:

```
class Game_Unit
class Game_Party < Game_Unit
```

There is our answer. Game_Party is a subclass of Game_Unit. For an analogy, think of it as a parent and a child. Game_Unit is the parent of Game_Party. The *super* in Game_Party's version of the method is a call to the parent method of the same name in Game_Unit. Execution-wise, this is technically what the Game_Party version actually says:

```
alive_members.empty? && ($game_party.in_battle || members.size > 0)
```

■ **Note** *super* can also accept parameters to limit what is called from the parent method. However, in RMVXA, you'll mostly be seeing *super* used without any parameters passed. In that case, it passes all of the method's arguments up to the superclass' method.

You may be wondering what the double "*and*" marks (ampersands) are for. They're one of Ruby's various operator expressions. You can find a full list of operators on RMVXA's Operator Expressions reference page. The two I'm personally interested in within the context of the basics are the && and || operators. && is another way to express and, while || is the equivalent of or. The difference between using the symbol operators and the word operators is essentially summarized on the cited reference page. Here's a relevant screenshot (Figure 14-2).

```
a && b || c    # => (a && b) || c
a || b && c    # =>  a || (b && c)
```

Figure 14-2. *A comparison of how Ruby handles a trio of variables, depending on where the operators are located*

&& has a greater priority than ||. So, if you have an expression that you can count on executing in a certain order, it may be preferable to use and/or instead. Our next task is to find alive_members. As we want the method definition, what we're looking for is on line 28 of Game_Unit.

```
def alive_members
  members.select {|member| member.alive? }
```

The expression contained within alive_members contains a new method, as it were. .select is part of Ruby's Enumerable module. This particular method accepts an object (in this case, |member|) that will be analyzed, based on the block (member.alive?) criteria. This method returns an array containing every object within the list (members) for which the block returns true. In other words, the alive_members array will contain a list of every party member that is alive. Being alive is defined by the alive? method, which can be found in line 565 of Game_BattlerBase.

```
def alive?
  exist? && !death_state?
```

This method contains another new Ruby idiom. Notice that death_state? has an exclamation mark to its left. That mark declares a state of opposition. In other words, the alive? method checks for death_state? to be false rather than true. We have nearly reached the bottom of this rabbit hole. exist? is only used to determine whether a certain battler is hidden or not (and, thus, only really applies to enemies, as Actors in battle always exist). So, let's just search for death_state? (note the absence of the exclamation mark). The very first result is what we have been looking for. As the comment box directly above the method notes, death_state? is used to check for the KO state.

```
def death_state?
  state?(death_state_id)
```

The method has a one-line expression that checks to see if the battler is afflicted with the Death state, as defined in the death_state_id method (the one right below death_state?, actually; it returns a value of 1). Trying to reinvent the wheel here is something you should only try when you gain greater expertise in Ruby. For now, tweaking that expression will suffice. The easiest way to do that is by using || or or to add new state? expressions.

■ **Note** Either operator will work in this case.

So, suppose you wanted to make it so that Paralysis (state #7 in the default state list in RMVXA) counts as an incapacitating state. First, go to the States tab and change it, so that it can only be removed at the end of battle. Then, return to the death_state? method and tweak it like so:

```
def death_state?
  state?(death_state_id) || state?(7)
```

To test whether the change is working or not, you can give one of the existing enemies a Paralysis-inducing skill (or give their normal attacks a 100% Paralysis State Rate) and then run a Battle Test. If you get a Game Over screen after being afflicted by Paralysis, you'll know that it is working correctly. Speaking of game overs, I have one last exercise to work through.

Adding a Menu to the Game Over Screen

This last exercise is going to involve some copy-pasting. Mainly, we're going to copy the RMVXA code that handles the Title screen's menu and integrate that into the class that governs the Game Over screen. The first order of business is finding the two classes. As it so happens, both the Title screen and the Game Over screen are governed by classes with the Scene prefix. Copy Scene_Title and Scene_Gameover to the Materials section of the Script Editor. Next, take a look at Scene_Gameover and analyze what is going on.

- Scene_Gameover starts with a method (called start) that calls to its parent in Scene_Base by use of super. Next, it executes three methods of its own.

- As a whole, the methods create the background that says "game over," handle the fade-out after the party is defeated and the subsequent fade-in to the Game Over screen, and play the appropriate music.

- There are several other methods that handle graphics processing within the class, but what we're interested in is the transition to Title screen method (goto_title).

As we want the game to cause a menu to pop up at the Game Over screen, instead of just cutting to the Title, we might as well go ahead and excise what we won't be using. Delete the goto_title method and then erase goto_title if Input.trigger?(:C) from the update method near the top of the class. With that done, we move over to Scene_Title. Our objective at the Scene_Title class is to figure out what methods are used to call up the Title screen's menu. If we take a look at the start method for Scene_Title, we see that six methods are called up. Our method of interest is create_command_window. A closer look at it (it starts on line 91) shows the following code:

```
def create_command_window
  @command_window = Window_TitleCommand.new
  @command_window.set_handler(:new_game, method(:command_new_game))
  @command_window.set_handler(:continue, method(:command_continue))
  @command_window.set_handler(:shutdown, method(:command_shutdown))
end
```

The first expression in the method draws a new window on the screen. Then each of the next three expressions handles a menu option via the `set_handler` method (located in `Window_Selectable`). `set_handler` accepts two parameters. The first parameter is the *handle* and the second parameter is the *method*. For example, the first `set_handler` expression in `create_command_window` calls the `command_new_game` method when the `:new_game` handle is invoked. This will become relevant in the next section. For now, the result, as you've almost certainly seen countless times during play-testing, is the Title menu that has three options. So, we know that we want to draw the Title menu into the Game Over screen. The next question becomes: *How* is this method drawing the window to the screen? If we compare the `start` methods of `Scene_Title` and `Scene_Gameover`, we see that the game over method doesn't draw a command window (`create_command_window`). You'll want to copy lines 88 through 128 of `Scene_Title` to your altered `Scene_Gameover` method in the Materials section. Then, add `create_command_window` to `Scene_Gameover`'s `start` method. It should look like the following:

```
def start
  super
  play_gameover_music
  fadeout_frozen_graphics
  create_background
  create_command_window
end
```

With that out of the way, you're done! Now, play-test your game and get into a situation that causes a game over. (It might be quicker to create an event that calls up the Game Over screen when you interact with it.) If you have followed these instructions, your Game Over screen should look like Figure 14-3.

Figure 14-3. *A screenshot of the Game Over screen, menu now included*

If you just wanted to have the Title screen menu in your game over, you are done.

Tweaking the Game Over Menu

However, what if you wanted to tweak the menu? As mentioned before, the menu window and options are handled in `create_command_window`. You may be thinking that removing an option from this method is all you would have to do. That is actually not true. If you do that, you'll still see the option in the game over menu. When you try to press the action button to get the option to do something, it will do nothing. Clearly, we must look elsewhere for the solution to this problem. The window itself is created and populated in Window_TitleCommand. However, altering that method will change the Title menu as well. Thus, you'll want to do the following:

1. Copy Window_TitleCommand to your Materials section.

2. Rename the copied class Window_GameoverCommand.

3. Hop over to your altered Scene_Gameover method and switch @command_window = Window_TitleCommand.new to @command_window = Window_GameoverCommand.new.

4. Back at Window_GameoverCommand, find the make_command_list method (it's near the bottom of the method).

The make_command_list method looks like this:

```
def make_command_list
  add_command(Vocab::new_game, :new_game)
  add_command(Vocab::continue, :continue, continue_enabled)
  add_command(Vocab::shutdown, :shutdown)
end
```

As you can see, this method is responsible for the three options that we see in the Title menu. To make the point, comment out (by typing in a single # before the line of code) the new_game command.. If you have followed my instructions correctly, the game over menu should now look like Figure 14-4.

Figure 14-4. *A screenshot of the game over menu after the changes*

On the other hand, if you wanted to add a menu option to that list (say, for example, the ability to go back to the Title screen), you would be best served by finding the add_command method, to see how it works. You could run a search and find it that way, but look at the class definition for Window_GameoverCommand at the top of the script page, and you'll see that this class is the child of Window_Command (this, of course, is also true in the case of Window_TitleCommand). Once at Window_Command, you needn't look far, for the add_command method starts on line 61 of the class. Look at the following to see the method in question:

```
#--------------------------------------------------------------------------
# * Add Command
#     name    : Command name
#     symbol  : Corresponding symbol
#     enabled : Activation state flag
#     ext     : Arbitrary extended data
#--------------------------------------------------------------------------
def add_command(name, symbol, enabled = true, ext = nil)
  @list.push({:name=>name, :symbol=>symbol, :enabled=>enabled, :ext=>ext})
end
```

The comment box above the method is pretty good about explaining what parameter goes where. For most options, you'll only be using the first two parameters. The command name is defined in the Vocab module (the specific terms list starts on line 113). The symbol used in the add_command method is the handle defined within set_handler. The Continue option also uses the third parameter, which determines whether or not you can select it from the menu. (When the player has no save files for the game, Continue will be grayed out.) .push is a method from Ruby's Array class. As the method name implies, .push sends an object to the end of an array (the array, in this case, being @list). Going back to Window_GameoverCommand, we can see the format of an add_command object that accepts two parameters.

```
add_command(Vocab::shutdown, :shutdown)
```

■ **Note** To summarize the menu logic: add_command adds options to menus while set_handler gives those options their functionality. As proven already, you need both to create a new menu option.

The Title screen option is called in the form to_title. So, you would write the following in make_command_list to add that command to Window_GameoverCommand.

```
add_command(Vocab::to_title, :to_title)
```

Place that one in between the two existent add_command expressions. Then, you would add the following line to create_command_window in Scene_Gameover, so that the option actually does something when the player interacts with it. I placed it between the Continue and Exit Game commands.

```
@command_window.set_handler(:to_title, method(:command_to_title))
```

Last, you need to add the command_to_title method itself, or the game will return an error telling you that the method is undefined.

■ **Note** I named the method command_to_title, to keep with the naming conventions used for this command in RMVXA. As it turns out, there *is* a preexisting method of the same name. More on that below.

As said in the note above, there's a preexisting method called command_to_title. In fact, running a search for the method will return only four results, two of them being the instances of the term we added for this exercise. The second result (line 48 of Scene_End) contains what we're looking for. Here's the method:

```
def command_to_title
  close_command_window
  fadeout_all
  SceneManager.goto(Scene_Title)
end
```

Copy-paste that method to the Scene_Gameover class you have tweaked, and we're done! Play-test your game and cause a game over. If you have done everything correctly, the screen should look like Figure 14-5.

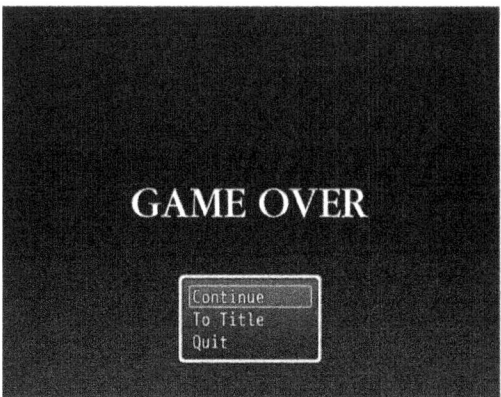

Figure 14-5. *A screenshot of the changed game over menu*

In closing, I humbly urge you to continue exploring the depths of RMVXA's Script Editor. The Appendix has a link to a list of scripts that can be used for RMVXA. If you want to investigate how something can be done, check to see if a script already exists for said functionality. There's nothing wrong with picking the brains of those who have more experience than you.

Summary

During the course of this chapter, we performed several basic scripting exercises that involved tweaking parts of the Script Editor to achieve things that aren't possible via eventing. Among them were causing a game over if the player's entire party is incapacitated by another status effect that isn't Death, tweaking the TP cap, and making sure that said tweaks were reflected properly within the game. In the final chapter of this book, I will cover miscellaneous concepts.

CHAPTER 15

More Tips and Tricks for RMVXA

I'd like to congratulate you for making it this far. This is the final chapter of the book. It has been an awesome journey full of learning experiences! Of course, this book is just a taste of the full potential of RPG Maker VX Ace (RMVXA). I urge you to continue reading and learning more about what makes this game-development engine tick. What better for a final chapter than a melting pot of tips and tricks that you can apply to your own games? The exercises in this chapter will use variable amounts of scripting, depending on what is needed. Without further ado, let's walk this final leg of our journey together.

Forcing Certain Party Members to Participate in a Battle

Our first exercise for this final chapter is inspired by a common role-playing game (RPG) convention: forced party compositions. If you have ever wanted to create a boss fight in which a certain party member must be present in the active party, this should be relevant to your interests. In RMVXA, the maximum active party size is four. A possible fifth (or more) party member is placed into the party reserves.

Tip The first four spots of your party represent your active party members. You can tell who is in the party reserves, based on the appearance of their status. The status of reserve party members is slightly transparent.

You can use the Formation option in the in-game menu to switch between your party members. Party members that are in the reserves gain a share of the experience gained in battle *if* (and only if) the Reserve Members' EXP check box is toggled in the System tab of the Database. In any case, here's our hypothetical situation:

> *In an alternate reality of our game, Eric starts with a full party of four members. The party arrives at Seaside as usual and eventually recruits Noah. As Noah is the fifth party member, he is placed at the bottom of the roster. That makes him a reserve member. Fast-forward to the encounter with Gemini. Noah will want to face off against his brother. If anyone is to stop his kin, he's reasoned, it should be he. If Noah happens to be in the active party, the battle starts as usual; otherwise, Noah will demand to be in the active party.*

Overview

For this exercise, you'll need the following:

- A new test map (the tileset and the size do not matter). Then, copy-paste the Gemini event from the first dungeon to our test map.

- An Autorun event that is only active when a switch is flipped. This event will use a scripted conditional branch to determine whether Noah is in the active party. If he is, we process the battle against Gemini. If he isn't, we have Noah say some words and use the Open Menu command to allow the player to change his/her active lineup.

- The Autorun will keep running until Noah is in the active party.

This is a rather easy event. The only thing that should even give you a second of pause by now is the single line that we have to use as a conditional branch. To find it, we must figure out how RMVXA handles party members internally.

Finding Out How RMVXA Handles Party Members

A good place to start figuring that out is the conveniently named Game_Party. We needn't go far, as we already see some promising code by line 70. Look at the following to see lines 63 to 74 of the Game_Party class.

```
#--------------------------------------------------------------------------
# * Get Battle Members
#--------------------------------------------------------------------------
def battle_members
  all_members[0, max_battle_members].select {|actor| actor.exist? }
end
#--------------------------------------------------------------------------
# * Get Maximum Number of Battle Members
#--------------------------------------------------------------------------
def max_battle_members
  return 4
end
```

In fact, the method we need happens to be battle_members. In essence, what the single line of code within that method does is find every available party member and then take the first one to four of them and place them into an array. This array is $game_party.battle_members.

■ **Note**　We use battle_members, as only the active party members can participate in battle. We want to see if Noah is part of that array or not.

Now, the next question is: How do we use that array? Click Help in RMVXA's Main Menu toolbar and run a search for Array. The first search result will be thus named. This is one of RMVXA's many Ruby reference pages. The array method we want to use is called include? (the question mark is not a typo). Figure 15-1 is a screenshot of what the reference file has to say about this particular method.

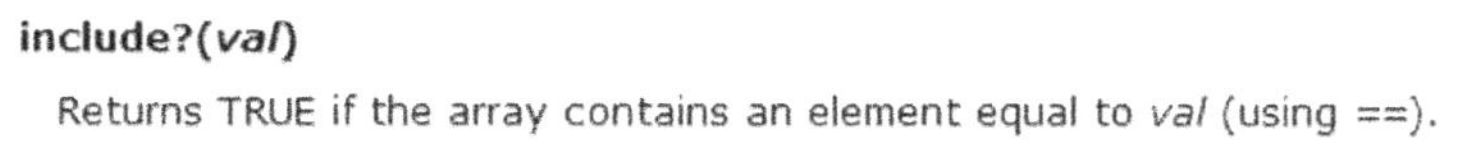

include?(*val*)

> Returns TRUE if the array contains an element equal to *val* (using ==).

Figure 15-1. *A screenshot of the* include? *array method*

That means our expression currently looks like this: $game_party.battle_members.include?(val). So close, yet so far. What do we put in val? We have to know if Noah is in the active party, so we must check for his actor ID. Recall from Chapter 12 (and, briefly noted, again in the previous chapter) that actor information arrays are called in RMVXA in the form $game_actors[actor_id]. So, Noah's array would be $game_actors[10]. That is the value we need to check for.

Creating the Forced Party Member Event

Following, I have placed the event commands belonging to the second half of page 1 of Gemini's event. It has been tweaked, so that, instead of calling a Battle Processing command, it flips on a switch that will trigger our Autorun event.

```
@>Text: 'Evil', 3, Normal, Bottom
:      : Heh, think you can surpass the power
:      : that has been granted to me? Prepare to
:      : suffer!
@>Change Battle BGM: 'Dungeon9', 100, 100
@>Control Switches: [0038:activepartymember] = ON
@>
```

When the activepartymember switch has been flipped on, this activates the Autorun event on the map, which will check to see if Noah is in the active party.

```
@>Conditional Branch: Script: $game_party.battle_members.include?($game_actors[10])
   @>Battle Processing: Gemini
   @>
: Else
   @>Text: 'Actor5', 6, Normal, Bottom
   :      : I wish to participate in this battle.
   @>Text: -, -, Normal, Bottom
   :      : Use the Formation option from the menu to add
   :      : Noah to your active party.
   @>Open Menu Screen
   @>
: Branch End
@>
```

The conditional branch uses the Script option and reads as follows:

```
$game_party.battle_members.include?($game_actors[10])
```

You can fit it all in the single line provided, but it will appear cut off in the event's contents list. This has no negative effects on the event itself. We can toggle "Set handling when conditions do not apply," to get the else statement to work with when Noah is not included in battle_members. Alternatively, we can have another conditional branch that reads: $game_party.battle_members.include?($game_actors[10]) == false. In either case, when Noah is not in the player's active party, he expresses a wish to participate in the battle at hand, and then a system message is displayed. You can add a color change command to that text (\C[n]; n is the value of color you wish to use). I'm partial to green for system messages (that would be n = 3), but you can use the color of your preference. After the message is displayed, we have the in-game menu pop up, allowing the player to bring in Noah from the reserves.

■ **Caution**   If Noah is not in the player's party at all, this event will infinitely loop, as it recognizes that Noah is not in battle_members but has no way of checking if Noah is in the party at all. You can use an *Actor in the Party* conditional branch to handle such an exception.

To properly test this event, you'll want to have an event that gives the player a full party and then adds Noah to the end of the party as a reserve. Check the following code for a sample event:

```
@>Change Party Member: Add [Natalie]
@>Change Party Member: Add [Terence]
@>Change Party Member: Add [Ernest]
@>Change Party Member: Add [Noah]
@>
```

You can place a nonplayer character (NPC) with these commands anywhere on the test map. You can talk with said NPC first, to fill up your party, and then test the rest of the events at leisure.

■ **Note**   Don't forget to set the player's starting position on your test map!

With all that said and done, this is the final chapter, and I have not yet discussed play-testing features. This is a good a time as any to do so.

Play-Testing Features

RMVXA has a pair of convenient and helpful features that are only available during play-testing. The first is known as the debugger. During play-testing, pressing F9 will bring up a screen similar to the one shown in Figure 15-2.

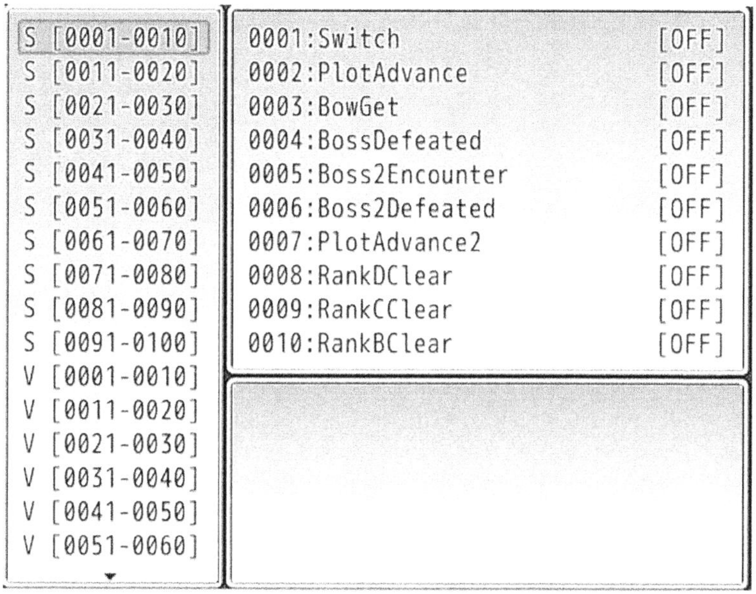

```
S [0001-0010]    0001:Switch          [OFF]
S [0011-0020]    0002:PlotAdvance      [OFF]
S [0021-0030]    0003:BowGet           [OFF]
S [0031-0040]    0004:BossDefeated      [OFF]
S [0041-0050]    0005:Boss2Encounter    [OFF]
S [0051-0060]    0006:Boss2Defeated     [OFF]
S [0061-0070]    0007:PlotAdvance2      [OFF]
S [0071-0080]    0008:RankDClear        [OFF]
S [0081-0090]    0009:RankCClear        [OFF]
S [0091-0100]    0010:RankBClear        [OFF]
V [0001-0010]
V [0011-0020]
V [0021-0030]
V [0031-0040]
V [0041-0050]
V [0051-0060]
       ▼
```

Figure 15-2. *A screenshot of the debugger in RMVXA*

The debugger contains a complete list of switches and variables present in your project. More important, you can see the state of each switch and variable and even tweak it for testing purposes. Perhaps you want to set Tree to 5 in our game off the bat, to see if the Autorun event triggers correctly. Maybe you want to see if Amanda acts appropriately once the player has beaten the appropriate rank of the arena. Instead of having to actually play through all of that, you can use the debugger to flip switches or change the value of variables. It is also a helpful reference when things go wrong in eventing, and you want to see what isn't setting itself properly. The other feature, while not as flashy, is useful all the same. By holding down the Ctrl key, you can clip through otherwise impassable terrain. My favorite use of ignoring passability is when I have accidentally made certain squares impassable when they should be passable. I can keep the squares in mind and just use Ctrl to bypass the accidental obstacles, instead of having to fix them then and there. Depending on what you are play-testing, this can be quite a time-saver. It's time for another exercise! If you want to make a desert that requires precise movement to get through successfully, you're going to love this one.

Of Deserts and Ghostly Locations

Deserts are a video game constant. Deserts that penalize the player who does not know the correct route to traverse them seem to be everywhere in games as well. You might be surprised to know that we can recycle events used in previous chapters to pull this off without a hitch. Don't believe me? Take a look at Figure 15-3, to see the map I'll be using for this exercise.

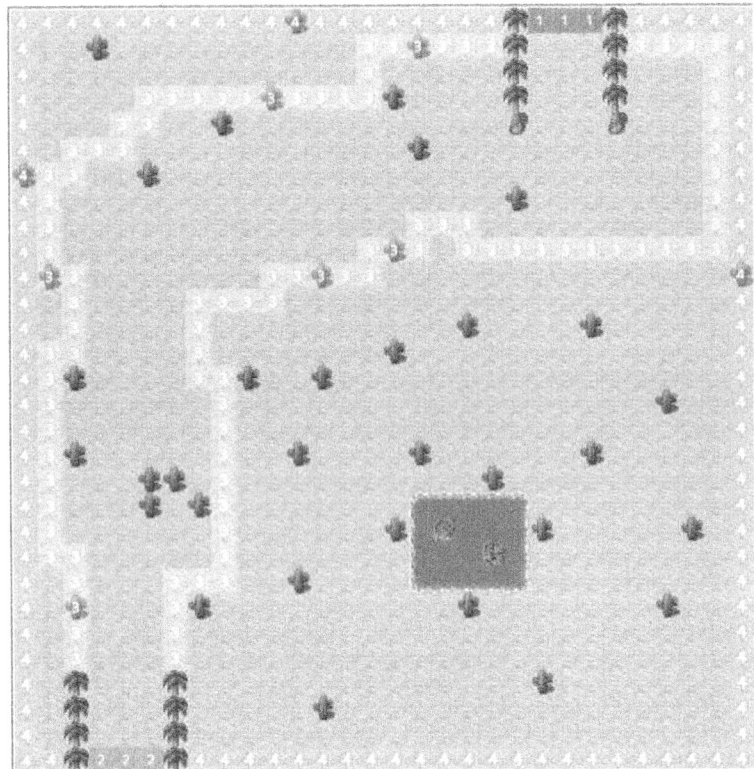

Figure 15-3. *A screenshot of the map to be used for this exercise*

The Desert Event

We need the following things to complete this exercise:

- A Region ID (I'm using 3) that will trace an invisible border around the map. Crossing that border will send the player back to the start of the area.

- A pair of Regions (1 and 2) that will transfer the player out of the desert area

- Some doodads to dot the map. I use cacti.

- A Parallel Process event that will handle all of the region-based shenanigans

As everything else is already established in the screenshot of the map, let's skip ahead to our Parallel Process event. It isn't anything that we haven't done before, as you'll quickly see.

```
@>Control Variables: [0002:X] = Player's Map X
@>Control Variables: [0003:Y] = Player's Map Y
@>Get Location Info: [0004], Region ID, Variable [0002][0003]
@>Conditional Branch: Variable [0004:Region] == 3
   @>Text: -, -, Normal, Bottom
   :      : You get lost in the desert!
   @>Transfer Player:[031:CHAP15EXE2] (004,028), Up
   @>
: Branch End
```

```
@>Conditional Branch: Variable [0004:Region] == 2
    @>Comment: Insert transfer event here.
    @>
: Branch End
@>Conditional Branch: Variable [0004:Region] == 1
    @>Comment: Insert transfer event here.
    @>
: Branch End
@>
```

If you can make teleportation puzzles, you can make deserts that cause the player to get lost and send him/her back to the start of the area as well! You may have noticed that I didn't use Region 4 at all. You could have a desert nomad sell the player some goggles or breathing apparatus that allows him/her to explore the inner parts of the desert. In that case, Region 3 would no longer warp the player back to the start of the area. That task would be transferred to Region 4, as it were. That lets the player explore the oasis, among other things. Let's move on to a similar exercise.

Forest Event Overview

Suppose you wanted to make an area like the Lost Woods in some of the *Legend of Zelda* games. That is to say, one in which you can move in one of several directions, only one of them correct. Going the wrong way will send you back to the start of the area. We can use Regions for that as well. However, what if I told you that we could pull this off using a single 17×13 map? Seems crazy, right? Let's get started!

For this exercise, we'll need the following:

- The aforementioned 17×13 map (Figure 15-4). It should have one Region for each cardinal direction, as in the following screenshot.

Figure 15-4. *A screenshot of the map that must be traversed in a certain order*

- A Parallel Process event that handles what happens when the player steps on a certain Region at a specific time

- A variable to quantify the player's progress, given that we're only using one area

That does it for needs, although we'll also probably want some graphics that appear, based on the player's progress into the labyrinth. We'll call the variable WoodsLocation. If the player goes in the correct direction, we increase the variable's value by one; otherwise, we zero it out. If the player can successfully get through five areas in a row, then he/she will have cleared the labyrinth. The reward can be reaching the inner part of the area or a treasure chest filled with a rare item. You'll want the Parallel Process event to have five pages. Each one will require that the WoodsLocation variable be at a value one higher than the page before. In other words, page 1 is unconditional, while page 2 requires the variable to be equal to 1. Page 3 requires the variable to be at 2, and so forth, up to page 5, which needs the variable at a value of 4. With all that said, we need to figure out what order the player has to walk through the labyrinth to clear it. I personally decided on right, right, left, down, up. Region-wise, that is 2, 2, 4, 3, 1.

Creating the Forest Event

Now that we know what we want our mysterious forest to do, all that's left is to actually write out the appropriate events.

■ **Tip** If you add this area to your own game, you'll want to come up with a way for the player to figure out in what direction he/she should go next. It could be a helpful NPC that gives the exact course to take or plants that appear as the player gets deeper into the labyrinth.

Following is the template for what each page of the Parallel Process event should look like:

```
@>Control Variables: [0002:X] = Player's Map X
@>Control Variables: [0003:Y] = Player's Map Y
@>Get Location Info: [0004], Region ID, Variable [0002][0003]
@>Conditional Branch: Variable [0004:Region] == 1
   @>Transfer Player:[032:CHAP15EXE3] (008,006)
   @>Control Variables: [0029:WoodsLocation] = 0
   @>
: Branch End
@>Conditional Branch: Variable [0004:Region] == 2
   @>Transfer Player:[032:CHAP15EXE3] (008,006)
   @>Control Variables: [0029:WoodsLocation] += 1
   @>
: Branch End
@>Conditional Branch: Variable [0004:Region] == 3
   @>Transfer Player:[032:CHAP15EXE3] (008,006)
   @>Control Variables: [0029:WoodsLocation] = 0
   @>
: Branch End
@>Conditional Branch: Variable [0004:Region] == 4
   @>Transfer Player:[032:CHAP15EXE3] (008,006)
   @>Control Variables: [0029:WoodsLocation] = 0
   @>
: Branch End
@>
```

When the player walks to the eastern exit (Region 2), the value of WoodsLocation is increased by 1. Otherwise, the variable is zeroed out. In either case, the player is transferred back to the center of the area. For each page, the correct entrance should be the one that increases the value of WoodsLocation.

■ **Caution**   Because we are working with a Parallel Process event, you want the player to be transferred *before* you change the value of WoodsLocation; otherwise, you'll run into weird interactions, such as the screen fading out twice in a row and WoodsLocation being reset, even if the player has stepped through the right area.

I added several plant events (using the Small Sprouts graphic in tab B of the Dungeon tileset) that are only visible when the value of WoodsLocation is at a certain number or higher. This will give a visual representation to the player that he/she is progressing. Figure 15-5 shows what the labyrinth looks like when WoodsLocation is equal to 5.

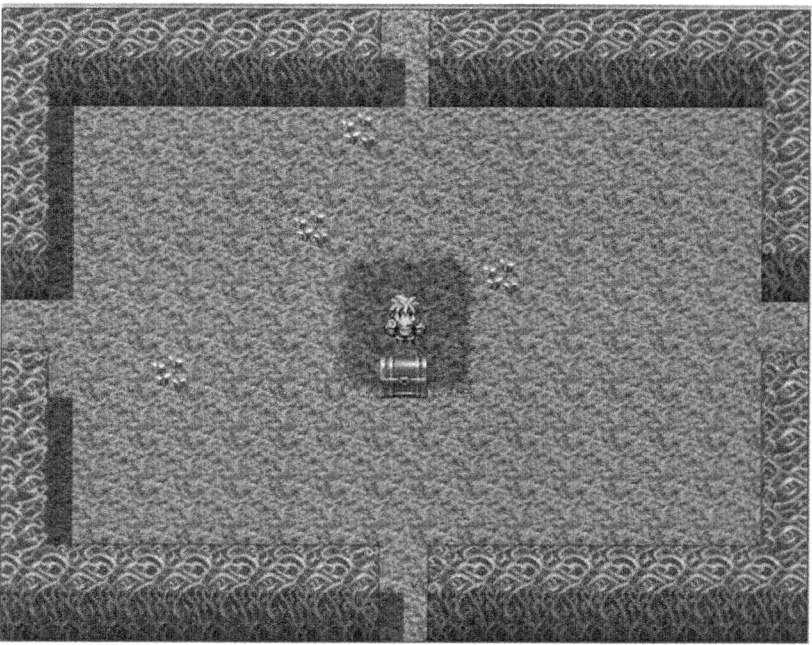

Figure 15-5. *A screenshot of the labyrinth state when WoodsLocation is equal to 5. I reward the player with a chest containing a powerful weapon*

That concludes this pair of exercises. A little information about vehicles follows, before we perform our next exercise.

Vehicles

I never covered vehicles during the course of creating our game, as we never had occasion to use them. Quite a few RPGs make do without a single vehicle, and others have vehicles that are not player-controlled. So, don't feel like you *have* to have vehicles in your game. RMVXA has three types of vehicles, the graphics of which can be changed in the

System tab of the Database. Each one of them can be used to navigate different types of terrains. In order of freedom of movement, they are as follows:

- *Boat*: To be honest, the default graphic is more of a canoe. In any case, the boat can cross shallow water (Pond and Sea in the Field tileset).

- *Ship*: A full-fledged vessel, such as in all of those pirate movies! The ship can cross shallow water and deep water.

- *Airship*: The default airship is more of a blimp or dirigible. The airship can travel over any terrain but can only land on solid ground. Additionally, an airship can fly over events. Airships are on a higher layer than even Above Characters events, so you'll want to use Parallel Process events for events involving them.

If you want to experiment with tweaking the passability of boats and ships, the relevant vehicle logic is handled in the Game_Map class. Figure 15-6 is a screenshot showing a test map that I created for the purpose of displaying each of RMVXA's vehicles.

Figure 15-6. *A screenshot of the test map I created to show off the three vehicles. From left to right, the different terrain tiles are Grass, Pond, Sea, Deep Sea*

You can set the starting position of a vehicle much as you can the player characters themselves. In addition, you can move a vehicle from one location to another instantly, by using the *Set Vehicle Location* event command. This is useful when you have the plot move the player from one part of the world to another instantly. It would only make sense that his/her ship would be docked at the new town and not stranded at the previous port (assuming, of course, that your player took the ship to the new port in the first place). The other vehicle-related event command is *Get On/Off Vehicle*, which does as the name implies.

░ **Note** In a rare exception to event commands that will crash your game if used incorrectly, you can use the Get On/Off Vehicle command just about anywhere and get away with it. It won't actually do anything, unless your player can leave the vehicle correctly. (It won't strand you in the middle of the ocean, for example).

Next, let's touch upon an enemy-related exercise. Mainly, making a battle in which there are two enemies, both of whom must be defeated on the same turn; otherwise, the survivor will revive his/her comrade.

Two of a Kind

In RPGs, this type of battle falls under the broad umbrella of what are considered to be gimmick battles. Basically, a gimmick battle is one in which only a certain strategy (or a limited number of strategies) can bring the player victory. A fight with a pair of twins, in which one revives the other, dissuades unfocused attacks and promotes a calculated approach to the task at hand. For this exercise, we'll use a pair of skeletons. For the sake of differentiation, copy the Skeleton entry in the Database into an empty slot and use the hue setting to change the graphic's colors a little. Then, change the new enemy's name to something else (such as Skeleton Lord or Skeleton Knight). Last, increase the new enemy's stats a bit. For reference, you can see a screenshot of the Skeleton Knight in Figure 15-7.

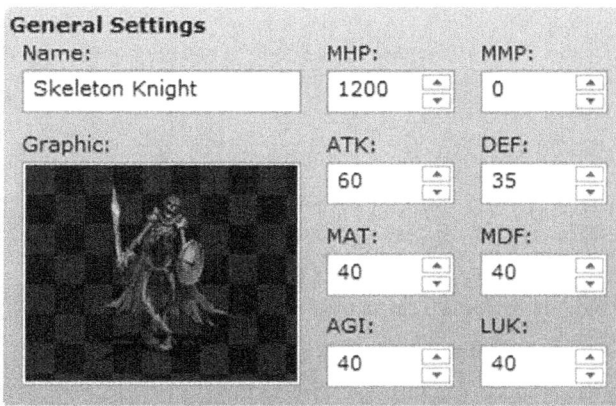

Figure 15-7. *A screenshot of the Skeleton Knight enemy that will accompany his lesser ally into battle*

Next, let's create a troop that has one Skeleton Knight and one Skeleton. In the troop event, you'll want to have a pair of event pages, one for each of the enemies. We will use double conditionals for the events themselves. (See Figure 15-8).

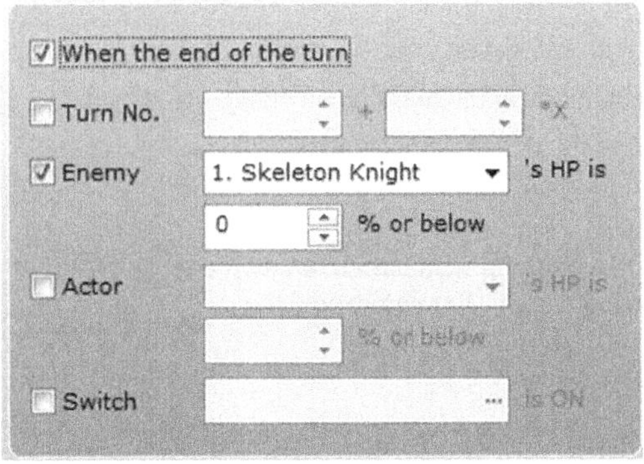

Figure 15-8. *The conditions for page 1 of the troop event. Page 2 requires that the other enemy (2. Skeleton) be at 0% HP or below, instead*

With that set up, we can fill out the pages themselves. Both of the pages will have a Span of Turn (so that they trigger once every turn) and a single Force Action event command.

```
Page 1's Force Action command is: [2. Skeleton], [Reanimate], Index 1.
Meanwhile, Page 2's Force Action command is: [1. Skeleton Knight], [Reanimate], Index 2.
```

To create Reanimate, I took the Raise spell and copied it to a new slot. Then, I zeroed out its MP cost and changed the damage formula from b.mhp/10 to b.mhp (turning the 10% HP heal into a full heal). That concludes this exercise! Let me end this section with a few interesting notes about Force Action.

- A skill used with Force Action can be executed even if the user doesn't have the MP to cast it.

- Similarly, the user doesn't even need to *have* the skill in his/her list to be forced into using it. I confirmed this particular fact by having Eric throw Thunder II spells around with Force Action.

- You can have a skill force the user to use another skill. If you're not careful, you could create a loop of skills that keep triggering infinitely until the battle is done or otherwise unwinnable (depending on what the skill in question does).

A Full House

While we're on the subject of troops and enemies, there's one other thing I've neglected to mention up to now. If you right-click a specific enemy's graphic within a troop, you get a single option named Appear Halfway. Clicking it causes the enemy to appear translucent in the troop display at the Database. If you begin a battle with some of the enemies in that state, they will not appear in the encounter. As the name of the option pretty much blurts out, you can use this to have enemies that appear during the course of a battle. This is useful in situations such as the following:

- A battle in which enemy reinforcements arrive at regular intervals

- An enemy that has a skill that causes allies to appear

- A battle with multiple waves of enemies. Defeat one wave to cause the next one to appear.

For this exercise, we will create a troop containing five Orcs. The first, third, and fifth Orcs will be present from the start of the battle. The second and fourth Orcs will appear in response to their defeated allies. Take a look at Figure 15-9.

Figure 15-9. *A screenshot of our horde of Orcs. Note how the second and fourth Orcs are nearly transparent, as compared to their allies*

The first troop event page should execute at the start of the battle. It gives the first and fifth Orcs the Immortal state. The second page is triggered when the first Orc drops to 0% HP or less, causing the second Orc to appear and the first one to be defeated. The last page is triggered when the fifth Orc drops to 0% HP or less, causing the fourth Orc to appear and the fifth one to be defeated. I will let you translate this into the relevant events. Just keep in mind that your event pages should have a span of Battle, as you don't want them to trigger more than once during the battle. Also, keeping in mind that death is prioritized over every other battle event in RMVXA, you want the new enemy to appear before the old one loses its immortality; otherwise, a clever player could use a skill that hits all enemies, bypassing the reinforcements completely by defeating all of them at the same time.

Amusingly, that used to happen all the time with older RPGs, given the limitations of programming. Players would just find sneaky ways to prevent reinforcement waves from appearing, by overtaxing the battle logic or employing any other such shenanigans.

Ye Olde RPG—A Treatise on Quest Experience

Japanese RPGs (with most of the exceptions being relatively recent titles) tend to give the player characters most, if not all, of their experience via combat. That was part of the reason why older Japanese RPGs were notorious for their grinding (repeatedly fighting monsters in the same area to get gold, experience, and items) and overall difficulty. Can't defeat any of the monsters outside of town? Don't have the gold to get items? Tough luck! Classic Western RPGs, such as *Wasteland* and the *Ultima* series, were actually somewhat better about that. Usually. That leads to my next topic.

Think back to the Rat Tail quest we created in the port town of Seaside for our players to complete. The player got gold out of it, but what if we wanted to offer experience as well? We could use the *Change EXP* event command to accomplish that task. Change EXP allows you to give experience points to (or take away from) a certain party member or the entire party (you can designate a specific actor ID using a variable as well). The value of EXP given or taken can be a fixed value or that of a variable. Last, you can toggle the "Show Level Up Message" check box, which will prompt the game to display the level-up box, if the experience gained from the command is enough to bump the character up one or more levels.

■ **Note**   *Change Level* can be used to much the same effect. In that event command, you are declaring how many levels you wish to add or subtract from the chosen character.

Using those two event commands, you give the player even more incentive to complete sidequests and also a way to progress in the game without having to battle monsters ceaselessly.

The Other Actor Event Commands

As it turns out, I've covered most of the event commands contained in the Actor section of the list. With that said, I haven't covered *all* of them. Here's a bulleted list of the ones I have glossed over until now.

- I didn't really mention *Change HP* or *Change MP*, as our only instances of out-of-combat healing were covered neatly by *Recover All*. However, those two commands are more versatile, as they allow you to increase *or* decrease the relevant stat. You could have a poisoned well that injures the party when it drinks from it, or a floating fairy that recovers the entire party's MP. The one thing to note is that you can make it so that damage inflicted with Change HP can't knock out its victim (by not toggling the "Allow Knockout" check box).

- *Change State*: This is something that you probably won't be using constantly. Most instances of adding or removing states from an actor are covered by skills and items on both sides of a battle. This could be useful for a damage floor that additionally inflicts a status effect, however.

- *Change Parameters*: In addition to experience and states, you can also permanently change an actor's stats, for better or worse. *The minimum for any stat except MP is 1. MP can be zeroed out.* An interesting use of this event command could be for a dungeon that disallows magic. Just make it so that the MP of every party member is set to 0 (ensuring that you write the value of each party member's MP to a specific variable beforehand), and you're set. *It would probably be easier to just make a Silence state and inflict it on the party when it enters the dungeon, to be fair.*

- *Change Skills*: These allow you to give or take away skills from a party member. For an actual video game example of this happening, see Garnet from *Final Fantasy* IX. She starts the game with a, quite frankly, ridiculous number of Eidolons (entities that can be summoned for powerful effects). The plot takes them away from her until a time when she regains them. You could have a similar thing happen in your game. Maybe your party's mage gets amnesia from witnessing a horrible event and forgets how to cast everything save the simplest cantrips. Or perhaps the game's villain seals away the knowledge of the one spell that could defeat him, forcing the party to find a way to unseal it, so that the party's magician can learn it once again.

- *Change Equipment*: This is perhaps the Actor event command I use least. It has its situational uses, but I'm not a huge fan. Essentially, it allows you to change an actor's current equipment. This is good to use when a member of your party is going to leave it permanently or semipermanently (in which case, losing the items it had equipped would be bad). Just have Change Equipment commands remove all of its gear and you're set. Note that this doesn't make items appear out of thin air. If you want to use this command to equip an actor with a new weapon he/she has found, it must actually be in his/her inventory (by use of Change Weapons), before you call for it to be equipped.

- In hindsight, we could have used *Change Name* instead of the script equivalent for our riddles back in Chapter 11. Basically, you choose which actor whose name you want to change and choose their new name. It's basically Name Input Processing, but without giving the player a chance to decide on the new name. *Change Nickname* is the same thing, but for nicknames instead of names.

- Last, *Change Class* allows you to change an actor's class. It's a bit quirky, because it drops your actor's level back to 1 (with the respective drop to parameters that this would cause) but doesn't cause him/her to forget any skills. This could be pretty neat for a class system like that of *Dragon Warrior III*. Imagine if Eric could learn every skill available to every class in the game!

The Bridge

As an interesting hypothetical situation, say that you want to make a bridge that meets both of the following conditions:

- It allows the player to walk under it.

- It allows the player to cross it.

If you were to place your bridge using map tiles, you would meet the second condition but not the first. If you were to use events to create your bridge, you'd run into a different problem. Namely, you would have to check for two different conditions. How do we solve this problem? We'll need the following items:

- A Parallel Process event that checks the player's location

- An event that has a graphic that will serve as our bridge tile

The first order of business is to figure out how the player will interact with the map containing the bridge. For example, take a look at Figure 15-10, to see the map I'm using for this exercise. The player's starting position is at the top of a staircase. While the player is atop this ledge, he/she should be able to walk on the bridge tiles. While the player is on the lower part of the area, he/she should be able to walk under the bridge. We need the bridge tile events to have two pages. Page 1 will have no conditions and will have a Below Characters priority. The second page will require that a certain switch be flipped on and have an Above Characters priority. The Parallel Process event will flip the switch on when the player walks down to the ground level and turn it back off when the player ascends to the ledge.

Figure 15-10. *A screenshot of the map used for this exercise. Note how the bridges connect directly with the ledges*

The first bridge uses the horizontal stone bridge tiles, while the second bridge uses the vertical stone bridge tiles. You can find both of the tiles in tab B of the Exterior tileset

---

■ **Caution** When working with bridge tiles, be warned that they have selective passability. So, if you want a bridge that goes from left to right, you need the horizontal tiles. Bridges that go north to south require the vertical tiles. Otherwise, the player will be unable to walk on your bridges as intended.

```
@>Control Variables: [0002:X] = Player's Map X
@>Control Variables: [0003:Y] = Player's Map Y
@>Conditional Branch: Variable [0003:Y] == 5
   @>Conditional Branch: Variable [0002:X] >= 2
      @>Conditional Branch: Variable [0002:X] <= 4
         @>Control Switches: [0040:BridgeAbove] = OFF
         @>
       : Branch End
      @>
    : Branch End
   @>
:Branch End
@>Conditional Branch: Variable [0003:Y] == 6
   @>Conditional Branch: Variable [0002:X] >= 2
```

```
    @>Conditional Branch: Variable [0002:X] <= 4
        @>Control Switches: [0040:BridgeAbove] = ON
        @>
      : Branch End
      @>
    : Branch End
    @>
  : Branch End
  @>
```

BridgeAbove is the switch that must be flipped on for the bridge tiles to allow the player to pass under them. You could also have a dungeon in which the player has to pull a lever, press a button, or otherwise cause a switch to be flipped. Once the switch is flipped, a bridge to advance deeper into the dungeon appears. All you would need in that case are the bridge tiles with a Below Characters priority and a requirement for a switch to be flipped, and the event that would flip that switch.

The Town Map

This is the end of the end. After this section, I will close out this chapter with the summary, and we will be done with the book. (You'll want to check the Appendix for helpful resources related to RMVXA and other such things.) How better to end a book about an RPG development engine than by explaining how to create a map? To complete this exercise, we'll need the following:

- A screenshot of the area for which we wish to have a map
- A picture of a symbol/marker denoting the player's location on the map
- A pair of common events governing the map logic
- An item to execute the map logic

I will be using the Port Town exterior for this exercise.

Preparing Our Map Pictures

The first order of business is figuring out how big the map has to be. Taking a screenshot of the game while you are play-testing will give you a fairly close estimate (I got 546×417). Next, go to the map editor and switch to Region Mode (this will conceal any events you have placed on the map).

■ **Note** This will have the unintended consequence of concealing doors as well, given that they are used in event graphics.

If not having doors displayed in the screenshot is unacceptable to you, there is a workaround.

1. Go into the Resource Manager (Hotkey: F10) and find the Graphics/Characters folder.
2. From there, scroll down to the !Door1 graphic set.
3. Click it and export it to the location of your choice.

4. Then, click Graphics/Tilesets.

5. Click Import and then find the !Door1 graphic set that you exported.

6. Last, go to the Tileset tab of the Database and assign !Door1 to the D tab of the Exterior tileset.

Now you can place doors to cover the entrances, for your screenshot needs. Just make sure to erase the graphics afterward! After concealing the map's events, zoom out the map until you can snap a screenshot of it in its entirety. (For the port town, a 1/2 scale will be sufficient.) Then, use your image editing software of choice (any will work, including Windows' own Paint application) to resize it to 546×417. Next, you'll want to make a picture that can be used as a marker for the player's current location. It should be small enough that it doesn't take up an excessive amount of space on the map, yet big enough that it can actually be seen. The marker that I created is 30×30 in size. Once we have both of our pictures, we need to add them to our Resource Manager. Find the Graphics/Pictures folder in the manager (curiously, RMVXA comes with no stock pictures) and import your two images to that folder accordingly.

Using the Show Picture Event Command

With that set up, it's time to use the *Show Picture* event command. Take a look at Figure 15-11 to see a screenshot of the event command, as displayed within RMVXA.

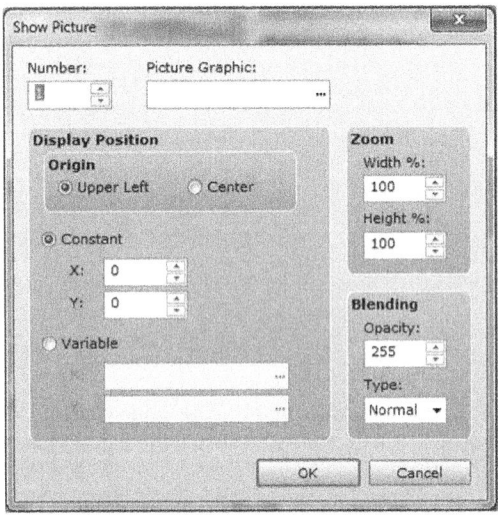

Figure 15-11. *A screenshot of the Show Picture event command*

You can assign a picture a control number. As the tool tip in RMVXA states: "Control number of the display picture. Those with the largest screen display number take precedence." Think of it like a stack of papers. The lower a picture's number, the deeper it is located within the stack. So, if we want our marker to be placed on top of the map, it must have a higher control number. With that said, you can pick any number from 1 to 100. The map could be 99, and the marker could be 100. To keep it simple, I'll give the map a 1 and the marker a 2. We can set which graphic is shown by selecting it with *Picture Graphic*. If you hadn't imported the two images to Graphics/Pictures accordingly, the browser window would be empty. For *Display Position*, we'll want the automap to be positioned at 0,0, with an Upper Left origin. *Origin* determines how the image is placed on the screen. If you choose Center, then it will be the map's center that is placed at 0,0. We don't want that. For our map marker, we will also use an Upper Left origin, but it will be positioned with the use of variables. Last, you can set *Blending* options. The lower the opacity of your picture, the more translucent it will appear. You can have additive or subtractive types of blending as well, which influence how the picture's colors look.

Creating Our Town Map Common Events

This is where it gets interesting. The general idea for our common events is the following:

- When the player uses the Map item, we want to determine the player's x and y coordinates. After that, we apply a multiplier to the X and Y variables.

- Afterward, we use a pair of Show Picture commands to display the map and the map marker.

What multiplier do we need? We have to correlate the pixel size of the map picture (546×417) with the tile size in the map editor (39×48). This is as easy as dividing the first value by the second for both X and Y. The multiplier for X is (546/39 = 14) and the multiplier for Y is (417/48 = 8.6875), which I rounded to two digits in the following code. Here's the first common event:

```
@>Control Switches: [0039:TurnOffMap] = ON
@>Control Variables: [0002:X] = Player's Map X
@>Control Variables: [0003:Y] = Player's Map Y
@>Control Variables: [0002:X] *= 14
@>Control Variables: [0003:Y] *= 8.69
@>Show Picture: 1, 'automap', Upper Left (0,0), (100%,100%), 255, Normal
@>Show Picture: 2, 'x', Upper Left (Variable [0002][0003]), (50%,50%), 255, Normal
@>
```

■ **Note**   You can use the Script option in Control Variables to write in decimal numbers. If you use the Constant option, decimals will be truncated.

I used a 50% zoom for the map marker, as, when displayed, 30×30 looks clunky on the map. As it stands, you can create a suitable item to hold the Map common event and then start up the game. However, you'll find that using the Map event will cause the screen to display the area map and map marker without a way to remove the pictures. That is what the TurnOffMap switch is for. When the switch is on, the second common event is processed. I give it a Parallel Process trigger, so that it is running concurrently until needed. The only role that the second common event has is to erase the pictures that have been created and flip off the TurnOffMap switch until it is needed once again.

```
@>Conditional Branch: The X Button is Being Pressed
   @>Erase Picture: 1
   @>Erase Picture: 2
   @>Control Switches: [0039:TurnOffMap] = OFF
   @>
: Branch End
@>
```

■ **Reminder**   The X button maps to the A key on your keyboard.

Erase Picture asks for a control number and erases the displayed image that has said number. That concludes this exercise. Give the player a Map item and test it out!

Variants on the Map Exercise

This is good and all, but following are some possible variants for you to think about as well.

1. **Make it so that the map marker moves as the player does.**

   - As you have almost certainly noticed, you can still control the character when the map is displayed.

   - To pull this off, all you need to do is copy-paste the part of the first common event that handles the X and Y variables and add a *Move Picture* event command directly below that.

   ```
   @>Control Variables: [0002:X] = Player's Map X
   @>Control Variables: [0003:Y] = Player's Map Y
   @>Control Variables: [0002:X] *= 14
   @>Control Variables: [0003:Y] *= 8.69
   @>Move Picture: 2, Upper Left (Variable [0002][00003]), (50%,50%),
      255, Normal, @15
   ```

2. **Make a mini-map of the area.**

   - I'm thinking in a manner similar to that of the Grinsia mini-map, where you have a semitransparent map in the upper-left corner.

   - This is actually relatively simple. We render the same map picture with the Upper Left origin but set the Zoom to 25% (which will shrink it to a quarter of its size). This drops it down to 137×105. Additionally, we set its Opacity to 128, as we want the mini-map to be somewhat see-through.

   - Then, we quarter the multipliers (which would become 3.5 and 2.17 for X and Y, respectively) for the map marker as well. I also dropped the marker's Zoom down to 25%, to keep it in line with the smaller map.

   - You could make an item that reveals an area's map to the player for a certain number of steps.

   - Keep in mind that you'll need a picture for each individual area in which you plan to have a mini-map. How would you handle an area like our interior structure map for the port town, where there are multiple different areas on the same map? That's an exercise for you.

Summary

This chapter covered a range of miscellaneous topics that were not covered in the book's previous chapters. Among them were creating a battle that requires a certain party member to participate, having encounters in which some of the enemies appear during the battle rather than at the start, and creating mazes within a single map, with the use of variables and Regions.

Useful Resources for RPG Maker VX Ace

This appendix is a compilation of helpful resources for just about anything related to your RPG Maker VX Ace (RMVXA) games. Do you need help with a certain idea that you have stuck in your head? Perhaps you could seek aid from one of the links listed under "Tutorials and General Help." Are you thinking of hiring someone to help you create your very own commercial game? Some of the other links should cover that. On that note, let us begin.

Tutorials and General Help for RMVXA

This section lists links to sites that contain tutorials and/or communities of people willing to help out aspiring role-playing game (RPG) designers. Game design, as with most things in life, is a constant process of renewal and learning new ways to tackle old (and not-so-old) problems.

> http://forums.rpgmakerweb.com: The official forum for Enterbrain's video game development engines, including RMVXA

> www.rpgmakerweb.com/support/products/tutorials: Also part of the official site. As the web link suggests, the site offers various tutorials perfect for beginners.

> www.rpgmakervxace.net: One of the most populated unofficial forums related to RMVXA on the Internet. If you can't find the answer you're looking for on the official site, this should be your next destination.

> http://rpgmaker.net/tutorials/rmvxace: Offers about three pages of tutorials on various topics of interest related to RMVXA

Note As it is the official site for RPG Maker, you'll notice quite a few references to it. Search engines will also steer you toward rpgmakerweb.com whenever they get a chance. Enterbrain has done a fairly good job of positioning itself as the universal destination for all things RPG Maker (which, given that it's the developer, is fair play). You can buy resource packs (music, art, etc.) from them, as well as a few other items of interest.

Art and Spriting

Need art for your RMVXA game? Want to learn how to create it yourself? I have you covered with three links. To be fair, art is easily my weakest asset when it comes to game design. However, a wise man once told me: "You need not know everything . . . only the people who *do*."

http://rpg-maker-artists.deviantart.com: A community on deviantART for RPG Maker artists. As a general statement, deviantART is an incredibly useful site for all things art. If you have an artistic inclination, you could join the community; otherwise, it is probably a good place to look for people who can create unique sprites and/or other pieces of art for your RMVXA games.

http://finalbossblues.com/pixel-tutorials: Offers a variety of cool tutorials for making your own pixel art. The tutorials are specifically targeted at RPG Maker XP, VX, and VX Ace users but should have relevance outside of the RPG Maker series as well. After all, art is art.

http://animatedbattlers.wordpress.com: Holder creates animated sprites to be used in scripted side-view battle systems in RMVXA. (Think of the view used in classic *Final Fantasy* games.) They look really awesome, so go check out what he has done, if you're interested in having a side-view battle system in your RPG.

Tutorials and References for Ruby

A veritable treasure trove of resources for Ruby exists on and off the Internet. Following are but some of the sites available:

www.codecademy.com/en/tracks/ruby: Codecademy's mission, as stated, is "Teaching the world how to code." It does an exemplary job at it, if I may be so bold as to offer an endorsement. It has course plans for several of the most popular programming languages, including Ruby.

https://rubymonk.com: Another site similar in principle to Codecademy, rubymonk, as the site name implies, is strictly for Ruby and Ruby on Rails tutorials.

www.ruby-doc.org: Perhaps the most comprehensive reference for Ruby, if you desire to dive into the world of Ruby programming. As stated on the site: "The ruby-doc.org Ruby documentation project is an effort by the Ruby community to provide complete and accurate documentation for the Ruby programming language." Thus, if you can't find a method contained in Ruby through the site, it probably doesn't exist!

http://rgss3doc.razelon.tk/en/rgss3/index.html: This links to the RGSS3 Reference Guide. I find it somewhat more convenient than trying to rummage through the RMVXA help files, but your mileage may vary on that.

Sounds and Music

No game is truly complete without an awesome soundtrack. Here are some links to musicians who can spruce up your project accordingly.

http://bc1281.wix.com/scythuz-music-web-1: Site of Benjamin Carr, a.k.a. Scythuz. I have had the pleasure of purchasing some of his tracks in the past. He delivers high-quality work at competitive rates. There is a contact page on his site, if you would like to commission some music tracks from him.

http://kainvinosec.com/: If you have ever poked your head into RPG Maker music, you've probably heard of Kain Vinosec. He wrote a very helpful music guide a while back and has several music packs for sale on the official RPG Maker site. Check out some of his samples and see if his work is right for your project.

http://gyrowolf.com/resources/: Gyrowolf has various music packs available on the official RPG Maker site and Amazon. A search for "gyrowolf music" on Google should return purchase links to said packs.

Video Game Writing Tutorials

The story and general flow of an RPG are two of its most important elements. Here are some links to sites that discuss video game writing:

> www.paladinstudios.com/2012/08/06/how-to-write-a-good-game-story-and-get-filthy-rich/

The article in question is from 2012, but it has a good treatise on writing a good story for your games.

> http://blog.rpgmakerweb.com/tutorials/design-by-layer-1/

> http://blog.rpgmakerweb.com/tutorials/design-by-layer-ii/

Nick Palmer wrote up a pair of helpful tutorials for writing an RPG story on the official RPG Maker blog.

■ **Note** If you require someone (or a group of someones) with whom to collaborate on a project, posting a thread in the official forums is never a bad idea. It may well be that you find like-minded individuals with design strengths to offset your weaknesses.

Scripts

These are perhaps the best way to add or change the functionality of your game. If you decide to cut your teeth on Ruby and its RGSS implementation within RMVXA, looking at other people's work is probably the best way to begin. Seeing what others before you have done is a great way to discover exactly what is and isn't possible within RMVXA.

> *RGSS3 Scripts (RMVXA) (*http://forums.rpgmakerweb.com/index.php?/forum/35-rgss3-scripts-rmvx-ace/*):* A subforum within the official RPG Maker site that lists scripts for use in RMVXA

> *Tsukihime's Change Currency Script (*www.rpgmakervxace.net/topic/9777-change-currency/*)*: Remember, back in Chapter 7, when I mentioned the graphical quirk involving currencies? You can use this script to fix that. Just use script calls, as explained in the comments section of the script, to switch from your default currency (G) to any other currency. Note, however, that this only changes the currency symbol.

> *Galv's Scripts (*http://galvs-scripts.com/*)*: Galv is but one of many skilled scripters within the RMVXA community. As of the time of writing, he has more than 50 scripts on his site, covering a variety of things you might need for your own game.

Note   If you are planning on releasing a commercial game, make sure that the scripts you are using are permitted in such a game. Most scripts list such licensing details in the comments section, but, when in doubt, don't hesitate to ask the scripter directly.

RMVXA Games

There's no shame in taking a look at the games created by your fellow RMVXA users and seeing what can be done with the engine. It may well be that you figure out how to do something new after seeing other games in action! On that note, following is a list of some of the RMVXA games that are available:

> *Crysalis (*www.rpgmakerweb.com/download/additional/sample-games*):* This particular game was created by Rene P. and is hosted on the official web site. It uses many of the stock graphics for RMVXA, so it's a good example of what can be done with this engine, from a raw game design perspective. It is free to download.

> *List of completed games on rpgmakervxace.net:* (www.rpgmakervxace.net/topic/16900-completed-games-list-updated-61114/): A large list of RMVXA games in the RMVXA community forums. Given the large number of games on the list, I did not check to see whether any of them are commercial (cost money). It is still very much worth a look.

Closing Notes

In closing, I'd like to emphasize that the RPG Maker community is filled with many talented and wonderful people. If you ever need help with anything related to RMVXA, don't hesitate to ask them for help. Just treat them with a modicum of respect (this is probably good advice relating to anybody, in the real world as on the Internet), and everything will be fine. Good luck with your endeavors, and may your games be awesome!

Index

▨ W, X, Y, Z

Get the eBook for only $10!

Now you can take the weightless companion with you anywhere, anytime. Your purchase of this book entitles you to 3 electronic versions for only $10.

This Apress title will prove so indispensible that you'll want to carry it with you everywhere, which is why we are offering the eBook in 3 formats for only $10 if you have already purchased the print book.

Convenient and fully searchable, the PDF version enables you to easily find and copy code—or perform examples by quickly toggling between instructions and applications. The MOBI format is ideal for your Kindle, while the ePUB can be utilized on a variety of mobile devices.

Go to www.apress.com/promo/tendollars to purchase your companion eBook.

Lightning Source UK Ltd.
Milton Keynes UK
UKOW05f0349080616

275864UK00015B/352/P